THE ANNOTATED
FRANKENSTEIN

THE ANNOTATED™
FRANKENSTEIN

Frankenstein by Mary Shelley

Introduction and Notes by
LEONARD WOLF

Art by MARCIA HUYETTE

With Maps, Drawings, and Photographs

Clarkson N. Potter, Inc./Publishers New York
Distributed by Crown Publishers, Inc.

This edition of Frankenstein *is dedicated to Mary Shelley, the "onlie begetter." She would have approved, I think, of a word of gratitude addressed to the shade of Boris Karloff.*

PUBLISHER'S NOTE

Through the years the popularity of Mary Shelley's *Frankenstein* has brought many editions into print. Inevitably this has resulted in some text variations. In order to ensure the authenticity of the text, we arranged with the Library of Congress in Washington, D.C., to microfilm a copy of the first edition. That text has been reproduced in this volume by the photo-offset process.

PHOTOGRAPH CREDITS: p. xi (top right, bottom left), courtesy National Portrait Gallery, London; pp. 14, 51, 225, 233 (bottom), 277, courtesy Mansell Collection, London; pp. ix, 69 (left), 138 (bottom right), 192, 202, 204, 211 (bottom right), courtesy Universal Pictures; p. 81, courtesy Pierpont Morgan Library, New York; pp. 61 (top left), 132, 138 (bottom left), courtesy French Government Tourist Office; p. 218, courtesy Auckland City Art Gallery; p. xi (top left), courtesy University of Texas Humanities Research Center Library; p. xx, courtesy Nottingham Museum, England; pp. 6, 146, courtesy Royal Academy, London; pp. xv, 2, courtesy Tate Gallery, London; pp. xvii, 66, 187, 263, 299, courtesy Columbia University, New York; p. xxiii, courtesy Richard Bratset; pp. 10, 11, 23, courtesy Metropolitan Toronto Library; p. 290, courtesy Sir John Soame's Museum, London; p. 296 (top), courtesy British Museum, London; pp. 291, 349 (top left), courtesy Limited Editions Club/Heritage Press, Avon, Connecticut; p. 289, courtesy Goethe Museum, Frankfort; pp. 29, 197, 281, courtesy Museum of Fine Arts, Boston; pp. xiii, 124, courtesy Duke University, North Carolina. Photographs by Leonard Wolf appear on the following pages: 68 (bottom left), 92, 96, 138 (top), 229 (left) 233 (top), 240, 241, 242. Special thanks to the Swiss National Library, Geneva.

Library of Congress Cataloging in Publication Data

Shelley, Mary Wollstonecraft Godwin, 1797–1851.
  The annotated Frankenstein.

  Bibliography: p.
  Filmography: p.
  Includes index.
  I. Wolf, Leonard. II. Title.
PZ3.S545An3   [PR5397]   823'.7   77-7458
ISBN 0-517-53071-6

ACKNOWLEDGMENTS

A book like *The Annotated Frankenstein* is only possible if its editor is fortunate, as I have been, in finding friends, colleagues, and perfect strangers who are willing to give their help. This note of acknowledgment is an insufficient measure of my thanks to them.

First, I want to thank Deborah Wolf, whose perceptions led me to what I hope is the heart of the *Frankenstein* matter. Then I want to thank James Rieger, Emily Sunstein, Richard Holmes, John Buxton, William Walling, Claire Tomalin, Martin Tropp, Muriel Spark, Radu Florescu, and Gerald Enscoe, most of whom I do not know but for whose scholarship, in a variety of fields, I am grateful.

My life has been made easier because of the insights, information, or detailed labor given to me by the following people: Renee Ashley; Robert Berg, Order Librarian at San Francisco State University; Professor Richard Bratset of San Francisco State University; Denis Broca; Caroline Butler; Leo Delucchi; the French Government Tourist Office; Dane Gleason; Daniel Goleman of *Psychology Today;* Susan Hart; Professor Daniel Knapp of San Francisco State University; the librarians and staff of the village of Cupar, and those of the town of Kirkwall, in Scotland; Evelyn McReady; Peter Mullins; Professor Edwin Nierenberg of San Francisco State University; James Richter; Evelyn Rocks, who worked on maps and on Mary Shelley's calendar; Theodore Roszak; Professor (and Doctor) Marc A. Rubenstein, who let me read his essay "My Accursed Origin" (*Studies in Romanticism*, vol. 10, no. 2), then talked with me about it when I most needed to know what he knew; Harlan Soeten, the Curator of the San Francisco Maritime Museum; Alexander Thompson Speirs, Printing Supervisor of the Fyfe Regional Council Print Department in Cupar; Professor Richard Trapp of San Francisco State University for his help to a man without Latin; Virginia Verrill; Stuart Vyse; Robin Wells, Curator of the Museum of Anthropology, San Francisco State University; and to Jack Stalker for the goose egg breakfast he gave to a stranger in Newton, Scotland.

Finally, Gail Gahagan, Dana Hoffman, and Susan Hart will know how grateful I am to them for the labor they put into this book.

A NOTE ON THE TEXT USED FOR THIS EDITION OF *FRANKENSTEIN*

Until 1974, when James Rieger issued his edition of the 1818 text of *Frankenstein*, Mary Shelley's great novel had been known chiefly in the various printings of the much revised 1831 edition. Since the revisions were Mary Shelley's, it becomes a fair question to ask why *The Annotated Frankenstein* should be based on the earlier work. The answer, for this editor, is that the 1818 edition preserves intact the initial vision that pushed her, in that wet 1816 summer, to put pen to paper. In it, *elle a poussé son cri* and the book, at its most successful, feels like the writing of an eighteen-year-old demibohemian in the grip of necessity Fifteen years later, she was a respectable widow striving for even more respectability. The 1831 edition reflects that change in her life.

The general direction of the second edition is to present the reader with a smoother, more socially presentable work. Victor, in 1831, is more luminously beautiful so that he can bear an even more idealized resemblance to the dead Percy Shelley. Walton, the young explorer, and Victor's alter ego, is given additional good intentions and refined sensibilities; while Victor's parents, Alphonse and Caroline Frankenstein, are steeped, in 1831, in a more intensely sugary domestic tranquillity than was their lot in 1818. But perhaps the most telling change in the second edition is in what we are told about the origins of Elizabeth, Victor's beautiful and ill-fated bride. In 1818 Elizabeth is cast as Victor's first cousin. In 1831, to avoid the slightest suggestion of incest, Elizabeth is turned into an aristocratic Milanese foundling, no blood relation to Victor, who is rescued from a poverty-stricken life by a condescending Caroline Beaufort Frankenstein who introduces the child into the Frankenstein household as a playmate—and destined bride—for Victor.

There are other changes correcting real or imagined angularities in the 1818 text, all of them noted in the present edition. But Mary Shelley's vision of horror made its first and, I think, its most compelling appearance in 1818. It is that vision, textually unchanged, that follows.

CONTENTS

INTRODUCTION

BORIS KARLOFF AS THE CREATURE.

1 Before there were movies, the creature on stage also died a number of inventive deaths. Elizabeth Nitchie, in her *Mary Shelley* (p. 225), says: "The Monster seemingly had as many lives as a cat, and each necessitated a different end. In 1823 at the English Opera House he perished in an avalanche, at the Coburg in a burning church. In 1826 he was killed by a thunderbolt in Paris and at the West London Theatre, he leapt into the crater of Mount Aetna at the Coburg, he died in an Arctic storm at the English Opera House. In the twentieth century, on the stage he committed suicide by a leap from a crag in 1927 and was shot to death in 1933."

We know Frankenstein's creature as if we had always known him: Boris Karloff, tall, lurching, mute, shabbily clad, a humanlike thing with a square head and electronic pegs sticking out of his neck and a look of baffled innocence on his face. We remember him best in the great scene in which, still giddy, still scarred by his newly acquired life, he stands, with his arms raised. His hands tremble as he tries to seize what some dim instinct tells him is important: light. An effulgence, a mystery. When he fails to seize it, he whimpers gently, and the rest of the film unreels its tale of incoherence, misplaced wisdom, cruel pride, and misunderstood love.

Since the James Whale–Boris Karloff production of *Frankenstein* (1931) there have been scores of sequels, film adaptations, cartoons, parodies, and travesties of the Frankenstein story. The range of film interpretations need not surprise us. The emblematic tale that Mary Shelley invented in 1816 had an equally varied stage life for nearly a century before film was invented.**1** By now, the name Frankenstein represents, in the popular imagination, an instantly recognizable myth. That the myth was created by Mary Shelley in a novel she wrote when she was eighteen years old is not quite so well known.

2   According to Mary Shelley. William A. Walling, in his *Mary Shelley* (p. 28), argues convincingly that Claire Clairmont, Mary Shelley's stepsister, was also there. That the younger woman is left out of Mary Shelley's account is not surprising when we consider, which we shall later, how she felt about Claire.

VILLA DIODATI.

Mary Shelley herself, in the Introduction to the 1831 edition of *Frankenstein* (p. v.) answers the question "How I, then a young girl, came to think of, and to dilate upon, so very hideous an idea?" It all happened, she tells us, in June 1816, on a rainy night when she and Percy Shelley spent an evening in the Villa Diodati, Lord Byron's home in Geneva. Byron was there, as was his physician and sometime friend, John Polidori. They were a young company. Byron, the oldest, was twenty-eight; Shelley was twenty-three; Mary Shelley, as we have seen, was eighteen. Polidori was twenty-one. In Mary Shelley's description of the eventful night, we are led to believe that it was a gathering of congenial people, whiling away a rainy evening. The mood was desultory. For a time they discussed some German horror tales that had come their way in a French translation titled *Les Fantasmagoriana*. Byron, always a Puritan sensualist, proposed that they do something useful:

"We will each write a ghost story," said Lord Byron; and his proposition was acceded to. There were four of us.**2**   The noble author began a tale, a fragment of which he printed at the end of his poem of Mazeppa. Shelley, more apt to embody ideas and sentiments in the radiance of brilliant imagery, and in the music of the most melodious verse that adorns our language, than to invent the machinery of a story, commenced one founded on the experiences of his early life. Poor Polidori had some terrible idea about a skull-headed lady, who was so punished for peeping through a keyhole—what to see I forget—something very shocking and wrong of course; but when she was reduced to a worse condition than the renowned Tom of Coventry, he did not know what to do with her, and was obliged to despatch her to the tomb of the Capulets, the only place for which she was fitted.

PERCY BYSSHE SHELLEY
BY EDWARD ELLECKER WILLIAMS.

MARY WOLLSTONECRAFT SHELLEY BY S. J. STUMK.

JOHN W. POLIDORI
BY F. G. GAINSFORD.

LORD BYRON BY T. PHILLIPS.

3 See note 2 on page 3 of the Preface.

4 But not asleep, and certainly not dreaming, as critics have frequently repeated. Mary Shelley specifically reports that she "did not sleep, nor could I be said to think." What she had was a vision, not a nightmare.

At first, Mary Shelley was not able to do much with the whimsical homework assignment. However, in the days that followed, she had still further stimuli. She tell us (p. ix) that

many and long were the conversations between Lord Byron and Shelley, to which I was a devout but nearly silent listener. During one of these, various philosophical doctrines were discussed, and among others the nature of the principle of life, and whether there was any probability of its ever being discovered and communicated. They talked of the experiments of Dr. Darwin,**3** (I speak not of what the Doctor really did, or said that he did, but, as more to my purpose, of what was then spoken of as having been done by him,) who preserved a piece of vermicelli in a glass case, till by some extraordinary means it began to move with voluntary motion. Not thus, after all, would life be given. Perhaps a corpse would be re-animated; galvanism had given token of such things; perhaps the component parts of a creature might be manufactured, brought together and endued with vital warmth.

It was after one such conversation that Mary Shelley received the donnée, the gift every artist prays for that seems to come from beyond the self. Lying in bed, her eyes tightly shut,**4** she saw

. . . the pale student of unhallowed arts kneeling beside the thing he had put together. I saw the hideous phantasm of a man stretched out, and then . . .

She opened her eyes in terror—as have generations of her readers since.

Though terror frequently chills the pages of *Frankenstein*, it is not properly a Gothic novel, the literary genre to which fear literature is usually assigned. Gothic fiction, which emerged as a distinct kind of writing in the mid-eighteenth century, has, as its usual central figure, an indisputably virginal young woman of genteel breeding who finds herself set down in a tangle of misfortunes, the most frightful of which is that she is being pursued, through caverns or castle, through ruins or abbeys, by a looming, dark male figure who has something terribly threatening to women on his mind. B. G. MacCarthy, writing in *The Female Pen* (1947), describes the Gothic ambience as made up of "dizzying battlements, dark and winding stairways, dark dungeons, instruments of torture, groans and gouts of blood, secret passages with many a suggestion of spectral life, ghostly music, tapestries which sway with the wind and which betray the secret watcher or the assassin."

Chap. 10th.

Day after day, week after week passed away on my return to Geneva and I had not the courage to commence my work. I feared the vengeance of the disappointed fiend, yet I was unable to overcome my repugnance to the task. My health which had hitherto declined was now much restored; & my spirits when unchecked by the memory of my unhappy promise, rose proportionably. My father saw this with pleasure and he turned his thoughts towards the best method of eradicating the remains of my melancholy, which every now and then would return by fits & with a devouring blackness over cast the approaching day. At these moments I took refuge in the most perfect solitude. Alone in a little boat I passed whole days on the lake watching the clouds & the ripple of the waves silent & listless. But the fresh air and bright sun seldom failed to restore me to some degree of composure & on my return I met the salutations of my friends with a readier smile, & a more cheerful heart.

It was after my return from one of these rambles that my father calling me aside thus addressed me.

FIRST PAGE OF *FRANKENSTEIN*, VOL. III, IN MARY SHELLEY'S OWN HAND.

In Horace Walpole's *Castle of Otranto* (1764), the so-called first of the English Gothic fictions, the pursuit has hovering over it a delicate whiff of incest; while in Matthew Lewis's *The Monk* (1796), there is nothing delicate about the incest at all. There, Father Ambrosio, pure as the driven snow as the book begins, discovers debauchery and makes a career of it. As the tale ends, he learns that the woman he has murdered to get at her daughter is really his mother, and that the maiden he has ravished and killed is his sister. In Ann Radcliffe's considerably more refined *Mysteries of Udolpho* (1794), the terrors that engage a reader frequently appear to be supernatural, though they never are; while in Charles Maturin's *Melmoth the Wanderer* (1820), perhaps the greatest Gothic fiction yet written, the full complexity of the Faustian bargain is ironically explored.

Curiously enough, despite the achievements of such men as Walpole, Lewis, and Maturin, Gothic fiction, almost from its inception, had a special attraction for women. Indeed, in the early days of the genre, reading Gothic novels or writing them became a middle-class female preoccupation—as if women, oppressed by needlepoint, whalebone stays, psychological frustrations, shame, and babies, found in the reading or writing of these fictions a way to signal to each other, and perhaps to the world of men, the shadowy outlines of their own pain.

There is plenty of female pain expressed by the figures that move through the pages of *Frankenstein*, but Mary Shelley was dealing with matters that were at once too biological and too personal to be contained in the Gothic formula of a young woman in flight from a man who has rape or worse on his mind.

Ellen Moers, in an important recent essay, has claimed for *Frankenstein* that it deals with "the motif of revulsion against newborn life, and the drama of guilt, dread, and flight surrounding birth and its consequences . . . *Frankenstein* seems to be distinctly a *woman*'s mythmaking on the subject of birth."

Frankenstein is that, and a good deal more. As the pages to come should amply demonstrate, we will see that the novel is a living artifact beneath whose surface we can see displayed the network of dangers that women face when they take the age-old risk of loving men. Mary Shelley, eighteen years old and scared, gave expression to in *Frankenstein*, an insight that is as simple as it is heartbreakingly true: that women have literally everything to fear from men. Below, or above, all the flattery of women as primordial life-givers, as instinctive nurturers, there

MARY WOLLSTONECRAFT
BY JOHN W. OPIE.

5 Sunday.

gleams this fact—that death sits on her side of the bed when a woman and a man make love. This is not rhetoric. One is talking about real death, the stern, cold reaper, and not the orgasmic "little death" invented by poets who were men. It comes down to this—that lovers risk babies, and babies can kill. It is a commonplace, an age-old fact that men and women both know, but which only women have to confront; and it is this fact, deeply experienced in Mary Shelley's life, that gives to *Frankenstein* its special eeriness.

Mary Wollstonecraft Shelley was born Mary Godwin on Wednesday, August 30, 1797, just five months after her politically radical parents, William Godwin and Mary Wollstonecraft, who did not believe in marriage, were married. Her parents had counted on "the animal" to be a boy, and had the name "William" in readiness. Mary Wollstonecraft's labor turned out to be unexpectedly long and difficult. It lasted from five o'clock in the morning until eleven-twenty that night, when William Godwin first heard the baby cry. Shortly afterward he was told that he was the father of a girl. William Godwin was then forty-one years old, and Mary Wollstonecraft, who had given him the only domestic happiness he had ever known, was thirty-eight.

Mary Wollstonecraft's difficult labor proved to be a presage of worse things to come. Though the baby emerged fully formed and well, the mother had difficulty expelling the placenta, and heroic, if ghastly, measures were taken to remove it. For eleven days, Mary Wollstonecraft lingered on after a distinguished obstetrician had spent hours plucking bits of the placenta from her womb. Her pain was extreme, and her death, in an age that only dimly understood antisepsis, was inevitable. She died reassuring William Godwin that he had been a good man. And he, whose lifelong literary style had been sedate, voluminous, reasonable, and calm, made this muted notation of her death in his journal: "September 10. Su.**5** 20 minutes before 8_____

_____

William Godwin, Mary Shelley's father, was born in 1756 into an intensely Calvinist family in Wisbech, England. As a young man, he tried his hand at preaching, but when he realized he had lost his faith, he turned to teaching instead, but that career came to an abrupt end when a school he projected failed to attract pupils. After these false starts, God-

6 Not for the first time. He had seen her in 1791 and in 1792 at various literary gatherings and had been rather put off by her. At one such meeting at which Tom Paine was present, Godwin had been irritated because Mary Wollstonecraft had been so voluble that he, Godwin, had had no opportunity to talk with Paine.

win tried his hand, this time more or less successfully, as a hack writer in London. He had a facile pen and turned out a novel called *Damon and Delia* in ten days; another one called *Italian Letters* was written in three weeks. A novel called *Imogen, a Pastoral Romance* took him a lugubrious four months to finish. Godwin was not particularly proud of these bread-and-butter efforts and was quite aware that such work was, as he put it, often "touched with the torpedo of mediocrity." One way or another, Godwin kept his head above water in the scribbling trade until, in 1793, he published his *Enquiry Concerning Political Justice*, which made him instantly famous. In an England demoralized by the consequences and the implications of the French Revolution, Godwin's *Enquiry*, which laid down a systematic critique of the evils of government (all government), as well as a projection of a libertarian future, might easily have had ugly political consequences for its author. Godwin took the necessary risks calmly and with great courage. As things worked out, he escaped with no more harm than to become famous overnight.

Three years later, still a social lion in London's radical circles, he met Mary Wollstonecraft,**6** then famous, in her turn, as the author of *A Vindication of the Rights of Woman.*

Mary Wollstonecraft, a brilliant, tempestuous, harried, frequently despondent and much abused woman, was born into a poverty-stricken family with genteel pretensions. Her father, a weaver who became a failed farmer, was undependable, a wife-beater, and a heavy drinker. Her mother, as Muriel Spark tells us in *Child of Light* (p. 10), was "a weak type of woman, [who] submitted to [her husband's] continual bullying, and Mary from an early age, acted as protector to the family meanwhile seizing what fragmentary opportunities of education came her way."

As soon as she reasonably could, Mary Wollstonecraft left home, supporting herself with the kind of scut labor that was available to poor but genteel women of her day. She worked as a rich woman's companion, as a tutor, as a schoolteacher, as a governess in a wealthy Irish family until her revulsion with so much servility drove her to London where she undertook to lead an independent life.

It was an all but unheard of decision, but with the help of Joseph Johnson, a kindly publisher who sent work her way, she established herself in the same literary-hack world where Godwin, too, had served an apprenticeship. It was in London that she, busy, active, and intellectually productive, made the first of

HENRY FUSELI, SELF-PORTRAIT.

the two great love mistakes of her life. In 1788, she fell in love with Henry Fuseli (Heinrich Füssli). Fuseli, fiftyish and married, was an expatriate Swiss with a prodigious talent and an ego to match. He was a vigorous sensualist, a bisexual who had once been the lover of the famous physiognomist Lavater. Fuseli was the sort of man who, writing an anonymous review of one of his own paintings, could trumpet that it was "a sublime scene . . . a happy effort of genius . . ." To which one may add that he was probably right.

Mary Wollstonecraft's fixation on Fuseli lasted nearly four years. Meanwhile her intellectual career moved forward by leaps and bounds. Her novel *Mary* and a collection of *Original Stories* were published in 1788. Her *Vindication of the Rights of Men* appeared in 1790, and in 1792, the work that made her famous was published: *A Vindication of the Rights of Woman*. Perhaps emboldened by her professional triumphs, Mary Wollstonecraft made one final and ill-starred effort to achieve some kind of union with Fuseli. In August 1792, she approached Fuseli's wife with an offer to join the Fuseli household as a platonic sharer in Fuseli's charisma. She seemed willing to leave Fuseli's stocky, but vigorous, body to the ministrations of Mrs. Fuseli while she, Mary Wollstonecraft, offered to be content with whatever spiritual light the genius might wish to diffuse in her direction. The offer was angrily rejected—Mary Wollstonecraft was shown out the door and forbidden to enter the house again.

It seemed a propitious time to leave London. Mary Wollstonecraft determined to go to France to gather material for a book on the Revolution, though in writing to her friend William Roscoe, she hinted jauntily that "at Paris, indeed, I might take a husband for the time being and get divorced when my truant heart longed again to nestle with its old friend; but this speculation has not yet entered into my plan."

In matters of love, need, not ripeness, is all. In Paris in 1793, Mary Wollstonecraft fell promptly into the sort of madcap love that very young people— and older romantics—still dream about. Her lover, Gilbert Imlay, was a fortyish, handsome, and not unintelligent American with whom, under the very shadow of the Terror, she conducted the most passionate—because at last fully sexual—affair of her life. Imlay, a dashing man, perhaps a captain, who had served in the American Revolution, was a competent author and an early abolitionist and sexual liberationist. Their affair was at first an ecstatic idyll for her; a delightful adventure for him. She adored him;

7   The journey produced a volume of astute travel letters, *Letters from Sweden* (1796). Claire Tomalin's tart comment on Imlay's tactic is that "there is an almost sublime effrontery about sending off a discarded mistress, newly recovered from a suicide attempt and accompanied by a small baby, on a difficult journey into unknown territory, to recoup your financial disasters for you and leave you free to enjoy the company of her rival without reproach: in his own way, Imlay was a man of resource" (*The Life and Death of Mary Wollstonecraft*, p. 179).

he liked her a lot. He was the love of her life; he was glad to be with her. The rest was easy to predict. As their transports became familiar and Imlay felt her love swarming all over him, he discovered that he was neglecting important business in Le Havre. By then she was pregnant. As her time approached, she followed him to Le Havre, where in May 1794 her baby, Fanny, was born.

From this point on, Imlay was forever on the move and unfaithful. But always, he was followed by a series of letters which, nearly two hundred years later, still make very bitter reading. It must have made even more dreadful reading for the young Mary Shelley, who found the letters neatly gathered together in a collection edited by her father, William Godwin, and published in the very year that Mary Shelley was born as the *Posthumous Works of the Author of a Vindication of the Rights of Woman*.

In 1795 the lovesick Mary Wollstonecraft was back in London with her baby Fanny, and it was there that she made her first suicide attempt by taking an overdose of laudanum. She was rescued, however, and enough of her relationship with Imlay was patched up so that she was willing to make a business trip for him into the Scandinavian countries.7

That done and back in England, the mess with Imlay was resumed. She wrote another series of beseeching letters, hoping that somehow the written word would restore their long-vanished love. Then there was another suicide note that began, "I write you now on my knees," and concluded:

Your treatment has thrown my mind into a state of chaos; yet I am serene. I go to find comfort, and my only fear is, that my poor body will be insulted by an endeavour to recal [sic] my hated existence. But I shall plunge into the Thames where there is the least chance of my being snatched from the death I seek.

God bless you! May you never know by experience what you have made me endure. Should your sensibility ever awake, remorse will find its way to your heart; and, in the midst of business and sensual pleasure, I shall appear before you, the victim of your deviation from rectitude.

It was a serious threat and she carried it out resolutely that very afternoon. She hired a boat and rowed herself out to Putney Bridge from which, in the rainy dusk of an October evening, she jumped, after first soaking the skirts of her dress to make sure that she would sink. She did not. Instead, she was rescued by passing boatmen "only to lament that,

8 For the sake of clarity, throughout this essay Mary Shelley will be referred to as Mary Shelley. Obviously at this point, and until she was married in 1816, she was still Mary Godwin.

when the bitterness of death was past, I was inhumanly brought back to life and misery."

She succumbed to one final reflex of hope and offered Imlay the same opportunity she had given to Mrs. Fuseli. She proposed a *ménage à trois:* Imlay, his new mistress, and herself. This time, there was nothing said about Plato.

Finally the affair tapered off and Mary Wollstonecraft resumed her life as a writer, until, in 1796, there came the meeting with Godwin followed by a gentler wooing, a kinder loving, and a brief, golden, if not always absolutely calm, marriage. Then came Mary Shelley's**8** birth, and Mary Wollstonecraft's brutal and lingering death.

For nearly four years Godwin struggled, with the help of servants and friends, to raise the infant Mary and her half sister, Fanny Imlay. Grown desperate, he made several clumsy marriage proposals to women who rejected him. Finally he was himself wooed and won by his next-door neighbor, a supposititious widow with green spectacles who won the shy philosopher's heart one evening in 1801 by observing to him from her balcony, "Is it possible that I behold the immortal Godwin?" It was possible, and the marriage between England's leading thinker and the woman whose extremely modest attainments included good cooking and a legible handwriting, was solemnized on December 21 of that same year.

It was not, from Mary Shelley's point of view, a fortuitous marriage. Her stepmother, Mary Jane Clairmont, had two children: Charles and Jane (later Claire) Clairmont. Godwin's child, Mary, was no relation to her, and Fanny Imlay was related to nobody in the household. Godwin, a brilliant thinker, turned out to be a very bad domestic manager. The family was constantly in money trouble.

When Mary Shelley was fifteen, on the grounds that she was suffering from ill health, but more likely to get her out of the clutches of her stepmother, she was sent off to Scotland where she stayed two years. When she returned to London, an intellectually awakened and handsome seventeen-year-old, she found that the poet Percy Bysshe Shelley was a frequent visitor to her father's house. Shelley was hardly known as yet but it was already clear that his genius was smoldering. Besides, he was a source of comfort to her impecunious father, to whom he lent substantial sums of money. It took hardly any time before Mary and the married Percy, who had written off his wife, Harriet Westbrook Shelley, as an intellectual

9 Edward John Trelawny, a close friend of Percy and Mary Shelley who later cooled in his affection for Mary, describes her in his *Recollection of the Last Days of Shelley and Byron* (p. 15) as follows: "The most striking feature in her face was her calm, grey eyes; she was rather under the English standard of a woman's height, very fair and light-haired, witty, social, and animated in the society of friends, though mournful in solitude; like Shelley, though in a minor degree, she had the power of expressing her thoughts in varied and appropriate words, derived from familiarity with the works of our vigorous old writers."

And Mary Cowden Clarke, in her *Recollections of Writers* (p. 38), describing Mary Shelley, writes: "Her well shaped golden head, almost always a little bent and drooping—her marble white shoulders and arms statuesquely visible in the perfectly plain black velvet dress which the custom of the time allowed to be cut low . . . her thoughtful earnest eyes; the short upper lip and intellectually curved mouth, with a certain close compressed and decisive expression while she listened, with a relaxation into fuller redness and mobility when speaking; her exquisitely formed, white, dimpled small hands, with rosy palms, and plumply commencing fingers, that tapered into tips as slender as those of a Vandyke portrait."

dud, were in love. The blonde pensive[9] young woman and the mercurial poet spent hours sitting on her mother's gravestone, talking profundities and holding hands. On July 28, 1814, the couple ran off together, much to the freethinking Godwin's consternation. For reasons no one has ever satisfactorily explained, Mary Shelley's stepsister, Jane (now Claire) Clairmont, joined the impassioned flight to the continent. Claire, with her dark, soulful, striking Gypsy beauty was to be with the Shelleys off and on for many years.

When the trio returned to England six weeks later, Mary Shelley was pregnant. Just the same, at Shelley's instigation (he dreamed of sexual communes), she involved herself in a somewhat ambiguous affair with the poet, and Shelley's friend, Thomas Jefferson Hogg. Her baby girl was born, prematurely, on February 22, 1815, and died two weeks later. Not two months later, Mary Shelley was pregnant again. Her second child, William, was born on January 24, 1816.

In the months that followed, the Shelleys were beset by money troubles, by the social pressure English gentility reserved for sinful lovers, and by Shelley's recurrent illness. They concluded at last that England was too uncomfortable to be endured. Accompanied once more by Claire, the Shelley

CLAIRE CLAIRMONT.

10 Byron wrote to his half sister Augusta, "Now don't scold—but what could I do? A foolish girl, in spite of all I could say or do would come after me . . . I was not in love nor have any possible love left for any, but I could not exactly play the Stoic with a woman who had scrambled eight hundred miles to un-philosophize me."

11 Actually, Mary Shelley's description seems to be a composite of events that took place on more than one night. James Rieger, in his edition of *Frankenstein* (pp. xvii–xviii), writes that "the available evidence indicates that 'poor Polidori,' not Byron, was Shelley's partner in the scientific conversation that precipitated Mary's germinal, nightmare image of the Monster."

ménage, on May 3, 1816, made its way to Geneva where the Shelleys took a house, the Maison Chapuis, on the shore of Lake Léman. Switzerland was chosen probably at Claire's insistence. In London, Claire, with artless lust, had offered herself to the poet Byron who was willing enough to have a casual affair. Now, pregnant and hoping to maintain the liaison, Claire pushed the Shelleys to go to Switzerland. Percy Shelley, who could see the intellectual advantages of a friendship with Byron, acquiesced in, or perhaps even connived at, the move.

The *Frankenstein* summer of 1816 turned out to be a resplendent one. The Shelleys did indeed meet Byron who, accompanied by his physician, John Polidori, rented the Villa Diodati, which was only a brief distance from the Maison Chapuis, and the two households visited each other frequently. On sunny days, Byron and Shelley, both avid sailors, explored places of interest around Lake Léman. For the others, there were walks, picnics, excursions. Mary Shelley studied hard, looked after little William, and developed an innocent friendship with Polidori, who was referred to, even by his friends, as "poor Poly." For a time Claire's liaison with Byron was resumed,**10** eagerly on her part, with a certain weariness on his.

We come back now to that famous rainy evening in Geneva. As Mary Shelley gives it to us from the vantage point of her 1831 respectable widowhood, it would appear to be one more pleasant occasion when good and high-minded friends sat about the fire and amused themselves by frightening one other in a safe place.

It is a Kodachrome snapshot,**11** redolent with pleasant memories, but as with any snapshot, there is an unseen context for the picture that now we must recall.

First, there is Mary Shelley herself. She was an eighteen-year-old woman who had had to live all her life with the knowledge that her own birth had killed her mother. To this must be added the uncertainty she undoubtedly lived with as an unmarried mother. No matter what advanced views she may have held about open marriages, she knew very well that Percy Shelley had abandoned a *wife* with two small children. How much more tenuous then must be a mistress's hold upon him?

Then, there was Byron, who had to contend that evening (or one like it) with the hungry light in Claire Clairmont's eye. He already loathed her, and to make things worse, she was carrying his baby. Byron knew what the world thought of him. He was its model of a fascinating monster: a genius, titled, las-

12 Writing of Polidori, Byron once observed that he was "exactly the kind of person to whom, if he fell overboard one would hold out a straw, to know if the old adage be true that drowning men catch at straws."

13 The friendship between Byron and Shelley had its own ambiguities. Byron admired the sweep and scope of Shelley's mind. Shelley, comparatively unknown as a poet, was exhilarated in Byron's presence even as he was occasionally nipped by jealousy for the older poet's great fame.

It may be that there was another undercurrent of feeling among the men in the room that night. Leslie A. Marchand, in *Byron: A Biography*, tells us that Byron was always drawn to the company of handsome younger men. Marchand writes: "How early Byron was aware of the sexual implication of these passionate friendships, it is difficult to know: possibly before he left Harrow, probably while he was at Cambridge, and certainly while he was in Greece on his first pilgrimage. There seems little doubt, if one considers dispassionately the total evidence now available, that a strong attraction to boys persisted in Byron from his Harrow days throughout his life."

14 In 1816, it was probably still a Platonic relationship. Richard Holmes, Shelley's most recent biographer, believes that "brought closely together by the mutual worries over Allegra [Claire's daughter by Byron] and Elise [the Swiss nursemaid in the Shelley household], Shelley and Claire became lovers during the nineteen days spent alone on the road to Venice, and at Este in August and September 1818, Claire conceived a child by Shelley" (Holmes, *Shelley: The Pursuit*, p. 482).

15 William Godwin, hysterically protective of his reputation, "forbade the Shelleys to go to Swansea or claim the body, and he himself was so discreet as to turn back his own journey at Bristol. No one went to see Fanny buried, and relatives were at first told that she had gone to Ireland; and later that she had died from a severe cold. Charles, her half brother [sic—he was her stepbrother], was still not informed of her death by the following summer" (Holmes, *Shelley: The Pursuit*, p. 347).

civious, lame. Sometimes he agreed with the world, and brooded about "the nightmare of [his] own delinquencies."

The other lines of feeling drawn between the people in the Villa Diodati on that famous night are almost too intricate to be drawn in detail. Polidori was jealous of Shelley's growing friendship with Byron. Byron treated Polidori like a plaything.**12** Mary Shelley was jealous of Byron, who took Shelley away from her for whole days at a time to go sailing.**13** Claire was yearning for Byron, but at the same time managed a strangely erotic relationship with Shelley with whom she often stayed up late at night when Mary was not feeling well. Shelley, in turn, comforted Claire by telling her tales of blood and gore until he rendered her hysterical, after which he put her tenderly to bed.**14**

The luminous *Frankenstein* summer ended for the Shelleys in May 1816, and they returned to England, where in the space of a few months (and while *Frankenstein* was still being written) their lives were suddenly touched by a couple of ugly deaths. Fanny Imlay, Mary Shelley's half sister, had come once more to the conclusion that she was not much loved in the Godwin household. She was not Godwin's daughter. She was not Mary Jane Clairmont's daughter. She judged, perhaps reasonably, that to be the object of everyone's duty and nobody's love was sufficient reason for suicide. On October 11, in a rundown Swansea hotel, she replayed a scene from her mother's life, but this time more convincingly. The overdose of laudanum she took killed her.**15**

Two months later, as Mary Shelley was finishing Chapter IV of *Frankenstein*, the news reached her and Shelley that Shelley's wife, Harriet, had been found floating in the Serpentine (an arch of the Thames), a suicide, and pregnant, though not with Shelley's child.

A little more than two weeks after Harriet Shelley's death, on December 29, Percy and Mary, neither of whom believed in the institution of marriage, were married, probably so that the poet might gain sufficient respectability in the transaction to impress the courts in which he was litigating the custody of his children by Harriet Shelley. That freethinker Godwin, who had been hostile to the Shelleys because of their scandalous elopement, was instantly reconciled to the newlyweds, and like any bourgeois gentleman, strutted with pleasure at their respectability.

On April 17, 1817, while Mary Shelley was pregnant with her third child, *Frankenstein* was finished. Though Percy Shelley worked hard in its behalf,

THE BAY OF LERICI, FROM WHICH SHELLEY
EMBARKED ON HIS FATAL JOURNEY.

the book did not find a publisher easily. Meanwhile little Clara Shelley was born in London on September 2, 1817. The baby died in Venice on September 24 of the same year. On March 11, 1818, *Frankenstein* was published anonymously by Lackington and Hughes, a not quite reputable house. The book was received with reasonably good, but occasionally harsh, reviews. *Blackwood's Magazine* admired the fiction, but when it became known that its author was a woman, it confessed that "for a man it was excellent, but for a woman it was wonderful." The *Quarterly Review* detested it, ranting that it was "a tissue of horrible and disgusting absurdity." Mary Shelley was launched on her career.

There is a Portuguese proverb that says, "God writes straight with crooked lines." Mary Shelley's career was launched just as she was assailed by new grief. Her son, William, died in Rome on June 7, 1819. Already pregnant when the beloved "Wilmouse" died, she gave birth to a son, Percy Florence Shelley, on November 12, 1819, in the city of Florence. He was the only one of her children who lived to become an adult.

She was not done yet with birth and death. On April 19, 1822, Allegra, Claire's five-year-old daughter by Byron, died in the Italian convent at Bagnacavello where she had been sent by her father. Two months later Mary Shelley herself came to the very brink of death after a miscarriage. Her life was probably saved by Shelley's quick thinking in that emergency. Then, on July 8, 1822, while she was still weak from the effects of her fifth pregnancy in eight years, she was dealt the unbearable blow. Percy Shelley, the avid sailor who had never learned to swim, was lost in a storm at sea off the Gulf of Spezia. Ten days later his sea-torn body was washed ashore.

Then followed a last flourish of the crooked lines. On August 16, Shelley's body was awkwardly cremated in a ceremony that was presided over by Edward Trelawny. Leigh Hunt was there, as was Byron. Byron, who could not stand the smell of burning flesh, avoided it by taking a swim. Trelawny saved Shelley's unburned heart from the furnace, intending to keep it as a souvenir, but Leigh Hunt, pleading the closeness of his friendship for Shelley, asked to have it. The result was that the stunned Mary Shelley, before she had had time to grasp the fact of her husband's death, was involved in an incredible correspondence with Hunt in which she pleaded for the heart. Hunt at first refused to give it up, but he was eventually, if grudgingly, persuaded, and Mary

16   The tower in the Protestant Cemetery in Rome beside which the poet was buried.

17   One should except from this judgment the brief but powerful novel *Matilda*, which was not published in Mary Shelley's lifetime. *Matilda*, a high-pitched tale of father-daughter incest, is nearly as excoriating as *Frankenstein* in what it suggests of Mary Shelley's emotional life in her golden years with Shelley.

18   There is a widespread view (publicly encouraged by Mary Shelley in her lifetime) that she did not remarry because she preferred to spend the rest of her life tending the flame of her husband's memory. But there is more reason to suppose that Mary Shelley, a widow at twenty-five, who had lived through five pregnancies in eight years, and whose mother had died in childbed, might shy away from further opportunities for pregnancy.

Shelley was allowed to sink into the rest of her life without any further need to claw or to beseech.

A sense of desolation, which had always been ready to assail her even while Percy Shelley lived, was for a long time her most persistent companion. Six months after his death she wrote in her *Journal* (p. 192), "Oh, Shelley, dear, lamented, beloved! help me, raise me, support me; let me not feel ever thus fallen and degraded! My imagination is dead, my genius lost, my energies sleep. Why am I not beneath that weed-grown tower?"**16**

But the force for survival reasserted itself, and she eventually resumed her self-education and her writing. With a small allowance from Shelley's father, combined with what she earned by her pen, she and her son, Percy Florence Shelley, managed to lead respectable, if unremarkable lives. Little that she wrote after *Frankenstein* has much except scholarly interest**17** to modern readers. The rest of her life, except for two or three not quite realized romantic flurries (one, more on her side than his, with the American writer Washington Irving), was just as unremarkable. Until she died, on February 1, 1851, she lived the quiet, productive, essentially bourgeois life of an English widow.**18**

In the Western tradition, tales of people making people can be found quite far back in the past. The Greeks had Hephaistos, the lame metalworker (Aphrodites' husband), who was credited with making female servants out of gold for himself. Lucian, a second-century Greek, tells the story of an Egyptian priest who also created a servant out of such materials as came to hand. The account of Pygmalion, the Greek sculptor, was, of course, well known to Mary Shelley. The Pygmalion tale, with its emphasis on the power of love to generate life, may have been especially interesting to her. It will be remembered that Pygmalion so detested women for their inconstancy that he abjured the sex forever, but erotic images of them kept pressing against his imagination until, to ease his woes, he carved himself an ivory statue of a woman that was so beautiful he fell desperately in love with it. Frustrated by the inert coldness of his creation, he prayed fervently to the gods for help, until Aphrodite, taking pity on him, turned the statue into living flesh.

One would suppose that the story of Prometheus would have had a great influence on *Frankenstein*. After all, the subtitle of Mary Shelley's fiction reads "The Modern Prometheus." But though she makes use of the *Prometheus plasticator* aspect of the story—

19   The assertion that *Frankenstein* is science fiction has been so frequently made that it has taken on the authority of a folk belief whose truth it may be foolhardy to resist. Nevertheless: *Frankenstein* is a psychological allegory in which the issues are, to use Norbert Wiener's great phrase, "the human use of human beings."

In 1891, Richard Garnett, in his introduction to Mary Shelley's *Tale and Stories* (p. vi), defines the moral issue perfectly. He writes: "Mary Shelley's original intention was probably that which would alone have occurred to most writers in her place. She meant to paint Frankenstein's monstrous creation as an object of unmitigated horror. The perception that he was an object of intense compassion as well imparted a moral value to what otherwise would have remained a daring flight of imagination. It has done more: it has helped to create, if it did not itself beget, a type of personage unknown to ancient fiction. The conception of a character at once justly execrable and truly pitiable is altogether modern." Garnett's is a fine assessment of Mary Shelley's achievement, but one would like to add that she created two such horrid and pitiable figures, not one.

Prometheus, the shaper, who made people out of clay—there is very little sustained effort in the fiction to exploit the myth. The Jewish tradition of the golem is also mentioned as a possible source for *Frankenstein*, but there is no evidence I can find to show that she knew the story. The golem tale that is best known to modern times is the one that credits the great Rabbi Löw, who lived in Prague at the end of the sixteenth century, with making a living creature out of clay. The story, if Mary Shelley did not know it, should have interested her, because Rabbi Löw animated his creature not by the power of intellect, but by invoking the power of God. Rabbi Löw, a very holy man, had acquired the secret of the *Shem ha-Meforash*, the unknowable, unspeakable name of God, and his clay creature was animated to protect the lives of the threatened Jewish community in Prague.

Another influence on *Frankenstein* that is frequently mentioned is the eighteenth- and early-nineteenth-century interest in automata. Certainly, there was a plethora of beautiful, mechanically animated toys being made in Europe in the decades before *Frankenstein*. There were peacocks that could spread their tails, mechanical pictures, ducks with all their tail feathers in place, talking dolls, peasants making shoes, bell-ringing monks, and jiggling skeletons. But charming as such toys might be, Mary Shelley's attention was on something else.

By a process that is in its own way fascinating, the story of *Frankenstein*, written by a young woman who was dealing with a particular set of female experiences and fears, has come to be read as a science fiction**19** allegory of the dangers of science. We are familiar with the film view of the case: white-coated, perhaps mad, scientists bending over to animate the creature's body in violation of a mysterious decree—"There are some things mankind is not permitted to know."

But science, despite Percy Shelley's name-dropping in the Preface he wrote to *Frankenstein*, is hardly visible in the novel. Mary Shelley, it is true, nods dutifully to the achievements of science in her day but she makes almost no effort to give to her tale that patina of verisimilitude that science fiction requires. Her protagonist, Victor, for example, is a semi-hemi-demi chemist and sometime anatomist who, after two years in college, is able, working in his private chambers, to discover the secret of life, a secret that had eluded the greatest human minds before he put his sophomore's attention to the problem. Mary

Shelley handles the matter with the aplomb of a writer. A couple of strokes of the pen and genius has behaved like genius! *Soit!*

Frankenstein does not touch us because Victor Frankenstein is a scientist but because his creature was born ugly, because Victor abandoned him, because the creature's life is spent in a long, long pilgrimage toward his father/mother's love. The issue is not the scientist's laboratory; rather it is the "workshop of filthy creation" in which love and birth, and their consequence—death—take place.

Just the same, *Frankenstein* does make a dark statement about science, because Mary Shelley intuited, long before Henry Adams put the matter elegantly to us, that the direction in which civilization moves is determined by what it understands of the nature of power. Force, Henry Adams called it—the occult force that modifies people in their relationship to the world. "The rays," Adams writes, "that Langley disowned, as well as those which he fathered, were occult, supersensual, irrational; they were a revelation of mysterious energy like that of the Cross; they were what, in terms of medieval science, were called immediate modes of the divine substance." That force, just in case this discussion has become suddenly abstruse, Adams recognized and named for what it was: sexual energy, and particularly the animating energy of woman. Writing of the Virgin, whose power he equates with that of Aphrodite, and to which he compares that of the "dynamo," Adams says:

She was goddess because of her force; she was the animated dynamo; she was reproduction—the greatest and most mysterious of all energies; all she needed was to be fecund (*The Education of Henry Adams*, p. 384).

The connection now becomes clear. In *Frankenstein* the energy toward fecundity, toward wholesome life such as might be expressed by love and responsible parenthood, is distorted by a life-offending egotism. Male egotism, as no doubt Mary Shelley experienced it, but, in the atomic and computer age, an egotism pure.

As fiction, *Frankenstein*, tends to be treated as a subliterary classic. Certainly, it is a work frequently lacking in skill. It would be easy enough to make a list of Mary Shelley's mistakes as a novelist: she overwrites; she makes relentless use of coincidence; her men and women (though not the creature) can be garrulous stick figures. But finally, there is the vision itself that, surmounting youthful uncertainty, inexperience, and wrongheadedness, leaves us with the sense that we have been taken by the hair and thrust into the presence of the awful truth. Muriel Spark, one of the wisest of the writers on *Frankenstein*, commenting on R. Glynn Grylls's view that "*Frankenstein* remains a period piece, of not very good date; historically interesting but not one of the living novels of the world," said that "a novel need not be mighty in order to be vital; it need not be a product of genius to survive as a classic." As a novel, *Frankenstein*, it must be admitted, is not mighty; on the other hand, it is a work that offers us a powerful and enduring vision. Surely genius was required for that.

There is a gnostic myth that tells us that God, gazing intently into the water of light, generated a female being called Barbelo. In her turn, Barbelo, gazing intently at God, bore a son who became the Lord of the Universe, after which, in a series of descents from light, the world went from bad to worse. If the tale is true, it may explain why, when we see Victor Frankenstein's creature lurching across the movie screen of a darkened theater, we intuit that we and the creature are in the right place. There he stands, lifting first his eyes and then his hands to the mysterious light, compelled into life by Mary Shelley's vision. His hands waver, but despite error and pain, despite confusion and terror, he keeps reaching upward to an eternal fire. True, his task and ours is hopeless, but that stumbling flesh has a responsibility to reach toward light is always clear.

1 *Frankenstein*. Literally the "stone of the Franks." Radu Florescu, in his *In Search of Frankenstein* (pp. 90–97), makes an extensive and unconvincing argument that Percy and Mary Shelley, accompanied by Claire Clairmont, visited Castle Frankenstein in the vicinity of Darmstadt early in September 1814 as they were making their way down the Rhine on their way back to England in the course of the Shelleys' elopement summer. Florescu's conspiracy theory holds that mention of the visit was later suppressed by both Mary Shelley and Claire Clairmont in order to defend Mary's claim to originality in having found the beginnings of her plot in a vision.

2 *Prometheus*. The story of Prometheus was particularly attractive to the Romantic Age, which had been stirred by two major events at the end of the eighteenth century: advancing industrialism and the French Revolution, both of which seemed to offer utopian promises. It saw him as embodying at once Christ's compassion toward mankind and the tragic heroism of Satan.

The myth of Prometheus as fire-bringer is well known. He was the Titan, in Greek lore, who stole fire from heaven and gave it to humanity. Zeus punished him for this act of generosity by fixing him to a rock in the Caucasus to which each day an eagle came to devour Prometheus's liver.

There is a lesser known aspect to the Prometheus myth: the story of *Prometheus plasticator*, in which Prometheus is seen as the creator of mankind. Christopher Small, in *Mary Shelley's Frankenstein* (p. 48), describes how Prometheus created man in three stages: "the shaping of man by Prometheus as sculptor, his endowment with life by a winged being who applies fire to his body, and his animation by Minerva, who brings his soul in the form of a butterfly or a bee." Percy Shelley, writing to Mary as early as October 25, 1814, included a quotation from Aeschylus's play *Prometheus Bound*. Byron later would be influenced by Shelley's translation of Aeschylus in the shaping of his own "Prometheus," written during the famous 1816 summer when Mary Shelley was writing *Frankenstein*. In Percy Shelley's notes to an early poem "Queen Mab," (1812–1815), Prometheus is by no means a heroic figure. There he is blamed for bringing fire to mankind and thereby seducing the human race to the foul vice of meat-eating. In later years, after the publication of *Frankenstein*, Shelley would write of Prometheus that "the only imaginary being resembling in any degree Prometheus, is Satan; and Prometheus is, in my judgement, a more poetical character than Satan, because, in addition to courage, and majesty, and firm and patient opposition to omnipotent force, he is susceptible of being described as exempt from the taints of ambition, envy, revenge, and a desire for personal aggrandisement . . . [Prometheus] is, as it were, the type of the highest perfection of moral and intellectual nature."

3 *Paradise Lost*. As will be noted later, *Paradise Lost* (1667) is frequently referred to in *Frankenstein*. Milton's poem often serves Mary Shelley as the lens through which she sees her own creation.

FRANKENSTEIN; [1]

OR,

THE MODERN PROMETHEUS. [2]

———◆———

IN THREE VOLUMES.

———◆———

Did I request thee, Maker, from my clay
To mould me man ? Did I solicit thee
From darkness to promote me ?——
                    PARADISE LOST. [3]

———

VOL. I.

———

London:

PRINTED FOR

LACKINGTON, HUGHES, HARDING, MAVOR, & JONES,
FINSBURY SQUARE.

———

1818.

WILLIAM GODWIN BY J. W. CHANDLER.

1 *William Godwin.* Godwin has already been dealt with in the introduction. Here it is only necessary to say that two of his novels, *Saint Leon* and especially *Caleb Williams,* had a direct influence on *Frankenstein.* Caleb Williams in Godwin's fiction is seen as overwhelmed by the forces of an unjust society whose enmity he himself starts into motion by his discovery of the guilty secret of Falkland, an otherwise kindly and decent gentleman. Falkland is so attached to the trappings of respectability that he undertakes an elaborate oppression of Caleb Williams as a way of keeping himself from exposure. Williams and Falkland, through the rest of the novel, dance about each other a ghastly dance of destiny. The secret and the oppression bind the two in an inexorable union that is only ended with Falkland's penitential death. *Saint Leon* is notable for its protagonist who has acquired both the elixir of life *and* the philosopher's stone.

1 *Preface.* The preface was entirely written by Percy Shelley, perhaps as part of his sense of obligation to the publishers, Lackington, Allen and Company of London, whom he had assured that "as to any mere inaccuracies of language, I should feel myself authorized to amend them when revising proofs." On October 23, 1817, he wrote to Lackington that "on my part I shall of course do my utmost (for my friend) . . . I have paid considerable attention to the correction of such few instances of baldness of style as necessarily occurs in the production of a very young writer."

James Rieger, in the introduction to his edition of *Frankenstein* (p. xix), offers the suggestion that Shelley meddled with Mary Shelley's prose enough so that "one hardly knows whether to regard him as editor or minor collaborator." This is, I think, an extreme judgment. The changes Mary Shelley accepted, though they are sometimes substantive, are no more or no less valuable than those that working writers accept from their editors. The donnée is unquestionably hers.

ERASMUS DARWIN.

2 *Darwin.* The physician Erasmus Darwin (1731–1802), grandfather of the more famous evolutionist Charles Darwin, was one of the most distinguished scientists of his age. A friend of the Godwin family, Darwin, a zestful womanizer and an audacious stut-

1 # PREFACE.

———

2 THE event on which this fiction is founded has been supposed, by Dr. Darwin, and some of the physiological writers of Germany, as not of impossible occurrence. I shall not be supposed as according the remotest degree of serious faith to such an imagination; yet, in assuming it as the basis of a work of fancy, I have not considered myself as merely weaving a series of supernatural terrors. The event on which the interest of the story depends is exempt from the disadvantages of a mere tale of spectres or enchantment. It was recommended by the novelty of the situations which it developes; and, however impossible as a physical fact, affords a point of view to the imagination for the delineating of human passions more comprehensive and commanding than any which the ordinary relations of existing events can yield.

I have thus endeavoured to preserve the truth of the elementary

terer, was capable of dominating any conversation despite his handicap. A corpulent man, Darwin gave sound advice to his contemporaries on diet. His famous prescription for the disease *pallor et tremor a timore* was "Opium. Wine. Food. Joy."

What is fascinating about Erasmus Darwin is that he was an early friend of Matthew Bolton, who would later become James Watt's partner in the further development of the steam engine, an invention proposed, in fact, some years earlier by Darwin himself. The list of Darwin's friends, most of them members of the Lunar Society (because it met before the full moon in order to save candlepower), reads like a committee of godfathers to the Industrial Revolution: Josiah Wedgwood, potter; James Keir, chemist; James Watt, engineer; Richard Lovell Edgeworth, inventor; and William Small, professor of natural philosophy.

In the Introduction to the 1831 edition of *Frankenstein*, Mary Shelley refers to the "experiments of Dr. Darwin . . . who preserved a piece of vermicelli in a glass case, till by some extraordinary means it began to move with voluntary motion." It is a curious reference, which has been illuminated for me by a personal communication from Darwin's biographer, Desmond King-Hele, who writes: "Mary Shelley's remarks can, I think, be regarded as recording a mixed-up remembrance by Byron and Shelley of what Darwin wrote in his first note to *The Temple of Nature*. It is entitled 'Spontaneous Vitality of Microscopic animals' . . . Darwin does refer (p. 3) to a 'paste composed of flour and water' in which 'the animalcules called eels' are seen in great abundance and gradually become larger, even in a 'sealed glass phial.' He also refers (p. 7) to the *vorticella* coming to life after being dried. Put this lot together and stir it, and you might arrive at Mary's report." Darwin's most famous works, *The Zoönomia* and *The Temple of Nature*, are treatises written in quite skillful if endless heroic couplets.

3 *principles of human nature.* Percy Shelley *cum* Mary is echoing Pope's dictum. "True wit is Nature to advantage dressed,/What oft was thought, but n'ere so well expressed." (Alexander Pope, "Essay on Criticism," part II, ll. 297–98.)

3 principles of human nature, while I have not scrupled to innovate upon their combinations. The *Iliad*, the tragic poetry of Greece,—Shakespeare, in the *Tempest* and *Midsummer Night's Dream*,—and most especially Milton, in *Paradise Lost*, conform to this rule; and the most humble novelist, who seeks to confer or receive amusement from his labours, may, without presumption, apply to prose fiction a licence, or rather a rule, from the adoption of which so many exquisite combinations of human feeling have resulted in the highest specimens of poetry.

The circumstance on which my story rests was suggested in casual conversation. It was commenced, partly as a source of amusement, and partly as an expedient for exercising any untried resources of mind. Other motives were mingled with these, as the work proceeded. I am by no means indifferent to the manner in which whatever moral tendencies exist in the sentiments or characters it contains shall affect the reader; yet my chief concern in this respect has been limited to the avoiding the enervating effects of the novels of the present day, and to the exhibition of the amiableness of domestic affection, and the excellence of universal virtue. The opinions which naturally spring from the

4 *German stories of ghosts.* The collection was the *Fantasmagoriana, ou Recueil d'Histoires d'Apparitions de Spectres, Revenans, Fantomes, etc.: Traduit de l'Allemand, par un Amateur* (Paris, 1812). The amateur was Jean Baptiste Benoit Eyvies (1767–1846). The book is a charming collection of ghostly tales more elegant and amusing than they are frightening.

Mary Shelley, though she does not remember the tales accurately, clearly found in them various plot elements that seemed especially significant to her; as, for instance, the story of the young ventriloquist whose trick it was to "animate" a head taken from a corpse. On the occasion of the tale, the head, stolen from a body recently buried, turns out to be that of the young mountebank's father.

5 *Two other friends.* Actually, there were more than two: Byron, Shelley, William Polidori, and Claire Clairmont, according to Mary Shelley's introduction to the 1831 edition of *Frankenstein*.

LORD BYRON IN SILHOUETTE
BY LEIGH HUNT.

6 *has been completed.* In one sense this is true. On the other hand, Polidori, taking off from a tale by Byron involving vampires, did later introduce into English literature the prototype of the elegant vampire in his *The Vampyre, A Tale*, published in 1819.

character and situation of the hero are by no means to be conceived as existing always in my own conviction; nor is any inference justly to be drawn from the following pages as prejudicing any philosophical doctrine of whatever kind.

It is a subject also of additional interest to the author, that this story was begun in the majestic region where the scene is principally laid, and in society which cannot cease to be regretted. I passed the summer of 1816 in the environs of Geneva. The season was cold and rainy, and in the evenings we crowded around a blazing wood fire, and occasionally

4 amused ourselves with some German stories of ghosts, which happenened to fall into our hands. These tales excited in us a playful

5 desire of imitation. Two other friends (a tale from the pen of one of whom would be far more acceptable to the public than any thing I can ever hope to produce) and myself agreed to write each a story, founded on some supernatural occurrence.

The weather, however, suddenly became serene; and my two friends left me on a journey among the Alps, and lost, in the magnificent scenes which they present, all memory of their ghostly visions. The following tale is the only one which

6 has been completed.

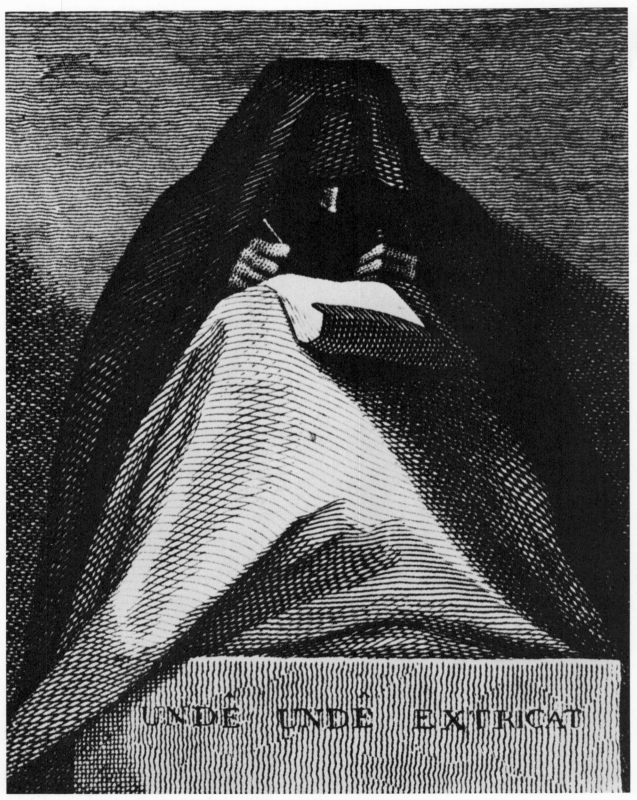

UNDÈ UNDÈ EXTRICAT

HOW, HOW TO ESCAPE BY HENRY FUSELI.

1 *Letter I*. Structurally, *Frankenstein* is in the popular eighteenth-century tradition of the epistolary novel. The letter-writing form that Fielding, Richardson, and Smollett used so effectively serves Mary Shelley, as it served them, in two ways: It gives an aura of verisimilitude to the action; and it permits her to manipulate the reader's point of view. Interestingly enough, when Bram Stoker came to write *Dracula* (1897) he too organized his novel as a series of letters and journal entries.

Mary Shelley's mother, Mary Wollstonecraft, and William Godwin, her father, were prolific letter writers who, at various stages of their relationship, wrote letters to each other though they lived next door. Percy and Mary Shelley were also voluminous correspondents.

2 Mrs. *Saville*. One of the pleasanter occupations that waits for a reader of *Frankenstein* is to speculate on just what kind of woman Mrs. Saville is. She is, after all, the recipient of the packet of letters in which, so goes Mary Shelley's fiction, the entire story of *Frankenstein* is contained.

From Robert Walton, the author of the letters, we will learn that Mrs. Saville is affectionate and tender; that she is married and has lovely children and that he, Walton, deeply loves her. And, because Walton spends so much time reminding Mrs. Saville of the details of his own youth, we must suppose that the brother and sister must have been separated as they were growing up; or that Mrs. Saville has a very poor memory.

There is a special poignancy too about Mary Shelley's conception of these unsent and perhaps unsendable letters written in the wastelands of the Arctic intended to be read in England by a comfortable English matron.

ST. PETERSBURGH.

3 *St. Petersburgh*. Saint Petersburg (modern Leningrad) was established in 1703 when the stones were set for the foundation of the Peter-Paul fortress, the

FRANKENSTEIN;

OR, THE

MODERN PROMETHEUS.

———

LETTER I.

2 *To Mrs.* SAVILLE, *England.*

3,4 St. Petersburgh, Dec. 11th, 17—.

YOU will rejoice to hear that no disaster has accompanied the commencement of an enterprise which you have regarded with such evil forebodings. I arrived here yesterday; and my first task is to assure my dear sister of my welfare, and increasing confidence in the success of my undertaking.

I am already far north of London; and as I walk in the streets of Petersburgh, I feel a cold northern breeze play upon my cheeks, which braces my nerves, and fills me with delight. Do you understand this feeling? This breeze, which has travelled from the regions towards which I am advancing, **5** gives me a foretaste of those icy climes. Inspirited by this wind of promise, my day dreams become more fervent and vivid. I try in vain to be persuaded that the pole is the seat of frost and desolation; it ever presents itself to my imagination as the region of beauty and delight. There, Margaret, the

city's first structure after Peter the Great had wrested this Black Sea coastal area from the Swedes during the northern wars. In building this city, Peter the Great hoped to make Russia more accessible to the modernizing influences of western Europe. For some time there existed between Archangel (previously, Russia's only access to European trade) and Saint Petersburg a rivalry for dominant position as a trade center, but by increasing duties on goods coming through Archangel and by compelling the merchant class to live in Saint Petersburg, the czar shifted the balance to his newly built city.

4 *December 11th, 17—*. See the "Chronology of Events in *Frankenstein*," to be found in the Appendix of this edition.

5 *icy climes*. Of all the many film treatments of the Frankenstein story, only the Christopher Isherwood television version makes use of this arctic setting.

6 *for ever visible*. Forever is a considerable exaggeration. Light and dark in those latitudes alternate in six-month periods.

7 *snow and frost are banished*. This curious notion of a warm-water polar region is not Mary Shelley's invention. M. K. Joseph, in his edition of *Frankenstein* (p. 236), writes that the "belief in a warm-water Polar Sea . . . is as old as the classical legends of the Hyperboreans, who lived an idyllic existence at the back of the North Wind."

George Best, in his "Discourse" in *Hakluyt's Voyages* (1589), gives a spirited theoretical defense of the theory that it must be warm at the poles. Arguing from how warm the sun in London is at noon in October, he goes on to say (pp. 272–73) that the "same force of heat it hath to them that dwell under the pole, the space almost of two months during the time of the Summer solstitium, and that without intermingling of any colde night . . . This heat of ours continueth but one houre, while the Sun is in that meridian, but theirs continueth a long time in one height . . . and by continuall accesse is still increased and strengthened. And thus by a similitude of the equall height of the Sun in both places appeareth the commodious and moderate heat of the regions under the poles."

6 sun is for ever visible; its broad disk just skirting the horizon, and diffusing a perpetual splendour. There—for with your leave, my sister, I will put some trust in preceding navigators— **7** there snow and frost are banished; and, sailing over a calm sea, we may be wafted to a land surpassing in wonders and in beauty every region hitherto discovered on the habitable globe. Its productions and features may be without example, as the phænomena of the heavenly bodies undoubtedly are in those undiscovered solitudes. What may not be expected in a country of eternal light? I may there discover

"PERPETUAL SPLENDOUR."

THE WARM WATER POLE.

8 *a little boat . . . his native river.* The image of the little boat is no accident. Boats had a lifelong and ultimately tragic fascination for Shelley, despite the fact that he could not swim. In Mary's journals we frequently learn that Shelley has gone boating, leaving her alone. In particular, Shelley was drawn to sailing along riverways, as he did in 1815 when he, Mary Shelley, Peacock, and Charles Clairmont traveled up the Thames. In 1816 he pursues the theme of rivers in a letter to Peacock: "If possible, we think of descending the Danube in a boat, of visiting Constantinople and Athens, then Rome and the Tuscan cities, and returning by the south of France, always following great rivers . . . rivers are not like roads, the work of the hands of man; they imitate mind, which wanders at will over pathless deserts, and flows through nature's loveliest recesses" (*Letters of Percy Bysshe Shelley*, p. 489–90). Mary Shelley's mother too was a practiced oarswoman.

9 *North Pacific Ocean.* Now we know which of the famous "passages" he means to find. He will not be the first to make the search for the Northeast Passage. In 1533, the task of organizing the first English search to find the Northeast Passage was entrusted to Sebastian Cabot, the son of Giovanni Caboto (John Cabot). Sebastian Cabot had the resounding title of "Governour of the Mysterie and Companie of the Merchants Adventurers for the Discoverie of Regions, Dominions, Islands and Places Unknowen." Three ships were sent off on the voyage: the *Bona Esperanza*, the *Edward Bonaventure*, and the *Bona Confidentia*. Only the *Bonaventure* returned from the unsuccessful voyage.

For readers of *Frankenstein*, there is a certain special interest in the fact that the *Bonaventure* got as far as Kholmogory, later called Archangel—Robert Walton's point of embarkation for his trip. The pilot of the *Bonaventure* and his crew traveled overland to

the wondrous power which attracts the needle; and may regulate a thousand celestial observations, that require only this voyage to render their seeming eccentricities consistent for ever. I shall satiate my ardent curiosity with the sight of a part of the world never before visited, and may tread a land never before imprinted by the foot of man. These are my enticements, and they are sufficient to conquer all fear of danger or death, and to induce me to commence this laborious voyage with the joy a child feels when he embarks **8** in a little boat, with his holiday mates, on an expedition of discovery up his native river. But, supposing all these conjectures to be false, you cannot contest the inestimable benefit which I shall confer on all mankind to the last generation, by discovering a passage near the pole to those countries, to reach which at present so many months are requisite; or by ascertaining the secret of the magnet, which, if at all possible, can only be effected by an undertaking such as mine.

These reflections have dispelled the agitation with which I began my letter, and I feel my heart glow with an enthusiasm which elevates me to heaven; for nothing contributes so much to tranquillize the mind as a steady purpose,—a point on which the soul may fix its intellectual eye. This expedition has been the favourite dream of my early years. I have read with ardour the accounts of the various voyages which have been made in the prospect **9** of arriving at the North Pacific Ocean through the seas which surround the

"THIS EXPEDITION HAS BEEN THE FAVOURITE DREAM OF MY EARLY YEARS."

Moscow, where they met Ivan the Terrible. Hakluyt, in his *Voyages*, reports that the great czar took a liking to "Master George Killingsworth's beard . . . as indeed at that time it was not only thicke, broad and yellow colored, but in length five foote and two inches of assize." The czar's congenial interest in an English seaman's beard led to the ensuing very profitable trade between Russia and England.

There was one other early English attempt to find a Northeast Passage. Jeanette Mirsky, writing in *To the Arctic*, p. 28, tells us that "in 1580 two tiny ships, the *George* of 40 tons, commanded by Arthur Pet, and the *William* of 20 tons, with Charles Jackman in command were sent to pierce the ice of the Kara Sea . . . Neither of these men lacked courage. Pet sailed through Yugor Strait, to the south of Vaygach, which for a time bore his name, only to be turned back by the continued ice and fog of the Kara Sea. Jackman never returned. Exploration to the eastward stopped; the Russia Company gave up all hope of accomplishing the Northeast Passage. Then it was forgotten in the beating of wings that carried hope exultingly to the west."

We will see in the course of *Frankenstein* what happens to Walton's expedition. In the real world, the Northeast Passage was finally traversed by Nils Adolf Erik, Baron Nordenskiöld, a Finn in the service of the king of Sweden. The Nordenskiöld expedition left Tromsø on July 18, 1878. On August 6, Nordenskiöld and his men entered Yugor Strait. For some two months, the vessels coasted the northernmost Russian coast, encountering a vast world of shifting ice, meeting with the hardy Chukchi natives for whom the "land of mist and snow" was home. On September 28, less than three months from the start of their expedition, with only one hundred and twenty miles to go before achieving their goal, they were stopped by immovable ice. For ten months, Nordenskiöld and his men lived in the frozen waste (by no means an isolated life—the Chukchi were constant and friendly visitors). With the coming of summer and the melting of the pack ice, the journey was resumed on July 18. Two days later, Nordenskiöld and his men entered the northernmost reaches of the Pacific, the first sailors to traverse the Northeast Passage.

10 *These volumes.* The best known of such volumes about voyages of discovery is no doubt Hakluyt's *Principal Navigations, Traffics, Voyages, and Discoveries of the English Nation,* published in 1589.

Samuel Purchas, in 1625, published a twenty-volume work, *Hakluyths Posthumus, or Purchas His Pilgrims,* in which are included accounts of the Hudson and the Baffin-Bylot expeditions. The books of travel and exploration that Mary Shelley read between the years 1814 and 1817 include: Mungo Park's *Travels in Africa,* Sir John Barrow's *Embassy to China, The Most Remarkable Year in the Life of Kotzebue, Containing His Exile into Siberia, By Himself,* translated by B. Beresford, *Voyages around the World* by George Baron Anson, and Evert Ides's *Three Years' Travels from Moscow Over-land to China.* An indicative entry in Mary Shelley's *Journal* for November 16, 1816 reads, "Draw, write [*Frankenstein*]; read old voyages."

11 *my father's dying injunction.* Walton is the first of various orphans about whom we will be reading. In *Frankenstein* there are either no whole families or families that are very quickly broken up. This paternal dying injunction, the only clue we have to Walton's relationship with his father, seems vindictive. Uncle Thomas, on the other hand, is "good," as is, of course, Margaret, in whom Walton confides.

The dying injunction is a favorite weapon in the arsenal of the Romantic novelist. There will be more of them as the story proceeds.

" . . . THROUGH THE SEAS
WHICH SURROUND THE POLE."

pole. You may remember, that a history of all the voyages made for purposes of discovery composed the whole of our good uncle Thomas's library. My education was neglected, yet I was passionately fond of read-

10 ing. These volumes were my study day and night, and my familiarity with them increased that regret which I had felt, as a child, on learning that

11 my father's dying injunction had forbidden my uncle to allow me to embark in a sea-faring life.

These visions faded when I perused, for the first time, those poets whose effusions entranced my soul, and lifted it to heaven. I also became a poet, and for one year lived in a Paradise of my own creation; I imagined that I also might obtain a niche in the temple where the names of Homer and Shakespeare are consecrated. You are well acquainted with my failure, and how

12 *I bore the disappointment.* As *Frankenstein* was being written, Percy Shelley had not yet been recognized for the great poet he would become. These words of Walton's echo Shelley's youthful letter to William Godwin, Mary Shelley's father, in the course of which Shelley introduced himself as the "son of a man of fortune in Sussex.—The habits of thinking of my Father and myself never coincided. . . . I could not descend to common life. The sublime interest of poetry, lofty and exalted achievements, the proselytism of the world, the equalization of its inhabitants were to me the soul of my soul" (*Letters of Percy Bysshe Shelley*, pp. 227–28). Shelley was nineteen at the time of this letter.

In December 1816, while Mary Shelley was at work on her masterpiece, Shelley's sense of himself was expressed in a letter to Leigh Hunt. He wrote that he had "powers deeply to interest or substantially improve, mankind," he felt himself "an outcast from human society; my name is execrated by all who would understand its entire import, . . . I am an object of compassion to a few more benevolent than the rest. All else abhor and avoid me." Mary Shelley, in her life with the poet, was to learn at very close hand how painful poetic disappointment could be.

13 *Six years.* When he was twenty-two. We will learn later (p. 16) that Walton is twenty-eight.

14 *I dedicated myself to this great enterprise.* Walton here calmly tells us of his polar passion and his preparations for achieving his goal. Nearly a hundred years later, Dr. Frederick A. Cook, in his book *My Attainment of the Pole* (1912), was to write, "I recall sitting alone one gloomy winter day. Opening a paper, I read that Parry was preparing his 1891 expedition to the Arctic. I cannot explain my sensations. It was as if a door to a prison cell had opened. I felt the first indomitable, commanding call of the Northland. To invade the Unknown, to assail the vastness of the white, frozen North—all that was latent in me, the impetus of that ambition born in childhood, perhaps before birth, and which had been stifled and starved, surged up tumultuously within me" (p. 27). Like the fictitious Walton, Cook went to elaborate lengths to prepare himself for polar exploration. He served on Parry's 1891 expedition to the Arctic, and later he hardened himself by scaling Mount McKinley. Sadly enough, Cook's account of his attainment reads like one long whine about the Parry conspiracy to rob him of the credit for the discovery.

PERCY BYSSHE SHELLEY.

12 heavily I bore the disappointment. But just at that time I inherited the fortune of my cousin, and my thoughts were turned into the channel of their earlier bent.

13 Six years have passed since I resolved on my present undertaking. I can, even **14** now, remember the hour from which I dedicated myself to this great enterprise. I commenced by inuring my body to hardship. I accompanied the whale-fishers on several expeditions to the North Sea; I voluntarily endured cold, famine, thirst, and want of sleep; I often worked harder than the common sailors during the day, and devoted my nights to the study of mathematics, the theory of medicine, and those branches of physical science from which a naval adventurer might derive the greatest practical advantage. Twice

15 *Greenland whaler.* Hans Egede's *A Description of Greenland* was published in the same year as *Frankenstein*. He tells us (p. 174) that the "goods and commodities Greenland affords for the entertainment of commerce or traffic are whale blubber or fat and whale bones, unicorn horns, reindeer skins and hides, seal and fox skins." Greenland whaling fleets were major providers of whale oil with which to light the lamps of Europe and America.

Egede's account of life in Greenland makes fascinating anthropological reading today. Egede was tempted to believe from some of their usages and ceremonies that native Greenlanders were descended from the Ten Tribes of Israel. For readers of *Frankenstein* the Greenland story of creation has special interest. It holds that the first man sprang spontaneously from the earth. This creature then begot himself a wife by copulating with a nearby hillock.

THE GREENLAND WHALERS.

I actually hired myself as an under-mate in a Greenland whaler, and acquitted myself to admiration. I must own I felt a little proud, when my captain offered me the second dignity in the vessel, and entreated me to remain with the greatest earnestness; so valuable did he consider my services.

And now, dear Margaret, do I not deserve to accomplish some great purpose. My life might have been passed in ease and luxury; but I preferred glory to every enticement that wealth placed in my path. Oh, that some encouraging voice would answer in the affirmative! My courage and my resolution is firm; but my hopes fluctuate, and my spirits are often depressed. I am about to proceed on a long and difficult voyage; the emergencies of which will demand all my fortitude: I am required not only to raise the spirits of others, but sometimes to sustain my own, when their's are failing.

This is the most favourable period for travelling in Russia. They fly quickly over the snow in their sledges; the motion is pleasant, and, in my opinion, far more agreeable than that of an English stage-coach. The cold is not excessive, if you are wrapt in furs, a dress which I have already adopted;

"THEY FLY QUICKLY."

"THE POST-ROAD."

16 *post-road.* A road built for the specific use of mail coaches.

17 *Archangel.* This port on the White Sea was for over a century Russia's only access to Western trade. It was founded by the English in 1583 as a base for the White Sea trade monopoly that had been granted to the Russian Company by Ivan the Terrible. It continued to be the center of trade between Europe and Russia until it was supplanted by Saint Petersburg.

for there is a great difference between walking the deck and remaining seated motionless for hours, when no exercise prevents the blood from actually freezing in your veins. I have no ambition to lose my life on the post-road between St. Petersburgh and Archangel.

I shall depart for the latter town in a fortnight or three weeks; and my intention is to hire a ship there, which can easily be done by paying the insurance for the owner, and to engage as many sailors as I think necessary among those who are accustomed to the whale-fishing. I do not intend to sail until the month of June: and when shall I return? Ah, dear sister, how can I answer this question? If I succeed, many, many months, perhaps years, will pass before you and I may meet. If I fail, you will see me again soon, or never.

Farewell, my dear, excellent, Margaret. Heaven shower down blessings on you, and save me, that I may again and again testify my gratitude for all your love and kindness.

Your affectionate brother,
R. WALTON.

LETTER II.

To Mrs. Saville, England.

Archangel, 28th March, 17—.

1 How slowly the time passes here, encompassed as I am by frost and snow; yet a second step is taken towards my enterprise. I have hired a vessel, and am occupied in collecting my sailors; those whom I have already engaged appear to be men on whom I can depend, and are certainly possessed of dauntless courage.

But I have one want which I have never yet been able to satisfy; and the absence of the object of which I **2** now feel as a most severe evil. I have no friend, Margaret: when I am glowing with the enthusiasm of success, there will be none to participate my joy; if I am assailed by disappointment, no one will endeavour to sustain me in dejection. I shall commit my thoughts to paper, it is true; but that is a poor medium for the communication of feeling. I desire the company of a man who could sympathize with me; whose eyes would reply to mine. You may deem me romantic, my dear sister, but I bitterly feel the want of a friend. I have no one near me, gentle yet courageous, possessed of a cultivated as well as of a capacious mind, whose tastes are like my own, to ap-

1 *frost and snow.* In this letter we are taken almost immediately into the ambience of Coleridge's *Ancient Mariner:* "And now there came both mist and snow, And it grew wondrous cold." For more on Coleridge's influence on *Frankenstein*, see page 18, note 13.

Cold, and particularly the massive presence of ice, is a powerful organizing element in *Frankenstein*. The story begins and ends in an icebound setting, and the major confrontation scene between Victor Frankenstein and his creature takes place on a glacier called the "sea of ice" in the Swiss Alps.

2 *I have no friend, Margaret.* Shelley, in one of his early letters to William Godwin, describes himself as "isolated and friendless" (*Letters*, p. 242). It is more likely, however, that Mary Shelley is here echoing lines in Mary Wollstonecraft's novel *MARY*, in which the heroine writes (pp. 141–42): "When overwhelmed by sorrow, I have met unkindness; I looked for some one to have pity on me; but found none!—The healing balm of sympathy is denied; I weep, a solitary wretch, and the hot tears scald my cheeks. I have not the medicine of life, the dear chimera I have so often chased, a friend."

3 *I am self-educated.* An accurate description of Mary Shelley's own education, though it may be argued that, as the daughter of William Godwin, her free-form education was likely to have been both wider and deeper than those of her contemporaries. Godwin, writing to William Baxter to whom he was sending the fourteen-year-old Mary for an extended Scottish visit, writes that "she has considerable talent . . . I am anxious that she be brought up (in this respect) like a philosopher, even like a cynic . . . I wish too that she should be *excited* to industry. She has occasionally great perseverance, but occasionally, too, she shows great need to be roused."

4 keeping. A painterly term for the ability to delineate things in their right proportion. In the Introduction to the 1831 edition of *Frankenstein*, our author tells us that her childhood "dreams were at once more fantastic and agreeable than my writings . . . my dreams were all my own; I accounted for them to nobody; they were my refuge when annoyed—my dearest pleasure when free."

5 *madly desirous of glory.* Like Walton. Curiously enough, this enterprising lieutenant never reappears in our tale.

6 *prejudices.* Presumably Russian prejudices and English endowments.

prove or amend my plans. How would such a friend repair the faults of your poor brother! I am too ardent in execution, and too impatient of difficulties. But it is a still greater evil to me that I am self-educated: for the first fourteen years of my life I ran wild on a common, and read nothing but our uncle Thomas's books of voyages. At that age I became acquainted with the celebrated poets of our own country; but it was only when it had ceased to be in my power to derive its most important benefits from such a conviction, that I perceived the necessity of becoming acquainted with more languages than that of my native country. Now I am twenty-eight, and am in reality more illiterate than many school-boys of fifteen. It is true that I have thought more, and that my day dreams are more extended and magnificent; but they want (as the painters call it) *keeping*; and I greatly need a friend who would have sense enough not to despise me as romantic, and affection enough for me to endeavour to regulate my mind.

Well, these are useless complaints; I shall certainly find no friend on the wide ocean, nor even here in Archangel, among merchants and seamen. Yet some feelings, unallied to the dross of human nature, beat even in these rugged bosoms. My lieutenant, for instance, is a man of wonderful courage and enterprise; he is madly desirous of glory. He is an Englishman, and in the midst of national and professional prejudices, unsoftened by cultivation, retains some of the noblest endowments

7 *The master.* There is room for some perplexity about the titles of the ships' personnel. On page 23, the master refers to Walton as the captain, though Walton's right to that distinction is not absolutely clear. Earlier, we have been introduced to a lieutenant, presumably a military rank on this civilian vessel. Harlan Soeten, curator of the San Francisco Maritime Museum, points out, however, that crews frequently served the military on civilian boats, and that it was perfectly possible for a man with a rank in one service to carry it with him to the other.

8 *spill blood.* This quality of mercy will occur later in another context. (See Vol. II, pp. 140 and 142.)

9 *prize-money.* Money made by capture of enemy vessels or by the plunder of enemy towns. One is a little less certain than Mary Shelley that the gentle ship's master "cannot endure to spill blood."

10 *to the match.* This episode of the generous master has very little connection with the rest of *Frankenstein* except as it gives us one more example of high-mindedness. The little tale may have its origins in Mary Shelley's reading, first, in Rousseau's *La Nouvelle Héloïse* and second, in Mary Wollstonecraft's *Letters From Sweden Etc. La Nouvelle Héloïse*, the original novel of sensibility, was much admired by the Shelleys (and the rest of Europe) for demonstrating how disinterested love was a superior experience to the coarser, if delightful, physical passions. In Rousseau's fiction, Lord Bomston, the English friend of the hero, Saint-Preux, offers to bestow a third, or even half his fortune on his poor but love-enchanted friend in order to make possible Saint-Preux's marriage with the beautiful Julie. And Mary Wollstonecraft, in her letters describing the esteem in which the king of Norway is held by his subjects, tells how that prince, at the behest of an officer dying at the battle of Quistram, undertook to look after the fiancée the officer left behind. The girl turned out to be pretty, the king was generous and promised to provide for any one she should marry. "She is since married, and he has not forgotten his promise."

of humanity. I first became acquainted with him on board a whale vessel: finding that he was unemployed in this city, I easily engaged him to assist in my enterprise.

7   The master is a person of an excellent disposition, and is remarkable in the ship for his gentleness, and the mildness of his discipline. He is, indeed, of so amiable a nature, that he will not hunt (a favourite, and almost the only amusement here), because he **8** cannot endure to spill blood. He is, moreover, heroically generous. Some years ago he loved a young Russian lady, of moderate fortune; and having **9** amassed a considerable sum in prize-money, the father of the girl consented **10** to the match. He saw his mistress once before the destined ceremony; but she was bathed in tears, and, throwing herself at his feet, entreated him to spare her, confessing at the same time that she loved another, but that he was poor, and that her father would never consent to the union. My generous friend reassured the suppliant, and on being informed of the name of her lover instantly abandoned his pursuit. He had already bought a farm with his money, on which he had designed to pass the remainder of his life; but he bestowed the whole on his rival, together with the remains of his prize-money to purchase stock, and then himself solicited the young woman's father to consent to her marriage with her lover. But the old man decidedly refused, thinking himself bound in honour to my friend; who, when he found the father inexorable, quitted his country,

11 *the shroud.* The ropes that stretch from the mast-head of a sailing ship to its sides.

12 *fixed as fate.* We will learn, as *Frankenstein* comes to its close, just how fixed is Walton's resolution.

13 *kill no albatross.* Indeed not. The albatross is an Antarctic bird.

This reference, from Coleridge's *The Rime of the Ancient Mariner*, makes it impossible for us to accept that the action of *Frankenstein* takes place at any time before September 1798, when the poem appeared in its first version in an edition of five hundred copies of a book called *Lyrical Ballads*, which contained poems by Coleridge and Wordsworth. Coleridge was not identified as the author of the *Rime.* The publication of *Lyrical Ballads*, with its famous preface by Wordsworth, is frequently cited as marking the advent of the Romantic movement in English literature.

We will see later that no date in the eighteenth century will be appropriate for the action of *Frankenstein*, but since it is Mary Shelley's obvious fictive intent that *Frankenstein* be taken as describing late-eighteenth-century events, it might be well for us to suspend our disbelief.

People who speculate on such matters think that Coleridge's albatross was the sooty albatross, a bird native to Antarctic waters.

Frankenstein and *The Rime of the Ancient Mariner* have much in common thematically, as we will see later.

14 *southern cape of Africa or America.* The Cape of Good Hope and the Strait of Magellan respectively.

nor returned until he heard that his former mistress was married according to her inclinations. " What a noble fellow !" you will exclaim. He is so ; but then he has passed all his life on board a vessel, and has scarcely an **11** idea beyond the rope and the shroud.

But do not suppose that, because I complain a little, or because I can conceive a consolation for my toils which I may never know, that I am wavering **12** in my resolutions. Those are as fixed as fate ; and my voyage is only now delayed until the weather shall permit my embarkation. The winter has been dreadfully severe ; but the spring promises well, and it is considered as a remarkably early season ; so that, perhaps, I may sail sooner than I expected. I shall do nothing rashly ; you know me sufficiently to confide in my prudence and considerateness whenever the safety of others is committed to my care.

I cannot describe to you my sensations on the near prospect of my undertaking. It is impossible to communicate to you a conception of the trembling sensation, half pleasurable and half fearful, with which I am preparing to depart. I am going to unexplored regions, to " the land of mist and **13** snow ;" but I shall kill no albatross, therefore do not be alarmed for my safety.

Shall I meet you again, after having traversed immense seas, and returned **14** by the most southern cape of Africa or America ? I dare not expect such success. yet I cannot bear to look on the reverse of the picture. Continue to write to me by every opportunity: I may receive your letters (though the chance is very doubtful) on some occasions when I need them most to support my spirits. I love you very tenderly. Remember me with affection, should you never hear from me again.

Your affectionate brother,

ROBERT WALTON.

LETTER III.

To Mrs. SAVILLE, England.

July 7th, 17—.

MY DEAR SISTER,

I WRITE a few lines in haste, to say that I am safe, and well advanced on my voyage. This letter will reach England by a merchant-man now on its homeward voyage from Archangel; more fortunate than I, who may not see my native land, perhaps, for many years. I am, however, in good spirits: my men are bold, and apparently firm of purpose; nor do the floating sheets of ice that continually pass us, indicating the dangers of the region towards which we are advancing, appear to dismay them. We have already reached a very high latitude; but it is the height of summer, and although not so warm as in England, the southern gales, which blow us speedily towards those shores which I so ardently desire to attain, breathe a degree of renovating warmth which I had not expected.

No incidents have hitherto befallen us, that would make a figure in a letter. One or two stiff gales, and the breaking of a mast, are accidents which experienced navigators scarcely remember to record; and I shall be well content, if nothing worse happen to us during our voyage.

Adieu, my dear Margaret. Be assured, that for my own sake, as well as your's, I will not rashly encounter danger. I will be cool, persevering, and prudent.

Remember me to all my English friends.

Most affectionately yours,

R. W.

1 *Letter IV.* The letter to come is the longest letter in the book. Indeed, all the rest of *Frankenstein* is contained in it, though the letter form merges into journal entries in Volume III, page 312.

2 *you will see me.* Walton's optimism is more prophetic than he realizes, as the reader will learn near the close of the book.

3 *the sea room.* Enough open sea in which a ship may maneuver.

4 *two o'clock.* In the afternoon.

5 *a low carriage.* The typical dogsled is drawn by ten to twenty dogs. They may be harnessed in single or double file or in a fan-shaped array.

SLED DOGS IN FAN-SHAPED HARNESS.

SLED DOGS HARNESSED IN TANDEM.

LETTER IV.

To Mrs. SAVILLE, *England.*

August 5th, 17—.

So strange an accident has happened to us, that I cannot forbear recording it, although it is very probable that **2** you will see me before these papers can come into your possession.

Last Monday (July 31st), we were nearly surrounded by ice, which closed in the ship on all sides, scarcely leaving her the sea room in which she **3** floated. Our situation was somewhat dangerous, especially as we were compassed round by a very thick fog. We accordingly lay to, hoping that some change would take place in the atmosphere and weather.

4 About two o'clock the mist cleared away, and we beheld, stretched out in every direction, vast and irregular plains of ice, which seemed to have no end. Some of my comrades groaned, and my own mind began to grow watchful with anxious thoughts, when a strange sight suddenly attracted our attention, and diverted our solicitude from our own situation. We perceived **5** a low carriage, fixed on a sledge and drawn by dogs, pass on towards the north, at the distance of half a mile: a being which had the shape of a man, but apparently of gigantic stature, sat in the sledge, and guided

6 *two hours.* Four P.M. On July 31, in the northern latitudes where the ship now is, there would be approximately eighteen hours of daylight, which perhaps explains why Walton gets only a few hours of sleep that night.

7 *ground sea.* The *Oxford English Dictionary* says that a ground sea is a "heavy sea in which large waves rise and dash upon the coast without apparent cause."

"THE ICE BROKE."

8 *within it.* That is, within the sledge.

the dogs. We watched the rapid progress of the traveller with our telescopes, until he was lost among the distant inequalities of the ice.

This appearance excited our unqualified wonder. We were, as we believed, many hundred miles from any land; but this apparition seemed to denote that it was not, in reality, so distant as we had supposed. Shut in, however, by ice, it was impossible to follow his track, which we had observed with the greatest attention.

6
7 About two hours after this occurrence, we heard the ground sea; and before night the ice broke, and freed our ship. We, however, lay to until the morning, fearing to encounter in the dark those large loose masses which float about after the breaking up of the ice. I profited of this time to rest for a few hours.

In the morning, however, as soon as it was light, I went upon deck, and found all the sailors busy on one side of the vessel, apparently talking to some one in the sea. It was, in fact, a sledge, like that we had seen before, which had drifted towards us in the night, on a large fragment of ice. Only one dog remained alive; but
8 there was a human being within it, whom the sailors were persuading to enter the vessel. He was not, as the other traveller seemed to be, a savage inhabitant of some undiscovered island, but an European. When I appeared on deck, the master said, "Here is our captain, and he will not allow you to perish on the open sea."

9 *a foreign accent.* English, modified by Swiss French.

10 *capitulated for.* To make conditions for a surrender.

11 *brandy.* The brandy is sensible, as, internally and externally, it stimulates the circulation.

The first aid for "the stranger" inevitably makes us remember the dream that Mary Shelley recorded in her *Journal* (March 19, 1815): "Dream that my baby came to life again; that it had only been cold, and that we rubbed it before the fire, and it lived. Awaken and find no baby" (p. 41).

On perceiving me, the stranger addressed me in English, although with **9** a foreign accent. " Before I come on board your vessel," said he, " will you have the kindness to inform me whither you are bound ?"

You may conceive my astonishment on hearing such a question addressed to me from a man on the brink of destruction, and to whom I should have supposed that my vessel would have been a resource which he would not have exchanged for the most precious wealth the earth can afford. I replied, however, that we were on a voyage of discovery towards the northern pole.

Upon hearing this he appeared satisfied, and consented to come on board. Good God! Margaret, if you had seen **10** the man who thus capitulated for his safety, your surprise would have been boundless. His limbs were nearly frozen, and his body dreadfully emaciated by fatigue and suffering. I never saw a man in so wretched a condition. We attempted to carry him into the cabin ; but as soon as he had quitted the fresh air, he fainted. We accordingly brought him back to the deck, and restored him to animation by rubbing **11** him with brandy, and forcing him to swallow a small quantity. As soon as he shewed signs of life, we wrapped him up in blankets, and placed him near the chimney of the kitchen-stove. By slow degrees he recovered, and ate a little soup, which restored him wonderfully.

Two days passed in this manner before he was able to speak ; and I often

12 *his sufferings had deprived him of understanding.* This is not the first time the sufferer has been deemed out of his mind. Indeed, madness is a recurrent subtheme of this work.

13 *"To seek one who fled from me."* Is Mary Shelley echoing the opening lines of Sir Thomas Wyatt's (1503–1542) famous love lament that begins, "They flee from me, that sometime did me seek,/With naked foot stalking in my chamber"? The poem in its entirety reads:

They flee from me, that sometime did me seek,
With naked foot, stalking in my chamber.
I have seen them, gentle, tame, and meek,
That now are wild, and do not remember
That sometime they put themselves in danger
To take bread at my hand; and now they range,
Busily seeking with a continual change.

Thanked be Fortune it hath been otherwise,
Twenty times better; but once in special,
In thin array, after a pleasant guise,
When her loose gown from her shoulders did fall,
And she me caught in her arms long and small,
And therewith all sweetly did me kiss
And softly said, "Dear heart, how like you this?"

It was no dream, I lay broad waking.
But all is turned, thorough my gentleness,
Into a strange fashion of forsaking;
And I have leave to go, of her goodness,
And she also to use newfangleness.
But since that I so kindely am served,
I fain would know what she hath deserved.

The poem will seem more directly applicable to the plot of *Frankenstein* a bit later.

If we recall that the cost of the wrong kind of love is one of Mary Shelley's themes, the link between the poem and the fiction will not seem so surprising.

12 feared that his sufferings had deprived him of understanding. When he had in some measure recovered, I removed him to my own cabin, and attended on him as much as my duty would permit. I never saw a more interesting creature: his eyes have generally an expression of wildness, and even madness; but there are moments when, if any one performs an act of kindness towards him, or does him any the most trifling service, his whole countenance is lighted up, as it were, with a beam of benevolence and sweetness that I never saw equalled. But he is generally melancholy and despairing; and sometimes he gnashes his teeth, as if impatient of the weight of woes that oppresses him.

When my guest was a little recovered, I had great trouble to keep off the men, who wished to ask him a thousand questions; but I would not allow him to be tormented by their idle curiosity, in a state of body and mind whose restoration evidently depended upon entire repose. Once, however, the lieutenant asked, Why he had come so far upon the ice in so strange a vehicle?

His countenance instantly assumed an aspect of the deepest gloom; and he **13** replied, "To seek one who fled from me."

"And did the man whom you pursued travel in the same fashion?"

"Yes."

"Then I fancy we have seen him; for, the day before we picked you up, we saw some dogs drawing a sledge, with a man in it, across the ice."

14 *dæmon.* The word used here for the first time in its usual sense will acquire a variety of interpretations in the course of our fiction.

15 *inquisitiveness of mine.* This exchange of civilities here in the arctic wastes is Mary Shelley's way of signaling to us that these men are both endowed with sensibility, a quality much admired in the Romantic age.

16 *up to the present day.* August 5.

This aroused the stranger's attention; and he asked a multitude of questions concerning the route which the **14** dæmon, as he called him, had pursued. Soon after, when he was alone with me, he said, "I have, doubtless, excited your curiosity, as well as that of these good people; but you are too considerate to make inquiries."

"Certainly; it would indeed be very impertinent and inhuman in me to **15** trouble you with any inquisitiveness of mine."

"And yet you rescued me from a strange and perilous situation; you have benevolently restored me to life."

Soon after this he inquired, if I thought that the breaking up of the ice had destroyed the other sledge? I replied, that I could not answer with any degree of certainty; for the ice had not broken until near midnight, and the traveller might have arrived at a place of safety before that time; but of this I could not judge.

From this time the stranger seemed very eager to be upon deck, to watch for the sledge which had before appeared; but I have persuaded him to remain in the cabin, for he is far too weak to sustain the rawness of the atmosphere. But I have promised that some one should watch for him, and give him instant notice if any new object should appear in sight.

Such is my journal of what relates **16** to this strange occurrence up to the present day. The stranger has gradually improved in health, but is very silent, and appears uneasy when any one except myself enters his cabin.

Yet his manners are so conciliating and gentle, that the sailors are all interested in him, although they have had very little communication with him. For my own part, I begin to love him as a brother; and his constant and deep grief fills me with sympathy and compassion. He must have been a noble creature in his better days, being even now in wreck so attractive and amiable.

I said in one of my letters, my dear Margaret, that I should find no friend on the wide ocean; yet I have found a man who, before his spirit had been broken by misery, I should have been happy to have possessed as the brother of my heart.

I shall continue my journal concerning the stranger at intervals, should I have any fresh incidents to record.

August 13th, 17—.

My affection for my guest increases every day. He excites at once my admiration and my pity to an astonishing degree. How can I see so noble a creature destroyed by misery without feeling the most poignant grief? He is so gentle, yet so wise; his mind is so cultivated; and when he speaks, although his words are culled with the choicest art, yet they flow with rapidity and unparalleled eloquence.

He is now much recovered from his illness, and is continually on the deck, apparently watching for the sledge that preceded his own. Yet, although unhappy, he is not so utterly occupied by his own misery, but that he interests himself deeply in the employments of others. He has asked me many questions concerning my design; and I have related my little history frankly to him. He appeared pleased with the confidence, and suggested several alterations in my plan, which I shall find exceedingly useful. There is no pedantry in his manner; but all he does appears to spring solely from the interest he instinctively takes in the welfare of those who surround him. He is often overcome by gloom, and then he sits by himself, and tries to overcome all that is sullen or unsocial in his humour. These paroxysms pass from him like a cloud from before the sun, though his dejection never leaves him. I have endeavoured to win his confidence; and I trust that I have succeeded. One day I mentioned to him the desire I had always felt of finding a friend who might sympathize with me, and direct me by his counsel. I said, I did not belong to that class of men who are offended by advice. "I am self-educated, and perhaps I hardly rely sufficiently upon my own powers. I wish therefore that my companion should be wiser and more experienced than myself, to confirm and support me; nor have I believed it impossible to find a true friend."

" I agree with you," replied the stranger, " in believing that friendship is not only a desirable, but a possible acquisition. I once had a friend, the most noble of human creatures, and am entitled, therefore, to judge respecting friendship. You have hope, and the world before you, and have no cause for despair. But I——I have lost

17 *a double existence.* An important note has been sounded here. The development of that double existence, though not precisely in the sense that Walton understands it, is one of the major themes in *Frankenstein*.

18 *August 19th.* Note that this fresh date is part of the continuation of Letter IV.

19 *the stranger.* The visitor has been on board the ship for nineteen days, and yet Walton continues to refer to him as "the stranger."

20 *a serpent to sting you.* Though the serpent reference is an independent cliché, the entire sentence is another reference to Milton's *Paradise Lost.*

THE TEMPTATION OF EVE BY WILLIAM BLAKE.

every thing, and cannot begin life anew."

As he said this, his countenance became expressive of a calm settled grief, that touched me to the heart. But he was silent, and presently retired to his cabin.

Even broken in spirit as he is, no one can feel more deeply than he does the beauties of nature. The starry sky, the sea, and every sight afforded by these wonderful regions, seems still to have the power of elevating his soul **17** from earth. Such a man has a double existence: he may suffer misery, and be overwhelmed by disappointments; yet when he has retired into himself, he will be like a celestial spirit, that has a halo around him, within whose circle no grief or folly ventures.

Will you laugh at the enthusiasm I express concerning this divine wanderer? If you do, you must have certainly lost that simplicity which was once your characteristic charm. Yet, if you will, smile at the warmth of my expressions, while I find every day new causes for repeating them.

18   August 19th, 17—.

19   Yesterday the stranger said to me, " You may easily perceive, Captain Walton, that I have suffered great and unparalleled misfortunes. I had determined, once, that the memory of these evils should die with me; but you have won me to alter my determination. You seek for knowledge and wisdom, as I once did; and I ardently hope that the gratification of your **20** wishes may not be a serpent to sting

21 *nature.* Human nature, as opposed to the "beauties of nature" for which, as we have seen (p. 29), this stranger has a special feeling.

you, as mine has been. I do not know that the relation of my misfortunes will be useful to you, yet, if you are inclined, listen to my tale. I believe that the strange incidents connected with it will **21** afford a view of nature, which may enlarge your faculties and understanding. You will hear of powers and occurrences, such as you have been accustomed to believe impossible: but I do not doubt that my tale conveys in its series internal evidence of the truth of the events of which it is composed."

You may easily conceive that I was much gratified by the offered communication; yet I could not endure that he should renew his grief by a recital of his misfortunes. I felt the greatest eagerness to hear the promised narrative, partly from curiosity, and partly from a strong desire to ameliorate his fate, if it were in my power. I expressed these feelings in my answer.

" I thank you," he replied, " for your sympathy, but it is useless; my fate is nearly fulfilled. I wait but for one event, and then I shall repose in peace. I understand your feeling," continued he, perceiving that I wished to interrupt him; " but you are mistaken, my friend, if thus you will allow me to name you; nothing can alter my destiny: listen to my history, and you will perceive how irrevocably it is determined.

He then told me, that he would commence his narrative the next day when I should be at leisure. This promise drew from me the warmest thanks. I have resolved every night, when I am not engaged, to record, as nearly as

22 *some future day!* With the conclusion of Letter IV, the thematic and narrative prologue to the central fiction ends. With Chapter I we begin our reading of *Frankenstein* itself, the narrative the stranger dictates to Walton over a period of one week (August 20 to August 26). Both Walton and the stranger go to great lengths to assure us that the stranger's account is both accurate and accurately transcribed.

possible in his own words, what he has related during the day. If I should be engaged, I will at least make notes. This manuscript will doubtless afford you the greatest pleasure: but to me, who know him, and who hear it from his own lips, with what interest and **22** sympathy shall I read it in some future day!

FRANKENSTEIN;

OR,

THE MODERN PROMETHEUS.

———

CHAPTER I.

1 I AM by birth a Genevese; and my family is one of the most distinguished of that republic. My ancestors had been for many years counsellors and
2 syndics; and my father had filled several public situations with honour and reputation. He was respected by all who knew him for his integrity and indefatigable attention to public business. He passed his younger days perpetually occupied by the affairs of his country; and it was not until the decline of life that he thought of marrying, and bestowing on the state sons who might carry his virtues and his name down to posterity.

As the circumstances of his marriage illustrate his character, I cannot refrain from relating them. One of his most intimate friends was a merchant, who, from a flourishing state, fell, through numerous mischances, into poverty. This man, whose name was Beaufort, was of a proud and unbending disposition, and could not bear to live in poverty and oblivion in the same country where he had formerly been distinguished for his rank and magnificence.

1 *Genevese.* In the 1831 edition of *Frankenstein*, Mary Shelley, though she retains this reference to Geneva, has the stranger say later in his narrative, "I . . . was born at Naples."

2 *syndics.* Municipal magistrates.

LUCERNE.

3 *Lucerne.* Mary Shelley, in her *History of a Six Weeks' Tour*, 1818 (pp. 48–50), says of Lucerne that it was the "principal town of the lake of that name . . . The journey to this place occupied rather more than two days. The country was flat and dull . . . Lucerne promised better things, and as soon as we arrived (August 23rd) we hired a boat, with which we proposed to coast the lake until we should meet with some suitable habitation." The scenery along Lake Lucerne, she found very impressive. She writes, "The high mountains encompassed us, darkening the waters . . . [this] lovely lake, these sublime mountains, and wild forests, seemed a fit cradle for a mind aspiring to high adventure and heroic deeds."

But the Swiss people had a different effect on her. She goes on to say, "The Swiss appeared to us then, and experience has confirmed our opinion, a people slow of comprehension and of action." Just the same, she would recall of Lucerne that its "sacred solitude and deep seclusion delighted us."

In 1816, when *Frankenstein* was being written, Lucerne had a population of between three and four thousand souls.

4 *begin the world.* To resume a business career.

5 *the Reuss.* The Reuss is the river that, issuing from Lake Lucerne, divides the city of Lucerne.

In early September 1814, the Shelley party traveled down the Reuss. Mary Shelley writes: "The Reuss is exceedingly rapid, and we descended several falls, one of more than eight feet. There is something very delicious in the sensation, when at one moment you are at the top of a fall of water, and before the second has expired you are at the bottom, still rushing on with the impulse which the descent has given. The waters of the Rhone are blue, those of the Reuss are of a deep green."

Having paid his debts, therefore, in the most honourable manner, he retreated **3** with his daughter to the town of Lucerne, where he lived unknown and in wretchedness. My father loved Beaufort with the truest friendship, and was deeply grieved by his retreat in these unfortunate circumstances. He grieved also for the loss of his society, and resolved to seek him out and endeavour **4** to persuade him to begin the world again through his credit and assistance.

Beaufort had taken effectual measures to conceal himself; and it was ten months before my father discovered his abode. Overjoyed at this discovery, he hastened to the house, which was **5** situated in a mean street, near the Reuss. But when he entered, misery and despair alone welcomed him. Beaufort had saved but a very small sum of money from the wreck of his fortunes; but it was sufficient to provide him with sustenance for some months, and in the mean time he hoped to procure some respectable employment in a merchant's house. The interval was consequently spent in inaction; his grief only became more deep and rankling, when he had leisure for reflection; and at length it took so fast hold of his mind, that at the end of three months he lay on a bed of sickness, incapable of any exertion.

His daughter attended him with the greatest tenderness; but she saw with despair that their little fund was rapidly decreasing, and that there was no other prospect of support. But Caroline Beaufort possessed a mind of an un-

6 *she plaited straw.* Into mats, baskets, or other woven work.

Mary Shelley's mother, in her *Thoughts on the Education of Daughters* (1786), wrote bitterly that "few are the modes of earning a subsistence [for women]," and Claire Tomalin, Mary Wollstonecraft's recent biographer, tells us that some of these ways were to be a "companion, schoolteacher, governess [and certain other occupations] such as hairdressing, millinery, mantua-making, midwifery, and dentistry" (*The Life and Death of Mary Wollstonecraft*, p. 41).

7 *protecting spirit.* Here it is the narrator's father who comes "like a protecting spirit." Later, there will be other spirits coming to aid and comfort him in the course of his own great sufferings (see Vol. III, p. 304).

8 *Geneva.* At the beginning of the nineteenth century, Geneva, on the banks of the Rhone where it issues from Lake Geneva, had a population of thirty thousand inhabitants. Geneva, of course, was the scene of that happy and productive summer in 1816 in the course of which the Shelley and Byron households frequented each other and during which *Frankenstein* was conceived and well begun.

Mary Shelley was frequently overwhelmed by the natural beauty of the mountain scenery in the vicinity of Geneva, but she was more reserved about the town itself, about which, in her *History of a Six Weeks' Tour* (pp. 100–101), she wrote, "There is nothing, however, in it that can repay you for the trouble of walking over its rough stones. The houses are high, the streets narrow, many of them on the ascent, and no public building of any beauty to attract your eye, or any architecture to gratify your taste." Nor did she think well of the Genevese, whom she regarded as "much inclined to puritanism" and not very bright.

9 *became his wife.* This form of paternalism mixed with self-interest has a long history. Erasmus Darwin had a friend who reared a couple of female orphans, meaning to marry one when she arrived at the right age. The young woman proved unwedable, and Darwin was consulted for advice in the matter (see Vol. II, p. 206, note 14 for an instance of Shelley's interest in raising young girls).

10 *When my father . . .* In the 1831 edition of *Frankenstein*, Mary Shelley interpolated seven pages here. In the rewritten version, Elizabeth, instead of being Victor's cousin, is made to be a foundling, and Victor's parents are described as having an even more perfect marriage than they have in the present edition.

Curiously enough, Mary Shelley, whose parents so looked forward to having a son that they had the name "William" ready for him when she was born, has Victor say, in her revision of *Frankenstein*, that "my mother had much desired to have a daughter."

common mould; and her courage rose to support her in her adversity. She **6** procured plain work; she plaited straw; and by various means contrived to earn a pittance scarcely sufficient to support life.

Several months passed in this manner. Her father grew worse; her time was more entirely occupied in attending him; her means of subsistence decreased; and in the tenth month her father died in her arms, leaving her an orphan and a beggar. This last blow overcame her; and she knelt by Beaufort's coffin, weeping bitterly, when my father entered the chamber. He came **7** like a protecting spirit to the poor girl, who committed herself to his care, and after the interment of his friend he **8** conducted her to Geneva, and placed her under the protection of a relation. Two years after this event Caroline **9** became his wife.

10 When my father became a husband and a parent, he found his time so occupied by the duties of his new situation, that he relinquished many of his public employments, and devoted himself to the education of his children. Of these I was the eldest, and the destined successor to all his labours and utility. No creature could have more tender parents than mine. My improvement and health were their constant care, especially as I remained for several years their only child. But before I continue my narrative, I must record an incident which took place when I was four years of age.

My father had a sister, whom he tenderly loved, and who had married

11 *her*. This is a misprint for *his* and was so corrected in the 1831 edition of *Frankenstein*.

12 *insect*. Here our narrator uses the word "insect" tenderly to describe the woman he loves. We will see later (Vol. II, p. 139) that he will hurl the same word as an epithet against his loathed creature. It is a telling coincidence that serves for an instant to identify the creature with Elizabeth.

early in life an Italian gentleman. Soon after her marriage, she had accom- **11** panied her husband into her native country, and for some years my father had very little communication with her. About the time I mentioned she died ; and a few months afterwards he received a letter from her husband, acquainting him with his intention of marrying an Italian lady, and requesting my father to take charge of the infant Elizabeth, the only child of his deceased sister. " It is my wish," he said, " that you should consider her as your own daughter, and educate her thus. Her mother's fortune is secured to her, the documents of which I will commit to your keeping. Reflect upon this proposition ; and decide whether you would prefer educating your niece yourself to her being brought up by a stepmother."

My father did not hestitate, and immediately went to Italy, that he might accompany the little Elizabeth to her future home. I have often heard my mother say, that she was at that time the most beautiful child she had ever seen, and shewed signs even then of a gentle and affectionate disposition. These indications, and a desire to bind as closely as possible the ties of domestic love, determined my mother to consider Elizabeth as my future wife; a design which she never found reason to repent.

From this time Elizabeth Lavenza became my playfellow, and, as we grew older, my friend. She was docile and good tempered, yet gay and playful as **12** a summer insect. Although she was lively and animated, her feelings were

13 *favourite animal.* The speaker's simile is intended to be loving, but it betrays his condescension. He sees Elizabeth as Mary Shelley thinks a man would want to see the woman he loved: intelligent but docile, imaginative but dutiful, gracious but humble.

14 *My brothers were considerably younger than myself.* Though the narrator's father has been described as at the "decline of life," this wide spacing of his children suggests a somewhat more than lingering vitality in him.

strong and deep, and her disposition uncommonly affectionate. No one could better enjoy liberty, yet no one could submit with more grace than she did to constraint and caprice. Her imagination was luxuriant, yet her capability of application was great. Her person was the image of her mind; her hazel eyes, although as lively as a bird's, possessed an attractive softness. Her figure was light and airy; and, though capable of enduring great fatigue, she appeared the most fragile creature in the world. While I admired her understanding and fancy, I loved to tend on her, as I should on a **13** favourite animal; and I never saw so much grace both of person and mind united to so little pretension.

Every one adored Elizabeth. If the servants had any request to make, it was always through her intercession. We were strangers to any species of disunion and dispute; for although there was a great dissimilitude in our characters, there was an harmony in that very dissimilitude. I was more calm and philosophical than my companion; yet my temper was not so yielding. My application was of longer endurance; but it was not so severe whilst it endured. I delighted in investigating the facts relative to the actual world; she busied herself in following the aërial creations of the poets. The world was to me a secret, which I desired to discover; to her it was a vacancy, which she sought to people with imaginations of her own.

14 My brothers were considerably younger than myself; but I had a friend in

"I NEVER SAW SO MUCH GRACE BOTH OF PERSON AND MIND UNITED TO SO LITTLE PRETENSION."

15 *a boy of singular talent.* Aaron Burr, later to be vice-president of the United States, visited the Godwin family on February 15, 1812. R. Glynn Grylls, in *Mary Shelley* (p. 17), quotes a letter of Burr's in which he writes: "Had only time to get to G[odwin]'s where dined. In the evening, William, the only *son* of W[illiam] Godwin, a lad of about 9 years old, gave his weekly lecture; having heard how Coleridge and others lectured, he would also lecture; and one of his sisters (Mary, I think) writes a lecture, which he reads from a little pulpit which they have erected for him. He went through it with great gravity and decorum."

16 *Orlando, Robin Hood, Amadis, and St. George.* Orlando is the main character in Ariosto's *Orlando Furioso*, which Shelley and Claire (Clairmont) were reading in April 1815. Amadis is the hero of the Spanish chivalric romance *Amadis de Gaula* by Vasco de Lobeida, which Mary Shelley read in Robert Southey's translation in March 1817. Saint George, of course, is the dragon slayer, patron saint of England. Robin Hood needs no annotation.

There is much in this description of Clerval that recalls Shelley's childhood storytelling to his younger sisters, though his stories were more often wild and fearful tales involving alchemists and tortoises, and such grotesque, macabre, and bloody images as he would later gather together in a Gothic tale called "Zastrozzi." In a letter to Godwin in June 1812, Percy Shelley (*Letters*, p. 303) writes that he "read romances & those of the most marvellous ones unremittingly."

T. J. Hogg tells us (in his *Life of Percy Bysshe Shelley*, p. 22) that many years after Shelley's death, his sister Helen remembered that as children "we dressed ourselves in strange costumes to personate spirits or fiends."

"MY PARENTS WERE INDULGENT, AND MY COMPANIONS AMIABLE."

one of my schoolfellows, who compensated for this deficiency. Henry Clerval was the son of a merchant of Geneva, an intimate friend of my father. **15** He was a boy of singular talent and fancy. I remember, when he was nine years old, he wrote a fairy tale, which was the delight and amazement of all his companions. His favourite study consisted in books of chivalry and romance; and when very young, I can remember, that we used to act plays composed by him out of these favourite books, the principal characters of **16** which were Orlando, Robin Hood, Amadis, and St. George.

No youth could have passed more happily than mine. My parents were indulgent, and my companions amiable. Our studies were never forced; and by some means we always had an end placed in view, which excited us to ardour in the prosecution of them. It was by this method, and not by emulation, that we were urged to application. Elizabeth was not incited to apply herself to drawing, that her companions might not outstrip her; but through the desire of pleasing her aunt, by the representation of some favourite scene done by her own hand. We learned Latin and English, that we might read the writings in those languages; and so far from study being made odious to us through punishment, we loved application, and our amusements would have been the labours of other children. Perhaps we did not read so many books, or learn languages so quickly, as those who are disciplined according to the ordinary methods; but

17 *destitute of companions at home.* We have already seen that Victor, our narrator, though he had brothers, also claims to have had a lonely home life.

18 *Natural philosophy.* What we would now call the physical sciences.

19 *Thonon.* An ancient Swiss town on the southern shore of Lake Geneva, which had some four thousand inhabitants in the early nineteenth century.

THONON.

20 *Cornelius Agrippa.* Heinrich Cornelius Agrippa (1486–1535) was a devotee of alchemy and occult studies in his youth. Agrippa, nominally a Catholic who died in that faith, was an early follower of Luther. Agrippa is notable too for his defense of women, a fact that may have been especially interesting to Mary Shelley, whose mother had written a *Vindication of the Rights of Woman.* The book that, most likely, interested Victor was Agrippa's *The Occult Philosophy* (1529).

21 *the theory which he attempts to demonstrate.* It is hard to know which theory Victor means here. Agrippa, after all, was interested in astrology, alchemy, and natural magic only as a young man. Toward the end of his life, he became a conservative thinker and could write: "It is better therefore and more profitable to be idiots and know nothing, to believe by Faith and Charity, and to become next unto God, than being lofty and proud through the subtilties [sic] of sciences to fall into the possession of the Serpent." But Victor, a young man, was excited by Agrippa's younger notions, as we will see.

what we learned was impressed the more deeply on our memories.

In this description of our domestic circle I include Henry Clerval; for he was constantly with us. He went to school with me, and generally passed the afternoon at our house; for being **17** an only child, and destitute of companions at home, his father was well pleased that he should find associates at our house; and we were never completely happy when Clerval was absent.

I feel pleasure in dwelling on the recollections of childhood, before misfortune had tainted my mind, and changed its bright visions of extensive usefulness into gloomy and narrow reflections upon self. But, in drawing the picture of my early days, I must not omit to record those events which led, by insensible steps to my after tale of misery: for when I would account to myself for the birth of that passion, which afterwards ruled my destiny, I find it arise, like a mountain river, from ignoble and almost forgotten sources; but, swelling as it proceeded, it became the torrent which, in its course, has swept away all my hopes and joys.

18 Natural philosophy is the genius that has regulated my fate; I desire therefore, in this narration, to state those facts which led to my predilection for that science. When I was thirteen years of age, we all went on a party of pleasure **19** to the baths near Thonon: the inclemency of the weather obliged us to remain a day confined to the inn. In this house I chanced to find a volume **20** of the works of Cornelius Agrippa. I **21** opened it with apathy; the theory which

22 *Victor*. This is the first mention of our protagonist's given name.

23 *from modern discoveries*. The most important headway made in chemistry during the last part of the eighteenth century concerned greater understanding of the nature of gases. Constituent parts of gases were determined by subjecting them to chemical reactions and analyzing the products by weight and volume. Several names are associated with this work:

HENRY CAVENDISH (1731–1810) pointed out the existence of several types of "air," which he distinguished according to their characteristics of weight, etc. In this way he discriminated fixed air (carbon dioxide), which he showed was heavier than ordinary air; he also pointed out the existence of inflammable air (hydrogen), which was ten times lighter than ordinary air.

JOSEPH PRIESTLEY (1733–1804), after his work in electricity, became involved in the study of gases and isolated several: nitric oxide, carbon monoxide, sulfur dioxide, hydrogen chloride, and ammonia.

ANTOINE-LAURENT LAVOISIER (1743–1794), drawing upon the work of his contemporaries as well as his own research, recognized that it was oxygen and not phlogiston that produced combustion. He set out in final form the reasoning and evidence that lead to this conclusion in his *Traité élémentaire de chimie* (1789).

he attempts to demonstrate, and the wonderful facts which he relates, soon changed this feeling into enthusiasm. A new light seemed to dawn upon my mind; and, bounding with joy, I communicated my discovery to my father. I cannot help remarking here the many opportunities instructors possess of directing the attention of their pupils to useful knowledge, which they utterly neglect. My father looked carelessly at the title-page of my book, and said, " Ah! Cornelius Agrippa! My dear **22** Victor, do not waste your time upon this; it is sad trash."

If, instead of this remark, my father had taken the pains to explain to me, that the principles of Agrippa had been entirely exploded, and that a modern system of science had been introduced, which possessed much greater powers than the ancient, because the powers of the latter were chimerical, while those of the former were real and practical; under such circumstances, I should certainly have thrown Agrippa aside, and, with my imagination warmed as it was, should probably have applied myself to the more rational theory of **23** chemistry which has resulted from modern discoveries. It is even possible, that the train of my ideas would never have received the fatal impulse that led to my ruin. But the cursory glance my father had taken of my volume by no means assured me that he was acquainted with its contents; and I continued to read with the greatest avidity.

When I returned home, my first care was to procure the whole works of this

24 *Paracelsus and Albertus Magnus.* Theophrastus Bombastus von Hohenheim Paracelsus (1493–1541) was a Swiss physician, with a reputation as an alchemist, whose theories are a blend of Greek philosophy, magic, and early experimental science.

Albertus Magnus (1193–1280) was a German philosopher of the Dominican Order who served as bishop of Regensburg. An early scientific investigator in botany and zoology, he is notable for being the teacher of Saint Thomas Aquinas. He is credited along with Aquinas for introducing an Aristotelian perspective into Christian thought.

The writings of both men were studied by the young Percy Shelley. In a letter to Godwin (June 3, 1812), Shelley writes, "I . . . pored over the reveries of Albertus Magnus, and Paracelsus, the former of which I read in Latin and probably gained more knowledge of that language from that source, than from all the discipline of Eton."

25 *the wild fancies of these writers.* What these are can only be conjectured. Perhaps Victor is thinking of Albertus Magnus's belief that there was a flow of causality from the stars that actually touched the human embryo, thus determining the course of its life; or Victor may have been moved by Paracelsus's view that the Creator of the world is a sort of divine alchemist whose work it is to separate things of the earth and heavens from unformed primal matter. In any case, the work of these writers was not wild in their day.

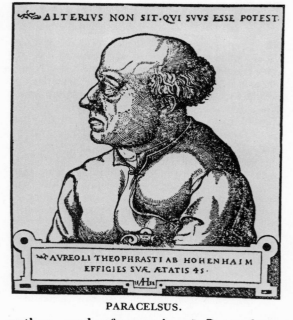

PARACELSUS.

THE ALCHEMIST'S LABORATORY.

26 *philosopher's stone.* For the alchemists it was an article of belief that if only the right procedures were followed, matter could be perfected. To this end, they postulated the existence of a philosopher's stone, the possession of which, it was said, would give its owner the power to transmute base metals into gold. The elixir of life was supposed to confer eternal life on the person who could distill it. The stone and the elixir play important parts in Godwin's novel *Saint Leon,* whose protagonist has access to them both. Saint Leon, being infinitely rich and immortal, is necessarily hard to sympathize with.

24 author, and afterwards of Paracelsus and Albertus Magnus. I read and studied the wild fancies of these writers with delight; they appeared to me treasures known to few beside myself; and although I often wished to communicate these secret stores of knowledge to my father, yet his indefinite censure of my favourite Agrippa always withheld me. I disclosed my discoveries to Elizabeth, therefore, under a promise of strict secrecy; but she did not interest herself in the subject, and I was left by her to pursue my studies alone.

It may appear very strange, that a disciple of Albertus Magnus should arise in the eighteenth century; but our family was not scientifical, and I had not attended any of the lectures given at the schools of Geneva. My dreams were therefore undisturbed by reality; and I entered with the greatest **26** diligence into the search of the philosopher's stone and the elixir of life.

27 *but what glory.* We have seen how Walton too is addressing himself to glory (see p. 13).

28 *ghosts or devils.* Percy Shelley was fascinated with occult phenomena, particularly with ghost- and devil-conjuring. T. J. Hogg writes of Shelley's occult pursuits in his *Life of Shelley* (p. 36): "Sometimes he watched the livelong nights for ghosts. At his father's house . . . he even planned how he might get admission to the vault, or charnel-house, at Warnham Church, and might sit there all night, harrowed by fear, yet trembling with expectation, to see one of the spiritualized owners of the bones piled around him."

Hogg further tells us that Shelley, on one occasion when he was at Eton, believed he was being pursued by the Devil. Another time, while taking one of his secret and solitary midnight walks, he tried to conjure a ghost with the help of a skull that he carried for the purpose. Hogg writes (p. 37): "he repeated his charm, and drank thrice from the skull. No ghost appeared, but for the credit of glamour-books, he did not doubt that the incantation failed from some mistake of his own."

Shelley himself characterized this period in his life in the autobiographical fifth stanza of "Hymn to Intellectual Beauty":

While yet a boy I sought for ghosts, and sped
    Through many a listening chamber, cave and ruin,
    And starlight wood, with fearful steps pursuing
Hopes of high talk with the departed dead.
I called on poisonous names with which our youth is fed.   (ll. 49–53)

He adds in the very next line, "I was not heard—I saw them not—" Several lines from Shelley's "Alastor; or, the Spirit of Solitude" also recall these ghost-raising activities:

I have made my bed
In charnels and on coffins, where black death
Keeps record of the trophies won from thee,
Hoping to still these obstinate questionings
Of thee and thine, by forcing some lone ghost
Thy messenger, to render up the tale
Of what we are.   (ll. 23–29)

Many years later, when Shelley had left behind his youthful interest in the occult, he still found the notion of ghosts compelling. In August 1816, Monk Lewis joined the Byron-Shelley circle. Shelley in a *Journal* entry (August 18, p. 57) writes: "We talk of Ghosts; neither Lord Byron nor Monk G. Lewis seem to believe in them; and they both agree, in the very face of reason, that none could believe in ghosts without also believing in God. I do not think that all the persons who profess to discredit these visitations really discredit them, or, if they do in the daylight, are not admonished by the approach of loneliness and midnight to think more respectably of the world of shadows."

See also page 38, note 16.

But the latter obtained my most undivided attention : wealth was an inferior **27** object ; but what glory would attend the discovery, if I could banish disease from the human frame, and render man invulnerable to any but a violent death !

Nor were these my only visions. The **28** raising of ghosts or devils was a promise liberally accorded by my favourite authors, the fulfilment of which I most eagerly sought ; and if my incantations were always unsuccessful, I attributed the failure rather to my own inexperience and mistake, than to a want of skill or fidelity in my instructors.

The natural phænomena that take place every day before our eyes did not escape my examinations. Distillation, **29** and the wonderful effects of steam, processes of which my favourite authors were utterly ignorant, excited my astonishment ; but my utmost wonder was engaged by some experiments on an air-pump, which I saw employed by a gentleman whom we were in the habit of visiting.

The ignorance of the early philosophers on these and several other points served to decrease their credit with me : but I could not entirely throw them aside, before some other system should occupy their place in my mind.

When I was about fifteen years old, **30** we had retired to our house near Belrive, when we witnessed a most violent and terrible thunder-storm. It advanced **31** from behind the mountains of Jura ; and the thunder burst at once with frightful loudness from various quarters of the heavens. I remained, while the storm

29 *the wonderful effects of steam.* James Watt in 1765 developed the separate condenser for improving the steam engine. Watt's relationship to other prime movers of the Industrial Revolution has already been noted. See page 4, note 2.

Erasmus Darwin, in his "Economy of Vegetation" (Bk I. ll. 289–96), prophesied the coming uses of steam as early as 1789:

Soon shall thy arm, UNCONQUER'D STEAM! afar
Drag the slow barge, or drive the rapid car;
Or on wide-waving wings expanded bear
The flying-chariot through the fields of air.
—Fair crews triumphant, leaning from above,
Shall wave their fluttering kerchiefs as they move;
Or warrior-bands alarm the gaping crowd,
And armies shrink beneath the shadowy cloud.

30 *Belrive.* A village on the south shore of Lake Geneva near the Shelleys' residence in Cologny.

31 *Jura.* A mountain range overlooking the south shore of Lake Geneva.

32 *blasted stump.* The image of this spectacularly blasted tree will recur again. It is one of Mary Shelley's more successful symbols.

lasted, watching its progress with curiosity and delight. As I stood at the door, on a sudden I beheld a stream of fire issue from an old and beautiful oak, which stood about twenty yards from our house; and so soon as the dazzling light vanished, the oak had disappeared, and nothing remained but a blasted stump. When we visited it the next morning, we found the tree shattered in a singular manner. It was not splintered by the shock, but entirely reduced to thin ribbands of wood. I never beheld any thing so utterly destroyed.

The catastrophe of this tree excited my extreme astonishment; and I eagerly inquired of my father the nature and origin of thunder and lightning. He replied, "Electricity;" describing at the same time the various effects of that power. He constructed a small electrical machine, and exhibited a few experiments; he made also a kite, with

"HE MADE ALSO A KITE."

33 *fluid from the clouds.* Lightning (indeed light itself) was regarded, according to Georg Ernest Stahl's (1660–1734) widely popular phlogiston theory, as a sort of fluid that was released as a consequence of combustion.

Benjamin Franklin's kite-flying experiment is well known. Mary Shelley may also have known of Joseph Priestley's *The History and Present State of Electricity* (1767), which shows the influence of Franklin, whose friend Priestley was. There is an entire chapter in Priestley's book on the medical uses of electricity. Among the examples he cites, this one may be of special interest to readers of *Frankenstein:* "The patient was a girl belonging to the foundling hospital, about seven years of age, who was first seized with a disorder occasioned by the worms, and at length by an universal rigidity of her muscles; so that her whole body felt more like that of a dead animal than a living one . . . about the middle of November, 1762, after all the usual medicines had failed, Dr. Watson began to electrify her . . . till the end of January following; when every muscle of her body was perfectly flexible."

Erasmus Darwin describes the effects of electricity in a crackling stanza of *The Botanic Garden* (pp. 349–56) that might have served as a model to the makers of the 1935 film, *The Bride of Frankenstein:*

Or, if one saw some fearless Beauty stand,
And touch the sparkling rod with graceful hand;
Through her fine limbs the mimic lightnings dart,
And flames innocuous eddy round her heart;
O'er her fair brow the kindling lustres glare,
Blue rays diverging from her bristling hair;
While some fond Youth the kiss ethereal sips,
And soft fires issue from their meeting lips.

(ll. 349–56)

In the 1831 edition of *Frankenstein*, Victor's father is described as "not scientific," and Victor receives instruction in electricity and galvanism from a "man of great research in natural philosophy."

DARWIN'S BOTANICAL CUPID.

33 a wire and string, which drew down that fluid from the clouds.

This last stroke completed the overthrow of Cornelius Agrippa, Albertus Magnus, and Paracelsus, who had so long reigned the lords of my imagination. But by some fatality I did not feel inclined to commence the study of any modern system; and this disinclination was influenced by the following circumstance.

My father expressed a wish that I should attend a course of lectures upon natural philosophy, to which I cheerfully consented. Some accident prevented my attending these lectures until the course was nearly finished. The lecture, being therefore one of the last, was entirely incomprehensible to me. The professor discoursed with the greatest fluency of potassium and boron, of sulphates and oxyds, terms to which I could affix no idea; and I

34 *Pliny and Buffon.* Pliny was a first-century naturalist (A.D. 23–79) whose *Historia Naturalis* is a compendium of knowledge of the natural world that existed up to his time. Mary Shelley would certainly have known of Percy Shelley's enthusiasm for Pliny, to whose works the young poet was introduced by Dr. James Lind, a physician who taught at Eton part time when Shelley was a student there. Dr. Lind, who had wide-ranging and sometimes semioccult interests, encouraged Shelley's readings in the sciences.

Buffon (1707–1788) was an early influence on the mind of Percy Shelley. As early as 1811, the poet undertook the translation of a Buffon treatise. Buffon was the author of the forty-four volume *Histoire Naturelle*, which Mary Shelley's journal shows she was reading in June and July 1817.

35 *at the age of seventeen.* If this is an impressive account of the intellectual achievements of a seventeen-year-old, we may be even more impressed by the wide range of Mary Shelley's own readings at the age of sixteen. In a single year she devoured nearly two hundred volumes of the works of a wide array of such demanding authors as Shakespeare, Goethe, Ovid (in Latin), Milton, Pope, Swift, Plutarch, Voltaire, and Rousseau. Henry H. Harper, editor of *Letters of Mary W. Shelley* (1918), writes (pp. 12–13), "For a girl of sixteen to read and intelligently study such a prodigious mass of learning in the space of twelve months shows a degree of application and mental precocity almost beyond human comprehension. This was followed by the reading of more than a hundred other volumes in English, Latin and Greek languages. Her ambition to keep pace with the mental development of the erudite Shelley never flagged."

36 *with ill health.* Ernest is one of Mary Shelley's less happy inventions. He never touches the plot of Frankenstein in any significant way. Ernest's ill health is, however, worth a comment. In the 1831 edition of *Frankenstein,* Ernest is reimagined as a robust lad with ambitions for a military career. The change reflects the fact that, by 1831, Percy Florence Shelley, Mary Shelley's only surviving child, was twelve years old. It may be that his mother, having repented of the name-magic she had inadvertently committed with William, chose not to give Percy the evil eye by retaining a sickly Ernest.

37 *William.* This child is, for the present editor, an overwhelming critical problem whose implication will be touched on in a later note (p. 97, note 3). For the moment it is enough to observe that Mary Shelley's father, brother, and infant son were all named William.

38 *studies.* While it is true that William Godwin, Mary Shelley's father, directed the education of his daughters, he did so fitfully and uncomfortably. Nor, in other respects, was our author's childhood anything like the idealized portrait the narrator gives us

became disgusted with the science of natural philosophy, although I still read **34** Pliny and Buffon with delight, authors, in my estimation, of nearly equal interest and utility.

My occupations at this age were principally the mathematics, and most of the branches of study appertaining to that science. I was busily employed in learning languages; Latin was already familiar to me, and I began to read some of the easiest Greek authors without the help of a lexicon. I also perfectly understood English and German. This is the list of my accom- **35** plishments at the age of seventeen; and you may conceive that my hours were fully employed in acquiring and maintaining a knowledge of this various literature.

Another task also devolved upon me, when I became the instructor of my brothers. Ernest was six years younger than myself, and was my principal pu- **36** pil. He had been afflicted with ill health from his infancy, through which Elizabeth and I had been his constant nurses: his disposition was gentle, but he was incapable of any severe appli- **37** cation. William, the youngest of our family, was yet an infant, and the most beautiful little fellow in the world; his lively blue eyes, dimpled cheeks, and endearing manners, inspired the tenderest affection.

Such was our domestic circle, from which care and pain seemed for ever banished. **38** My father directed our studies, and my mother partook of our enjoyments. Neither of us possessed the slightest pre-eminence over the other;

here. Mary Jane Godwin, Mary Shelley's stepmother, is described by George Woodcock, Godwin's biographer, as a woman "devoid of all the Godwinian virtues . . . She was jealous and possessive to a degree . . . she showed a marked preference for her own [children]." Woodcock adds gloomily that the "Godwin household was never harmonious, and there is no reasonable doubt that Mary Jane's attitude was the principal cause of this disharmony" (*William Godwin*, pp. 182, 183–84). Godwin's friends described her variously as an implacable gossip, a prying woman, and as a "pustule of vanity."

the voice of command was never heard amongst us; but mutual affection engaged us all to comply with and obey the slightest desire of each other.

CHAPTER II.

1 *Ingolstadt*. The German University of Ingolstadt, founded in 1410, was notable for its medical school. Though the university no longer exists in Ingolstadt, the town still boasts a Museum of Medical History housed in what was once the Anatomy Building.

Ingolstadt was a dangerous place to send the seventeen-year-old scion of a quiet bourgeois family. It was in Ingolstadt that Dr. Adam Weishaupt, in May 1776, founded the Illuminist Society, whose doctrine, writes Richard Holmes in *Shelley: The Pursuit* (pp. 52–53), "was one of militant egalitarianism, the destruction of private property, religion, and 'superstitious' social forms such as marriage. Their methods were essentially conspiratorial, based on the Masonic type of secret lodges, and with a tradition of antinomian underground movement dating back to a medieval Spanish sect of the same name."

2 *scarlet fever*. An acute childhood illness caused by a streptococcus infection. While scarlet fever is usually a mild disease, it can turn alarmingly severe, as it is complicated by other illnesses such as rheumatic fever, meningitis, and kidney disease.

Here, in this 1818 edition of our text, Elizabeth has a mild form of the disease, but in the 1831 edition, Mary Shelley punished her with a severe case of scarlet fever. One suspects that the change was intended to intensify the identification between Elizabeth and Mary Shelley who, we recall, was by her birth responsible for her own mother's death.

WHEN I had attained the age of seventeen, my parents resolved that I should become a student at the university of

1 Ingolstadt. I had hitherto attended the schools of Geneva ; but my father thought it necessary, for the completion of my education, that I should be made acquainted with other customs than those of my native country. My departure was therefore fixed at an early date ; but, before the day resolved upon could arrive, the first misfortune of my life occurred—an omen, as it were, of my future misery.

2 Elizabeth had caught the scarlet fever ; but her illness was not severe, and she quickly recovered. During her confinement, many arguments had been urged to persuade my mother to refrain from attending upon her. She had, at first, yielded to our entreaties ; but when she heard that her favourite was recovering, she could no longer debar herself from her society, and entered her chamber long before the danger of infection was past. The consequences of this imprudence were fatal. On the third day my mother sickened ; her fever was very malignant, and the looks of her attendants prognosticated the worst event. On her death-bed the fortitude and benignity of this admirable woman did not de-

3 *your union.* See pp. 35–36 when this wish is first expressed.

4 *in another world.* This idealized death contrasts sharply with the long and horrid dying of Mary Shelley's mother, Mary Wollstonecraft, who died of childbed complications ten days after Mary Shelley was born. The specific cause of her death was an infection brought on by the medical measures taken to remove the placenta, which failed to descend after the baby was born. In an age when there were no anesthetics or antiseptics available, Dr. Poignard, the obstetrician, labored with his fingertips for some five hours to remove the bits of the fragmented placenta from the womb. A few days later, the much weakened mother suffered the further indignity of having puppies attached to her overflowing breasts to draw off her excess milk. Later still, suffering from blood poisoning, and possibly gangrene, she lay in bed muttering incoherently. At one point, the dying woman, who, despite her radical convictions, had never lost her faith in God, exclaimed, "Oh Godwin, I am in heaven," to which Godwin, her husband, ever the rationalist replied, "You mean, my dear, that your symptoms are a little easier." Claire Tomalin, in *The Life of Mary Wollstonecraft* (p. 225), writes, "There is something peculiarly horrible about this third death [the other two were suicide attempts—L.W.] of Mary's buzzed about by doctors and well-meaning intellectuals, painful, long drawn out and lacking in peace and dignity."

The fact that it was peculiarly a woman's death was not lost either on Mary Wollstonecraft's contemporaries, nor on her daughter, the frequently pregnant Mary Shelley.

If we see Elizabeth in the role of a daughter, as I think we are intended to, the sequence of illnesses resulting in the death of a mother bears a striking similarity to Mary Shelley's birth and the subsequent death of *her* mother. Seen from that point of view, we may conjecture that the fictional Elizabeth's more than exceptional sweetness to the surviving Frankensteins served Mary Shelley as a self-exculpating fantasy.

sert her. She joined the hands of Elizabeth and myself: "My children," she said, "my firmest hopes of future happiness were placed on the prospect of **3** your union. This expectation will now be the consolation of your father. Elizabeth, my love, you must supply my place to your younger cousins. Alas! I regret that I am taken from you; and, happy and beloved as I have been, is it not hard to quit you all? But these are not thoughts befitting me; I will endeavour to resign myself cheerfully to death, and will indulge a hope of **4** meeting you in another world."

She died calmly; and her countenance expressed affection even in death. I need not describe the feelings of those whose dearest ties are rent by that most irreparable evil, the void that presents itself to the soul, and the despair that is exhibited on the countenance. It is so long before the mind can persuade itself that she, whom we saw every day, and whose very existence appeared a part of our own, can have departed for ever—that the brightness of a beloved eye can have been extinguished, and the sound of a voice so familiar, and dear to the ear, can be hushed, never more to be heard. These are the reflections of the first days; but when the lapse of time proves the reality of the evil, then the actual bitterness of grief commences. Yet from whom has not that rude hand rent away some dear connexion; and why should I describe a sorrow which all have felt, and must feel? The time at length arrives, when grief is rather an indulgence than a necessity; and

CAROLINE BEAUFORT FRANKENSTEIN.

the smile that plays upon the lips, although it may be deemed a sacrilege, is not banished. My mother was dead, but we had still duties which we ought to perform; we must continue our course with the rest, and learn to think ourselves fortunate, whilst one remains whom the spoiler has not seized.

My journey to Ingolstadt, which had been deferred by these events, was now again determined upon. I obtained from my father a respite of some weeks. This period was spent sadly; my mother's death, and my speedy departure, depressed our spirits; but Elizabeth endeavoured to renew the spirit of cheerfulness in our little society. Since the death of her aunt, her mind had acquired new firmness and vigour. She determined to fulfil her duties with the greatest exactness; and she felt that that most imperious duty, of rendering her uncle and cousins happy, had devolved upon her. She consoled me, amused her uncle, instructed my brothers; and I never beheld her so enchanting as at this time, when she was continually endeavouring to contribute to the happiness of others, entirely forgetful of herself.

The day of my departure at length arrived. I had taken leave of all my friends, excepting Clerval, who spent the last evening with us. He bitterly lamented that he was unable to accompany me: but his father could not be persuaded to part with him, intending that he should become a partner with him in business, in compliance with his favourite theory, that learning was superfluous in the commerce of

"HENRY HAD A REFINED MIND."

5 *chaise*. A light, two-wheeled carriage.

ordinary life. Henry had a refined mind ; he had no desire to be idle, and was well pleased to become his father's partner, but he believed that a man might be a very good trader, and yet possess a cultivated understanding.

We sat late, listening to his complaints, and making many little arrangements for the future. The next morning early I departed. Tears gushed from the eyes of Elizabeth ; they proceeded partly from sorrow at my departure, and partly because she reflected that the same journey was to have taken place three months before, when a mother's blessing would have accompanied me.

5   I threw myself into the chaise that was to convey me away, and indulged in the most melancholy reflections. I, who had ever been surrounded by amiable companions, continually engaged in endeavouring to bestow mutual plea-

"MY DEPARTURE" (DRAWING BY CHEVALIER
FOR 1831 EDITION FRANKENSTEIN).

6 *"old familiar faces."* The phrase is taken from Charles Lamb's (1775–1834) poem, "The Old Familiar Faces" (1798), but in that context, it is used as a refrain that calls up grievous personal losses. The second stanza of Lamb's poem is sufficiently grim for the occasion, but it must have been especially painful for Mary Shelley whose life it almost seems to be describing directly:

Where are they gone, the old familiar faces?

I had a mother, but she died, and left me,
Died prematurely in a day of horrors—
All, all are gone, the old familiar faces.

I have had playmates, I have had companions,
In my days of childhood, in my joyful schooldays,—
All, all are gone, the old familiar faces.

I have been laughing, I have been carousing,
Drinking late, sitting late, with my bosom cronies,—
All, all are gone, the old familiar faces.

I loved a Love once, fairest among women:
Closed are her doors on me, I must not see her,—
All, all are gone, the old familiar faces.

I have a friend, a kinder friend has no man:
Like an ingrate, I left my friend abruptly;
Left him, to muse on the old familiar faces.

Ghost-like, I paced round the haunts of my childhood.
Earth seemed a desert I was bound to traverse,
Seeking to find the old familiar faces.

Friend of my bosom, thou more than a brother,
Why wert not thou born in my father's dwelling?
So might we talk of the old familiar faces—

How some they have died, and some they have left me,
And some are taken from me; all are departed,—
All, all are gone, the old familiar faces.

Charles Lamb was at the center of an intellectually influential circle that included Coleridge, Southey, and Hazlitt as well as, later, Mary Shelley's father, William Godwin.

sure, I was now alone. In the university, whither I was going, I must form my own friends, and be my own protector. My life had hitherto been remarkably secluded and domestic; and this had given me invincible repugnance to new countenances. I loved my brothers, Elizabeth, and Clerval: **6** these were " old familiar faces;" but I believed myself totally unfitted for the company of strangers. Such were my reflections as I commenced my journey; but as I proceeded, my spirits and hopes rose. I ardently desired the acquisition of knowledge. I had often, when at home, thought it hard to remain during my youth cooped up in one place, and had longed to enter the world, and take my station among other human beings. Now my desires were complied with, and it would, indeed, have been folly to repent.

"I COMMENCED MY JOURNEY."

HORTVS ACADEMICO-MEDICVS INGOLSTADIENSIS.

THE UNIVERSITY AS VICTOR SAW IT.

7 *long and fatiguing.* From Geneva to Ingolstadt is a journey of some five hundred miles. Given the hazards and the conditions of eighteenth-century roads, Victor, unless he traveled day and night, must have taken no less than two weeks to make the journey.

8 *white steeple.* The clock tower of Ingolstadt's fifteenth-century Münster, like the cathedral itself, is of red brick trimmed with white stone. It is possible that Mary Shelley, never having visited Ingolstadt, deduced the tower was white from black-and-white sketches she may have seen.

I had sufficient leisure for these and many other reflections during my jour-
7 ney to Ingolstadt, which was long and
8 fatiguing. At length the high white steeple of the town met my eyes. I alighted, and was conducted to my solitary apartment, to spend the evening as I pleased.

The next morning I delivered my letters of introduction, and paid a visit to some of the principal professors, and among others to M. Krempe, professor of natural philosophy. He received me with politeness, and asked me several questions concerning my progress in the different branches of science appertaining to natural philosophy. I mentioned, it is true, with fear and

THE WALLED CITY, INGOLSTADT,
VIEW FROM THE SOUTH.

MODERN INGOLSTADT:
A STREET SCENE.

trembling, the only authors I had ever read upon those subjects. The professor stared: " Have you," he said, " really spent your time in studying such nonsense ?"

I replied in the affirmative. " Every minute," continued M. Krempe with warmth, " every instant that you have wasted on those books is utterly and entirely lost. You have burdened your memory with exploded systems, and useless names. Good God! in what desert land have you lived, where no one was kind enough to inform you that these fancies, which you have so greedily imbibed, are a thousand years old, and as musty as they are ancient? I little expected in this enlightened and scientific age to find a disciple of Albertus Magnus and Paracelsus. My dear Sir, you must begin your studies entirely anew."

So saying, he stept aside, and wrote down a list of several books treating of natural philosophy, which he desired me to procure, and dismissed me, after

FORMER UNIVERSITY BUILDINGS:
MODERN INGOLSTADT.

"A LITTLE SQUAT MAN, WITH A GRUFF
VOICE AND REPULSIVE COUNTENANCE."

mentioning that in the beginning of the following week he intended to commence a course of lectures upon natural philosophy in its general relations, and that M. Waldman, a fellow-professor, would lecture upon chemistry the alternate days that he missed.

I returned home, not disappointed, for I had long considered those authors useless whom the professor had so strongly reprobated; but I did not feel much inclined to study the books which I procured at his recommendation. M. Krempe was a little squat man, with a gruff voice and repulsive countenance; the teacher, therefore, did not prepossess me in favour of his doctrine. Besides, I had a contempt for the uses of modern natural philosophy. It was very different, when the masters of the science sought immortality and power; such views, although futile, were grand: but now the scene was changed. The ambition of the inquirer seemed to limit itself to the annihilation of those visions on which my interest in science was chiefly founded. I was required to exchange chimeras of boundless grandeur for realities of little worth.

Such were my reflections during the first two or three days spent almost in solitude. But as the ensuing week commenced, I thought of the information which M. Krempe had given me concerning the lectures. And although I could not consent to go and hear that little conceited fellow deliver sentences out of a pulpit, I recollected what he had said of M. Waldman, whom I had never seen, as he had hitherto been out of town.

Partly from curiosity, and partly

9 *repulsive countenance*. Krempe's ugliness, we are meant to believe, is a sign that all is not well with his soul. In the epoch in which *Frankenstein* was being written, Johann Kaspar Lavater's *Speculations in Physiognomy* was still in vogue. Lavater, like Lombroso later, had a system that purported to enable one to read character from physiognomic hints supplied by nature. Lavater, early in his life, was an intimate friend of Henry Fuseli.

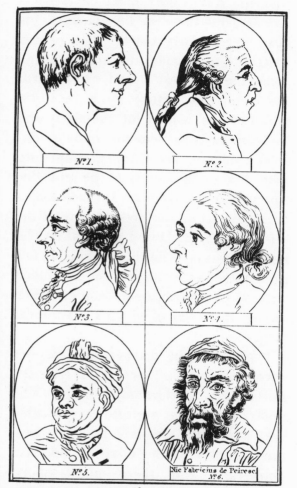

PLATE III OF LAVATER'S PHYSIOGNOMY (1867).

DESCRIPTION OF PLATE III.

Number 1.

THIS outline, from a bust of Cicero, appears to me an almost perfect model of congeniality; the whole has the character of penetrating acuteness, an extraordinary though not a great profile. All is acute; all is sharp: discerning, searching, less benevolent than satirical, elegant, conspicuous, subtle.

Number 2.

Another congenial countenance. Too evidently nature for it to be mistaken for ideal, or the invention and emendation of art. Such a forehead does not betoken the rectilinear, but the nose thus bent. Such an upper lip, such an open, eloquent mouth! The forehead does not lead us to expect high poetical genius; but acute punctuality, and the stability of retentive memory. It is impossible to suppose this a common countenance.

Number 3.

The forehead and nose not congenial. The nose shows the very acute thinker. The lower part of the forehead, on the contrary, especially the distance between the eyebrow and eye, do not betoken this high degree of mental power. The stiff position of the whole is much at variance with the eye and mouth, but particularly with the nose. The whole, the eyebrow excepted, speaks a calm, peaceable, mild character.

Number 4.

The harmony of the mouth and nose is self-evident. The forehead is too good, too comprehensive, for this very limited under part of the countenance. The whole bespeaks a harmless character; nothing delicate nor severe.

Number 5.

We have here a high bold forehead, with a short-seeming blunt nose, and a fat double chin. How do these harmonize! It is almost a general law of nature, that where the eyes are strong drawn, and the eyebrows near, the eyebrows must also be strong. This countenance, merely by its harmony, its prominent congenial traits, is expressive of sound, clear understanding; the countenance of reason.

Number 6.

The perfect countenance of a politician. Faces which are thus pointed from the eyes to the chin always have lengthened noses, and never possess large, open, powerful, and piercing eyes. Their firmness partakes of obstinacy, and they rather follow intricate plans than the dictates of common-sense.

M. WALDMAN.

10 *microscope.* The Dutchman Anton van Leeuwenhoek (1632–1723) is credited with the invention of the microscope. Van Leeuwenhoek's researches into the lives of the "very little animalcules" he observed with his microscope did much to weaken the prevalent notion of spontaneous generation by showing that such creatures as weevils and fleas were actually hatched from eggs invisible to the naked eye, which had been laid by adult flying insects.

11 *the air we breathe.* The contributions of Priestley and Watt to the study of gases have already been noted (see p. 43, note 29 and p. 44, note 33). William Harvey (1578–1657), who is credited with the discovery of the circulation of the blood, was a physician, not a chemist. In 1628 he published *Exercitatio Anatomica de Motu Cordis et Sanguinis in Animalibus*, which set forth the evidence supporting his theory of the function of the heart's valves. How eighteenth-century chemists could do all that Waldman claims for them in the last sentence of this paragraph is not clear.

from idleness, I went into the lecturing room, which M. Waldman entered shortly after. This professor was very unlike his colleague. He appeared about fifty years of age, but with an aspect expressive of the greatest benevolence; a few gray hairs covered his temples, but those at the back of his head were nearly black. His person was short, but remarkably erect; and his voice the sweetest I had ever heard. He began his lecture by a recapitulation of the history of chemistry and the various improvements made by different men of learning, pronouncing with fervour the names of the most distinguished discoverers. He then took a cursory view of the present state of the science, and explained many of its elementary terms. After having made a few preparatory experiments, he concluded with a panegyric upon modern chemistry, the terms of which I shall never forget:—

" The ancient teachers of this science," said he, " promised impossibilities, and performed nothing. The modern masters promise very little; they know that metals cannot be transmuted, and that the elixir of life is a chimera. But these philosophers, whose hands seem only made to dabble in dirt, and their eyes to pour over **10** the microscope or crucible, have indeed performed miracles. They penetrate into the recesses of nature, and shew how she works in her hiding places. They ascend into the heavens; they have discovered how the blood **11** circulates, and the nature of the air we breathe. They have acquired new and

12 *the greatest affability and kindness.* This brief sketch of Professor Waldman may have had its model in the poet Shelley's memories of Dr. James Lind (see p. 45, note 34).

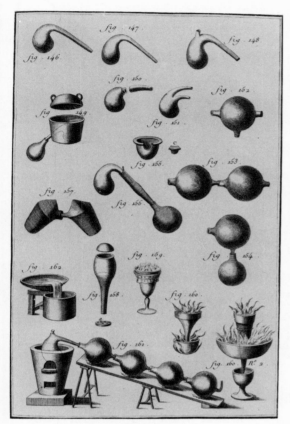

CHEMISTRY.

almost unlimited powers; they can command the thunders of heaven, mimic the earthquake, and even mock the invisible world with its own shadows."

I departed highly pleased with the professor and his lecture, and paid him a visit the same evening. His manners in private were even more mild and attractive than in public; for there was a certain dignity in his mien during his lecture, which in his own **12** house was replaced by the greatest affability and kindness. He heard with attention my little narration concerning my studies, and smiled at the names of Cornelius Agrippa, and Paracelsus, but without the contempt that M. Krempe had exhibited. He said, that " these were men to whose indefatigable zeal modern philosophers were indebted for most of the foundations of their knowledge. They had left to us, as an easier task, to give new names, and arrange in connected classifications, the facts which they in a great degree had been the instruments of bringing to light. The labours of men of genius, however erroneously directed, scarcely ever fail in ultimately turning to the solid advantage of mankind." I listened to his statement, which was delivered without any presumption or affectation; and then added, that his lecture had removed my prejudices against modern chemists; and I, at the same time, requested his advice concerning the books I ought to procure.

" I am happy," said M. Waldman, " to have gained a disciple; and if your application equals your ability, I

"CHARACTERS" IN CHEMISTRY.

have no doubt of your success. Chemistry is that branch of natural philosophy in which the greatest improvements have been and may be made; it is on that account that I have made it my peculiar study; but at the same time I have not neglected the other branches of science. A man would make but a very sorry chemist, if he attended to that department of human knowledge alone. If your wish is to become really a man of science, and not merely a petty experimentalist, I should advise you to apply to every branch of natural philosophy, including mathematics."

He then took me into his laboratory,

13 *the list of books.* Our author is as silent about the details of this list as she was about the repulsive Dr. Krempe's.

"VARIOUS MACHINES."

and explained to me the uses of his various machines; instructing me as to what I ought to procure, and promising me the use of his own, when I should have advanced far enough in the science not to derange their mechanism. He 13 also gave me the list of books which I had requested; and I took my leave.

Thus ended a day memorable to me; it decided my future destiny.

CHAPTER III.

FROM this day natural philosophy, and particularly chemistry, in the most comprehensive sense of the term, became nearly my sole occupation. I read with ardour those works, so full of genius and discrimination, which modern inquirers have written on these subjects. I attended the lectures, and cultivated the acquaintance, of the men of science of **1** the university; and I found even in M. Krempe a great deal of sound sense and real information, combined, it is true, with a repulsive physiognomy and manners, but not on that account the less valuable. In M. Waldman I found a true friend. His gentleness was never tinged by dogmatism; and his instructions were given with an air of frankness and good nature, that banished every idea of pedantry. It was, perhaps, the amiable character of this man that inclined me more to that branch of natural philosophy which he professed, than an intrinsic love for the science itself. But this state of mind had place only in the first steps towards knowledge: the more fully I entered into the science, the more exclusively I pursued it for its own sake. That application, which at first had been a matter of duty and resolution, now became so ardent and eager, that the stars often disappeared in the light of morn-

1 *the university*. It is interesting to compare the details of Victor's scientific studies and of his life at the university with T. J. Hogg's account in *The Life of Shelley* (pp. 55–56) of his first glimpse of Shelley's rooms at Oxford: "Books, boots, papers, shoes, philosophical instruments, clothes, pistols, linens, crockery, ammunition, and phials innumerable, with money, stockings, prints, crucibles, bags, and boxes, were scattered on the floor and in every place; as if the young chemist, in order to analyse the mystery of creation, had endeavoured first to reconstruct the primeval chaos. The tables, and especially the carpet, were already stained with large spots of various hues, which frequently proclaimed the agency of fire. An electrical machine, an air-pump, the galvanic trough, a solar microscope, and large glass jars and receivers, were conspicuous amidst the mass of matter . . .

"He [Shelley] then proceeded, with much eagerness and enthusiasm, to show me the various instruments, especially the electrical apparatus; turning round the handle very rapidly, so that the fierce, crackling sparks flew forth; and presently standing upon the stool with glass feet, he begged me to work the machine until he was filled with the fluid so that his long, wild locks bristled and stood on end. Afterwards he charged a powerful battery of several jars; labouring with vast energy, and discoursing with increasing vehemence of the marvelous powers of electricity, of thunder and lightning; describing an electrical kite that he had made at home, and projecting another and an enormous one, or rather a combination of many kites, that would draw down from the sky an immense volume of electricity, the whole ammunition of a mighty thunderstorm; and this being directed to some point would there produce the most stupendous results."

ing whilst I was yet engaged in my laboratory.

As I applied so closely, it may be easily conceived that I improved rapidly. My ardour was indeed the astonishment of the students; and my proficiency, that of the masters. Professor Krempe often asked me, with a sly smile, how Cornelius Agrippa went on? whilst M. Waldman expressed the most heartfelt exultation in my progress. Two years passed in this manner, during which I paid no visit to Geneva, but was engaged, heart and soul, in the pursuit of some discoveries, which I hoped to make. None but those who have experienced them can conceive of the enticements of science. In other studies you go as far as others have gone before you, and there is nothing more to know; but in a scientific pursuit there is continual food for discovery and wonder. A mind of moderate capacity, which closely pursues one study, must infallibly arrive at great proficiency in that study; and I, who continually sought the attainment of one object of pursuit, and was solely wrapt

2 up in this, improved so rapidly, that, at the end of two years, I made some discoveries in the improvement of some chemical instruments, which procured me great esteem and admiration at the university. When I had arrived at this point, and had become as well acquainted with the theory and practice of natural philosophy as depended on the lessons of any of the professors at Ingolstadt, my residence there being no longer conducive to my improvements, I thought of returning to my friends

and my native town, when an incident happened that protracted my stay.

One of the phænonema which had peculiarly attracted my attention was the structure of the human frame, and, indeed, any animal endued with life. Whence, I often asked myself, did the principle of life proceed? It was a bold question, and one which has ever been considered as a mystery; yet with how many things are we upon the brink of becoming acquainted, if cowardice or carelessness did not restrain our inquiries. I revolved these circumstances in my mind, and determined thenceforth to apply myself more particularly to those branches of natural philosophy which relate to physiology. Unless I had been animated by an almost supernatural enthusiasm, my application to this study would have been irksome, and almost intolerable. To examine the causes of life, we must first have recourse to death. I became acquainted with the science of anatomy: but this was not sufficient; I must also observe the natural decay and corruption of the human body. In my education my father had taken the greatest precautions that my mind should be impressed with no supernatural horrors. I do not ever remember to have trembled at a tale of superstition, or to have feared the apparition of a spirit. Darkness had no effect upon my fancy; and a church-yard was to me merely the receptacle of bodies deprived of life, which, from being the seat of beauty and strength, had become food for the worm. Now I was led to examine the cause and progress of this decay, and forced to spend days and

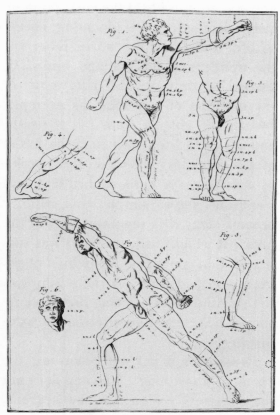

"THE STRUCTURE
OF THE HUMAN FRAME" A.

"THE STRUCTURE
OF THE HUMAN FRAME" B.

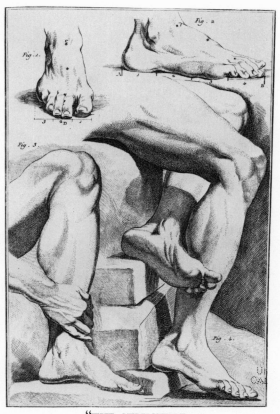

"THE STRUCTURE
OF THE HUMAN FRAME" C.

3 *capable of bestowing animation.* This overwhelming achievement comes to us at the end of a series of paragraphs in which our author, with considerable dexterity, has avoided giving us any details. The evasion is not surprising, since Victor has here surpassed the achievement of the "wisest men since the creation of the world." Under the circumstances, the eighteen-year-old Mary Shelley may be excused from the responsibility of telling us how it was that Victor arrived at success.

nights in vaults and charnel houses. My attention was fixed upon every object the most insupportable to the delicacy of the human feelings. I saw how the fine form of man was degraded and wasted; I beheld the corruption of death succeed to the blooming cheek of life; I saw how the worm inherited the wonders of the eye and brain. I paused, examining and analysing all the minutiæ of causation, as exemplified in the change from life to death, and death to life, until from the midst of this darkness a sudden light broke in upon me—a light so brilliant and wondrous, yet so simple, that while I became dizzy with the immensity of the prospect which it illustrated, I was surprised that among so many men of genius, who had directed their inquiries towards the same science, that I alone should be reserved to discover so astonishing a secret.

Remember, I am not recording the vision of a madman. The sun does not more certainly shine in the heavens, than that which I now affirm is true. Some miracle might have produced it, yet the stages of the discovery were distinct and probable. After days and nights of incredible labour and fatigue, I succeeded in discovering the cause of generation and life; nay, more, I became myself capable of bestowing animation upon lifeless matter.

The astonishment which I had at first experienced on this discovery soon gave place to delight and rapture. After so much time spent in painful labour, to arrive at once at the summit of my desires, was the most gratifying consummation of

4 *like the Arabian.* The reference is to the "Fourth Voyage of Sinbad" in *The Arabian Nights.* There we learn that Sinbad, after various dangerous adventures, finds refuge with a friendly king who loads Sinbad with honors and gifts, not the least among them being a beautiful young wife. For a time Sinbad lives and delights in the lap of luxury, but his happiness is disturbed when he learns that the custom of the country in which he is so happy a dweller requires that, when one of the partners in a marriage dies, the other be promptly buried alive with the dead spouse.

Sinbad, quite properly, begins to worry about his wife's health. Sure enough, not much later, his wife becomes ill and dies, and Sinbad, with a small supply of food and water, is enclosed with her body in a subterranean cavern in which there are the remains of the other luckless couples that preceded them. For a while, the resourceful Sinbad survives by killing, for their food and water, the surviving partner of later couples lowered into the cavern. One day Sinbad is led toward a spot of light that he assiduously follows and finds himself at last outside the charnel cavern, free and safe once more.

THE FOURTH VOYAGE OF ES-SINDIBAD OF THE SEA.

Afterwards, however, I comforted myself, and said, Perhaps I shall die before her: and no one knoweth which will precede and which will follow. And I proceeded to beguile myself with occupations.⁵⁵

And but a short time had elapsed after that when my wife fell sick, and she remained so a few days, and died. So the greater number of the people assembled to console me, and to console her family for her death; and the King also came to console me for the loss of her, as was their custom. They then brought for her a woman to wash her, and they washed her, and decked her with the richest of her apparel, and ornaments of gold, and necklaces and jewels. And when they had attired my wife, and put her in the bier, and carried her and gone with her to that mountain, and lifted up the stone from the mouth of the pit, and cast her into it, all my companions, and the family of my wife, advanced to bid me farewell and to console me for the loss of my life. I was crying out among them, I am a foreigner, and am unable to endure your custom! But they would not hear what I said, nor pay any regard to my words. They laid hold upon me and bound me by force, tying with me seven cakes of bread and a jug of sweet water, according to their custom, and

SINBAD DESCENDING INTO THE PIT.

my toils. But this discovery was so great and overwhelming, that all the steps by which I had been progressively led to it were obliterated, and I beheld only the result. What had been the study and desire of the wisest men since the creation of the world, was now within my grasp. Not that, like a magic scene, it all opened upon me at once: the information I had obtained was of a nature rather to direct my endeavours so soon as I should point them towards the object of my search, than to exhibit that object already accomplished. I **4** was like the Arabian who had been buried with the dead, and found a

5 *informed of the secret.* An interesting, if unlikely, idea. How Walton, a sailor and a failed poet, who has confessed that he is self-educated, could be expected to understand the scientific complexities of Victor's secret strains one's powers of belief.

VICTOR (HENRY FUSELI'S
BUST OF BRUTUS).

passage to life aided only by one glimmering, and seemingly ineffectual light.

I see by your eagerness, and the wonder and hope which your eyes express, my friend, that you expect to be informed of the secret with which I am acquainted; that cannot be: listen patiently until the end of my story, and you will easily perceive why I am reserved upon that subject. I will no lead you on, unguarded and ardent as I then was, to your destruction and infallible misery. Learn from me, if not by my precepts, at least by my example, how dangerous is the acquirement of knowledge, and how much happier that man is who believes his native town to be the world, than he who aspires to become greater than his nature will allow.

When I found so astonishing a power placed within my hands, I hesitated a long time concerning the manner in which I should employ it. Although I possessed the capacity of bestowing animation, yet to prepare a frame for the reception of it, with all its intricacies of fibres, muscles, and veins, still remained a work of inconceivable difficulty and labour. I doubted at first whether I should attempt the creation of a being like myself or one of simpler organization; but my imagination was too much exalted by my first success to permit me to doubt of my ability to give life to an animal as complex and wonderful as man. The materials at present within my command hardly appeared adequate to so arduous an undertaking; but I doubted not that

6 *of a gigantic stature.* Mary Shelley seems unbothered by this assertion. Her readers may wonder where Victor found the larger-than-life-size parts needed to make an eight-foot-high, properly proportioned being. As we will see, Victor overcomes this difficulty not once, but almost twice. One may wonder too that it seems not to have occurred to Victor that an eight-foot-high being might not fit into the ordinary scheme of things.

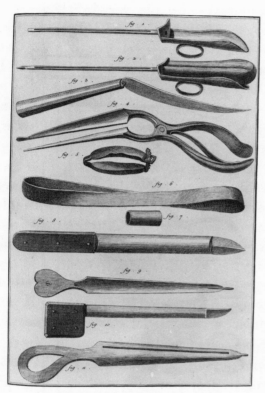

EIGHTEENTH-CENTURY SURGICAL
IMPLEMENTS.

7 *ideal bounds.* Imaginary limits.

8 *A new species.* It is possible to read Victor's speech here as an extraordinary expression of hubris—to believe that he, alone and unaided, could "pour a torrent of light into our dark world"; that he, all by himself, would find the means to reject the work of death. Certainly, Victor's speech is extravagant, and it is not made any less prideful by the gloating "a new species would bless me as its creator and source." But it is also possible to read this passage as Mary Shelley's first hint to us that she intends at least a touch of satire of the biblical account of the Creation of humankind.

At a level not quite so lofty, the tone and content of Victor's speech can make one think of the braggadocio of abused children fantasizing how they will one day do something that will earn them love.

I should ultimately succeed. I prepared myself for a multitude of reverses; my operations might be incessantly baffled, and at last my work be imperfect: yet, when I considered the improvement which every day takes place in science and mechanics, I was encouraged to hope my present attempts would at least lay the foundations of future success. Nor could I consider the magnitude and complexity of my plan as any argument of its impracticability. It was with these feelings that I began the creation of a human being. As the minuteness of the parts formed a great hindrance to my speed, I resolved, contrary to my first **6** intention, to make the being of a gigantic stature; that is to say, about eight feet in height, and proportionably large. After having formed this determination, and having spent some months in successfully collecting and arranging my materials, I began.

No one can conceive the variety of feelings which bore me onwards, like a hurricane, in the first enthusiasm of success. Life and death appeared to **7** me ideal bounds, which I should first break through, and pour a torrent of **8** light into our dark world. A new species would bless me as its creator and source; many happy and excellent natures would owe their being to me. No father could claim the gratitude of his child so completely as I should deserve their's. Pursuing these reflections, I thought, that if I could bestow animation upon lifeless matter, I might in process of time (although I now found it impossible) renew life where death

9 *One secret.* That is, that he is capable of bestowing "animation upon lifeless matter."

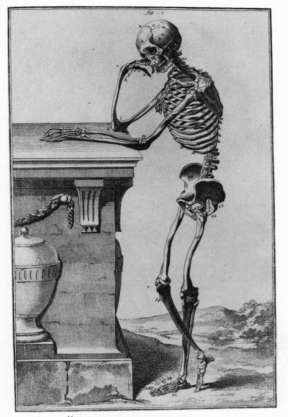

"I COLLECTED BONES . . .
SECRETS OF THE HUMAN FRAME."

"A SOLITARY CHAMBER . . . AT THE TOP
OF THE HOUSE," INGOLSTADT.

had apparently devoted the body to corruption.

These thoughts supported my spirits, while I pursued my undertaking with unremitting ardour. My cheek had grown pale with study, and my person had become emaciated with confinement. Sometimes, on the very brink of certainty, I failed; yet still I clung to the hope which the next day or the next **9** hour might realize. One secret which I alone possessed was the hope to which I had dedicated myself; and the moon gazed on my midnight labours, while, with unrelaxed and breathless eagerness, I pursued nature to her hiding places. Who shall conceive the horrors of my secret toil, as I dabbled among the unhallowed damps of the grave, or tortured the living animal to animate the lifeless clay? My limbs now tremble, and my eyes swim with the remembrance; but then a resistless, and almost frantic impulse, urged me forward; I seemed to have lost all soul or sensation but for this one pursuit. It was indeed but a passing trance, that only made me feel with renewed acuteness so soon as, the unnatural stimulus ceasing to operate, I had returned to my old habits. I collected bones from charnel houses; and disturbed, with profane fingers, the tremendous secrets of the human frame. In a solitary chamber, or rather cell, at the top of the house, and separated from all the other apartments by a gallery and staircase, I kept my workshop of filthy creation; my eyeballs were starting from their sockets in attending to the details of my employment. **10** The dissecting room and the slaugh-

"WORKSHOP OF FILTHY CREATION."

10 *slaughter-house*. Here the uneasy suggestion seems to be that Victor employed animal parts for his creation.

11 *my eyes were insensible*. This detail lets Walton know just how engrossed Victor was. Walton has earlier told us (p. 29) that Victor was an ardent admirer of nature.

ter-house furnished many of my materials; and often did my human nature turn with loathing from my occupation, whilst, still urged on by an eagerness which perpetually increased, I brought my work near to a conclusion.

The summer months passed while I was thus engaged, heart and soul, in one pursuit. It was a most beautiful season; never did the fields bestow a more plentiful harvest, or the vines yield a more luxuriant vintage: but my eyes were insensible to the charms of nature. And the same feelings which made me neglect the scenes around me caused me also to forget those friends who were so many miles absent,

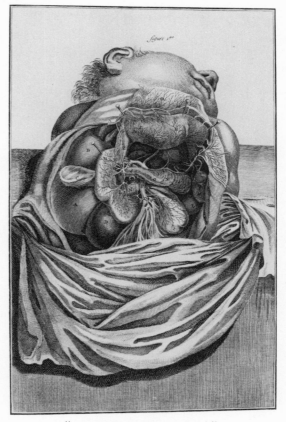

"THE DISSECTING ROOM."

and whom I had not seen for so long a time. I knew my silence disquieted them; and I well remembered the words of my father: " I know that while you are pleased with yourself, you will think of us with affection, and we shall hear regularly from you. You must pardon me, if I regard any interruption in your correspondence as a proof that your other duties are equally neglected."

I knew well therefore what would be my father's feelings; but I could not tear my thoughts from my employment, loathsome in itself, but which had taken an irresistible hold of my imagination. I wished, as it were, to procrastinate all that related to my feelings of affection until the great object, which swallowed up every habit of my nature, should be completed.

I then thought that my father would be unjust if he ascribed my neglect to vice, or faultiness on my part; but I am now convinced that he was justified in conceiving that I should not be altogether free from blame. A human being in perfection ought always to preserve a calm and peaceful mind, and never to allow passion or a transitory desire to disturb his tranquillity. I do not think that the pursuit of knowledge is an exception to this rule. If the study to which you apply yourself has a tendency to weaken your affections, and to destroy your taste for those simple pleasures in which no alloy can possibly mix, then that study is certainly unlawful, that is to say, not befitting the human mind. If this rule were always observed; if no man allow-

12 *had not been destroyed.* The Godwinian, and grandiloquent, prose of this paragraph comes unhesitatingly to its inflated conclusion. Fortunately, our author notices that her occasional habit of rushing on has overtaken her and brings herself to an abrupt stop. Many years later, Mary Shelley, writing to Thomas Henry Payne, would admit wryly that the "truth is, though I can rein my spoken words I find all the woman directs my written ones, and the pen in my hand, I gallop over fence and ditch without pity for my reader—*ecce signum!*" (*The Romance of Mary Shelley*, p. 78.)

13 *summer, passed.* Victor is now twenty.

14 *by his favourite employment.* This portrait of the toiling Victor resembles, in certain details, the description Joseph Weizenbaum gives us of the compulsive computer programmer. Weizenbaum, in his *Computer Power and Human Reason* (p. 116), writes: "Wherever computer centers have become established, bright young men of disheveled appearance, often with sunken glowing eyes, can be seen sitting at computer consoles, their arms tensed and waiting to fire with their fingers, already poised to strike, at the buttons and keys on which their attention seems to be as riveted as a gambler's on the rolling dice. When not so transfixed, they often sit at tables strewn with computer printouts over which they pore like possessed students of a cabalistic text. They work until they nearly drop, twenty, thirty hours at a time. Their food, if they arrange it, is brought to them . . . If possible, they sleep on cots near the computer. But only for a few hours—then back to the console or the printouts. Their rumpled clothes, their unwashed and unshaven faces, and their uncombed hair all testify that they are oblivious to their bodies and the world in which they move. They exist . . . only through and for the computers. These are computer bums, compulsive programmers. They are an international phenomenon."

12 ed any pursuit whatsoever to interfere with the tranquillity of his domestic affections, Greece had not been enslaved; Cæsar would have spared his country; America would have been discovered more gradually; and the empires of Mexico and Peru had not been destroyed.

But I forget that I am moralizing in the most interesting part of my tale; and your looks remind me to proceed.

My father made no reproach in his letters; and only took notice of my silence by inquiring into my occupations more particularly than before. **13** Winter, spring, and summer, passed away during my labours; but I did not watch the blossom or the expanding leaves — sights which before always yielded me supreme delight, so deeply was I engrossed in my occupation. The leaves of that year had withered before my work drew near to a close; and now every day shewed me more plainly how well I had succeeded. But my enthusiasm was checked by my anxiety, and I appeared rather like one doomed by slavery to toil in the mines, or any other unwholesome trade, than an artist **14** occupied by his favourite employment. Every night I was oppressed by a slow fever, and I became nervous to a most painful degree; a disease that I regretted the more because I had hitherto enjoyed most excellent health, and had always boasted of the firmness of my nerves. But I believed that exercise and amusement would soon drive away such symptoms; and I promised myself both of these, when my creation should be complete.

CHAPTER IV.

It was on a dreary night of November, that I beheld the accomplishment of my toils. With an anxiety that almost amounted to agony, I collected the instruments of life around me, that I might infuse a spark of being into the lifeless thing that lay at my feet. It was already one in the morning; the rain pattered dismally against the panes, and my candle was nearly burnt out, when, by the glimmer of the half-extinguished light, I saw the dull yellow eye of the creature open; it breathed hard, and a convulsive motion agitated its limbs.

How can I describe my emotions at this catastrophe, or how delineate the wretch whom with such infinite pains and care I had endeavoured to form? His limbs were in proportion, and I had selected his features as beautiful. Beautiful!—Great God! His yellow skin scarcely covered the work of muscles and arteries beneath; his hair was of a lustrous black, and flowing; his teeth of a pearly whiteness; but these luxuriances only formed a more horrid contrast with his watery eyes, that seemed almost of the same colour as the dun

"HIS LIMBS WERE IN PROPORTION."

"I COLLECTED THE INSTRUMENTS OF LIFE AROUND ME, THAT I MIGHT INFUSE
A SPARK OF BEING INTO THE LIFELESS THING THAT LAY AT MY FEET."

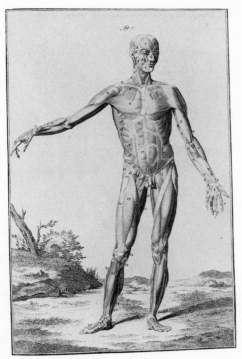

"WORK OF MUSCLES
AND ARTERIES BENEATH."

1 *straight black lips.* In Percy Shelley's poem *The Wandering Jew* (1810), we are told that Victorio, the Jew, encounters a demonic witch who had "black tumid lips—array'd/In livid fiendish smiles of joy." Shelley's witch, however, had "Projecting teeth of mouldy blue."

2 *nearly two years.* Victor is now nearly twenty-one years old.

white sockets in which they were set,
1 his shrivelled complexion, and straight black lips.

The different accidents of life are not so changeable as the feelings of human nature. I had worked hard for
2 nearly two years, for the sole purpose of infusing life into an inanimate body. For this I had deprived myself of rest and health. I had desired it with an ardour that far exceeded moderation; but now that I had finished, the beauty of the dream vanished, and breathless horror and disgust filled my heart. Unable to endure the aspect of the being I had created, I rushed out of the room, and continued a long time traversing my bed-chamber, unable to

"I RUSHED OUT OF THE ROOM" (DRAWING BY CHEVALIER FOR 1831 EDITION FRANKENSTEIN).

3 *compose my mind to sleep.* In a book replete with astonishments, Victor's behavior here is one of the most astonishing—the creator fleeing from his creation; the father-mother revolted by the infant.

Ellen Moers, one of the earliest critics to recognize the psychological implications of this bizarre flight, says of it, "Mary Shelley's book [becomes] most interesting, most powerful, and most feminine: in the motif of revulsion against new-born life, and the drama of guilt, dread, and flight surrounding birth and its consequences." If one recalls the details of Mary Shelley's own birth and *its* consequences, Victor's panic, though it remains incredible as fiction, takes on resonance as a symbol of the author's pain.

Moers, too, is certainly right when she connects the moment of the monster's stirring into life with the entry in Mary Shelley's journal of March 19, 1815, in which Mary Shelley writes, "Dreamed that my little baby came to life again, that it had only been cold, and that we rubbed it before the fire, and it lived. Awake and find no baby."

It will be remembered that Victor too, when he is taken off the ice by Walton, is rubbed into life with brandy and placed before the fire (see p. 24).

A couple of final details: in January of the year in which *Frankenstein* was begun, Mary Shelley had given birth to her son William; by December of that same year, she was pregnant again. At the same time her stepsister Claire, who was part of the Shelley household, conceived and gave birth to Byron's illegitimate daughter.

4 *with horror.* This complex and terrifying dream, with its strong hint of incest, has a literary antecedent in the prophetic dream that Saint-Preux, the protagonist in Rousseau's *La Nouvelle Héloïse*, has about his beloved Julie. Saint-Preux has gone to bed, bitterly regretting the loss to him of Julie, who is now another man's wife. Just before he falls asleep, he finds himself wishing for Julie's death (pp. 364–65). "Would that she were dead! I dared cry that out in a fit of rage. . . . At least I should have the hope of rejoining her. . . . She lives, her life is my death, and her happiness is my torment."

Then, in his sleep, he dreams. "I thought I saw [Julie's] worthy mother on her death bed, her daughter on her knees before her, bathed in tears, kissing her hands and receiving her last breath. . . . I tried to raise my eyes and look at [Julie's mother]; I saw her no more. In her place I saw Julie. I saw her; I recognized her although her face was covered with a veil. I gave a shriek, I rushed forward to put aside the veil, I could not reach it, I stretched forth my arms, I tormented myself, but I touched nothing.

" 'Friend, be calm,' [Julie] said to me in a faint voice. 'The terrible veil covers me. No hand can put it aside.' "

More immediately, Victor's dream seems to hint at a fear of incest, a theme that Mary Shelley would deal with directly in her novel *Matilda*, undertaken soon after she finished *Frankenstein*. Notable too is the fact that in this (the 1818) edition of *Frankenstein* Victor

3 compose my mind to sleep. At length lassitude succeeded to the tumult I had before endured; and I threw myself on the bed in my clothes, endeavouring to seek a few moments of forgetfulness. But it was in vain: I slept indeed, but I was disturbed by the wildest dreams. I thought I saw Elizabeth, in the bloom of health, walking in the streets of Ingolstadt. Delighted and surprised, I embraced her; but as I imprinted the first kiss on her lips, they became livid with the hue of death; her features appeared to change, and I thought that I held the corpse of my dead mother in my arms; a shroud enveloped her form, and I saw the grave-worms crawling in the folds of the flannel. I started from my sleep with horror; **4** a cold dew covered my forehead, my teeth chattered, and every limb became convulsed; when, by the dim and yellow light of the moon, as it forced its way through the window-shutters, I beheld the wretch—the miserable monster whom I had created. He held up the curtain of the bed; and his eyes, if eyes they may be called. were fixed on me. His jaws opened, and he muttered some inarticulate sounds, while a grin wrinkled his cheeks. He might have spoken, but I did not hear; one hand was stretched out, seemingly to detain me, but I escaped, and rushed down stairs. I took refuge in the court-yard belonging to the house which I inhabited; where I remained during the rest of the night, walking up and down in the greatest agitation, listening attentively, catching and fearing each sound as if

"I THOUGHT THAT I HELD THE CORPSE OF MY DEAD MOTHER IN MY ARMS."

and Elizabeth are first cousins. We may guess that the too-close blood ties made Mary Shelley uncomfortable, because in the 1831 edition, Elizabeth is rewritten as an unrelated foundling whom Victor's father brings into the Frankenstein household.

Percy Shelley, too, like many Romantic writers, found the subject of incest fascinating. The lovers Laon and Cythna, in his *Revolt of Islam* (1817) were, in the first edition of that poem, brother and sister. The incest was necessary, Shelley wrote, "to startle the reader from the trance of ordinary life."

Another interesting connection may be noted. Percy Shelley was at work on *The Revolt of Islam* while Mary Shelley was writing *Frankenstein*. In Canto III, stanza 26, of *The Revolt*, Laon describes a particularly grisly dream in which he sees

A woman's shape, now lank and cold and blue,
  The dwelling of the many-coloured worm,
Hung there; the white and hollow cheek I drew
  To my dry lips . . . whose was that withered form?
Alas, alas! it seemed that Cythna's ghost
  Laughed in those looks, and that the flesh was warm
Within my teeth!

Whether Percy Shelley borrowed his imagery from his wife, or whether she took hers from him, is an open question.

5 *could not have conceived.* The loathliness of the creature is at once a most effective and perplexing detail. The problems it raises will be referred to in detail later.

6 *its white steeple and clock.* See p. 52, note 8.

THE TOWN CATHEDRAL,
WITH CLOCK TOWER.

it were to announce the approach of the demoniacal corpse to which I had so miserably given life.

Oh! no mortal could support the horror of that countenance. A mummy again endued with animation could not be so hideous as that wretch. I had gazed on him while unfinished; he was ugly then; but when those muscles and joints were rendered capable of motion, it became a thing such as **5** even Dante could not have conceived.

I passed the night wretchedly. Sometimes my pulse beat so quickly and hardly, that I felt the palpitation of every artery; at others, I nearly sank to the ground through languor and extreme weakness. Mingled with this horror, I felt the bitterness of disappointment: dreams that had been my food and pleasant rest for so long a space, were now become a hell to me; and the change was so rapid, the overthrow so complete!

Morning, dismal and wet, at length dawned, and discovered to my sleepless and aching eyes the church of Ingol- **6** stadt, its white steeple and clock, which indicated the sixth hour. The porter opened the gates of the court, which had that night been my asylum, and I issued into the streets, pacing them with quick steps, as if I sought to avoid the wretch whom I feared every turning of the street would present to my view. I did not dare return to the apartment which I inhabited, but felt impelled to hurry on, although wetted **7** by the rain, which poured from a black and comfortless sky.

I continued walking in this manner for some time, endeavouring, by bodily

7 *a black and comfortless sky.* This is only the first of many such downpours. As in much Romantic fiction, weather frequently plays a role in establishing or maintaining mood.

8 *"Doth close behind him tread."* From Coleridge's *Ancient Mariner.* Coleridge was a frequent visitor to the Godwin household. Mary Shelley and her stepsister, Claire, are reported to have had memories of hiding behind the living room sofa, listening to Coleridge recite the *Rime of the Ancient Mariner.*

9 *diligences.* Carriages used as public conveyances.

10 *Swiss diligence.* That is, it came from Switzerland.

exercise, to ease the load that weighed upon my mind. I traversed the streets, without any clear conception of where I was, or what I was doing. My heart palpitated in the sickness of fear; and I hurried on with irregular steps, not daring to look about me:

> Like one who, on a lonely road,
>   Doth walk in fear and dread,
> **And,** having once turn'd round, walks on,
>   And turns no more his head;
> Because he knows a frightful fiend
> **8**　　Doth close behind him tread.

Continuing thus, I came at length opposite to the inn at which the various **9** diligences and carriages usually stopped. Here I paused, I knew not why; but I remained some minutes with my eyes fixed on a coach that was coming towards me from the other end of the street. As it drew nearer, I observed **10** that it was the Swiss diligence: it stopped just where I was standing; and, on the door being opened, I perceived Henry Clerval, who, on seeing me, instantly sprung out. " My dear Frankenstein," exclaimed he, " how glad I am to see you! how fortunate that you should be here at the very moment of my alighting!

Nothing could equal my delight on seeing Clerval; his presence brought back to my thoughts my father, Elizabeth, and all those scenes of home so dear to my recollection. I grasped his hand, and in a moment forgot my horror and misfortune; I felt suddenly, and for the first time during many months, calm and serene joy. I welcomed my

11 *without Greek*. The reference is to a scene in Goldsmith's *The Vicar of Wakefield* (p. 129) in which the principal of the university of Louvain boasts: " 'You see me, young man, I never learned Greek, and I don't find that I have ever missed it. I have had a doctor's cap and gown without Greek; I have ten thousand florins a year without Greek; I eat heartily without Greek; and, in short,' continued he, 'as I don't know Greek, I do not believe there is any good in it.' "

12 *watching*. Keeping awake.

friend, therefore, in the most cordial manner, and we walked towards my college. Clerval continued talking for some time about our mutual friends, and his own good fortune in being permitted to come to Ingolstadt. " You may easily believe," said he, " how great was the difficulty to persuade my father that it was not absolutely necessary for a merchant not to understand any thing except book-keeping; and, indeed, I believe I left him incredulous to the last, for his constant answer to my unwearied entreaties was the same as that of the Dutch schoolmaster in the Vicar of Wakefield : ' I have ten thousand florins a year without Greek, I eat heartily without Greek.' But his affection for me at length overcame his dislike of learning, and he has permitted me to undertake a voyage of discovery to the land of knowledge."

" It gives me the greatest delight to see you ; but tell me how you left my father, brothers, and Elizabeth."

" Very well, and very happy, only a little uneasy that they hear from you so seldom. By the bye, I mean to lecture you a little upon their account mysel.—But, my dear Frankenstein," continued he, stopping short, and gazing full in my face, " I did not before remark how very ill you appear; so thin and pale; you look as if you had been watching for several nights."

" You have guessed right; I have lately been so deeply engaged in one occupation, that I have not allowed myself sufficient rest, as you see: but I hope, I sincerely hope, that all these employments are now at an end, and that I am at length free."

I trembled excessively; I could not endure to think of, and far less to allude to the occurrences of the preceding night. I walked with a quick pace, and we soon arrived at my college. I then reflected, and the thought made me shiver, that the creature whom I had left in my apartment might still be there, alive, and walking about. I dreaded to behold this monster; but I feared still more that Henry should see him. Entreating him therefore to remain a few minutes at the bottom of the stairs, I darted up towards my own room. My hand was already on the lock of the door before I recollected myself. I then paused; and a cold shivering came over me. I threw the door forcibly open, as children are accustomed to do when they expect a spectre to stand in waiting for them on the other side; but nothing appeared. I stepped fearfully in: the apartment was empty; and my bedroom was also freed from its hideous guest. I could hardly believe that so great a good-fortune could have befallen me; but when I became assured that my enemy had indeed fled, I clapped my hands for joy, and ran down to Clerval.

We ascended into my room, and the servant presently brought breakfast; but I was unable to contain myself. It was not joy only that possessed me; I felt my flesh tingle with excess of sensitiveness, and my pulse beat rapidly.

13 *in a fit*. Percy Shelley, a frequent user of laudanum, was given to such seizures. On June 18 of the famous *Frankenstein* summer of 1816, the Shelley-Byron group was gathered around Byron who was reciting Coleridge's *Christabel* from memory. Byron reached the passage in which Coleridge describes the Lady Geraldine, the serpent woman of the poem:

> Behold! her bosom and half her side,
> Hideous, deformed, and pale of hue—
> A sight to dream of, not to tell!
> And she is to sleep by Christabel!

At these words, Shelley, in the grip of a hallucination, burst from the room. He was followed by the physician, John William Polidori, who succeeded finally in quieting him. It happened that Shelley, who had been looking at Mary Shelley during Byron's reading, had been overwhelmed by an image of a woman who had eyes in her breasts instead of nipples.

PERCY BYSSHE SHELLEY
BY EDWARD ELLECKER WILLIAMS.

I was unable to remain for a single instant in the same place; I jumped over the chairs, clapped my hands, and laughed aloud. Clerval at first attributed my unusual spirits to joy on his arrival; but when he observed me more attentively, he saw a wildness in my eyes for which he could not account; and my loud, unrestrained, heartless laughter, frightened and astonished him.

" My dear Victor," cried he, " what, for God's sake, is the matter? Do not laugh in that manner. How ill you are! What is the cause of all this?

" Do not ask me," cried I, putting my hands before my eyes, for I thought I saw the dreaded spectre glide into the room; " *he* can tell.—Oh, save me! save me!" I imagined that the monster seized me; I struggled furiously, **13** and fell down in a fit.

Poor Clerval! what must have been his feelings? A meeting, which he anticipated with such joy, so strangely turned to bitterness. But I was not the witness of his grief; for I was lifeless, and did not recover my senses for a long, long time.

This was the commencement of a nervous fever, which confined me for several months. During all that time Henry was my only nurse. I afterwards learned that, knowing my father's advanced age, and unfitness for so long a journey, and how wretched my sickness would make Elizabeth, he spared them this grief by concealing the extent of my disorder. He knew that I could not have a more kind and at-

14 *raved incessantly*. This is the first of several mental lapses that will affect the narrator in the course of the story.

Erasmus Darwin's suggested treatments for madness included emetics, cathartics, warm baths, large doses of opium, and electric shock (King-Hele, *Erasmus Darwin*, p. 76).

15 *a divine spring*. The creature was given life in November, when Victor was nearly twenty-one. It is now at least five months later.

tentive nurse than himself; and, firm in the hope he felt of my recovery, he did not doubt that, instead of doing harm, he performed the kindest action that he could towards them.

But I was in reality very ill; and surely nothing but the unbounded and unremitting attentions of my friend could have restored me to life. The form of the monster on whom I had bestowed existence was for ever before **14** my eyes, and I raved incessantly concerning him. Doubtless my words surprised Henry: he at first believed them to be the wanderings of my disturbed imagination; but the pertinacity with which I continually recurred to the same subject persuaded him that my disorder indeed owed its origin to some uncommon and terrible event.

By very slow degrees, and with frequent relapses, that alarmed and grieved my friend, I recovered. I remember the first time I became capable of observing outward objects with any kind of pleasure, I perceived that the fallen leaves had disappeared, and that the young buds were shooting forth from the, trees that shaded my window. It **15** was a divine spring; and the season contributed greatly to my convalescence. I felt also sentiments of joy and affection revive in my bosom; my gloom disappeared, and in a short time I became as cheerful as before I was attacked by the fatal passion.

" Dearest Clerval," exclaimed I, " how kind, how very good you are to me. This whole winter, instead of being spent in study, as you promised yourself, has been consumed in my sick room. How shall I ever repay you? I feel the greatest remorse for the disappointment of which I have been the occasion; but you will forgive me."

" You will repay me entirely, if you do not discompose yourself, but get well as fast as you can; and since you appear in such good spirits, I may speak to you on one subject, may I not?"

I trembled. One subject! what could it be? Could he allude to an object on whom I dared not even think?

" Compose yourself," said Clerval, who observed my change of colour, " I will not mention it, if it agitates you; but your father and cousin would be very happy if they received a letter from you in your own hand-writing. They hardly know how ill you have been, and are uneasy at your long silence."

" Is that all? my dear Henry. How could you suppose that my first thought would not fly towards those dear, dear friends whom I love, and who are so deserving of my love."

" If this is your present temper, my friend, you will perhaps be glad to see a letter that has been lying here some days for you: it is from your cousin, I believe."

CHAPTER V.

CLERVAL then put the following letter into my hands.

1   " *To* V. FRANKENSTEIN.

" MY DEAR COUSIN,

" I cannot describe to you the uneasiness we have all felt concerning your health. We cannot help imagining that your friend Clerval conceals the extent of your disorder: for it is now several months since we have seen your hand-writing; and all this time you have been obliged to dictate your letters to Henry. Surely, Victor, you must have been exceedingly ill; and this makes us all very wretched, as much so nearly as after the death of your dear mother. My uncle was almost persuaded that you were indeed dangerously ill, and could hardly be restrained from undertaking a journey to Ingolstadt. Clerval always writes that you are getting better; I eagerly hope that you will confirm this intelligence soon in your own hand-writing; for indeed, indeed, Victor, we are all very miserable on this account. Relieve us from this fear, and we shall be the happiest creatures in the world. Your father's health is now so vigorous, that he appears ten years younger since last winter. Ernest also is so much improved, that you would hardly know him: he is now nearly sixteen, and has

1 *"To V. Frankenstein."* In 1831 this letter was completely rewritten. Ernest's health, for example, was so much improved that he is described, in 1831, as thinking seriously of becoming a soldier, much to Alphonse Frankenstein's distress.

2 *robust and active.* Here is a curious bit of news, that the health of Victor's father and mother improved just about the time when the creature was endowed with life. What the coincidence means is beyond this editor's speculation.

3 *a judge.* That is, that Ernest should become a lawyer so that, with his father's connections, he might be made a judge.

Mary Shelley's strictures against lawyers are partly youthful commonplaces, but they may also reflect her bitterness at the constant litigation in which Percy Shelley was involved regarding first his inheritance and then the custody of his children by his first wife, Harriet.

"DO YOU NOT REMEMBER JUSTINE MORITZ?"

2 lost that sickly appearance which he had some years ago; he is grown quite robust and active.

" My uncle and I conversed a long time last night about what profession Ernest should follow. His constant illness when young has deprived him of the habits of application; and now that he enjoys good health, he is continually in the open air, climbing the hills, or rowing on the lake. I therefore proposed that he should be a farmer; which you know, Cousin, is a favourite scheme of mine. A farmer's is a very healthy happy life; and the least hurtful, or rather the most beneficial profession of any. My uncle had an idea of his being educated as an advocate, that through his interest he might **3** become a judge. But, besides that he is not at all fitted for such an occupation, it is certainly more creditable to cultivate the earth for the sustenance of man, than to be the confidant, and sometimes the accomplice, of his vices; which is the profession of a lawyer. I said, that the employments of a prosperous farmer, if they were not a more honourable, they were at least a happier species of occupation than that of a judge, whose misfortune it was always to meddle with the dark side of human nature. My uncle smiled, and said, that I ought to be an advocate myself, which put an end to the conversation on that subject.

" And now I must tell you a little story that will please, and perhaps amuse you. Do you not remember Justine Moritz? Probably you do not; I will relate her history, therefore, in a

4 *treated her very ill.* It has been observed that while there are many fathers in *Frankenstein*, there are comparatively few mothers. One mother, Victor's, is simply good, while the other, this one, is unnatural. This simplified polarity is not surprising in the work of a writer whose own mother died giving her birth and who had, as Muriel Spark puts it in her *Child of Light* (p. 17), "an admitted dislike of Mrs. Godwin whom she secretly compared with the illustrious mother she had never known except by hearsay."

5 *My aunt.* Victor's mother.

6 *refined and moral.* Even as Mary Shelley was writing these words there lived in the Shelley household in Geneva a new Swiss maidservant, Elise Foggi. Elise was to play a complex role in the lives of Mary and Percy Shelley. Already a mother out of wedlock when she entered the Shelley's service, she became pregnant by Paolo, the Shelleys' coachman, in 1818. The Shelleys urged the two to marry and they did, though they were dismissed just the same. On December 27, 1818, a child named Elena Adelaide Shelley was born in Naples and registered as the daughter of Percy B. Shelley. There is considerable uncertainty about the identity of the child's mother. Richard Holmes, in his biography of Shelley (*Shelley, the Pursuit*, pp. 481–84), makes a summary of the various possibilities that might explain the mystery child who died on June 9, 1820.

Holmes surveys the evidence that the child might be the poet's daughter by Claire Clairmont or by the nursemaid, Elise Foggi. Both women, it seems clear, are likely candidates for that motherhood, but Holmes does not give either of them the unequivocal honor. In any case, Paolo, the dismissed coachman, made use of the scandal implicit in the events surrounding the child's birth to blackmail the poet.

7 *the beauty of Angelica.* Angelica is the heroine of Ariosto's *Orlando Furioso*. Shelley was reading Ariosto in 1815. Mary Shelley did not get to it until 1818 when, with her husband, she used Ariosto as a text for studying Italian.

few words. Madame Moritz, her mother, was a widow with four children, of whom Justine was the third. This girl had always been the favourite of her father; but, through a strange perversity, her mother could not endure her, and, after the death of M. Moritz, treated her very ill. My aunt observed this; and, when Justine was twelve years of age, prevailed on her mother to allow her to live at her house. The republican institutions of our country have produced simpler and happier manners than those which prevail in the great monarchies that surround it. Hence there is less distinction between the several classes of its inhabitants; and the lower orders being neither so poor nor so despised, their manners are more refined and moral. A servant in Geneva does not mean the same thing as a servant in France and England. Justine, thus received in our family, learned the duties of a servant; a condition which, in our fortunate country, does not include the idea of ignorance, and a sacrifice of the dignity of a human being.

" After what I have said, I dare say you well remember the heroine of my little tale: for Justine was a great favourite of your's; and I recollect you once remarked, that if you were in an ill humour, one glance from Justine could dissipate it, for the same reason that Ariosto gives concerning the beauty of Angelica—she looked so frank-hearted and happy. My aunt conceived a great attachment for her, by which she was induced to give her an education superior to that which she had at first

8 *made any professions.* That is, made no spoken demonstrations of her gratitude.

9 *was very ill.* Presumably of the same scarlet fever that had threatened Elizabeth's life and killed Victor's mother.

10 *her brothers and sister died.* These wholesale infant mortalities were not uncommon. Mary Shelley herself in the course of her seven-year relationship with Percy Shelley was pregnant five times, but only one child of their union, Percy Florence Shelley, grew to manhood.

intended. This benefit was fully repaid; Justine was the most grateful little creature in the world : I do not

8 mean that she made any professions, I never heard one pass her lips; but you could see by her eyes that she almost adored her protectress. Although her disposition was gay, and in many respects inconsiderate, yet she paid the greatest attention to every gesture of my aunt. She thought her the model of all excellence, and endeavoured to imitate her phraseology and manners, so that even now she often reminds me of her.

" When my dearest aunt died, every one was too much occupied in their own grief to notice poor Justine, who had attended her during her illness with the most anxious affection. Poor

9 Justine was very ill; but other trials were reserved for her.

10 " One by one, her brothers and sister died; and her mother, with the exception of her neglected daughter, was left childless. The conscience of the woman was troubled; she began to think that the deaths of her favourites was a judgment from heaven to chastise her partiality. She was a Roman Catholic; and I believe her confessor confirmed the idea which she had conceived. Accordingly, a few months after your departure for Ingoldstadt, Justine was called home by her repentant mother. Poor girl! she wept when she quitted our house: she was much altered since the death of my aunt; grief had given softness and a winning mildness to her manners, which had before been remarkable for vivacity. Nor was her

11 *my dear aunt*. This entire tale of poor Justine strains credulity. If Justine, as we are told, lived in the Frankenstein household from the time she was twelve, and, furthermore, tended Victor's mother during the course of her fatal illness, it seems beyond all likelihood that Victor would be so little aware of her existence as to need all this identifying detail.

12 *five years of age*. We learned earlier (p. 45) that William was an infant about the time that Victor was seventeen. Victor is nearly sixteen years older than his youngest brother. William, then, is now about seven years old.

The choice of the name Biron for Louisa need not surprise us. Claire Clairmont, who was living in the Shelley household, was carrying Lord Byron's child during many of the months in which Mary Shelley was writing *Frankenstein*.

residence at her mother's house of a nature to restore her gaiety. The poor woman was very vacillating in her repentance. She sometimes begged Justine to forgive her unkindness, but much oftener accused her of having caused the deaths of her brothers and sister. Perpetual fretting at length threw Madame Moritz into a decline, which at first increased her irritability, but she is now at peace for ever. She died on the first approach of cold weather, at the beginning of this last winter. Justine has returned to us; and I assure you I love her tenderly. She is very clever and gentle, and extremely pretty; as I mentioned before, her mien and her expressions continually remind

11 me of my dear aunt.

" I must say also a few words to you, my dear cousin, of little darling William. I wish you could see him; he is very tall of his age, with sweet laughing blue eyes, dark eye-lashes, and curling hair. When he smiles, two little dimples appear on each cheek, which are rosy with health. He has already had one or two little *wives*, but Louisa Biron is his favourite, a pretty little girl of

12 five years of age.

" Now, dear Victor, I dare say you wish to be indulged in a little gossip concerning the good people of Geneva. The pretty Miss Mansfield has already received the congratulatory visits on her approaching marriage with a young Englishman, John Melbourne, Esq. Her ugly sister, Manon, married M. Duvillard, the rich banker, last autumn. Your favourite schoolfellow, Louis Manoir, has suffered several mis-

"DEAR, DEAR ELIZABETH!"

fortunes since the departure of Clerval from Geneva. But he has already recovered his spirits, and is reported to be on the point of marrying a very lively pretty Frenchwoman, Madame Tavernier. She is a widow, and much older than Manoir; but she is very much admired, and a favourite with every body.

" I have written myself into good spirits, dear cousin; yet I cannot conclude without again anxiously inquiring concerning your health. Dear Victor, if you are not very ill, write yourself, and make your father and all of us happy; or——I cannot bear to think of the other side of the question; my tears already flow. Adieu, my dearest cousin.

"   Elizabeth Lavenza.
" Geneva, March 18th, 17—."

" Dear, dear Elizabeth !" I exclaimed when I had read her letter, " I will write instantly, and relieve them from the anxiety they must feel." I wrote, and this exertion greatly fatigued me; but my convalescence had commenced, and proceeded regularly. In another fortnight I was able to leave my chamber.

One of my first duties on my recovery was to introduce Clerval to the several professors of the university. In doing this, I underwent a kind of rough usage, ill befitting the wounds that my mind had sustained. Ever since the fatal night, the end of my labours, and the beginning of my misfortunes, I had conceived a violent antipathy even to the name of natural philosophy. When

13 *the room which had previously been my laboratory.*
Given what Victor has been up to, one wonders at
Henry's heroic lack of curiosity about what he must
have found as he was removing the apparatus from
Victor's rooms.

I was otherwise quite restored to health,
the sight of a chemical instrument
would renew all the agony of my nervous symptoms. Henry saw this, and
had removed all my apparatus from
my view. He had also changed my
apartment; for he perceived that I had
13 acquired a dislike for the room which
had previously been my laboratory.
But these cares of Clerval were made
of no avail when I visited the professors.   M. Waldman inflicted torture
when he praised, with kindness and
warmth, the astonishing progress I had
made in the sciences. He soon perceived that I disliked the subject; but,
not guessing the real cause, he attributed my feelings to modesty, and
changed the subject from my improvement to the science itself, with a desire, as I evidently saw, of drawing me
out. What could I do? He meant to.
please, and he tormented me. I felt as
if he had placed carefully, one by one, in
my view those instruments which were
to be afterwards used in putting me to
a slow and cruel death. I writhed.
under his words, yet dared not exhibit
the pain I felt. Clerval, whose eyes
and feelings were always quick in discerning the sensations of others, declined the subject, alleging, in excuse,
his total ignorance; and the conversation took a more general turn. I
thanked my friend from my heart, but
I did not speak. I saw plainly that he
was surprised, but he never attempted
to draw my secret from me; and although I loved him with a mixture of
affection and reverence that knew no
bounds, yet I could never persuade

myself to confide to him that event which was so often present to my recollection, but which I feared the detail to another would only impress more deeply.

M. Krempe was not equally docile; and in my condition at that time, of almost insupportable sensitiveness, his harsh blunt encomiums gave me even more pain than the benevolent approbation of M. Waldman. " D—n the fellow!" cried he; " why, M. Clerval, I assure you he has outstript us all. Aye, stare if you please; but it is nevertheless true. A youngster who, but a few years ago, believed Cornelius Agrippa as firmly as the gospel, has now set himself at the head of the university; and if he is not soon pulled down, we shall all be out of countenance.—Aye, aye," continued he, observing my face expressive of suffering, " M. Frankenstein is modest; an excellent quality in a young man. Young men should be diffident of themselves, you know, M. Clerval; I was myself when young: but that wears out in a very short time."

M. Krempe had now commenced an eulogy on himself, which happily turned the conversation from a subject that was so annoying to me.

Clerval was no natural philosopher. His imagination was too vivid for the minutiæ of science. Languages were his principal study; and he sought, by acquiring their elements, to open a field for self-instruction on his return to Geneva. Persian, Arabic, and Hebrew, gained his attention, after he had made himself perfectly master of Greek and Latin. For

14   *winter and snow arrived.* The creature is nearly a year old; Victor is entering his twenty-third year.

"ENVIRONS OF INGOLSTADT."

CASTLE IN INGOLSTADT.

my own part, idleness had ever been irksome to me; and now that I wished to fly from reflection, and hated my former studies, I felt great relief in being the fellow-pupil with my friend, and found not only instruction but consolation in the works of the orientalists. Their melancholy is soothing, and their joy elevating to a degree I never experienced in studying the authors of any other country. When you read their writings, life appears to consist in a warm sun and garden of roses,—in the smiles and frowns of a fair enemy, and the fire that consumes your own heart. How different from the manly and heroical poetry of Greece and Rome.

Summer passed away in these occupations, and my return to Geneva was fixed for the latter end of autumn; but being delayed by several accidents, **14** winter and snow arrived, the roads were deemed impassable, and my journey was retarded until the ensuing spring. I felt this delay very bitterly; for I longed to see my native town, and my beloved friends. My return had only been delayed so long from an unwillingness to leave Clerval in a strange place, before he had become acquainted with any of its inhabitants. The winter, however, was spent cheerfully; and although the spring was uncommonly late, when it came, its beauty compensated for its dilatoriness.

The month of May had already commenced, and I expected the letter daily which was to fix the date of my departure, when Henry proposed a pedestrian tour in the environs of Ingoldstadt that I might bid a personal farewell to the country I had so long inhabited.   I acceded with pleasure to this proposition: I was fond of exercise, and Clerval had always been my favourite companion in the rambles of this nature that I had taken among the scenes of my native country.

We passed a fortnight in these perambulations: my health and spirits had long been restored, and they gained additional strength from the salubrious air I breathed, the natural incidents of our progress, and the conversation of my friend.   Study had before secluded me from the intercourse of my fellow-creatures, and rendered me unsocial; but Clerval called forth the better feelings of my heart; he again taught me to love the aspect of nature, and the cheerful faces of children.   Excellent friend! how sincerely did you love me, and endeavour to elevate my mind, until it was on a level with your own. A selfish pursuit had cramped and narrowed me, until your gentleness and affection warmed and opened my senses; I became the same happy creature who, a few years ago, loving and beloved by all, had no sorrow or care.   When happy, inanimate nature had the power of bestowing on me the most delightful sensations.   A serene sky and verdant fields filled me with ecstacy.   The present season was indeed divine; the flowers of spring bloomed in the hedges, while those of summer were already in bud: I was undisturbed by thoughts which during the preceding year had pressed upon me, notwithstanding my endeavours to throw them off, with an invincible burden.

15 *he invented tales.* We have already seen Clerval's aptitude for such tale-telling (p. 38. See also p. 94).

Henry rejoiced in my gaiety, and sincerely sympathized in my feelings: he exerted himself to amuse me, while he expressed the sensations that filled his soul. The resources of his mind on this occasion were truly astonishing: his conversation was full of imagination; and very often, in imitation

15 of the Persian and Arabic writers, he invented tales of wonderful fancy and passion. At other times he repeated my favourite poems, or drew me out into arguments, which he supported with great ingenuity.

We returned to our college on a Sunday afternoon: the peasants were dancing, and every one we met appeared gay and happy. My own spirits were high, and I bounded along with feelings of unbridled joy and hilarity.

CHAPTER VI.

On my return, I found the following letter from my father:—

" *To* V. FRANKENSTEIN.

" MY DEAR VICTOR,

" You have probably waited impatiently for a letter to fix the date of your return to us; and I was at first tempted to write only a few lines, merely mentioning the day on which I should expect you. But that would be a cruel kindness, and I dare not do it. What would be your surprise, my son, when you expected a happy and gay welcome, to behold, on the contrary, tears and wretchedness? And how, Victor, can I relate our misfortune? Absence cannot have rendered you callous to our joys and griefs; and how shall I inflict pain on an absent child? I wish to prepare you for the woeful news, but I know it is impossible; even now your eye skims over the page, to seek the words which are to convey to you the horrible tidings.

" William is dead!—that sweet child, whose smiles delighted and warmed my heart, who was so gentle, yet so gay! Victor, he is murdered!

" I will not attempt to console you; but will simply relate the circumstances of the transaction.

" Last Thursday (May 7th) I, my

MODERN PLAINPALAIS.

1 *Plainpalais*. Mary Shelley, in her *History of a Six Weeks' Tour* (p. 101), tells us that "to the south of the town [Geneva] is the promenade of the Genevese, a grassy plain planted with a few trees, and called Plainpalais. Here a small obelisk is erected to the glory of Rousseau."

2 *five in the morning*. A Friday, May 8.

niece, and your two brothers, went to **1** walk in Plainpalais. The evening was warm and serene, and we prolonged our walk farther than usual. It was already dusk before we thought of returning; and then we discovered that William and Ernest, who had gone on before, were not to be found. We accordingly rested on a seat until they should return. Presently Ernest came, and inquired if we had seen his brother: he said, that they had been playing together, that William had run away to hide himself, and that he vainly sought for him, and afterwards waited for him a long time, but that he did not return.

" This account rather alarmed us, and we continued to search for him until night fell, when Elizabeth conjectured that he might have returned to the house. He was not there. We returned again, with torches; for I could not rest, when I thought that my sweet boy had lost himself, and was exposed to all the damps and dews of night: Elizabeth also suffered extreme anguish. **2** About five in the morning I discovered my lovely boy, whom the night before I had seen blooming and active in health, stretched on the grass livid and motionless: the print of the murderer's finger was on his neck.

" He was conveyed home, and the anguish that was visible in my countenance betrayed the secret to Elizabeth. She was very earnest to see the corpse. At first I attempted to prevent her; but she persisted, and entering the room where it lay, hastily examined the neck

3 *my beloved William.* Mary Shelley's choice of the name William for this child has already been noted. One wonders about the curious warp in her mind that allowed the mother of six-month-old William, who was crawling about her feet at the time she was writing *Frankenstein*, to bestow his name on the creature's first victim.

of the victim, and clasping her hands exclaimed, ' O God! I have murdered my darling infant!'

" She fainted, and was restored with extreme difficulty. When she again lived, it was only to weep and sigh. She told me, that that same evening Willia mhad teazed her to let him wear a very valuable miniature that she possessed of your mother. This picture is gone, and was doubtless the temptation which urged the murderer to the deed. We have no trace of him at present, although our exertions to discover him are unremitted; but they will not restore my beloved William.

3

" Come, dearest Victor; you alone can console Elizabeth. She weeps continually, and accuses herself unjustly as the cause of his death; her words pierce my heart. We are all unhappy; but will not that be an additional motive for you, my son, to return and be our comforter? Your dear mother! Alas, Victor! I now say, Thank God she did not live to witness the cruel, miserable death of her youngest darling!

"Come, Victor; not brooding thoughts of vengeance against the assassin, but with feelings of peace and gentleness, that will heal, instead of festering the wounds of our minds. Enter the house of mourning, my friend, but with kindness and affection for those who love you, and not with hatred for your enemies.

" Your affectionate and afflicted father,

ALPHONSE FRANKENSTEIN.

" Geneva, May 12th, 17—."

4 *my friends.* Used in the sense of one who belongs to the same community, as here Victor's family.

Clerval, who had watched my countenance as I read this letter, was surprised to observe the despair that succeeded to the joy I at first expressed **4** on receiving news from my friends. I threw the letter on the table, and covered my face with my hands.

" My dear Frankenstein," exclaimed Henry, when he perceived me weep with bitterness, " are you always to be unhappy? My dear friend, what has happened ?"

I motioned to him to take up the letter, while I walked up and down the room in the extremest agitation. Tears also gushed from the eyes of Clerval, as he read the account of my misfortune.

" I can offer you no consolation, my friend," said he ; " your disaster is irreparable. What do you intend to do ?"

" To go instantly to Geneva : come with me, Henry, to order the horses."

During our walk, Clerval endeavoured to raise my spirits. He did not do this by common topics of consolation, but by exhibiting the truest sympathy. " Poor William !" said he, " that dear child ; he now sleeps with his angel mother. His friends mourn and weep, but he is at rest : he does not now feel the murderer's grasp ; a sod covers his gentle form, and he knows no pain. He can no longer be a fit subject for pity ; the survivors are the greatest sufferers, and for them time is the only consolation. Those maxims of the Stoics, that death was no evil, and that the mind of man ought to be superior to despair on the eternal ab-

5 *Cato.* Marcus Porcius Cato (95–46B.C.), the Roman Stoic philosopher. Plutarch, in his *Lives,* tells the following story about Cato: "When he was but a child, he was asked, one day, whom he loved most? and he answered, his brother. The person who put the question, then asked him, whom he loved next? and again he said, his brother; whom in the third place? and still it was, his brother: and so on till he put no more questions to him about it. This affection increased with his years, insomuch that when he was twenty years old, if he supped, if he went out into the country, if he appeared in the forum, Caepio [his brother] must be with him. . . . While he was with the army in Macedonia, he had notice by letter that his brother Caepio was fallen sick at Aenus in Thrace. The sea was extremely rough, and no large vessel to be had. He ventured, however, to sail from Thessalonica in a small passage-boat, with two friends and three servants and, having very narrowly escaped drowning, arrived at Aenus just after Caepio expired. On this occasion Cato showed the sensibility of a brother, rather than the fortitude of a philosopher. He wept, he groaned, he embraced the dead body; and, besides these and other tokens of the greatest sorrow, he spent vast sums upon the funeral" (pp. 525, 527). One cannot believe that Clerval's fulsome consolation could do much to lift anyone's spirits.

6 *cabriole.* A light two-seated carriage with a folding top drawn by a single horse. The usual word is cabriolet.

7 *nearly six years.* Victor then is nearly twenty-three; the creature, nearly two years old.

5 sence of a beloved object, ought not to be urged. Even Cato wept over the dead body of his brother."

Clerval spoke thus as we hurried through the streets; the words impressed themselves on my mind, and I remembered them afterwards in solitude. But now, as soon as the horses **6** arrived, I hurried into a cabriole, and bade farewell to my friend.

My journey was very melancholy. At first I wished to hurry on, for I longed to console and sympathize with my loved and sorrowing friends; but when I drew near my native town, I slackened my progress. I could hardly sustain the multitude of feelings that crowded into my mind. I passed through scenes familiar to my youth, **7** but which I had not seen for nearly six years. How altered every thing might be during that time? One sudden and desolating change had taken place; but a thousand little circumstances might have by degrees worked other alterations which, although they were done more tranquilly, might not be the less decisive. Fear overcame me; I dared not advance, dreading a thousand name-

"FAMILIAR TO MY YOUTH."

LAUSANNE.

8　*Lausanne.* A Swiss city on the northern shore of Lake Geneva. In Mary Shelley's day the town had a population of fourteen thousand.

In 1816 Byron and Shelley, but not Mary, visited Lausanne in order to see the historian Edward Gibbon's (1737–1794) house.

9　*"the palaces of nature."* In 1816 Mary and Percy Shelley both had seen the manuscript of the third canto of Byron's *Childe Harold's Pilgrimage,* in which Byron describes Childe Harold taking his leave of the Rhineland and its beauties. In stanza sixty-two Byron writes:

But these recede. Above me are the Alps
The palaces of Nature, whose vast walls
Have pinnacled in clouds their snowy scalps,
And throned Eternity in icy halls
Of cold sublimity, where forms and falls
The avalanche—the thunderbolt of snow!
All that expands the spirit, yet appals,
Gather around these summits, as to show
　　How Earth may pierce to Heaven, yet leave
　　　vain man below.

"MY NATIVE TOWN."

10　*Mont Blanc.* See Volume II, page 134, note 18.

less evils that made me tremble, although I was unable to define them.

8　I remained two days at Lausanne, in this painful state of mind. I contemplated the lake: the waters were placid; all around was calm, and the snowy **9** mountains, " the palaces of nature," were not changed. By degrees the calm and heavenly scene restored me, and I continued my journey towards Geneva.

The road ran by the side of the lake, which became narrower as I approached my native town. I discovered more distinctly the black sides of Jura, and **10** the bright summit of Mont Blanc; I wept like a child: " Dear mountains! my own beautiful lake! how do you welcome your wanderer? Your summits are clear; the sky and lake are blue and placid. Is this to prognosticate peace, or to mock at my unhappiness?"

I fear, my friend, that I shall render myself tedious by dwelling on these preliminary circumstances; but they were days of comparative happiness, and I think of them with pleasure. My

THE SUMMIT OF MONT BLANC.

11 *thy lovely lake.* Victor's tourist enthusiasm for his home country is a reflection of Mary Shelley's own delight in the presence of the mountains.

"IT WAS COMPLETELY DARK
WHEN I ARRIVED IN THE ENVIRONS
OF GENEVA."

12 *Secheron.* The suburb where the Shelley household stayed (at the Hôtel d'Angleterre) on their arrival in Geneva on May 14, 1816. At the beginning of June they took a house at Montalègre, near Byron's Villa Diodati.

13 *lightnings playing.* Once again lightning is deployed as an omen, as it was on page 43.

In one of those letters that became part of her *History of a Six Weeks' Tour* (p. 99), Mary Shelley writes: "The thunderstorms that visit us are grander and more terrific than I have ever seen before. We watch them as they approach from the opposite side of the lake, observing the lightning play among the clouds in various parts of the heavens, and dart in jagged figures upon the piny heights of Jura, dark with the shadow of the overhanging clouds, while perhaps the sun is shining cheerily upon us. One night we enjoyed a finer storm than I had ever before beheld. The lake was lit up, the pines on Jura made visible, and all the scene illuminated for an instant, when a pitchy blackness succeeded, and the thunder came in frightful burst over our heads amid the darkness."

country, my beloved country! who but a native can tell the delight I took in again beholding thy streams, thy mountains, and, more than all, thy lovely lake.

11

Yet, as I drew nearer home, grief and fear again overcame me. Night also closed around; and when I could hardly see the dark mountains, I felt still more gloomily. The picture appeared a vast and dim scene of evil, and I foresaw obscurely that I was destined to become the most wretched of human beings. Alas! I prophesied truly, and failed only in one single circumstance, that in all the misery I imagined and dreaded, I did not conceive the hundredth part of the anguish I was destined to endure.

It was completely dark when I arrived in the environs of Geneva; the gates of the town were already shut; and I was obliged to pass the night at **12** Secheron, a village half a league to the east of the city. The sky was serene; and, as I was unable to rest, I resolved to visit the spot where my poor William had been murdered. As I could not pass through the town, I was obliged to cross the lake in a boat to arrive at Plainpalais. During this short voyage **13** I saw the lightnings playing on the summit of Mont Blanc in the most beautiful figures. The storm appeared to approach rapidly; and, on landing, I ascended a low hill, that I might observe its progress. It advanced; the heavens were clouded, and I soon felt the rain coming slowly in large drops, but its violence quickly increased.

I quitted my seat, and walked on, although the darkness and storm in-

14 *Salève.* Le Salève, a series of limestone precipices, rises on the southeast side of Geneva to more than 3,100 feet above the lake.

Mary Shelley wrote (*Letters*, p. 19): "Another Sunday recreation for the citizens is an excursion to the top of Mont Saleve. This hill is within a league of the town, and rises perpendicularly from the cultivated plain. It is ascended on the other side, and I should judge from its situation that your toil is rewarded by a delightful view of the course of the Rhone and Arve, and of the shores of the lake."

15 *the Alps of Savoy.* The *Encyclopaedia Britannica* for 1797 says of the alps of Savoy that they are "in general very barren, many of the highest are perpetually covered with ice and snow. Thunder in summer is not an unusual occurrence. In the ice-valleys of these mountains the air is extremely cold, even in July and August."

16 *Belrive.* As noted earlier, a village on the south shore of Lake Geneva.

17 *Copêt.* Modern-day Coppet, a village of six hundred inhabitants on the northern shore of Lake Geneva, best known, in the summer of 1816, for being the home of Mme. de Staël, the famous "blue stocking."

Percy Shelley, in a letter to T. J. Hogg, writes, "Mme. de Staël is here & a number of literary people whom I have not seen, & indeed have no great curiosity to see" (*Letters of Percy Bysshe Shelley*, p. 356).

18 *the filthy dæmon.* Two years and nearly fifty pages have passed since last we saw this interesting creature.

creased every minute, and the thunder burst with a terrific crash over my **14** head. It was echoed from Salêve, the **15** Juras, and the Alps of Savoy; vivid flashes of lightning dazzled my eyes, illuminating the lake, making it appear like a vast sheet of fire; then for an instant every thing seemed of a pitchy darkness, until the eye recovered itself from the preceding flash. The storm, as is often the case in Switzerland, appeared at once in various parts of the heavens. The most violent storm hung exactly north of the town, over that part of the lake which lies **16** betweeen the promontory of Belrive **17** and the village of Copêt. Another storm enlightened Jura with faint flashes; and another darkened and sometimes disclosed the Môle, a peaked mountain to the east of the lake.

While I watched the storm, so beautiful yet terrific, I wandered on with a hasty step. This noble war in the sky elevated my spirits; I clasped my hands, and exclaimed aloud, " William, dear angel! this is thy funeral, this thy dirge!" As I said these words, I perceived in the gloom a figure which stole from behind a clump of trees near me; I stood fixed, gazing intently: I could not be mistaken. A flash of lightning illuminated the object, and discovered its shape plainly to me; its gigantic stature, and the deformity of its aspect, more hideous than belongs to humanity, instantly informed **18** me that it was the wretch, the filthy dæmon to whom I had given life. What did he there? Could he be (I shuddered at the conception) the mur-

MONT SALÈVE.

"NO ONE CAN CONCEIVE
THE ANGUISH I SUFFERED."

derer of my brother? No sooner did that idea cross my imagination, than I became convinced of its truth; my teeth chattered, and I was forced to lean against a tree for support. The figure passed me quickly, and I lost it in the gloom. Nothing in human shape could have destroyed that fair child. *He* was the murderer! I could not doubt it. The mere presence of the idea was an irresistible proof of the fact. I thought of pursuing the devil; but it would have been in vain, for another flash discovered him to me hanging among the rocks of the nearly perpendicular ascent of Mont Salêve, a hill that bounds Plainpalais on the south. He soon reached the summit, and disappeared.

I remained motionless. The thunder ceased; but the rain still continued, and the scene was enveloped in an impenetrable darkness. I revolved in my mind the events which I had until now sought to forget: the whole train of my progress towards the creation; the appearance of the work of my own hands alive at my bed side; its departure. Two years had now nearly elapsed since the night on which he first received life; and was this his first crime? Alas! I had turned loose into the world a depraved wretch, whose delight was in carnage and misery; had he not murdered my brother?

No one can conceive the anguish I suffered during the remainder of the night, which I spent, cold and wet, in the open air. But I did not feel the inconvenience of the weather; my imagination was busy in scenes of evil and

19 *my own vampire*. Victor's observation that the creature is his own vampire is a direct reflection of one aspect of European vampire lore, which holds that the first victims of a newly created vampire are his closest kin.

It has been noted that one of the consequences of the evening conversations conducted by the Byron-Shelley households during bad weather that famous summer of 1816 was the later publication of John Polidori's *The Vampyre*. Byron too in his *Giaour* makes a fearsome allusion to the vampire. By 1816, when Mary Shelley was writing *Frankenstein*, *The Giaour* had been through more than fifteen editions.

The eighteenth century saw a resurgence of interest in the vampire. There were frequent "true" accounts of the appearance of vampires throughout Europe. The most famous consideration of vampirism was by Dom Calmet, the French priest, whose *Traité Sur les Apparitions des Ésprits* was published in 1751 in Paris.

What Mary Shelley could not have known is that Harriet Shelley, who at the time *Frankenstein* was being written was still Percy Shelley's wife, had written to her friend Catherine Nugent, as she was about to give birth to her second child: "Next month I shall be confined. He [Shelley] will not be near me. No, he cares not for me now. He never asks after me or sends me word how he going on. In short, the man I once loved is dead. This is a vampire. His character is blasted for ever" (Shelley's *Letters*, p. 421).

despair. I considered the being whom I had cast among mankind, and endowed with the will and power to effect purposes of horror, such as the deed which he had now done, nearly in the light of my own vampire, my own spirit let loose from the grave, and forced to destroy all that was dear to me.

Day dawned; and I directed my steps towards the town. The gates were open; and I hastened to my father's house. My first thought was to discover what I knew of the murderer, and cause instant pursuit to be made. But I paused when I reflected on the story that I had to tell. A being whom I myself had formed, and endued with life, had met me at midnight among the precipices of an inaccessible mountain. I remembered also the nervous fever with which I had been seized just at the time that I dated my creation, and which would give an air of delirium to a tale otherwise so utterly improbable. I well knew that if any other had communicated such a relation to me, I should have looked upon it as the ravings of insanity. Besides, the strange nature of the animal would elude all pursuit, even if I were so far credited as to persuade my relatives to commence it. Besides, of what use would be pursuit? Who could arrest a creature capable of scaling the overhanging sides of Mont Salêve? These reflections determined me, and I resolved to remain silent.

It was about five in the morning when I entered my father's house. I told the servants not to disturb the family, and went into the library to attend their usual hour of rising.

20 *Six years.* He is now twenty-three.

21 *three months ago.* Three months is an unlikely number. We are now in mid- or late June. The family's grief began on May 5 when William was murdered (see Vol. II, p. 206). Ernest's happy "three months ago" would, then, have been in March.

22 *his misfortunes.* Victor seems not to have heard his brother answering precisely this question on the previous page. Ernest, in turn, ignores it now.

20 Six years had elapsed, passed as a dream but for one indelible trace, and I stood in the same place where I had last embraced my father before my departure for Ingoldstadt. Beloved and respectable parent! He still remained to me. I gazed on the picture of my mother, which stood over the mantle-piece. It was an historical subject, painted at my father's desire, and represented Caroline Beaufort in an agony of despair, kneeling by the coffin of her dead father. Her garb was rustic, and her cheek pale; but there was an air of dignity and beauty, that hardly permitted the sentiment of pity. Below this picture was a miniature of William; and my tears flowed when I looked upon it. While I was thus engaged, Ernest entered: he had heard me arrive, and hastened to welcome me. He expressed a sorrowful delight to see me: " Welcome, my dearest Victor," said he." Ah! I wish you had come **21** three months ago, and then you would have found us all joyous and delighted. But we are now unhappy; and, I am afraid, tears instead of smiles will be your welcome. Our father looks so sorrowful: this dreadful event seems to have revived in his mind his grief on the death of Mamma. Poor Elizabeth also is quite inconsolable." Ernest began to weep as he said these words.

" Do not," said I, " welcome me thus; try to be more calm, that I may not be absolutely miserable the moment I enter my father's house after so long an absence. But, tell me, how does **22** my father support his misfortunes? and how is my poor Elizabeth?"

" She indeed requires consolation; she accused herself of having caused the death of my brother, and that made her very wretched. But since the murderer has been discovered———"

" The murderer discovered! Good God! how can that be? who could attempt to pursue him? It is impossible; one might as well try to overtake the winds, or confine a mountain-stream with a straw."

" I do not know what you mean; but we were all very unhappy when she was discovered. No one would believe it at first; and even now Elizabeth will not be convinced, notwithstanding all the evidence. Indeed, who would credit that Justine Moritz, who was so amiable, and fond of all the family, could all at once become so extremely wicked?"

" Justine Moritz! Poor, poor girl, is she the accused? But it is wrongfully; every one knows that; no one believes it, surely, Ernest?"

" No one did at first; but several circumstances came out, that have almost forced conviction upon us: and her own behaviour has been so confused, as to add to the evidence of facts a weight that, I fear, leaves no hope for doubt. But she will be tried to-day, and you will then hear all."

He related that, the morning on which the murder of poor William had been discovered, Justine had been taken ill, and confined to her bed; and, after several days, one of the servants, happening to examine the apparel she had worn on the night of the murder, had discovered in her pocket the picture of

23 *human being.* Victor, then, is clear in his own mind that the creature is nonhuman.

my mother, which had been judged to be the temptation of the murderer. The servant instantly shewed it to one of the others, who, without saying a word to any of the family, went to a magistrate; and, upon their deposition, Justine was apprehended. On being charged with the fact, the poor girl confirmed the suspicion in a great measure by her extreme confusion of manner.

This was a strange tale, but it did not shake my faith; and I replied earnestly, " You are all mistaken; I know the murderer. Justine, poor, good Justine, is innocent."

At that instant my father entered. I saw unhappiness deeply impressed on his countenance, but he endeavoured to welcome me cheerfully; and, after we had exchanged our mournful greeting, would have introduced some other topic than that of our disaster, had not Ernest exclaimed, " Good God, Papa! Victor says that he knows who was the murderer of poor William."

" We do also, unfortunately," replied my father; " for indeed I had rather have been for ever ignorant than have discovered so much depravity and ingratitude in one I valued so highly."

" My dear father, you are mistaken; Justine is innocent."

" If she is, God forbid that she should suffer as guilty. She is to be tried to-day, and I hope, I sincerely hope, that she will be acquitted."

This speech calmed me. I was firmly convinced in my own mind that Justine, **23** and indeed every human being, was

24 *slight and graceful*. A shy, or sly, description of Mary Shelley herself.

guiltless of this murder. I had no fear, therefore, that any circumstantial evidence could be brought forward strong enough to convict her; and, in this assurance, I calmed myself, expecting the trial with eagerness, but without prognosticating an evil result.

We were soon joined by Elizabeth. Time had made great alterations in her form since I had last beheld her. Six years before she had been a pretty, good-humoured girl, whom every one loved and caressed. She was now a woman in stature and expression of countenance, which was uncommonly lovely. An open and capacious forehead gave indications of a good understanding, joined to great frankness of disposition. Her eyes were hazel, and expressive of mildness, now through recent affliction allied to sadness. Her hair was of a rich dark auburn, her

24 complexion fair, and her figure slight and graceful. She welcomed me with the greatest affection. " Your arrival, my dear cousin," said she, " fills me with hope. You perhaps will find some means to justify my poor guiltless Justine. Alas! who is safe, if she be convicted of crime? I rely on her innocence as certainly as I do upon my own. Our misfortune is doubly hard to us; we have not only lost that lovely darling boy, but this poor girl, whom I sincerely love, is to be torn away by even a worse fate. If she is condemned, I never shall know joy more. But she will not, I am sure she will not; and then I shall be happy again, even after the sad death of my little William."

" She is innocent, my Elizabeth,"

25 *partiality*. That is, prejudice.

said I, " and that shall be proved ; fear nothing, but let your spirits be cheered by the assurance of her acquittal."

" How kind you are ! every one else believes in her guilt, and that made me wretched ; for I knew that it was impossible : and to see every one else prejudiced in so deadly a manner, rendered me hopeless and despairing."   She wept.

" Sweet niece," said my father, " dry your tears.   If she is, as you believe, innocent, rely on the justice of our judges, and the activity with which I shall prevent the slightest shadow of
25 partiality."

CHAPTER VII.

WE passed a few sad hours, until eleven o'clock, when the trial was to commence. My father and the rest of the family being obliged to attend as witnesses, I accompanied them to the court. During the whole of this wretched mockery of justice, I suffered living torture. It was to be decided, whether the result of my curiosity and lawless devices would cause the death of two of my fellow-beings: one a smiling babe, full of innocence and joy; the other far more dreadfully murdered, with every aggravation of infamy that could make the murder memorable in horror. Justine also was a girl of merit, and possessed qualities which promised to render her life happy: now all was to be obliterated in an ignominious grave; and I the cause! A thousand times rather would I have confessed myself guilty of the crime ascribed to Justine; but I was absent when it was committed, and such a declaration would have been considered as the ravings of a madman, and would not have exculpated her who suffered through me.

The appearance of Justine was calm. She was dressed in mourning; and her countenance, always engaging, was rendered, by the solemnity of her feelings, exquisitely beautiful. Yet she

1 *eleven o'clock*. A.M.

2 *a smiling babe*. William, as we have seen, was seven or eight years old at his death—hardly a babe.

3 *by thousands.* One wonders where or how thousands could have gazed at her, unless she had been trundled through the streets on a cart to her prison.

4 *eight o'clock.* A.M.

appeared confident in innocence, and did not tremble, although gazed on and **3** execrated by thousands; for all the kindness which her beauty might otherwise have excited, was obliterated in the minds of the spectators by the imagination of the enormity she was supposed to have committed. She was tranquil, yet her tranquillity was evidently constrained; and as her confusion had before been adduced as a proof of her guilt, she worked up her mind to an appearance of courage. When she entered the court, she threw her eyes round it, and quickly discovered where we were seated. A tear seemed to dim her eye when she saw us; but she quickly recovered herself, and a look of sorrowful affection seemed to attest her utter guiltlessness.

The trial began; and after the advocate against her had stated the charge, several witnesses were called. Several strange facts combined against her, which might have staggered any one who had not such proof of her innocence as I had. She had been out the whole of the night on which the murder had been committed, and towards morning had been perceived by a market-woman not far from the spot where the body of the murdered child had been afterwards found. The woman asked her what she did there; but she looked very strangely, and only returned a confused and unintelligible answer. She returned to the house about **4** eight o'clock; and when one inquired where she had passed the night, she replied, that she had been looking for the child, and demanded earnestly, if

5 *nine o'clock.* P.M.

any thing had been heard concerning him. When shewn the body, she fell into violent hysterics, and kept her bed for several days. The picture was then produced, which the servant had found in her pocket; and when Elizabeth, in a faltering voice, proved that it was the same which, an hour before the child had been missed, she had placed round his neck, a murmur of horror and indignation filled the court.

Justine was called on for her defence. As the trial had proceeded, her countenance had altered. Surprise, horror, and misery, were strongly expressed. Sometimes she struggled with her tears; but when she was desired to plead, she collected her powers, and spoke in an audible although variable voice :—

" God knows," she said, " how entirely I am innocent. But I do not pretend that my protestations should acquit me: I rest my innocence on a plain and simple explanation of the facts which have been adduced against me; and I hope the character I have always borne will incline my judges to a favourable interpretation, where any circumstance appears doubtful or suspicious."

She then related that, by the permission of Elizabeth, she had passed the evening of the night on which the murder had been committed, at the house of an aunt at Chêne, a village situated at about a league from Geneva. On
5　her return, at about nine o'clock, she met a man, who asked her if she had seen any thing of the child who was lost. She was alarmed by this account, and passed several hours in looking for

6 *to rest or sleep*. Here Justine is described as being unable to rest or sleep. See Volume II, page 208, note 18, for the contradiction that, therefore, results.

him, when the gates of Geneva were shut, and she was forced to remain several hours of the night in a barn belonging to a cottage, being unwilling to call up the inhabitants, to whom she was well known. Unable to rest or sleep, she quitted her asylum early, that she might again endeavour to find my brother. If she had gone near the spot where his body lay, it was without her knowledge. That she had been bewildered when questioned by the marketwoman, was not surprising, since she had passed a sleepless night, and the fate of poor William was yet uncertain. Concerning the picture she could give no account.

"I know," continued the unhappy victim, "how heavily and fatally this one circumstance weighs against me, but I have no power of explaining it; and when I have expressed my utter ignorance, I am only left to conjecture concerning the probabilities by which it might have been placed in my pocket. But here also I am checked. I believe that I have no enemy on earth, and none surely would have been so wicked as to destroy me wantonly. Did the murderer place it there? I know of no opportunity afforded him for so doing; or if I had, why should he have stolen the jewel, to part with it again so soon?

"I commit my cause to the justice of my judges, yet I see no room for hope. I beg permission to have a few witnesses examined concerning my character; and if their testimony shall not overweigh my supposed guilt, I must be condemned, although I would

7 *her own mother.* This is something we were not told when Elizabeth wrote to Victor about Justine earlier. In that letter (p. 87) we learned that Justine became ill after the death of Madame Frankenstein. Indeed, if Justine's judges had read Elizabeth's earlier letter, they would have learned from it that Justine's mother had accused Justine of causing the deaths of her siblings. Mercifully, Elizabeth suppresses the detail.

pledge my salvation on my innocence."

Several witnesses were called, who had known her for many years, and they spoke well of her; but fear, and hatred of the crime of which they supposed her guilty, rendered them timorous, and unwilling to come forward. Elizabeth saw even this last resource, her excellent dispositions and irreproachable conduct, about to fail the accused, when, although violently agitated, she desired permission to address the court.

" I am," said she, " the cousin of the unhappy child who was murdered, or rather his sister, for I was educated by and have lived with his parents ever since and even long before his birth. It may therefore be judged indecent in me to come forward on this occasion ; but when I see a fellow-creature about to perish through the cowardice of her pretended friends, I wish to be allowed to speak, that I may say what I know of her character. I am well acquainted with the accused. I have lived in the same house with her, at one time for five, and at another for nearly two years. During all that period she appeared to me the most amiable and benevolent of human creatures. She nursed Madame Frankenstein, my aunt, in her last illness with the greatest affection and care; and 7 afterwards attended her own mother during a tedious illness, in a manner that excited the admiration of all who knew her. After which she again lived in my uncle's house, where she was beloved by all the family. She was warmly attached to the child who is now dead, and acted towards him like a most affectionate mother. For my own part, I do not hesitate to say, that, notwithstanding all the evidence produced against her, I believe and rely on her perfect innocence. She had no temptation for such an action: as to the bauble on which the chief proof rests, if she had earnestly desired it, I should have willingly given it to her; so much do I esteem and value her."

Excellent Elizabeth! A murmur of approbation was heard; but it was excited by her generous interference, and not in favour of poor Justine, on whom the public indignation was turned with renewed violence, charging her with the blackest ingratitude. She herself wept as Elizabeth spoke, but she did not answer. My own agitation and anguish was extreme during the whole trial. I believed in her innocence; I knew it. Could the dæmon, who had (I did not for a minute doubt) murdered my brother, also in his hellish sport have betrayed the innocent to death and ignominy. I could not sustain the horror of my situation; and when I perceived that the popular voice, and the countenances of the judges, had already condemned my unhappy victim, I rushed out of the court in agony. The tortures of the accused did not equal mine; she was sustained by innocence, but the fangs of remorse tore my bosom, and would not forego their hold.

I passed a night of unmingled wretchedness. In the morning I went to the court; my lips and throat were parched. I dared not ask the fatal question; but I was known, and the officer guessed

8 *The ballots had been thrown.* The word "ballot" has its origin in the Italian diminutive for a ball, "*ballotta*." The *Oxford English Dictionary* describes "the method or system of secret voting, originally by means of small balls placed in an urn or box." Usually, the balls were made of wood or ivory, and, of course, the black ones meant a negative verdict.

8 the cause of my visit. The ballots had been thrown; they were all black, and Justine was condemned.

I cannot pretend to describe what I then felt. I had before experienced sensations of horror; and I have endeavoured to bestow upon them adequate expressions, but words cannot convey an idea of the heart-sickening despair that I then endured. The person to whom I addressed myself added, that Justine had already confessed her guilt. " That evidence," he observed, " was hardly required in so glaring a case, but I am glad of it; and, indeed, none of our judges like to condemn a criminal upon circumstantial evidence, be it ever so decisive."

When I returned home, Elizabeth eagerly demanded the result.

" My cousin," replied I, " it is decided as you may have expected; all judges had rather that ten innocent should suffer, than that one guilty should escape. But she has confessed."

This was a dire blow to poor Elizabeth, who had relied with firmness upon Justine's innocence. " Alas!" said she, " how shall I ever again believe in human benevolence? Justine, whom I loved and esteemed as my sister, how could she put on those smiles of innocence only to betray; her mild eyes seemed incapable of any severity or ill-humour, and yet she has committed a murder."

Soon after we heard that the poor victim had expressed a wish to see my cousin. My father wished her not to go; but said, that he left it to her own judgment and feelings to decide.

9 *confessed a lie.* Justine here blames her confessor. This easy anti-Catholicism may reflect the degree to which Mary Shelley shared both her father's and her husband's antireligious bias. What is more likely is that she simply reached for a cliché of British (and Protestant) Gothic fiction in which dark and villainous monks and nuns abound.

One wonders how Justine, a devout and well-instructed Catholic, could fail to know that an absolution gained by a false confession was more likely to ensure her perdition than it would prevent it.

" Yes," said Elizabeth, " I will go, although she is guilty ; and you, Victor, shall accompany me : I cannot go alone." The idea of this visit was torture to me, yet I could not refuse.

We entered the gloomy prison-chamber, and beheld Justine sitting on some straw at the further end ; her hands were manacled, and her head rested on her knees. She rose on seeing us enter ; and when we were left alone with her, she threw herself at the feet of Elizabeth, weeping bitterly. My cousin wept also.

" Oh, Justine !" said she, " why did you rob me of my last consolation. I relied on your innocence ; and although I was then very wretched, I was not so miserable as I am now."

" And do you also believe that I am so very, very wicked ? Do you also join with my enemies to crush me ?" Her voice was suffocated with sobs.

" Rise, my poor girl," said Elizabeth, " why do you kneel, if you are innocent ? I am not one of your enemies ; I believed you guiltless, notwithstanding every evidence, until I heard that you had yourself declared your guilt. That report, you say, is false ; and be assured, dear Justine, that nothing can shake my confidence in you for a moment, but your own confession."

9 " I did confess ; but I confessed a lie. I confessed, that I might obtain absolution ; but now that falsehood lies heavier at my heart than all my other sins. The God of heaven forgive me ! Ever since I was condemned, my confessor has besieged me ; he threatened and menaced, until I almost began to think that I was the monster that he said I was. He threatened excommunication and hell fire in my last moments, if I continued obdurate. Dear lady, I had none to support me; all looked on me as a wretch doomed to ignominy and perdition. What could I do? In an evil hour I subscribed to a lie; and now only am I truly miserable."

She paused, weeping, and then continued—" I thought with horror, my sweet lady, that you should believe your Justine, whom your blessed aunt had so highly honoured, and whom you loved, was a creature capable of a crime which none but the devil himself could have perpetrated. Dear William! dearest blessed child! I soon shall see you again in heaven, where we shall all be happy; and that consoles me, going as I am to suffer ignominy and death."

" Oh, Justine! forgive me for having for one moment distrusted you. Why did you confess? But do not mourn, my dear girl; I will every where proclaim your innocence, and force belief. Yet you must die; you, my playfellow, my companion, my more than sister. I never can survive so horrible a misfortune."

" Dear, sweet Elizabeth, do not weep. You ought to raise me with thoughts of a better life, and elevate me from the petty cares of this world of injustice and strife. Do not you, excellent friend, drive me to despair."

" I will try to comfort you; but this, I fear, is an evil too deep and poignant

VOLUME I/CHAPTER VII 119

10 *not consolation*. Certainly not. Elizabeth as a comforter must rank with those who consoled poor Job. Evidently Mary Shelley also disliked Elizabeth's speech because in the 1831 edition of *Frankenstein* she cut it severely.

to admit of consolation, for there is no hope. Yet heaven bless thee, my dearest Justine, with resignation, and a confidence elevated beyond this world. Oh! how I hate its shews and mockeries! when one creature is murdered, another is immediately deprived of life in a slow torturing manner; then the executioners, their hands yet reeking with the blood of innocence, believe that they have done a great deed. They call this *retribution*. Hateful name! When that word is pronounced, I know greater and more horrid punishments are going to be inflicted than the gloomiest tyrant has ever invented to satiate **10** his utmost revenge. Yet this is not consolation for you, my Justine, unless indeed that you may glory in escaping from so miserable a den. Alas! I would I were in peace with my aunt and my lovely William, escaped from a world which is hateful to me, and the visages of men which I abhor."

Justine smiled languidly. " This, dear lady, is despair, and not resignation. I must not learn the lesson that you would teach me. Talk of something else, something that will bring peace, and not increase of misery."

During this conversation I had retired to a corner of the prison-room, where I could conceal the horrid anguish that possessed me. Despair! Who dared talk of that? The poor victim, who on the morrow was to pass the dreary boundary between life and death, felt not as I did, such deep and bitter agony. I gnashed my teeth, and ground them together, uttering a groan that came from my inmost soul. Jus-

11 *never-dying worm.* The phrase "never-dying worm," referring to remorse, goes far back in English literature. The *Oxford English Dictionary* cites Hampole's *Psalter* (1340), i, I "the sow through assent gets the worm that never shall die." There are other entries, but the most likely immediate source of the phrase was either Milton's *Paradise Lost* (Book VI, lines 731–36)

[I] shall soon,
Armed with thy might, rid Heaven of these rebelled,
To their prepared ill mansion driven down,
To chains of darkness and th' undying worm,
That from thy just obedience could revolt,
Whom to obey is happiness entire

or the lines from Byron's "Bride of Abydos," (1813), II. xxvii:

And, oh! that pang where more than madness lies!
The worm that will not sleep—and never dies.

tine started. When she saw who it was, she approached me, and said, " Dear Sir, you are very kind to visit me; you, I hope, do not believe that I am guilty."

I could not answer. " No, Justine," said Elizabeth ; " he is more convinced of your innocence than I was ; for even when he heard that you had confessed, he did not credit it."

" I truly thank him. In these last moments I feel the sincerest gratitude towards those who think of me with kindness. How sweet is the affection of others to such a wretch as I am ! It removes more than half my misfortune; and I feel as if I could die in peace, now that my innocence is acknowledged by you, dear lady, and your cousin."

Thus the poor sufferer tried to comfort others and herself. She indeed gained the resignation she desired. **11** But I, the true murderer, felt the never-dying worm alive in my bosom, which allowed of no hope or consolation. Elizabeth also wept, and was unhappy; but her's also was the misery of innocence, which, like a cloud that passes over the fair moon, for a while hides, but cannot tarnish its brightness. Anguish and despair had penetrated into the core of my heart; I bore a hell within me, which nothing could extinguish. We staid several hours with Justine; and it was with great difficulty that Elizabeth could tear herself away. " I wish," cried she, " that I were to die with you ; I cannot live in this world of misery."

Justine assumed an air of cheerfulness, while she with difficulty repressed her bitter tears. She embraced Elizabeth, and said, in a voice of half-suppressed emotion, " Farewell, sweet lady, dearest Elizabeth, my beloved and only friend ; may heaven in its bounty bless and preserve you ; may this be the last misfortune that you will ever suffer. Live, and be happy, and make others so."

As we returned, Elizabeth said, " You know not, my dear Victor, how much I am relieved, now that I trust in the innocence of this unfortunate girl.   I never could again have known peace, if I had been deceived in my reliance on her.   For the moment that I did believe her guilty, I felt an anguish that I could not have long sustained. Now my heart is lightened.   The innocent suffers ; but she whom I thought amiable and good has not betrayed the trust I reposed in her, and I am consoled.

Amiable cousin ! such were your thoughts, mild and gentle as your own dear eyes and voice.   But I—I was a wretch, and none ever conceived of the misery that I then endured.

END OF VOL. I.

FRANKENSTEIN;

OR,

THE MODERN PROMETHEUS.

IN THREE VOLUMES.

Did I request thee, Maker, from my clay
To mould me man ? Did I solicit thee
From darkness to promote me ?——
PARADISE LOST.

VOL. II.

London :

PRINTED FOR
LACKINGTON, HUGHES, HARDING, MAVOR, & JONES,
FINSBURY SQUARE.

1818.

Chap. 13th

Nothing is more painful than when the mind has been worked up by a quick & succession of events, for a dead calm and of inaction and certainty to follows which deprives the soul both of hope or fear. Justine died — she rested. And I was alive. the blood flowed freely in my veins but a weight of despair & remorse pressed on my heart which nothing could remove. our house was a house of mourning. My fathers health was deeply shaken by the horror of the recent events; Eliza beth was sad and desponding. she no longer took delight in her ordinary occupa tions all pleasure seemed to her sacri ledge towards the dead — eternal woe and tears she then thought was the just tribute she ought to pay to inno cence thus blasted & destroyed. Sleep fled from my eyes. I wandered like an evil spirit for I had committed deeds of mischief beyond description horrible, and more much more I persuaded my self) was yet in store yet my heart overflowed with kind ness and goodness — I had begun life

FIRST PAGE OF FRANKENSTEIN, VOL. II, IN MARY SHELLEY'S OWN HAND.

FRANKENSTEIN;

OR, THE

MODERN PROMETHEUS.

—◆—

CHAPTER I.

NOTHING is more painful to the human mind, than, after the feelings have been worked up by a quick succession of events, the dead calmness of inaction and certainty which follows, and deprives the soul both of hope and fear. Justine died; she rested; and I was alive. The blood flowed freely in my veins, but a weight of despair and remorse pressed on my heart, which nothing could remove. Sleep fled from my eyes; I wandered like an evil spirit, for I had committed deeds of mischief beyond description horrible, and more, much more, (I persuaded myself) was yet behind. Yet my heart overflowed with kindness, and the love of virtue. I had begun life with benevolent intentions, and thirsted for the moment when I should put them in practice, and make myself useful to my fellow-beings. Now all was blasted: instead of that serenity of conscience, which allowed me to look back upon the past with self-satisfaction, and from thence to gather promise of new hopes, I was

---

1 *Justine died.* The short life and undeserved death of this young woman whose name is Justine has caused Mario Praz to observe (in *The Romantic Agony*, p. 114) that "the innocent woman, imprisoned, tried and executed, is called—by an odd coincidence—Justine, like de Sade's unhappy virtuous heroine." De Sade's heroine moves through the pages of *Justine* (1797) retaining her sexual innocence though she has been ravaged by any number of men in any number of ways. At the end of de Sade's tale, God strikes the long-suffering Justine with lightning just as she has finished telling her story to the pampered courtesan her less determinedly virtuous sister has become.

Though I cannot find evidence that Mary Shelley had read de Sade—it would not be surprising if she had suppressed the fact—there is a persistent undercurrent of dark sexuality in *Frankenstein* that makes Praz's remark seem like something more than a chance hit.

We know for certain that Byron, at least, had a secret copy of *Justine* in his possession in April 1816, only a few months before he met the Shelleys in Geneva. (See Marchand, *Byron: a Biography*, v.II, p. 559, note 1.)

2 *behind.* This is a puzzling locution. Its intent seems to be to say "much more was yet to come." Perhaps our author intended a metaphor, as in "More, much more . . . was yet behind the veil of the future."

3 *with benevolent intentions.* This language will be echoed later in a surprising context. See pages 140 and 142.

4 *first shock.* That is, of the animation of the creature.

5 *The shutting of the gates.* The locked gates of the city are not imagined by Mary Shelley. In one of the letters included in her *History of a Six Weeks' Tour* she writes (p. 101), "The town [Geneva] is surrounded by a wall, the three gates of which are shut exactly at ten o'clock, when no bribery (as in France) can open them."

In Murray's *Handbook for Travellers' in Switzerland* (1838), we read that "the gates of Geneva are shut at ten in the evening, and a small toll is exacted up to midnight, after which it is doubled. In former times they finally closed before midnight, and it will be remembered that it was the accident of being shut out one evening, on his return from a walk in the country, that induced Rosseau to fly from his native town and tyrannical master, whom he, as a truant apprentice, feared to face."

seized by remorse and the sense of guilt, which hurried me away to a hell of intense tortures, such as no language can describe.

This state of mind preyed upon my health, which had entirely recovered from the first shock it had sustained. **4** I shunned the face of man; all sound of joy or complacency was torture to me; solitude was my only consolation— deep, dark, death-like solitude.

My father observed with pain the alteration perceptible in my disposition and habits, and endeavoured to reason with me on the folly of giving way to immoderate grief. " Do you think, Victor," said he, " that I do not suffer also? No one could love a child more than I loved your brother;" (tears came into his eyes as he spoke); " but is it not a duty to the survivors, that we should refrain from augmenting their unhappiness by an appearance of immoderate grief? It is also a duty owed to yourself; for excessive sorrow prevents improvement or enjoyment, or even the discharge of daily usefulness, without which no man is fit for society."

This advice, although good, was totally inapplicable to my case; I should have been the first to hide my grief, and console my friends, if remorse had not mingled its bitterness with my other sensations. Now I could only answer my father with a look of despair, and endeavour to hide myself from his view.

About this time we retired to our house at Belrive. This change was particularly agreeable to me. **5** The shutting of the gates regularly at ten o'clock, and the impossibility of remaining on the lake

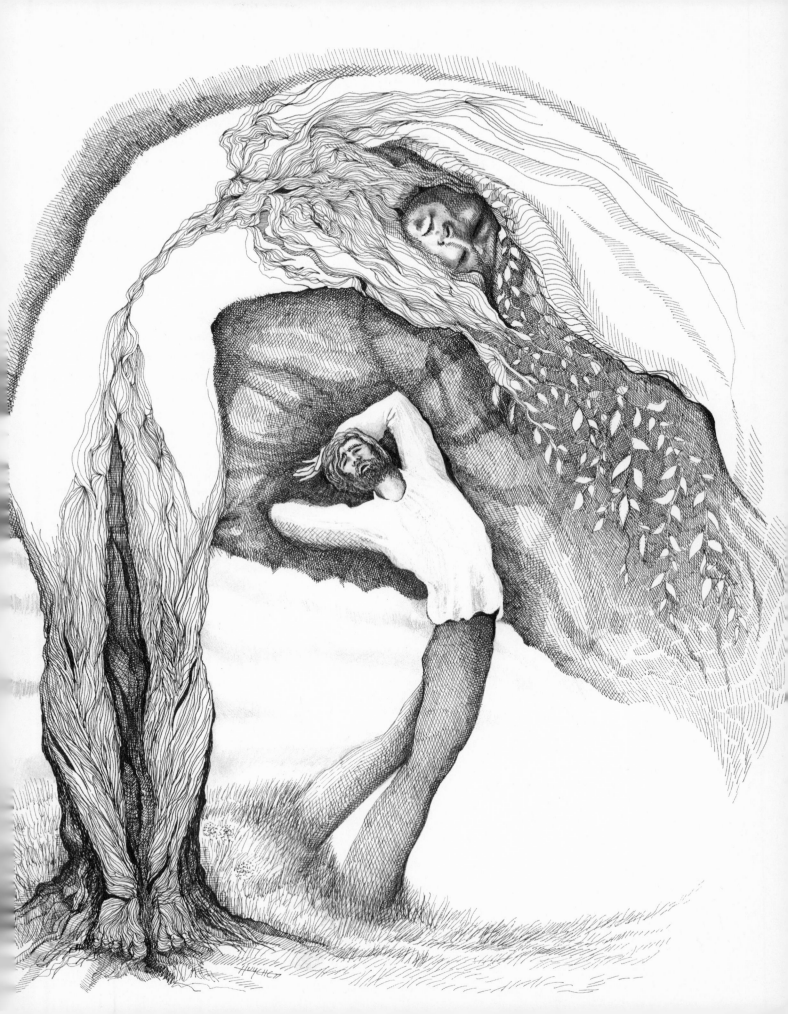

6 *many hours upon the water*. Percy Shelley's love of boating has already been mentioned. In an 1816 letter included in Mary Shelley's *History of a Six Weeks' Tour* (p. 95), she writes: "You know our attachment to water excursions. We have hired a boat, and every evening, at about six o'clock, we sail on the lake, which is delightful, whether we glide over a glassy surface or are speeded along by a strong wind. The waves of this lake never afflict me with that sickness that deprives me of all enjoyment in a sea-voyage; on the contrary, the tossing of our boat raises my spirits and inspires me with unusual hilarity." Victor's mood is, of course, anything but hilarious.

7 *for ever*. This is the first of several suggestions of suicide that will occur in the pages to come. Percy Shelley, who thought frequently of suicide, went so far as to ask his friend Trelawny to get a lethal dose of arsenic for him.

As Mary Shelley was writing, she may well have recalled an episode in 1813, during her own illicit and tempestuous courtship, when Shelley, believing that Godwin was contriving to separate the young lovers, burst into the Godwin household. Mary Jane Godwin describes the scene: "He looked extremely wild. He pushed me aside with extreme violence, and entering, walked straight to Mary. 'They wish to separate us, my beloved; but Death shall unite us,' and offered her a bottle of laudanum. 'By this you can escape from tyranny; and this,' taking a small pistol from his pocket, 'shall reunite me to you.' Poor Mary turned as pale as a ghost, and my poor silly [Jane-Claire], who is so timid even at trifles, at the sight of the pistol filled the room with her shrieks . . . With tears streaming down her cheeks, [Mary] entreated him to calm himself" (Dowden's *Life of Shelley*, II Appendix A, p. 544).

It should be added that suicide was a popular Romantic temptation, especially after the publication of Goethe's *Sorrows of Young Werther* (1774), in which Werther moves toward suicide in the most lingering slow motion. In Rousseau's *La Nouvelle Héloïse*, Saint-Preux urges suicide in the following terms: "Oh let us die, my sweet friend. Let us die, beloved of my heart! What shall we do henceforward with an insipid youth now that we have exhausted all of its delights."

Suicides in literature are one thing. On October 10, 1816, Fanny Imlay, Mary Shelley's half sister, who had led a depressed and depressing life in the Godwin ménage, killed herself in a Swansea inn by taking an overdose of laudanum. On December 10 of the same year, Harriet Shelley, who was still legally Percy Shelley's wife, and whom he had abandoned to join Mary, was found floating in the Serpentine, a suicide. She was, according to a newspaper account, "well advanced" in pregnancy by someone other than Shelley. Mary Shelley's mother too, as has been noted in the introduction, was no stranger to suicidal impulses. In her first suicide attempt. Mary Wollstonecraft used laudanum.

after that hour, had rendered our residence within the walls of Geneva very irksome to me. I was now free. Often, after the rest of the family had retired for the night, I took the boat, **6** and passed many hours upon the water. Sometimes, with my sails set, I was carried by the wind ; and sometimes, after rowing into the middle of the lake, I left the boat to pursue its own course, and gave way to my own miserable reflections. I was often tempted, when all was at peace around me, and I the only unquiet thing that wandered restless in a scene so beautiful and heavenly, if I except some bat, or the frogs, whose harsh and interrupted croaking was heard only when I approached the shore—often, I say, I was tempted to plunge into the silent lake, that the waters might close over me and my calamities for ever. **7** But I was restrained, when I thought of the heroic and suffering Elizabeth, whom I tenderly loved, and whose existence was bound up in mine. I thought also of my father, and surviving brother : should I by my base desertion leave them exposed and unprotected to the malice of the fiend whom I had let loose among them?

At these moments I wept bitterly, and wished that peace would revisit my mind only that I might afford them consolation and happiness. But that could not be. Remorse extinguished every hope. I had been the author of unalterable evils ; and I lived in daily fear, lest the monster whom I had created should perpetrate some new wickedness. I had an obscure feeling that all was not over, and that he would still commit some signal crime, which by its enormity should almost efface the recollection of the past. There was always scope for fear, so long as any thing I loved remained behind. My abhorrence of this fiend cannot be conceived. When I thought of him, I gnashed my teeth, my eyes became inflamed, and I ardently wished to extinguish that life which I had so thoughtlessly bestowed. When I reflected on his crimes and malice, my hatred and revenge burst all bounds of moderation. I would have made a pilgrimage to the highest peak of the Andes, could I, when there, have precipitated him to their base. I wished to see him again, that I might wreak the utmost extent of anger on his head, and avenge the deaths of William and Justine.

Our house was the house of mourning. My father's health was deeply shaken by the horror of the recent events. Elizabeth was sad and desponding; she no longer took delight in her ordinary occupations; all pleasure seemed to her sacrilege toward the dead; eternal woe and tears she then thought was the just tribute she should pay to innocence so blasted and destroyed. She was no longer that happy creature, who in earlier youth wandered with me on the banks of the lake, and talked with ecstacy of our future prospects. She had become grave, and often conversed of the inconstancy of fortune, and the instability of human life.

" When I reflect, my dear cousin," said she, " on the miserable death of Justine Moritz, I no longer see the world and its works as they before appeared

8 *for each other's blood.* Elizabeth, as lugubrious as she is tearful, is repeating the simplistic view of mankind with which she comforted Justine earlier (see Vol. I, p. 119, note 10).

9 *the death of any human being.* Percy and Mary Shelley were both opposed to capital punishment.

to me. Before, I looked upon the accounts of vice and injustice, that I read in books or heard from others, as tales of ancient days, or imaginary evils; at least they were remote, and more familiar to reason than to the imagination; but now misery has come home, and men appear to me as monsters thirst- **8** ing for each other's blood. Yet I am certainly unjust. Every body believed that poor girl to be guilty; and if she could have committed the crime for which she suffered, assuredly she would have been the most depraved of human creatures. For the sake of a few jewels, to have murdered the son of her bene-factor and friend, a child whom she had nursed from its birth, and appeared to love as if it had been her own! I **9** could not consent to the death of any human being; but certainly I should have thought such a creature unfit to remain in the society of men. Yet she was innocent. I know, I feel she was innocent; you are of the same opinion, and that confirms me. Alas! Victor, when falsehood can look so like the truth, who can assure themselves of certain happiness? I feel as if I were walking on the edge of a precipice, to-wards which thousands are crowding, and endeavouring to plunge me into the abyss. William and Justine were assassinated, and the murderer escapes; he walks about the world free, and per-haps respected. But even if I were condemned to suffer on the scaffold for the same crimes, I would not change places with such a wretch."

I listened to this discourse with the extremest agony. I, not in deed, but

10 *he now proposed.* This trip, described in the pages that follow as a family excursion, is, in the 1831 edition of *Frankenstein*, taken by Victor alone.

11 *the valley of Chamounix.* The choice of the vale of Chamounix as the setting for the scenes that are to come is one of Mary Shelley's happier literary decisions. The Shelleys visited Chamounix in the course of the *Frankenstein* summer (1816). They departed from Montalègre on July 21, and for both of them the magnificence of the natural scenery proved overwhelming. Mary Shelley's *Journal* would later serve for many of the images she made use of in her fiction. One might, in fact, read the following pages as alternate versions of her first impression recorded in the *Journal*. Her *Journal* (p. 52) describes their arrival into the vale of Chamounix: "The mountains assumed a more formidable appearance, and the glaciers approach nearer to the road. . . . As we went along we heard a sound like the rolling of distant thunder, and we beheld an avalanche rush down a ravine of the rocks; it stopped midway, but, in its course, forced a torrent from its bed, which now fell to the base of the mountain." Interestingly enough, this family excursion was undertaken without the child William, who was left in the care of Elise Foggi, the Swiss maidservant (see Vol. I, p. 86, note 6).

in effect, was the true murderer. Elizabeth read my anguish in my countenance, and kindly taking my hand said, " My dearest cousin, you must calm yourself. These events have affected me, God knows how deeply; but I am not so wretched as you are. There is an expression of despair, and sometimes of revenge, in your countenance, that makes me tremble. Be calm, my dear Victor; I would sacrifice my life to your peace. We surely shall be happy: quiet in our native country, and not mingling in the world, what can disturb our tranquillity?"

She shed tears as she said this, distrusting the very solace that she gave; but at the same time she smiled, that she might chase away the fiend that lurked in my heart. My father, who saw in the unhappiness that was painted in my face only an exaggeration of that sorrow which I might naturally feel, thought that an amusement suited to my taste would be the best means of restoring to me my wonted serenity. It was from this cause that he had removed to the country; and, induced by **10** the same motive, he now proposed that we should all make an excursion to **11** the valley of Chamounix. I had been there before, but Elizabeth and Ernest never had; and both had often expressed an earnest desire to see the scenery of this place, which had been described to them as so wonderful and sublime. Accordingly we departed from Geneva on this tour about the middle of the month of August, nearly two months after the death of Justine.

The weather was uncommonly fine;

12 *in a carriage.* This description of the excursion to Chamounix very closely parallels the Shelleys' own 1816 visit. They too traveled by carriage the first day, following the river Arve. In her *Journal* (p. 51), Mary Shelley says: "The scene assumes here also a more savage and colossal character; the valley becomes narrow, affording no more space than is sufficient for the river and the road. The pines descend to the banks, imitating with their regular spires the pyramidal crags which lift themselves far above the regions of the forest."

13 *the river Arve.* The Arve is a cold and muddy stream fed by glaciers. Percy Shelley, in one of his *Letters* (pp. 494, 496), writes of the valley of the Arve: "The Valley of the Arve (strictly speaking it extends to that of Chamouni) [sic] gradually increases in magnificence and beauty, until, at a place called Servoz [sic], where Mount Blanc and its connected mounts limit one side of the valley, it exceeds and renders insignificant all that I had before seen, or imagined.

"For an hour, we proceed along the valley of the Arve—a valley surrounded on all sides by immense mountains whose jagged precipices were intermixed on high with dazzling snow: Their base was still covered with the eternal forest which perpetually grew darker & profounder as it approached the regions of snow."

14 *waterfalls.* On the first day of her visit to Chamounix, Mary Shelley reports in her *Journal* (p. 51) that she saw two waterfalls: "They were no more than mountain rivulets, but the height from which they fell, at least 200 feet, made them assume a character inconsistent with the smallness of the stream. The first fell in two parts, and struck first on an enormous rock resembling precisely some colossal Egyptian statue of a female deity; it struck the head of the visionary image, and, gracefully dividing, then fell in folds of foam, more like cloud than water, imitating a veil of the most exquisite woof; it united then, concealing the lower part of the statue, and hiding itself in a winding of its channel, burst into a deeper fall, and crossed our route in its path towards the Arve. The other waterfall was more continuous, and larger; the violence with which it fell made it look rather like some shape which an exhalation had assumed than like water, for it fell beyond the mountain, which appeared dark behind it, as it might have appeared behind an evanescent cloud."

Percy Shelley, in his *Letters* (p. 496), also notes waterfalls. He says that "the character of the scenery continues the same, the mountains perpetually becoming more elevated, & exhibiting at every turn of the road more craggy summits, loftier waterfalls, wider extent of forests, darker & more deep recesses."

and if mine had been a sorrow to be chased away by any fleeting circumstance, this excursion would certainly have had the effect intended by my father. As it was, I was somewhat interested in the scene; it sometimes lulled, although it could not extinguish my grief. During the first day we travelled in a carriage. In the morning we had seen the mountains at a distance, towards which we gradually advanced. We perceived that the valley through which we wound, and which was formed by the river Arve, whose course we followed, closed in upon us by degrees; and when the sun had set, we beheld immense mountains and precipices overhanging us on every side, and heard the sound of the river raging among rocks, and the dashing of waterfalls around.

MONT BLANC: A TWENTIETH-CENTURY APPROACH TO "AWFUL MAJESTY."

15 *another race of beings.* This description of the Alps as a world proper to a superhuman race adds dimension to the symbolic meaning of the creature. See Volume I, page 67, for a previous mention of another race of beings. There we learn that Victor dreamed of creating a new species of humanity. Here, confronting the mountains, he thinks of them as the appropriate habitat of beings who are primordial and powerful. Later (Vol. III, p. 246), Victor's fear that his creature may beget a "race of devils" prompts him to the act that produces the catastrophe of *Frankenstein*. The decline from the "new species" of Volume I to the "race of devils" in Volume III is, of course, in Victor's own mind, and it tells us a good deal about what being a father meant to him. One begins with hopes for a new species; one toils in the "workshop of filthy creation"; and one ends with a "race of devils." Altogether, as Mary Shelley has Victor see it, fatherhood is a loathsome and thankless task.

16 *the bridge of Pelissier.* Percy Shelley, writing to T. L. Peacock (*Letters of Percy Bysshe Shelley*, p. 501), says that "we repassed Pont Pelissier a wooden bridge over the Arve & the ravine of the Arve. We repassed the pine forests which overhang the defile, the Chateau of St. Michel a haunted ruin built on the edge of a precipice & shadowed over the Eternal forest."

17 *Servox.* In Mary Shelley's *Journal* (p. 54), we are told that "the hills of the Vale of Servoz [sic] are covered with pines, intermixed by cultivated lawns. On one mountain that stands in the middle there are the ruins of a castle."

Percy Shelley, in a letter to Peacock, writes: "We repassed the vale of Servoz [sic], a vale more beautiful because more luxuriant than that of Chamouni [sic]" (*Letters of Percy Bysshe Shelley*, p. 501).

The next day we pursued our journey upon mules; and as we ascended still higher, the valley assumed a more magnificent and astonishing character. Ruined castles hanging on the precipices of piny mountains; the impetuous Arve, and cottages every here and there peeping forth from among the trees, formed a scene of singular beauty. But it was augmented and rendered sublime by the mighty Alps, whose white and shining pyramids and domes towered above all, as belonging to another earth, the habitations of another race of beings.

We passed the bridge of Pelissier, where the ravine, which the river forms, opened before us, and we began to ascend the mountain that overhangs it. Soon after we entered the valley of Chamounix. This valley is more wonderful and sublime, but not so beautiful and picturesque as that of Servox, through which we had just passed. The high and snowy mountains were its immediate boundaries; but we saw no more ruined castles and fertile fields. Immense glaciers approached the road; we heard the rumbling thunder of the falling avelânche, and marked the

"THE VALLEY OF CHAMOUNIX."

A MODERN VIEW OF MONT BLANC.

18 *Mont Blanc.* Mont-Blanc is the highest mountain in the Alps; it was first scaled by a Chamounix physician, Dr. Paccard, in 1786.

Mont-Blanc was a source of excitement to the Romantic poets, many of whom were, or felt the need to feel, exalted in its presence. Percy Shelley observed that the "immensity of these aerial summits excited, when they suddenly burst upon the sight, a sentiment of extatic [sic] wonder, not unallied to madness" (*Letters of Percy Bysshe Shelley*, p. 497).

"MONT BLANC OVERLOOKED THE VALLEY."

19   aiguilles. The French word for "needles." It is also used to describe sharply pointed mountain peaks.

18 smoke of its passage. Mont Blanc, the supreme and magnificent Mont Blanc, raised itself from the surround-**19**ing *aiguilles*, and its tremendous *dome* overlooked the valley.

During this journey, I sometimes joined Elizabeth, and exerted myself to point out to her the various beauties of the scene. I often suffered my mule to lag behind, and indulged in the misery of reflection. At other times I spurred on the animal before my companions, that I might forget them, the world, and, more than all, myself. When at a distance, I alighted, and threw myself on the grass, weighed down by horror and despair. At eight in the evening I arrived at Chamounix. My father and Elizabeth were very much fatigued; Ernest, who accompanied us, was delighted, and in high spirits: the only circumstance that detracted from his pleasure was the south wind, and the rain it seemed to promise for the next day.

We retired early to our apartments, but not to sleep; at least I did not. I remained many hours at the window, watching the pallid lightning that played above Mont Blanc, and listening to the rushing of the Arve, which ran below my window.

CHAPTER II.

THE next day, contrary to the prognostications of our guides, was fine, although clouded. We visited the source
1 of the Arveiron, and rode about the
2 valley until evening. These sublime and magnificent scenes afforded me the greatest consolation that I was capable of receiving. They elevated me from all littleness of feeling; and although they did not remove my grief, they subdued and tranquillized it. In some degree, also, they diverted my mind from the thoughts over which it had brooded for the last month. I returned in the evening, fatigued, but less unhappy, and conversed with my family with more cheerfulness than had been my custom for some time. My father was pleased, and Elizabeth overjoyed. "My dear cousin," said she, "you see what happiness you diffuse when you are happy; do not relapse again!"

The following morning the rain poured down in torrents, and thick mists hid the summits of the mountains. I rose early, but felt unusually melancholy. The rain depressed me; my old feelings recurred, and I was miserable. I knew how disappointed my father would be at this sudden change, and I wished to avoid him until I had recovered myself so far as to

1 *the Arveiron.* An affluent of the Arve river, which is fed by glacial waters. Percy Shelley, writing to Thomas Love Peacock about a visit he and Mary Shelley made, says: "Yesterday morning we went to the source of the Arveiron. It is about a league from the village [of Chamounix]—the river rolls impetuously from an arch of ice, & spreads itself in many streams over a vast space of the valley ravaged & laid bare by its inundations. The glacier by which its waters are nourished overhangs this cavern & the plain, & the forests of pines which surround it with terrible precipices of solid ice" (*The Letters of Percy Bysshe Shelley*, p. 498).

2 *sublime and magnificent scenes.* Victor is elevated by the sublimity of his surroundings, but we have seen (p. 133, note 15) how Mary Shelley has made Victor able to glimpse in these mountains aspects of the terror he has turned loose on the world. In giving Victor these divided feelings, Mary Shelley may have been influenced by a letter Percy Shelley wrote to his friend Peacock (a letter which she made a copy of) in which Shelley writes: "Do you who assert the supremacy of Ahriman [the chief of the forces of darkness in the Zoroastrian religion] image him throned among these desolating snows, among these palaces of death & frost, sculptured in this their terrible magnificence by the unsparing hand of necessity, & that he casts around him the first essays of his final usurpation avalanches, torrents, rocks & thunders—and above all, these deadly glaciers at once the proofs & the symbols of his reign.—Add to this the degradation of the human species, who in these regions are half-deformed or idiotic & all of whom are deprived of anything that can excite interest & admiration. This is a part of the subject more mournful & less sublime" (*The Letters of Percy Bysshe Shelley*, p. 499).
Shelley's letter was written on July 22, 1816. Mary Shelley began working on *Frankenstein* in mid-June of that year.

3 *inured myself*. Victor shares this attribute with Walton who, it will be remembered, inured himself to hardship by serving in the Greenland fisheries. Later (p. 202), we will see that the creature too is weather-hardy.

4 *Montanvert*. Percy Shelley was as affected by these glaciers as Victor is here. He writes: "On the other side rises the immense glacier of Montanvert, 50 miles in extent occupying a chasm among the mountains of inconceivable height & of forms so pointed & abrupt that they seem to pierce the sky. . . . These glaciers flow perpetually into the valley ravaging in their slow but irresistible progress the pastures & the forests which surround them, & performing a work of desolation in ages which a river of lava might accomplish in an hour, but far more irretrievably—for where the ice has once been the hardiest plant refuses to grow. . . . [The glacier presents] the most vivid image of desolation that it is possible to conceive. No one dares to approach it, for the enormous pinnacles of ice perpetually fall, & are perpetually reproduced.—The pines of the forest which bounds it at one extremity are overthrown & shattered;—there is something inexpressibly dreadful in the aspect of the few branchless trunks which nearest to the ice rifts still stand in the uprooted soil. The meadows perish overwhelmed with sand & stones" (*Letters of Percy Bysshe Shelley*, pp. 498–99).

And Mary Shelley: "Nothing can be more desolate than the ascent of this mountain; the trees in many places have been torn away by avalanches, and some half leaning over others, intermingled with stones, present the appearance of vast and dreadful desolation" (*Journal*, p. 53).

It took the Shelley party—including Claire—three hours to reach Montanvert from the valley below. The modern visitor can take a funicular that reaches Montanvert in twenty minutes.

be enabled to conceal those feelings that overpowered me. I knew that they would remain that day at the inn ; **3** and as I had ever inured myself to rain, moisture, and cold, I resolved to **4** go alone to the summit of Montanvert. I remembered the effect that the view of the tremendous and ever-moving glacier had produced upon my mind when I first saw it. It had then filled me with a sublime ecstacy that gave wings to the soul, and allowed it to soar from the obscure world to light and joy. The sight of the awful and majestic in nature had indeed always the effect of solemnizing my mind, and causing me to forget the passing cares of life. I determined to go alone, for I was well acquainted with the path, and the presence of another would destroy the solitary grandeur of the scene.

The ascent is precipitous, but the path is cut into continual and short windings, which enable you to surmount the perpendicularity of the mountain. It is a scene terrifically desolate. In a thousand spots the traces of the winter avelanche may be perceived, where trees lie broken and strewed on the ground ; some entirely destroyed, others bent, leaning upon the jutting rocks of the mountain, or transversely upon other trees. The path, as you ascend higher, is intersected by ravines of snow, down which stones continually roll from above ; one of them is particularly dangerous, as the slightest sound, such as even speaking in a loud voice, produces a concussion of air sufficient to draw destruction upon

5 *but mutability*! One wonders what the raptly attentive Walton in 17—made of this sudden drift in Victor's thoughts, which makes him quote a poem of Percy Shelley's written in 1815. The whole poem, in a modern edition, reads:

"Mutability"

We are as clouds that veil the midnight moon;
  How restlessly they speed, and gleam, and quiver,
Streaking the darkness radiantly!—yet soon
  Night closes round, and they are lost for ever:

Or like forgotten lyres, whose dissonant strings
  Give various response to each varying blast,
To whose frail frame no second motion brings
  One mood or modulation like the last.

We rest.—A dream has power to poison sleep;
  We rise.—One wandering thought pollutes the day;
  We feel, conceive or reason, laugh or weep;
  Embrace fond woe, or cast our cares away;

It is the same!—For, be it joy or sorrow,
  The path of its departure still is free:
Man's yesterday may ne'er be like his morrow;
  Nought may endure but Mutability.

6 *nearly noon.* Precisely the time when the Shelley party, with *"beaucoup de monde,"* reached it on July 25, 1816.

"THE SEA OF ICE."

the head of the speaker. The pines are not tall or luxuriant, but they are sombre, and add an air of severity to the scene. I looked on the valley beneath; vast mists were rising from the rivers which ran through it, and curling in thick wreaths around the opposite mountains, whose summits were hid in the uniform clouds, while rain poured from the dark sky, and added to the melancholy impression I received from the objects around me. Alas! why does man boast of sensibilities superior to those apparent in the brute; it only renders them more necessary beings. If our impulses were confined to hunger, thirst, and desire, we might be nearly free; but now we are moved by every wind that blows, and a chance word or scene that that word may convey to us.

We rest; a dream has power to poison sleep.
  We rise; one wand'ring thought pollutes the day.
We feel, conceive, or reason; laugh, or weep,
  Embrace fond woe, or cast our cares away;
It is the same: for, be it joy or sorrow,
  The path of its departure still is free.
Man's yesterday may ne'er be like his morrow;
  5   Nought may endure but mutability!

6   It was nearly noon when I arrived at the top of the ascent. For some time I sat upon the rock that overlooks the sea of ice. A mist covered both that and the surrounding mountains. Presently a breeze dissipated the cloud, and I descended upon the glacier. The surface is very uneven, rising like the waves of a troubled sea, descending low, and interspersed by rifts that sink deep. The field of ice is almost a

BENEATH THE SEA OF ICE.

7 *crossing it*. The Shelley party did not cross the Mer de Glace as Mary Shelley's journal entry of July 25 (p. 53) notes: "This is the most desolate place in the world; iced mountains surround it; no sign of vegetation appears . . . We went on the ice; it is traversed by irregular crevices, whose sides of ice appear blue, while the surface is of a dirty white" (*Journal*, p. 53).

A CONTEMPORARY VIEW OF
THE MER DE GLACE.

8 *Wandering spirits*. This invocation to spirits is one of several. It should be noted that neither Victor nor the creature ever call upon God directly. Elizabeth uses God's name but only in conventional locutions and never in direct prayer. Clearly Mary Shelley, though she wants to give her characters transcendental needs, would not let them acknowledge the presence of God in their universe. This is not surprising from a young woman who shared her father's and her husband's atheism.

league in width, but I spent nearly two

7 hours in crossing it. The opposite mountain is a bare perpendicular rock. From the side where I now stood Montanvert was exactly opposite, at the distance of a league; and above it rose Mont Blanc, in awful majesty. I remained in a recess of the rock, gazing on this wonderful and stupendous scene. The sea, or rather the vast river of ice, wound among its dependent mountains, whose aerial summits hung over its recesses. Their icy and glittering peaks shone in the sunlight over the clouds. My heart, which was before sorrowful, now swelled with something like joy;

8 I exclaimed—" Wandering spirits, if indeed ye wander, and do not rest in your narrow beds, allow me this faint happiness, or take me, as your companion, away from the joys of life."

As I said this, I suddenly beheld the figure of a man, at some distance, advancing towards me with superhuman speed. He bounded over the crevices in the ice, among which I had walked

"I SUDDENLY BEHELD
THE FIGURE OF A MAN."

9 *vile insect*! Not a fortunate phrase with which to describe a creature who stands eight feet tall.

10 *this reception*. Despite the swollen rhetoric in which both of the protagonists indulge, this is a compelling moment, as the father-mother-creator greets his infant with murderous intent. Magnificently conceived as this scene is, it has never been exploited in any of the film versions of the novel. Though these are the first words Victor and the readers of *Frankenstein* hear from the creature, they are not the first he speaks to another person in his life. For those, see page 191.

with caution; his stature also, as he approached, seemed to exceed that of man. I was troubled: a mist came over my eyes, and I felt a faintness seize me; but I was quickly restored by the cold gale of the mountains. I perceived, as the shape came nearer, (sight tremendous and abhorred!) that it was the wretch whom I had created. I trembled with rage and horror, resolving to wait his approach, and then close with him in mortal combat. He approached; his countenance bespoke bitter anguish, combined with disdain and malignity, while its unearthly ugliness rendered it almost too horrible for human eyes. But I scarcely observed this; anger and hatred had at first deprived me of utterance, and I recovered only to overwhelm him with words expressive of furious detestation and contempt.

"Devil!" I exclaimed, "do you dare approach me? and do not you fear the fierce vengeance of my arm wreaked **9** on your miserable head? Begone, vile insect! or rather stay, that I may trample you to dust! and, oh, that I could, with the extinction of your miserable existence, restore those victims whom you have so diabolically murdered!"

10 "I expected this reception," said the dæmon. "All men hate the wretched; how then must I be hated, who am miserable beyond all living things! Yet you, my creator, detest and spurn me, thy creature, to whom thou art bound by ties only dissoluble by the annihilation of one of us. You purpose to kill me. How dare you sport thus with life? Do your duty towards me, and I will

11 *extinguish the spark.* This language echoes that on page 128, where Victor, merely thinking of the creature, gnashes his teeth and expresses much the same wish.

12 *devoted.* In the sense here, and frequently later, devoted means consecrated.

13 *Remember, thou.* It is clear from the context of this paragraph that the shift from the "you" to the "thou" form of address is intended to heighten the God-Adam analogy that the creature will shortly develop. In *Paradise Lost*, which is very much on Mary Shelley's mind here, both God and Adam use the "thou" form (see Book VIII of *Paradise Lost*, pp. 190–94).

In Genesis 3:8–13, God addresses Adam as "You" while Adam replies "thou." Certainly the God-Adam Victor-creature analogy is implicit in *Frankenstein* from the first moment when Victor succeeds in animating his creature, but Mary Shelley seems not to exploit the biblical parallels nearly as much as she does the Miltonic ones. Still, one would not be wrong to think that, buried beneath the surface of the fiction, there is at least a tentative satire of the creation story as it is found in the Old Testament.

do mine towards you and the rest of mankind. If you will comply with my conditions, I will leave them and you at peace; but if you refuse, I will glut the maw of death, until it be satiated with the blood of your remaining friends."

" Abhorred monster! fiend that thou art! the tortures of hell are too mild a vengeance for thy crimes. Wretched devil! you reproach me with your creation; come on then, that I **11** may extinguish the spark which I so negligently bestowed."

My rage was without bounds; I sprang on him, impelled by all the feelings which can arm one being against the existence of another.

He easily eluded me, and said,

" Be calm! I entreat you to hear me, before you give vent to your hatred on **12** my devoted head. Have I not suffered enough, that you seek to increase my misery? Life, although it may only be an accumulation of anguish, is dear to **13** me, and I will defend it. Remember, thou hast made me more powerful than thyself; my height is superior to thine; my joints more supple. But I will not be tempted to set myself in opposition to thee. I am thy creature, and I will be even mild and docile to my natural lord and king, if thou wilt also perform thy part, the which thou owest me. Oh, Frankenstein, be not equitable to every other, and trample upon me alone, to whom thy justice, and even thy clemency and affection, is most due. Remember, that I am thy creature: I ought to be thy Adam; but I am rather the fallen angel, whom thou

"I AM THY CREATURE, AND I WILL BE EVEN MILD AND DOCILE TO MY NATURAL LORD AND KING, IF THOU WILT ALSO PERFORM THY PART, THE WHICH THOU OWEST ME."

14 *love and humanity.* Compare this speech with Victor's on the first page of Volume II.

drivest from joy for no misdeed. Every where I see bliss, from which I alone am irrevocably excluded. I was benevolent and good; misery made me a fiend. Make me happy, and I shall again be virtuous."

" Begone! I will not hear you. There can be no community between you and me; we are enemies. Begone, or let us try our strength in a fight, in which one must fall."

" How can I move thee? Will no entreaties cause thee to turn a favourable eye upon thy creature, who implores thy goodness and compassion. Believe me, Frankenstein: I was bene-

14   volent; my soul glowed with love and humanity: but am I not alone, miserably alone? You, my creator, abhor me; what hope can I gather from your fellow-creatures, who owe me nothing? they spurn and hate me. The desert mountains and dreary glaciers are my refuge. I have wandered here many days; the caves of ice, which I only do not fear, are a dwelling to me, and the only one which man does not grudge. These bleak skies I hail, for they are kinder to me than your fellow-beings. If the multitude of mankind knew of my existence, they would do as you do, and arm themselves for my destruction. Shall I not then hate them who abhor me? I will keep no terms with my enemies. I am miserable, and they shall share my wretchedness. Yet it is in your power to recompense me, and deliver them from an evil which it only remains for you to make so great, that not only you and your fa-

15 *Thus I relieve thee.* The whole of this long speech by the creature is a fascinating interplay of tones in which ferocious threats alternate with the most pathetic pleading—the whole finely mitigated by compassion. The gesture of the hand placed over Victor's eyes coupled with the creature's concern for Victor's more delicate constitution ("the temperature of this place is not fitting to your fine sensations") are manifestations of Mary Shelley's triumphant imagination. That the creature fails to honor the contract implied by his speech is beside the point.

mily, but thousands of others, shall be swallowed up in the whirlwinds of its rage. Let your compassion be moved, and do not disdain me. Listen to my tale: when you have heard that, abandon or commiserate me, as you shall judge that I deserve. But hear me. The guilty are allowed, by human laws, bloody as they may be, to speak in their own defence before they are condemned. Listen to me, Frankenstein. You accuse me of murder; and yet you would, with a satisfied conscience, destroy your own creature. Oh, praise the eternal justice of man! Yet I ask you not to spare me: listen to me; and then, if you can, and if you will, destroy the work of your hands."

" Why do you call to my remembrance circumstances of which I shudder to reflect, that I have been the miserable origin and author? Cursed be the day, abhorred devil, in which you first saw light! Cursed (although I curse myself) be the hands that formed you! You have made me wretched beyond expression. You have left me no power to consider whether I am just to you, or not. Begone! relieve me from the sight of your detested form."

15   " Thus I relieve thee, my creator," he said, and placed his hated hands before my eyes, which I flung from me with violence; " thus I take from thee a sight which you abhor. Still thou canst listen to me, and grant me thy compassion. By the virtues that I once possessed, I demand this from you. Hear my tale; it is long and strange, and the temperature of this place is

16   *For the first time*. It has been a long wait. There is something of a cinematic tenderness in this image of the perplexed parent and his hulking offspring clumping through the crevasses of a glacier together searching for a place to get in out of the rain.

17   *had lighted*. The creature's filial tenderness is in sharp contrast with Victor's rigid hostility.

There was, indeed, a hut in the vicinity of the Sea of Ice, built for the convenience of tourists.

not fitting to your fine sensations; come to the hut upon the mountain. The sun is yet high in the heavens; before it descends to hide itself behind yon snowy precipices, and illuminate another world, you will have heard my story, and can decide. On you it rests, whether I quit for ever the neighbourhood of man, and lead a harmless life, or become the scourge of your fellow-creatures, and the author of your own speedy ruin."

As he said this, he led the way across the ice: I followed. My heart was full, and I did not answer him; but, as I proceeded, I weighed the various arguments that he had used, and determined at least to listen to his tale. I was partly urged by curiosity, and compassion confirmed my resolution. I had hitherto supposed him to be the murderer of my brother, and I eagerly sought a confirmation or denial of this opinion. **16** For the first time, also, I felt what the duties of a creator towards his creature were, and that I ought to render him happy before I complained of his wickedness. These motives urged me to comply with his demand. We crossed the ice, therefore, and ascended the opposite rock. The air was cold, and the rain again began to descend: we entered the hut, the fiend with an air of exultation, I with a heavy heart, and depressed spirits. But I consented to listen; and, seating myself by the fire which my **17** odious companion had lighted, he thus began his tale.

1 *Chapter III*. We enter now the third of the narratives that make up the story of *Frankenstein:* the creature's autobiography.

2 *my being*. Mary Shelley in the next several pages develops the Adam-creature analogy. Milton's rendition of Adam's coming to consciousness in Eden is her model with the difference that Adam awoke to find a gentle God as mentor for his perplexities. In every respect, the creature's experience is rooted in the harsher, natural world of sensation, hunger, and weather. The difference between the two forms of awakening to consciousness is not lost on Mary Shelley, and it helps make this and the suceeding pages among the best in her fiction. The creature wakes without sponsorship, a victim of his sensations, unattended, inexplicably conscious but with no sense of self. He is oppressed by the disabilities of existence without having any of its mitigating joys.

Milton describes Adam's waking in Eden as follows (*Paradise Lost*, pp. 188–89):

"For man to tell how human life began
Is hard; for who himself beginning knew?
Desire with thee still longer to converse
Induced me. As new-waked from soundest sleep,
Soft on the flowery herb I found me laid,
In balmy sweat, which with his beams the Sun
Soon dried, and on the reeking moisture fed.
Straight toward Heaven my wondering eyes I turned,
And gazed a while the ample sky, till, raised
By quick instinctive motion, up I sprung,
As thitherward endeavouring, and upright
Stood on my feet. About me round I saw
Hill, dale, and shady woods, and sunny plains,
And liquid lapse of murmuring streams; by these,
Creatures that lived and moved, and walked or flew,
Birds on the branches warbling: all things smiled;
With fragrance and with joy my heart o'erflowed.
Myself I then perused, and limb by limb
Surveyed, and sometimes went, and sometimes ran
With supple joints, as lively vigour led;
But who I was, or where, or from what cause,
Knew not. To speak I tried, and forthwith spake;
My tongue obeyed, and readily could name
Whate'er I saw. 'Thou Sun,' said I, 'fair light,
And thou enlightened Earth, so fresh and gay,
Ye hills and dales, ye rivers, woods, and plains,
And ye that live and move, fair creatures, tell,

"**I**T is with considerable difficulty that
2 I remember the original æra of my being : all the events of that period appear confused and indistinct. A strange multiplicity of sensations seized me, and I saw, felt, heard, and smelt, at the same time; and it was, indeed, a long time before I learned to distinguish between the operations of my various senses. By degrees, I remember, a stronger light pressed upon my nerves, so that I was obliged to shut my eyes. Darkness then came over me, and troubled me ; but hardly had I felt this, when, by opening my eyes, as I now suppose, the light poured in upon me again. I walked, and, I believe, descended ; but I presently found a great alteration in my sensations. Before, dark and opaque bodies had surrounded me, impervious to my touch or sight ; but I now found that I could wander on at liberty, with no obstacles which I could not either **3** surmount or avoid. The light became more and more oppressive to me ; and, the heat wearying me as I walked, I sought a place where I could receive shade. This was the forest near Ingoldstadt ; and here I lay by the side of a brook resting from my fatigue, until I felt tormented by hunger and thirst. This roused me from my nearly

Tell, if ye saw, how came I thus, how here?
Not of myself; by some great Maker then,
In goodness and in power pre-eminent.
Tell me, how may I know him, how adore,
From whom I have that thus I move and live,
And feel that I am happier than I know?'
While thus I called, and strayed I knew not whither,
From where I first drew air, and first beheld
This happy light, when answer none returned,
On a green shady bank, profuse of flowers,
Pensive I sat me down. There gentle sleep
First found me, and with soft oppression seized
My drowsed sense, untroubled, though I thought
I then was passing to my former state
Insensible, and forthwith to dissolve:
When suddenly stood at my head a dream,
Whose inward apparition gently moved
My fancy to believe I yet had being,
And lived. One came, methought, of shape divine,
And said, "Thy mansion wants thee, Adam; rise"

3 *surmount or avoid.* Here we learn that the creature finds no barriers insurmountable. Now we know how, moments after he came to life, he was able to leave Victor's walled lodgings.

4 *were insufficient.* Whether Victor, his creator, had had the foresight to have oversize clothes made for the eight-foot-tall creature but they were too lightweight for the weather, or whether they were simply too small, we are not told.

dormant state, and I ate some berries which I found hanging on the trees, or lying on the ground. I slaked my thirst at the brook; and then lying down, was overcome by sleep.

" It was dark when I awoke; I felt cold also, and half-frightened as it were instinctively, finding myself so desolate. Before I had quitted your apartment, on a sensation of cold, I had covered myself with some clothes; but **4** these were insufficient to secure me from the dews of night. I was a poor, helpless, miserable wretch; I knew, and could distinguish, nothing; but,

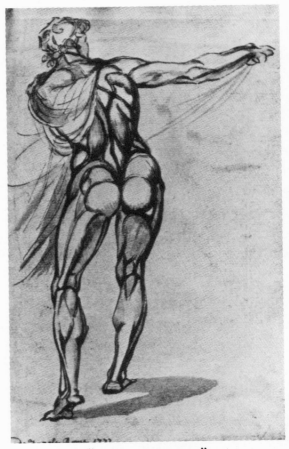

"I FELT COLD ALSO"
(FUSELI'S NUDE MAN FROM THE BACK).

5 *cloak*. However misfortunate the creature is in other things, he frequently, as we will see, benefits from the most astonishing coincidences, such as finding this huge cloak just exactly when he needs it.

feeling pain invade me on all sides, I sat down and wept.

" Soon a gentle light stole over the heavens, and gave me a sensation of pleasure. I started up, and beheld a radiant form rise from among the trees. I gazed with a kind of wonder. It moved slowly, but it enlightened my path; and I again went out in search of berries. I was still cold, when under one of the trees I found a huge cloak, with which I covered myself, and sat down upon the ground. No distinct ideas occupied my mind; all was confused. I felt light, and hunger, and thirst, and darkness; innumerable sounds rung in my ears, and on all sides various scents saluted me: the only object that I could distinguish was the bright moon, and I fixed my eyes on that with pleasure.

" Several changes of day and night passed, and the orb of night had greatly lessened when I began to distinguish my sensations from each other. I gradually saw plainly the clear stream that supplied me with drink, and the trees that shaded me with their foliage. I was delighted when I first discovered that a pleasant sound, which often saluted my ears, proceeded from the throats of the little winged animals who had often intercepted the light from my eyes. I began also to observe, with greater accuracy, the forms that surrounded me, and to perceive the boundaries of the radiant roof of light which canopied me. Sometimes I tried to imitate the pleasant songs of the birds, but was unable. Sometimes I wished to ex-

6 *sweet and enticing.* In November, while the sparrows and blackbirds might still be there, the thrushes would certainly be gone. In any case they would no longer be singing since song is part of the springtime mating behavior of these birds in those latitudes.

press my sensations in my own mode, but the uncouth and inarticulate sounds which broke from me frightened me into silence again.

" The moon had disappeared from the night, and again, with a lessened form, shewed itself, while I still remained in the forest. My sensations had, by this time, become distinct, and my mind received every day additional ideas. My eyes became accustomed to the light, and to perceive objects in their right forms; I distinguished the insect from the herb, and, by degrees, one herb from another. I found that the sparrow uttered none but harsh notes, whilst those of the black-

6 bird and thrush were sweet and enticing.

" One day, when I was oppressed by cold, I found a fire which had been left by some wandering beggars, and was overcome with delight at the warmth I experienced from it. In my joy I thrust my hand into the live embers, but quickly drew it out again with a cry of pain. How strange, I thought, that the same cause should produce such opposite effects! I examined the materials of the fire, and to my joy found it to be composed of wood. I quickly collected some branches; but they were wet, and would not burn. I was pained at this, and sat still watching the operation of the fire. The wet wood which I had placed near the heat dried, and itself became inflamed. I reflected on this; and, by touching the various branches, I discovered the cause, and busied myself in collecting a great quantity of wood, that I might dry it, and have a

"I WAS DELIGHTED WHEN I FIRST DISCOVERED THAT A PLEASANT SOUND . . . PROCEEDED FROM THE THROATS OF THE LITTLE WINGED ANIMALS."

7 *offals.* Used here in the sense of refuse—leftovers.

plentiful supply of fire. When night came on, and brought sleep with it, I was in the greatest fear lest my fire should be extinguished. I covered it carefully with dry wood and leaves, and placed wet branches upon it; and then, spreading my cloak, I lay on the ground, and sunk into sleep.

" It was morning when I awoke, and my first care was to visit the fire. I uncovered it, and a gentle breeze quickly fanned it into a flame. I observed this also, and contrived a fan of branches, which roused the embers when they were nearly extinguished. When night came again, I found, with pleasure, that the fire gave light as well as heat; and that the discovery of this element was useful to me in my

7 food; for I found some of the offals that the travellers had left had been roasted, and tasted much more savoury than the berries I gathered from the trees. I tried, therefore, to dress my food in the same manner, placing it on the live embers. I found that the berries were spoiled by this operation, and the nuts and roots much improved.

" Food, however, became scarce; and I often spent the whole day searching in vain for a few acorns to assuage the pangs of hunger. When I found this, I resolved to quit the place that I had hitherto inhabited, to seek for one where the few wants I experienced would be more easily satisfied. In this emigration, I exceedingly lamented the loss of the fire which I had obtained through accident, and knew not how to re-produce it. I gave several hours to the serious consideration of this diffi-

8 *Pandæmonium*. Pandæmonium was in Milton's account (Book I of *Paradise Lost*) the capital city of the damned built by the fallen angels under the supervision of Mammon. The city was designed by Mulciber, who before his fall was famous in Heaven for his structures. Pandæmonium was, no doubt, an improvement on the Lake of Fire in which the legions of the damned floated in their first hours in Hell.

culty; but I was obliged to relinquish all attempt to supply it; and, wrapping myself up in my cloak, I struck across the wood towards the setting sun. I passed three days in these rambles, and at length discovered the open country. A great fall of snow had taken place the night before, and the fields were of one uniform white; the appearance was disconsolate, and I found my feet chilled by the cold damp substance that covered the ground.

" It was about seven in the morning, and I longed to obtain food and shelter; at length I perceived a small hut, on a rising ground, which had doubtless been built for the convenience of some shepherd. This was a new sight to me; and I examined the structure with great curiosity. Finding the door open, I entered. An old man sat in it, near a fire, over which he was preparing his breakfast. He turned on hearing a noise; and, perceiving me, shrieked loudly, and, quitting the hut, ran across the fields with a speed of which his debilitated form hardly appeared capable. His appearance, different from any I had ever before seen, and his flight, somewhat surprised me. But I was enchanted by the appearance of the hut: here the snow and rain could not penetrate; the ground was dry; and it presented to me then as exquisite and divine a retreat as Pandæmonium appeared to the dæmons of hell after their sufferings in the lake of fire. I greedily devoured the remnants of the shepherd's breakfast, which consisted of bread, cheese, milk, and wine; the

9 *I did not like*. The creature, we will see, is altogether a teetotaler. However, in the film *The Bride of Frankenstein* (1935), we see him introduced to the delights of wine and tobacco with considerable comic effect. The comedy becomes hilarious in Mel Brooks's movie *Young Frankenstein* (1974).

10 *wallet*. In its older sense, the word describes a large leather case or knapsack.

11 *of these*. That is, cottages.

"THIS HOVEL."

9 latter, however, I did not like. Then overcome by fatigue, I lay down among some straw, and fell asleep.

" It was noon when I awoke; and, allured by the warmth of the sun, which shone brightly on the white ground, I determined to recommence my travels; and, depositing the remains of the pea-

10 sant's breakfast in a wallet I found, I proceeded across the fields for several hours, until at sunset I arrived at a village. How miraculous did this appear! the huts, the neater cottages, and stately houses, engaged my admiration by turns. The vegetables in the gardens, the milk and cheese that I saw placed at the windows of some of the cottages, allured my appetite. One of

11 the best of these I entered; but I had hardly placed my foot within the door, before the children shrieked, and one of the women fainted. The whole village was roused; some fled, some attacked me, until, grievously bruised by stones and many other kinds of missile weapons, I escaped to the open country, and fearfully took refuge in a low hovel, quite bare, and making a wretched appearance after the palaces I had beheld in the village. This hovel, however, joined a cottage of a neat and pleasant appearance; but, after my late dearly-bought experience, I dared not enter it. My place of refuge was constructed of wood, but so low, that I could with difficulty sit upright in it. No wood, however, was placed on the earth, which formed the floor, but it was dry; and although the wind entered it by innumerable chinks, I found it an agreeable asylum from the snow and rain.

12   *tolerably warm.* Mary Shelley's description of the creature's refuge has in it all the details that an unhappy child might imagine for himself in a secret hiding place, equipped with all things needful, including running water.

" Here then I retreated, and lay down, happy to have found a shelter, however miserable, from the inclemency of the season, and still more from the barbarity of man.

" As soon as morning dawned, I crept from my kennel, that I might view the adjacent cottage, and discover if I could remain in the habitation I had found. It was situated against the back of the cottage, and surrounded on the sides which were exposed by a pig-stye and a clear pool of water. One part was open, and by that I had crept in; but now I covered every crevice by which I might be perceived with stones and wood, yet in such a manner that I might move them on occasion to pass out: all the light I enjoyed came through the stye, and that was sufficient for me.

" Having thus arranged my dwelling, and carpeted it with clean straw, I retired; for I saw the figure of a man at a distance, and I remembered too well my treatment the night before, to trust myself in his power. I had first, however, provided for my sustenance for that day, by a loaf of coarse bread, which I purloined, and a cup with which I could drink, more conveniently than from my hand, of the pure water which flowed by my retreat. The floor was a little raised, so that it was kept perfectly dry, and by its vicinity to the chimney of the cottage it was tolerably warm.

12

" Being thus provided, I resolved to reside in this hovel, until something should occur which might alter my determination. It was indeed a paradise, compared to the bleak forest, my former

13 *to be*. This is a touch of upper-middle-class snobbery. Both Mary and the poet Shelley, in their letters and journals, complain incessantly of the un-couth and boorish European peasant. In the revised 1831 edition of *Frankenstein*, Elizabeth Lavenza is the foster child of peasants among whose children the nobly-born Elizabeth stands out in sharp contrast: "This child was thin, and very fair. Her hair was the brightest living gold, and, despite the poverty of her clothing, seemed to set a crown of distinction on her head. Her brow was clear and ample, her blue eyes cloudless, and her lips and the moulding of her face so expressive of sensibility and sweetness, that none could behold her without looking on her as of a distinct species."

It is interesting to compare this description with one which appears in a letter written by Shelley to Peacock during the *Frankenstein* summer. In it, Shel-ley describes an incident that occurred in the Swiss village of Nernier during the Shelley-Byron boat trip. "We sat on a wall beside the lake, looking at some children who were playing at a game of ninepins. The children here appeared in an extraordinary way de-formed and diseased. Most of them were crooked, and with enlarged throats; but one little boy had such exquisite grace in his mien and motions, as I never before saw equalled in a child. His countenance was beautiful for the expression with which it overflowed. There was a mixture of pride and gentleness in his eyes and lips, the indications of sensibility, which his education will probably pervert to misery or seduce to crime", (*Letters of Percy Bysshe Shelley*, p. 481).

residence, the rain-dropping branches, and dank earth. I ate my breakfast with pleasure, and was about to remove a plank to procure myself a little water, when I heard a step, and, looking through a small chink, I beheld a young creature, with a pail on her head, pass-ing before my hovel. The girl was young and of gentle demeanour, unlike what I have since found cottagers and farm-house servants to be. Yet she was meanly dressed, a coarse blue pet-ticoat and a linen jacket being her only garb; her fair hair was plaited, but not adorned; she looked patient, yet sad. I lost sight of her; and in about a quarter of an hour she return-ed, bearing the pail, which was now partly filled with milk. As she walked along, seemingly incommoded by the burden, a young man met her, whose countenance expressed a deeper de-spondence. Uttering a few sounds with an air of melancholy, he took the pail from her head, and bore it to the cot-tage himself. She followed, and they disappeared. Presently I saw the young man again, with some tools in his hand, cross the field behind the cottage; and the girl was also busied, sometimes in the house, and sometimes in the yard.

" On examining my dwelling, I found that one of the windows of the cottage had formerly occupied a part of it, but the panes had been filled up with wood. In one of these was a small and almost imperceptible chink, through which the eye could just penetrate. Through this crevice, a small room was visible, white-washed and clean, but very bare of furniture. In one

14 *an instrument.* What that instrument is we will learn later. In the film *The Bride of Frankenstein*, it was a violin.

corner, near a small fire, sat an old man, leaning his head on his hands in a disconsolate attitude. The young girl was occupied in arranging the cottage; but presently she took something out of a drawer, which employed her hands, and she sat down beside the old man, **14** who, taking up an instrument, began to play, and to produce sounds, sweeter than the voice of the thrush or the nightingale. It was a lovely sight, even to me, poor wretch! who had never beheld aught beautiful before. The silver hair and benevolent countenance of the aged cottager, won my reverence; while the gentle manners of the girl enticed my love. He played a sweet mournful air, which I perceived drew tears from the eyes of his amiable companion, of which the old man took no notice, until she sobbed audibly; he then pronounced a few sounds, and the fair creature, leaving her work, knelt at his feet. He raised her, and smiled with such kindness and affection, that I felt sensations of a peculiar and overpowering nature: they were a mixture of pain and pleasure, such as I had never before experienced, either from hunger or cold, warmth or food; and I withdrew from the window, unable to bear these emotions.

" Soon after this the young man returned, bearing on his shoulders a load of wood. The girl met him at the door, helped to relieve him of his burden, and, taking some of the fuel into the cottage, placed it on the fire; then she and the youth went apart into a nook of the cottage, and he shewed her a large loaf and a piece of cheese. She seemed

15 *my human neighbours*. This is a bit of splendidly realized writing. There are few images of loneliness in literature that are quite as persuasive as this one of the creature pressing, as it were, his nose to the window of domestic joy; at once alert to what he is missing and constrained not to make his presence known.

pleased; and went into the garden for some roots and plants, which she placed in water, and then upon the fire. She afterwards continued her work, whilst the young man went into the garden, and appeared busily employed in digging and pulling up roots. After he had been employed thus about an hour, the young woman joined him, and they entered the cottage together.

" The old man had, in the mean time, been pensive; but, on the appearance of his companions, he assumed a more cheerful air, and they sat down to eat. The meal was quickly dispatched. The young woman was again occupied in arranging the cottage; the old man walked before the cottage in the sun for a few minutes, leaning on the arm of the youth. Nothing could exceed in beauty the contrast between these two excellent creatures. One was old, with silver hairs and a countenance beaming with benevolence and love: the younger was slight and graceful in his figure, and his features were moulded with the finest symmetry; yet his eyes and attitude expressed the utmost sadness and despondency. The old man returned to the cottage; and the youth, with tools different from those he had used in the morning, directed his steps across the fields.

" Night quickly shut in; but, to my extreme wonder, I found that the cottagers had a means of prolonging light, by the use of tapers, and was delighted to find, that the setting of the sun did not put an end to the pleasure I experienced in watching **15** my human neighbours. In the evening, the young girl and her companion were employed in various occupations which I did not understand; and the old man again took up the instrument, which produced the divine sounds that had enchanted me in the morning. So soon as he had finished, the youth began, not to play, but to utter sounds that were monotonous, and neither resembling the harmony of the old man's instrument or the songs of the birds; I since found that he read aloud, but at that time I knew nothing of the science of words or letters.

" The family, after having been thus occupied for a short time, extinguished their lights, and retired, as I conjectured, to rest.

CHAPTER IV.

" I LAY on my straw, but I could not sleep. I thought of the occurrences of the day. What chiefly struck me was the gentle manners of these people; and I longed to join them, but dared not. I remembered too well the treatment I had suffered the night before from the barbarous villagers, and resolved, whatever course of conduct I might hereafter think it right to pursue, that for the present I would remain quietly in my hovel, watching, and endeavouring to discover the motives which influenced their actions.

" The cottagers arose the next morning before the sun. The young woman arranged the cottage, and prepared the food; and the youth departed after the first meal.

" This day was passed in the same routine as that which preceded it. The young man was constantly employed out of doors, and the girl in various laborious occupations within. The old man, whom I soon perceived to be blind, employed his leisure hours on his instrument, or in contemplation. Nothing could exceed the love and respect which the younger cottagers exhibited towards their venerable companion. They performed towards him every little office of affection and duty with gentleness; and he rewarded them by his benevolent smiles.

1 *to be blind.* In the 1935 film *The Bride of Frankenstein*, the blind man, transformed into a hermit instead of a father of a family, as here, teaches the creature to say a few words, how to smoke a cigar, and how to drink wine. The cigar and the wine delight the creature, and his pleasure is exploited by the filmmakers for considerable comic effect. In the 1974 Mel Brooks production of *Young Frankenstein*, the scene is parodied. The hermit, endeavoring to light the creature's cigar, lights one of his guest's fingers instead. When they drink to each other's health, they smash the cups they have clinked together.

1

2 *wretched.* This benign but wretched family needs to be seen in the tradition of Romantic melancholy. Robert Kiely, in *The Romantic Novel in England,* page 158, quotes Maccauley on Byron: "He continued to repeat that to be wretched is the destiny of all; that to be eminently wretched, is the destiny of the eminent." The family in whom our creature is interested are only moderately miserable, and yet their low-key grief makes them "interesting" to their envious and unknown friend.

3 *poverty.* In the first years of their liaison Mary and Percy Shelley, while they were not absolutely poor, did indeed suffer the evils of British upper-class poverty. Percy Shelley, as the heir-apparent to a vast fortune, should have been richer than he was, but his assets were tied up in litigations over the course of many years, and there were times when he was so fearful of process servers, that he had, literally, to hide from them. Mary Shelley, on the other hand, had experienced up close the consequences of her father's spendthrift impracticality. But neither Mary nor Percy ever "suffered the pangs of hunger." More usually they lived comfortable, if sometimes financially pressed, lives.

" They were not entirely happy. The young man and his companion often went apart, and appeared to weep. I saw no cause for their unhappiness; but I was deeply affected by it. If such lovely creatures were miserable, it was less strange that I, an imperfect and solitary being, should be wretched. Yet why were these gentle beings unhappy? They possessed a delightful house (for such it was in my eyes), and every luxury; they had a fire to warm them when chill, and delicious viands when hungry; they were dressed in excellent clothes; and, still more, they enjoyed one another's company and speech, interchanging each day looks of affection and kindness. What did their tears imply? Did they really express pain? I was at first unable to solve these questions; but perpetual attention, and time, explained to me many appearances which were at first enigmatic.

" A considerable period elapsed before I discovered one of the causes of the uneasiness of this amiable family; it was poverty: and they suffered that evil in a very distressing degree. Their nourishment consisted entirely of the vegetables of their garden, and the milk of one cow, who gave very little during the winter, when its masters could scarcely procure food to support it. They often, I believe, suffered the pangs of hunger very poignantly, especially the two younger cottagers; for several times they placed food before the old man, when they reserved none for themselves.

" This trait of kindness moved me sensibly. I had been accustomed, during the night, to steal a part of their store for my own consumption; but when I found that in doing this I inflicted pain on the cottagers, I abstained, and satisfied myself with berries, nuts, and roots, which I gathered from a neighbouring wood.

" I discovered also another means through which I was enabled to assist their labours. I found that the youth spent a great part of each day in collecting wood for the family fire; and, during the night, I often took his tools, the use of which I quickly discovered, and brought home firing sufficient for the consumption of several days.

" I remember, the first time that I did this, the young woman, when she opened the door in the morning, appeared greatly astonished on seeing a great pile of wood on the outside. She uttered some words in a loud voice, and the youth joined her, who also expressed surprise. I observed, with pleasure, that he did not go to the forest that day, but spent it in repairing the cottage, and cultivating the garden.

" By degrees I made a discovery of still greater moment. I found that these people possessed a method of communicating their experience and feelings to one another by articulate sounds. I perceived that the words they spoke sometimes produced pleasure or pain, smiles or sadness, in the minds and countenances of the hearers. This was indeed a godlike science, and I ardently desired to become acquainted with it. But I was baffled in every attempt I made for this purpose. Their

4 fire, milk, bread, *and* wood. As we will soon see, the creature is one of the world's most talented autodidacts. Here it is pleasing to recall a tale told by Herodotus about one of the world's earliest linguistic experiments. Psammetichus, an ancient Egyptian king, wishing to discover whether the Phrygians or Egyptians were the most ancient people, devised, according to Herodotus, the following experiment: "He [Psammetichus] took at random, from an ordinary family, two newly born infants and gave them to a shepherd to be brought up amongst his flocks, under strict orders that no one should utter a word in their presence. They were to be kept by themselves in a lonely cottage, and the shepherd was to bring in goats from time to time, to see that the babies had enough milk to drink, and to look after them in any other way that was necessary. All these arrangements were made by Psammetichus because he wished to find out what word the children would first utter, once they had grown out of their meaningless baby-talk. The plan succeeded; two years later the shepherd, who during that time had done everything he had been told to do, happened one day to open the door of the cottage and go in, when both children, running up to him with hands outstretched, pronounced the word 'becos' . . . Psammetichus ordered the children to be brought to him, and when he himself heard them say 'becos' he determined to find out to what language the word belonged. His inquiries revealed that it was the Phrygian for 'bread' " (Herodotus, *The Histories*, pp. 102–3).

pronunciation was quick; and the words they uttered, not having any apparent connexion with visible objects, I was unable to discover any clue by which I could unravel the mystery of their reference. By great application, however, and after having remained during the space of several revolutions of the moon in my hovel, I discovered the names that were given to some of the most familiar objects of discourse: I learned and applied the words *fire, milk, bread,* and *wood.* I learned also the names of the cottagers themselves. The youth and his companion had each of them several names, but the old man had only one, which was *father.* The girl was called *sister,* or *Agatha;* and the youth *Felix, brother,* or *son.* I cannot describe the delight I felt when I learned the ideas appropriated to each of these sounds, and was able to pronounce them. I distinguished several other words, without being able as yet to understand or apply them; such as *good, dearest, unhappy.*

" I spent the winter in this manner. The gentle manners and beauty of the cottagers greatly endeared them to me: when they were unhappy, I felt depressed; when they rejoiced, I sympathized in their joys. I saw few human beings beside them; and if any other happened to enter the cottage, their harsh manners and rude gait only enhanced to me the superior accomplishments of my friends. The old man, I could perceive, often endeavoured to encourage his children, as sometimes I found that he called them, to cast off their melancholy. He

5 *little white flower.* In the vicinity of Ingolstadt, as well as most areas in the temperate zone, this would be the crocus.

6 *outhouse.* A building detached from the cottage.

would talk in a cheerful accent, with an expression of goodness that bestowed pleasure even upon me. Agatha listened with respect, her eyes sometimes filled with tears, which she endeavoured to wipe away unperceived ; but I generally found that her countenance and tone were more cheerful after having listened to the exhortations of her father. It was not thus with Felix. He was always the saddest of the groupe ; and, even to my unpractised senses, he appeared to have suffered more deeply than his friends. But if his countenance was more sorrowful, his voice was more cheerful than that of his sister, especially when he addressed the old man.

" I could mention innumerable instances, which, although slight, marked the dispositions of these amiable cottagers. In the midst of poverty and want, Felix carried with pleasure to his **5** sister the first little white flower that peeped out from beneath the snowy ground. Early in the morning before she had risen, he cleared away the snow that obstructed her path to the milk-house, drew water from the well, **6** and brought the wood from the outhouse, where, to his perpetual astonishment, he found his store always replenished by an invisible hand. In the day, I believe, he worked sometimes for a neighbouring farmer, because he often went forth, and did not return until dinner, yet brought no wood with him. At other times he worked in the garden ; but, as there was little to do in the frosty season, he read to the old man and Agatha.

7 *transparent pool!* This reversal of the Narcissus theme is clearly intended. Narcissus, it will be remembered, spurned the love of Echo, causing her death. In revenge, Nemesis, the goddess of justice, caused Narcissus to fall madly in love with his own image, seen reflected in a quiet pool. The infatuation was hopeless and he pined away until the gods, taking pity on him, transformed him into the flower we call *narcissus*.

Our author may also be recalling how Eve, in Milton's *Paradise Lost* (Book IV, ll. 23–32), describes her own first sight of herself reflected in a pool in Paradise:

. . . I thither went
With unexperienced thought, and laid me down
On the green bank, to look into the clear
Smooth lake, that to me seemed another sky.
As I bent down to look, just opposite
A shape within the wat'ry gleam appeared,
Bending to look on me. I started back,
It started back; but pleased I soon returned,
Pleased, it returned as soon with answering looks
Of sympathy and love.

" This reading had puzzled me extremely at first; but, by degrees, I discovered that he uttered many of the same sounds when he read as when he talked. I conjectured, therefore, that he found on the paper signs for speech which he understood, and I ardently longed to comprehend these also; but how was that possible, when I did not even understand the sounds for which they stood as signs? I improved, however, sensibly in this science, but not sufficiently to follow up any kind of conversation, although I applied my whole mind to the endeavour: for I easily perceived that, although I eagerly longed to discover myself to the cottagers, I ought not to make the attempt until I had first become master of their language; which knowledge might enable me to make them overlook the deformity of my figure; for with this also the contrast perpetually presented to my eyes had made me acquainted.

" I had admired the perfect forms of my cottagers—their grace, beauty, and delicate complexions: but how was I terrified, when I viewed myself in a transparent pool! At first I started back, unable to believe that it was indeed I who was reflected in the mirror; and when I became fully convinced that I was in reality the monster that I am, I was filled with the bitterest sensations of despondence and mortification. Alas! I did not yet entirely know the fatal effects of this miserable deformity.

" As the sun became warmer, and the light of day longer, the snow vanished, and I beheld the bare trees and the black earth. From this time Felix was more employed; and the heart-moving indications of impending famine disappeared. Their food, as I afterwards found, was coarse, but it was wholesome; and they procured a sufficiency of it. Several new kinds of plants sprung up in the garden, which they dressed; and these signs of comfort increased daily as the season advanced.

" The old man, leaning on his son, walked each day at noon, when it did not rain, as I found it was called when the heavens poured forth its waters. This frequently took place; but a high wind quickly dried the earth, and the season became far more pleasant than it had been.

" My mode of life in my hovel was uniform. During the morning I attended the motions of the cottagers; and when they were dispersed in various occupations, I slept: the remainder of the day was spent in observing my friends. When they had retired to rest, if there was any moon, or the night was star-light, I went into the woods, and collected my own food and fuel for the cottage. When I returned, as often as it was necessary, I cleared their path from the snow, and performed those offices that I had seen done by Felix. I afterwards found that these labours, performed by an invisible hand, greatly astonished them; and once or twice I heard them, on these occasions, utter the words *good spirit*, *wonderful;* but I did not then understand the signification of these terms.

FRONTISPIECE TO FABLES BY LA FONTAINE.

8 *the ass and the lap-dog.* The story is told in La Fontaine's *Fables* (1668–1678). The donkey, having observed that the lap dog was petted and handled by his master and mistress because of his affectionate ways, decided to imitate the tiny beast. Waiting until his master was in a good mood, the donkey approached him and tried to caress his cheek with his hoof. The donkey was well beaten for his pains.

How the creature came to know of this fable, since La Fontaine is not included in his book list, is a mystery—unless he read Aesop's earlier version. Writing of "The Ass and the Lap Dog" may have reminded Mary Shelley of her elopement journey with Percy Shelley when he purchased an ass at the ass market in Paris so that it might carry Mary and Claire Clairmont on their trip to Uri on Lake Lucerne. The ass turned out to be so weak that for the last part of the journey it was necessary for the poet to carry it in his arms.

" My thoughts now became more active, and I longed to discover the motives and feelings of these lovely creatures ; I was inquisitive to know why Felix appeared so miserable, and Agatha so sad. I thought (foolish wretch !) that it might be in my power to restore happiness to these deserving people. When I slept, or was absent, the forms of the venerable blind father, the gentle Agatha, and the excellent Felix, flitted before me. I looked upon them as superior beings, who would be the arbiters of my future destiny. I formed in my imagination a thousand pictures of presenting myself to them, and their reception of me. I imagined that they would be disgusted, until, by my gentle demeanour and conciliating words, I should first win their favour, and afterwards their love.

" These thoughts exhilarated me, and led me to apply with fresh ardour to the acquiring the art of language. My organs were indeed harsh, but supple ; and although my voice was very unlike the soft music of their tones, yet I pronounced such words as I understood with tolerable ease. It was **8** as the ass and the lap-dog ; yet surely the gentle ass, whose intentions were affectionate, although his manners were rude, deserved better treatment than blows and execration.

" The pleasant showers and genial warmth of spring greatly altered the aspect of the earth. Men, who before this change seemed to have been hid in caves, dispersed themselves, and were employed in various arts of cultivation. The birds sang in more cheer-

9 *Happy, happy earth!* The creature, like Victor, his creator, has a Romantic sensibility and is responsive to the more genial shows of nature.

ful notes, and the leaves began to bud forth on the trees. Happy, happy earth ! fit habitation for gods, which, so short a time before, was bleak, damp, and unwholesome. My spirits were elevated by the enchanting appearance of nature ; the past was blotted from my memory, the present was tranquil, and the future gilded by bright rays of hope, and anticipations of joy.

CHAPTER V.

" **I** now hasten to the more moving part of my story. I shall relate events that impressed me with feelings which, from what I was, have made me what I am.

" Spring advanced rapidly; the weather became fine, and the skies cloudless. It surprised me, that what before was desert and gloomy should now bloom with the most beautiful flowers and verdure. My senses were gratified and refreshed by a thousand scents of delight, and a thousand sights of beauty.

" It was on one of these days, when my cottagers periodically rested from labour—the old man played on his guitar, and the children listened to him—I observed that the countenance of Felix was melancholy beyond expression: he sighed frequently; and once his father paused in his music, and I conjectured by his manner that he inquired the cause of his son's sorrow. Felix replied in a cheerful accent, and the old man was recommencing his music, when some one tapped at the door.

" It was a lady on horseback, accompanied by a countryman as a guide. The lady was dressed in a dark suit, and covered with a thick black veil. Agatha asked a question; to which the stran-

1 *what I am*. The creature, in the best Godwinian style, is presented to us as having been created essentially "good." Humankind, in Godwin's view, was naturally perfectible so long as it exercised its reason. Evil came about in the world because of prejudice and/or unreason. See the many pages on which the creature argues his primordial innocence, and that he has been driven to evil only because of what was done to him (pp. 193, 194, 202–3, 209–10, 213).

2 *Spring advanced*. If, as appears likely, it is now April, the creature is six months old.

3 *guitar*. We see now what the instrument was with which the old man soothed or intensified the melancholy feelings of his children.

4 *a lovely pink*. The distance from the creature's chink to the door is either very small or else his eyes are very sharp for him to be able to see so much from his hiding place.

ger only replied by pronouncing, in a sweet accent, the name of Felix. Her voice was musical, but unlike that of either of my friends. On hearing this word, Felix came up hastily to the lady; who, when she saw him, threw up her veil, and I beheld a countenance of angelic beauty and expression. Her hair of a shining raven black, and curiously braided; her eyes were dark, but gentle, although animated; her features of a regular proportion, and her complexion wondrously fair, each cheek tinged **4** with a lovely pink.

" Felix seemed ravished with delight when he saw her, every trait of sorrow vanished from his face, and it instantly expressed a degree of ecstatic joy, of which I could hardly have believed it capable; his eyes sparkled, as his cheek flushed with pleasure; and at that moment I thought him as beautiful as the stranger. She appeared affected by different feelings; wiping a few tears from her lovely eyes, she held out her hand to Felix, who kissed it rapturously, and called her, as well as I could distinguish, his sweet Arabian. She did not appear to understand him, but smiled. He assisted her to dismount, and, dismissing her guide, conducted her into the cottage. Some conversation took place between him and his father; and the young stranger knelt at the old man's feet, and would have kissed his hand, but he raised her, and embraced her affectionately.

" I soon perceived, that although the stranger uttered articulate sounds, and appeared to have a language of her own, she was neither understood by, or

5 *Agatha*. This line is the only hint we have that the creature has fallen in love with Agatha. Though nothing is made of this moment of tenderness, it seems clear that the sight of the unattached Agatha in the presence of the reunited lovers stirs the creature to the sexual musings whose consequences we will later discover. At this moment, certainly, Agatha in the presence of the reunited lovers is *de trop*—as Claire Clairmont was in the Shelley household for too many years.

6 *the others*. The creature's intellectual prowess is spectacular. As we will see, he moves from these primitive language lessons to the most sophisticated competence. It is a feat almost as dramatic as, in later years, the boy Tarzan would perform on the coast of Africa where he taught himself to read and write by deciphering the meaning of twenty-six "bugs" he found crawling across the pages of a child's primer. Edgar Rice Burroughs, in *Tarzan of the Apes* (1912), p. 49, tells the story without blushing: "Squatting upon his haunches on the table top in the cabin his father had built—his smooth, brown, naked little body bent over the book which rested in his strong slender hands, and his great shock of long, black hair falling about his well-shaped head and bright, intelligent eyes—Tarzan of the apes, little primitive man, presented a picture filled, at once, with pathos and with promise—an allegorical figure of the primordial groping through the black night of ignorance toward the light of learning.

"His little face was tense in study, for he had partially grasped, in a hazy, nebulous way, the rudiments of a thought which was destined to prove the key and the solution to the puzzling problem of the strange little bugs.

"In his hands was a primer opened at a picture of a little ape similar to himself, but covered, except for hands and face, with strange, colored fur, for such he thought the jacket and trousers to be. Beneath the picture were three little bugs—BOY

"And now he had discovered in the text upon the page that these three were repeated many times in the same sequence. Slowly he turned the pages, scanning the pictures and the text for a repetition of the combination b-o-y. Presently he found it beneath a picture of another little ape and a strange animal which went upon four legs like the jackal and resembled him not at all: A BOY AND A DOG

"There they were, the three little bugs which always accompanied the little ape.

"And so he progressed very, very slowly, for it was a hard and laborious task which he had set himself without knowing it—a task which might seem to you or me impossible—learning to read without having the slightest knowledge of letters or written language, or the faintest idea that such things existed."

---

herself understood, the cottagers. They made many signs which I did not comprehend; but I saw that her presence diffused gladness through the cottage, dispelling their sorrow as the sun dissipates the morning mists. Felix seemed peculiarly happy, and with smiles of delight welcomed his Arabian. Agatha, the ever-gentle Agatha, kissed the hands of the lovely stranger; and, pointing to her brother, made signs which appeared to me to mean that he had been sorrowful until she came. Some hours passed thus, while they, by their countenances, expressed joy, the cause of which I did not comprehend. Presently I found, by the frequent recurrence of one sound which the stranger repeated after them, that she was endeavouring to learn their language; and the idea instantly occurred to me, that I should make use of the same instructions to the same end. The stranger learned about twenty words at the first lesson, most of them indeed were those which I had before understood, but I profited by the others.

" As night came on, Agatha and the Arabian retired early. When they separated, Felix kissed the hand of the stranger, and said, 'Good night, sweet Safie.' He sat up much longer, conversing with his father; and, by the frequent repetition of her name, I conjectured that their lovely guest was the subject of their conversation. I ardently desired to understand them, and bent every faculty towards that purpose, but found it utterly impossible.

" The next morning Felix went out to his work; and, after the usual occupations of Agatha were finished, the Arabian sat at the feet of the old man, and, taking his guitar, played some airs so entrancingly beautiful, that they at once drew tears of sorrow and delight from my eyes. She sang, and her voice flowed in a rich cadence, swelling or dying away, like a nightingale of the woods.

When she had finished, she gave the guitar to Agatha, who at first declined it. She played a simple air, and her voice accompanied it in sweet accents, but unlike the wondrous strain of the stranger. The old man appeared enraptured, and said some words, which Agatha endeavoured to explain to Safie, and by which he appeared to wish to express that she bestowed on him the greatest delight by her music.

The days now passed as peaceably as before, with the sole alteration, that joy had taken place of sadness in the countenances of my friends. Safie was always gay and happy; she and I improved rapidly in the knowledge of language, so that in two months I began to comprehend most of the words uttered by my protectors.

In the meanwhile also the black ground was covered with herbage, and the green banks interspersed with innumerable flowers, sweet to the scent and the eyes, stars of pale radiance among the moonlight woods; the sun became warmer, the nights clear and balmy; and my nocturnal rambles were an extreme pleasure to me, although they were considerably shortened by the late setting and early rising of the sun; for I never ventured abroad during daylight, fearful of meeting with the same

7 *improved more rapidly*. The creature's jealousy of Safie is perhaps the only successful moment of deliberate humor in the novel.

There is little reason for the creature to boast. French is, after all, his "native" tongue, and he has been acquiring it in that period most fit for language study—his infancy. Safie, on the other hand, has to deal with Turkish as an impediment to her learning, not to mention the embarrassments produced by love.

VOLNEY.

8 Ruins of Empires. Constantin François de Chassebœuf, comte de Volney, was born in 1757, and died in 1820. His *Les Ruines, ou Méditations sur les Révolutions des Empires* was published in 1791. A passionate lover of liberty, and an ardent supporter of the French Revolution, Volney was, nevertheless, tried for being a royalist and spent ten months in prison. *Les Ruines* is a rationalist's lively attack against received religion, whether Jewish, Christian, or Islamic. Volney was a most extraordinary man who, well before Richard F. Burton achieved fame as a scholar-adventurer in the Arab world, decided to immerse himself in the civilization of the Middle East. Volney, while still quite young, made the long journey from Egypt to Syria. To prepare himself for the journey (like our Walton preparing himself for his destiny), Volney practiced horsemanship, undertook long walks, leaped over ditches, and trained himself to live without food. Volney, among his many other wanderings, found his way to the United States and produced a volume describing its climate and soil.

9 *of its original inhabitants*. Volney's view of the original inhabitants, as he developed it in his appendix to *Tableau du Climat et du Sol des États-Unis*, is considerably less sympathetic to them than Mary Shelley's. Volney writes: "[There] the Indians of the

treatment as I had formerly endured in the first village which I entered.

"My days were spent in close attention, that I might more speedily master the language; and I may boast that I **7** improved more rapidly than the Arabian, who understood very little, and conversed in broken accents, whilst I comprehended and could imitate almost every word that was spoken.

While I improved in speech, I also learned the science of letters, as it was taught to the stranger; and this opened before me a wide field for wonder and delight.

"The book from which Felix instruct-**8** ed Safie was Volney's *Ruins of Empires*. I should not have understood the purport of this book, had not Felix, in reading it, given very minute explanations. He had chosen this work, he said, because the declamatory style was framed in imitation of the eastern authors. Through this work I obtained a cursory knowledge of history, and a view of the several empires at present existing in the world; it gave me an insight into the manners, governments, and religions of the different nations of the earth. I heard of the slothful Asiatics; of the stupendous genius and mental activity of the Grecians; of the wars and wonderful virtue of the early Romans—of their subsequent degeneration—of the decline of that mighty empire; of chivalry, christianity, and kings. I heard of the discovery of the American hemisphere, and wept with Safie over the **9** hapless fate of its original inhabitants.

"These wonderful narrations inspired me with strange feelings. Was man, indeed, at once so powerful, so virtuous,

Alleghenies were for me a new and bizarre experience. Imagine nearly nude bodies darkened by the sun and the air, glistening with grease and smoke, bare headed with coarse straight limp black hair, their faces masked with black, blue or red . . . a nostril pierced to hold a copper or silver ring, . . . a little square of cloth covering the pubic area, another covering the tailbone, thighs and legs bare, or sometimes covered with what the English called leggings, shoes of smoked hide on their feet. . .

"This is only a sketch of the tableau and I am showing its better side, because if one wants to see the whole thing, one needs to add that in the morning men and women wander through the streets with the sole purpose of finding whiskey; that having sold first their furs, then their jewelry, then their clothing, they continue to search for drink like beggars, never ceasing their libations until they have absolutely lost their faculties. Sometimes there are burlesque scenes, as when they cling to the cup with both hands trying to drink in the manner of apes, or when they gargle their delicious and *funeste* liquor . . . sometimes they take their women by their heads, pour the whiskey down their throats, making at the same time their gross caresses. Sometimes these moments are followed by afflicting scenes in which they finally lose all sense, all reason and turn furious and stupid or fall dead drunk in the dust or in the mud . . . On the ninth of August four o'clock in the afternoon, twenty paces from me, one of these savages stabbed his wife with four blows of his knife."

It needs to be added that Volney was as disenchanted with his own civilization as he was with that of the Indians. Whatever his revulsion, he set himself to a careful study of Indian life and produced a vocabulary of the Miami language.

10 *disgust and loathing.* There is a certain echo in the preceding sentences of Gulliver's reaction to his own species after his salubrious experience in the land of the Houyhnhnms. Having described the vice and bloodshed of the human world to his kindly Houyhnhnm master in chapters five through nine of *Gulliver's Travels*, Gulliver suddenly realizes that humans are, in fact, the same species as the detestable Yahoos, "perhaps a little more civilized and qualified with the Gift of Speech; but making no other Use of Reason, than to improve and multiply those Vices, whereof their Brethren in this Country had only the Share that Nature allotted them. When I happened to behold the Reflection of my own Form in a Lake or Fountain, I turned away my Face in Horror and detestation of myself; and could not endure the Sight of a common Yahoo" (*The Writings of Jonathan Swift*, p. 243).

On November 9 and 11, 1816, as we know from Mary Shelley's *Journals*, Percy Shelley read aloud from *Gulliver's Travels*; and *Gulliver's Travels* is listed as one of the books that Mary Shelley read during 1816.

and magnificent, yet so vicious and base? He appeared at one time a mere scion of the evil principle, and at another as all that can be conceived of noble and godlike. To be a great and virtuous man appeared the highest honour that can befall a sensitive being; to be base and vicious, as many on record have been, appeared the lowest degradation, a condition more abject than that of the blind mole or harmless worm. For a long time I could not conceive how one man could go forth to murder his fellow, or even why there were laws and governments; but when I heard details of vice and bloodshed, my wonder ceased, and I **10** turned away with disgust and loathing.

" Every conversation of the cottagers now opened new wonders to me. While I listened to the instructions which Felix bestowed upon the Arabian, the strange system of human society was explained to me. I heard of the division of property, of immense wealth and squalid poverty; of rank, descent, and noble blood.

" The words induced me to turn towards myself. I learned that the possessions most esteemed by your fellow-creatures were, high and unsullied descent united with riches. A man might be respected with only one of these acquisitions; but without either he was considered, except in very rare instances, as a vagabond and a slave, doomed to waste his powers for the profit of the chosen few. And what was I? Of my creation and creator I was absolutely ignorant; but I knew that I possessed no money, no friends, no kind of property. I was, besides, endowed with a figure hideously deformed and loathsome; I was not even of the same nature as man. I was more agile than they, and could subsist upon coarser diet; I bore the extremes of heat and cold with less injury to my frame; my stature far exceeded their's. When I looked around, I saw and heard of none like me. Was I then a monster, a blot upon the earth, from which all men fled, and whom all men disowned?

" I cannot describe to you the agony that these reflections inflicted upon me; I tried to dispel them, but sorrow only increased with knowledge. Oh, that I had for ever remained in my native wood, nor known or felt beyond the sensations of hunger, thirst, and heat!

" Of what a strange nature is knowledge! It clings to the mind, when it has once seized on it, like a lichen on the rock. I wished sometimes to shake off all thought and feeling; but I learned that there was but one means to overcome the sensation of pain, and that was death—a state which I feared yet did not understand. I admired virtue and good feelings, and loved the gentle manners and amiable qualities of my cottagers; but I was shut out from intercourse with them, except through means which I obtained by stealth, when I was unseen and unknown, and which rather increased than satisfied the desire I had of becoming one among my fellows. The gentle words of Agatha, and the animated smiles of the charming Arabian, were not for me. The mild exhortations of the old man, and

11 *distinguished nothing.* Though the poignancy of a creature without memory or childhood is touched on in the various film versions of *Frankenstein*, it has been developed most effectively in the movie *The Mind of Mr. Soames*, which tells the story of Jonathan Soames, born in a coma and kept alive until he reached adulthood when he was made conscious by means of electrotherapy. The film, while only modestly interesting in other respects, catches vividly the pain of consciousness entering an adult mind for the first time.

12 *my protectors.* This is a splendidly imagined fictional moment. The pathos of the creature's fantasy relationship to this idealized family has already been touched on. For the creature to think of them now as *his* protectors is one of the subtler ways Mary Shelley has found for compounding the unhappy being's pain.

the lively conversation of the loved Felix, were not for me. Miserable, unhapp wretch!

" Other lessons were impressed upon me even more deeply. I heard of the difference of sexes; of the birth and growth of children; how the father doated on the smiles of the infant, and the lively sallies of the older child; how all the life and cares of the mother were wrapt up in the precious charge; how the mind of youth expanded and gained knowledge; of brother, sister, and all the various relationships which bind one human being to another in mutual bonds.

" But where were my friends and relations? No father had watched my infant days, no mother had blessed me with smiles and caresses; or if they had, all my past life was now a blot, a blind **11** vacancy in which I distinguished nothing. From my earliest remembrance I had been as I then was in height and proportion. I had never yet seen a being resembling me, or who claimed any intercourse with me. What was I? The question again recurred, to be answered only with groans.

" I will soon explain to what these feelings tended; but allow me now to return to the cottagers, whose story excited in me such various feelings of indignation, delight, and wonder, but which all terminated in additional love **12** and reverence for my protectors (for so I loved, in an innocent, half painful self-deceit, to call them).

CHAPTER VI.

" SOME time elapsed before I learned the history of my friends. It was one which could not fail to impress itself deeply on my mind, unfolding as it did a number of circumstances each interesting and wonderful to one so utterly inexperienced as I was.

" The name of the old man was De Lacey. He was descended from a good family in France, where he had lived for many years in affluence, respected by his superiors, and beloved by his equals. His son was bred in the service of his country; and Agatha had ranked with ladies of the highest distinction. A few months before my arrival, they had lived in a large and luxurious city, called Paris, surrounded by friends, and possessed of every enjoyment which virtue, refinement of intellect, or taste, accompanied by a moderate fortune, could afford.

" The father of Safie had been the cause of their ruin. He was a Turkish merchant, and had inhabited Paris for many years, when, for some reason which I could not learn, he became obnoxious to the government. He was seized and cast into prison the very day that Safie arrived from Constantinople to join him. He was tried, and condemned to death. The injustice of his sentence was very flagrant; all Paris

"HE WAS A TURKISH MERCHANT."

CONSTANTINOPLE.

1 *the trial.* How Felix, who was presumably "in the service of his country," managed to be at the trial during working hours, we must not presume to ask.

was indignant; and it was judged that his religion and wealth, rather than the crime alleged against him, had been the cause of his condemnation.

1   " Felix had been present at the trial ; his horror and indignation were uncontrollable, when he heard the decision of the court.   He made, at that moment, a solemn vow to deliver him, and then looked around for the means.   After many fruitless attempts to gain admittance to the prison, he found a strongly grated window in an unguarded part of the building, which lighted the dungeon of the unfortunate Mahometan ; who, loaded with chains, waited in despair the execution of the barbarous sentence.   Felix visited the grate at night, and made known to the prisoner his intentions in his favour. The Turk, amazed and delighted, endeavoured to kindle the zeal of his deliverer by promises of reward and wealth.   Felix rejected his offers with contempt; yet when he saw the lovely Safie, who was allowed to visit her father, and who, by her gestures, expressed her lively gratitude, the youth could not help owning to his own mind, that the captive possessed a treasure which would fully reward his toil and hazard.

" The Turk quickly perceived the impression that his daughter had made on the heart of Felix, and endeavoured to secure him more entirely in his interests by the promise of her hand in marriage, so soon as he should be conveyed to a place of safety.   Felix was too delicate to accept this offer; yet he looked forward to the probability of

2 *to procure the implements of writing.* How the creature did all this, we are left to imagine. One has to admire what is either Mary Shelley's innocence, or her audacity, as she repeatedly makes demands on her readers to ignore the problems of the real world, which ordinarily limit even a fictional character's behavior. What were the writing implements? Pens, ink, pencils? How did the creature manage to get close enough to the letters to copy them?

On the other hand, if we have accepted the story of the creature's education-through-a-peephole, we may not be entitled to ask our carping questions. Perhaps the answer to them has to be that the creature, and Mary Shelley, his true creator, were both geniuses.

"THE LOVELY SAFIE."

that event as to the consummation of his happiness.

" During the ensuing days, while the preparations were going forward for the escape of the merchant, the zeal of Felix was warmed by several letters that he received from this lovely girl, who found means to express her thoughts in the language of her lover by the aid of an old man, a servant of her father's, who understood French. She thanked him in the most ardent terms for his intended services towards her father ; and at the same time she gently deplored her own fate.

" I have copies of these letters ; for I found means, during my residence in **2** the hovel, to procure the implements of writing ; and the letters were often in the hands of Felix or Agatha. Before I depart, I will give them to you, they will prove the truth of my tale ;

3 *made a slave by the Turks*. It is possible that Safie's mother was taken in slavery by the corsairs, pirates usually based in the seaside towns of North Africa such as Algiers and Tunis, who lived by plundering the merchant vessels sailing in the Mediterranean as well as the coastal cities of Spain, Italy, France, and sometimes England and Ireland. Their Christian captives became slaves and the women frequently found themselves in a Turkish harem. These pirates were so skillful that the Turks made use of them in their navy, where the pirate leaders often became admirals. The famous pirate Barbarossa became a Turkish admiral in this way.

"RECOMMENDED BY HER BEAUTY."

4 *now reduced*. This description of the position of the "female followers of Mahomet" may reflect some of Mary Wollstonecraft's remarks in *A Vindication of the Rights of Woman*: "In the true style of Mahometanism, they [women] are treated as a kind of subordinate beings, and not as a part of the human species" (Poston edition, p. 8). Or: "In the true Mahometan strain . . . to deprive us of souls, and insinuate that we were beings only designed by sweet attractive grace, and docile blind obedience, to gratify the senses of man" (Poston edition, p. 19).

5 *her religion*. The Christian religion.

but at present, as the sun is already far declined, I shall only have time to repeat the substance of them to you.

" Safie related, that her mother was **3** a Christian Arab, seized and made a slave by the Turks; recommended by her beauty, she had won the heart of the father of Safie, who married her. The young girl spoke in high and enthusiastic terms of her mother, who, born in freedom spurned the bondage **4** to which she was now reduced. She instructed her daughter in the tenets **5** of her religion, and taught her to aspire to higher powers of intellect, and an independence of spirit, forbidden to the female followers of Mahomet. This lady died; but her lessons were indelibly impressed on the mind of Safie, who sickened at the prospect of again returning to Asia, and the being im- **6** mured within the walls of a haram, allowed only to occupy herself with puerile amusements, ill suited to the temper of her soul, now accustomed to grand ideas and a noble emulation for virtue. The prospect of marrying a Christian, and remaining in a country

"TAUGHT HER TO ASPIRE TO HIGHER POWERS OF INTELLECT."

"WITHIN THE WALLS OF A HARAM."

6 *haram*. This is the typical European view of the Turkish harem, but not at all a correct one according to *The Harem*, published in 1937, by N. M. Penzer, a book that examines this institution at great length. He writes: "So far from being a palace of women lazing about marble halls awaiting their master's pleasure, the *harem* was a little world of its own, governed with the utmost deliberation and care, not by a man at all, but by a woman. Every member of it had her exact duties to perform, and was forced to comply with all the rules and regulations that in many respects were as strict and rigid as in a convent" (p. 14).

7 *aided the deceit*. Whatever Felix's other virtues as a son and brother may be, he shows reckless judgment here in making willing accomplices of his father and sister.

8 *Mont Cenis to Leghorn.*

MONT CENIS: an Alpine pass a few miles north of the Italian border.

LEGHORN: an Italian port city forty miles west of Florence, also known as Livorno. In the eighteenth century it was part of the duchy of Tuscany. During World War II, it lost two of its important Renaissance buildings to German bombardment—its cathedral and its synagogue.

where women were allowed to take a rank in society, was enchanting to her.

" The day for the execution of the Turk was fixed ; but, on the night previous to it, he had quitted prison, and before morning was distant many leagues from Paris. Felix had procured passports in the name of his father, sister, and himself. He had previously communicated his plan to the **7** former, who aided the deceit by quitting his house, under the pretence of a journey, and concealed himself, with his daughter, in an obscure part of Paris.

" Felix conducted the fugitives through France to Lyons, and across **8** Mont Cenis to Leghorn, where the merchant had decided to wait a favourable opportunity of passing into some part of the Turkish dominions.

" Safie resolved to remain with her father until the moment of his departure, before which time the Turk renewed his promise that she should be united to his deliverer ; and Felix remained with them in expectation of that event ; and in the mean time he enjoyed the society of the Arabian, who exhibited towards him the simplest and tenderest affection. They conversed with one another through the means of an interpreter, and sometimes with the interpretation of looks ; and Safie sang to him the divine airs of her native country.

" The Turk allowed this intimacy to take place, and encouraged the hopes of the youthful lovers, while in his heart he had formed far other plans. He loathed the idea that his daughter should be united to a Christian ; but he feared the resentment of Felix if he

9 *for escape*. The Turk, left to his own devices, is effectively a free man. The word *escape* hardly fits his situation.

should appear lukewarm ; for he knew that he was still in the power of his deliverer, if he should choose to betray him to the Italian state which they inhabited. He revolved a thousand plans by which he should be enabled to prolong the deceit until it might be no longer necessary, and secretly to take his daughter with him when he departed. His plans were greatly facilitated by the news which arrived from Paris.

" The government of France were greatly enraged at the escape of their victim, and spared no pains to detect and punish his deliverer. The plot of Felix was quickly discovered, and De Lacey and Agatha were thrown into prison. The news reached Felix, and roused him from his dream of pleasure. His blind and aged father, and his gentle sister, lay in a noisome dungeon, while he enjoyed the free air, and the society of her whom he loved. This idea was torture to him. He quickly arranged with the Turk, that if the latter should find a favourable opportunity for escape before Felix could return to Italy, Safie should remain as a boarder at a convent at Leghorn ; and then, quitting the lovely Arabian, he hastened to Paris, and delivered himself up to the vengeance of the law, hoping to free De Lacey and Agatha by this proceeding.

" He did not succeed. They remained confined for five months before the trial took place ; the result of which deprived them of their fortune, and condemned them to a perpetual exile from their native country.

" They found a miserable asylum

10 *maintenance*. Up to this point, the details we get are from the point of view of the De Laceys. In the pages below, they are told from Safie's viewpoint.

in the cottage in Germany, where I discovered them. Felix soon learned that the treacherous Turk, for whom he and his family endured such unheard-of oppression, on discovering that his deliverer was thus reduced to poverty and impotence, became a traitor to good feeling and honour, and had quitted Italy with his daughter, insultingly sending Felix a pittance of money to aid him, as he said, in some plan of

10 future maintenance.

" Such were the events that preyed on the heart of Felix, and rendered him, when I first saw him, the most miserable of his family. He could have endured poverty, and when this distress had been the meed of his virtue, he would have gloried in it: but the ingratitude of the Turk, and the loss of his beloved Safie, were misfortunes more bitter and irreparable. The arrival of the Arabian now infused new life into his soul.

" When the news reached Leghorn, that Felix was deprived of his wealth and rank, the merchant commanded his daughter to think no more of her lover, but to prepare to return with him to her native country. The generous nature of Safie was outraged by this command; she attempted to expostulate with her father, but he left her angrily, reiterating his tyrannical mandate.

" A few days after, the Turk entered his daughter's apartment, and told her hastily, that he had reason to believe that his residence at Leghorn had been divulged, and that he should speedily be delivered up to the French govern-

11 *some jewels.* These jewels are carefully specified as belonging to Safie, as if our author were very anxious not to have us think the beautiful Arabian is a sneak-thief. The sum of money too is specified as "small," as if pilferage, not theft, was the crime.

Later we will see that Victor too takes jewels and money with him for a journey (Vol. III, p. 300).

12 *of her lover.* Even the most ardent admirer of *Frankenstein* must concede that the Safie-Felix-Agatha-De Lacey interlude is much too long. Nor is one's patience soothed by knowing that just such silken departures from a central plot are very much in the tradition of the sorts of terror fiction that Mary Shelley knew best.

Having said that the De Lacey interpolation is too long, it is still possible to see it as aptly serving Mary Shelley's theme. The De Laceys were, after all, the creature's first sustained view of humankind. From his yearning vantage point beside the chink in his wall, they seemed to him to be the inhabitants of paradise. Despite their initial wistfulness without Safie, they were all love and tenderness. With her, the cottage turned entirely to sweetness and light. When the creature is spurned by these beloved beings, their fear of him deprives him abruptly not *of* paradise, because he was never in it, but of his voyeur's glimpse of it. Adam, when he was expelled from Eden, left it in the company of Eve. The creature, in or out of happiness, is, each time, alone.

ment; he had, consequently, hired a vessel to convey him to Constantinople, for which city he should sail in a few hours. He intended to leave his daughter under the care of a confidential servant, to follow at her leisure with the greater part of his property, which had not yet arrived at Leghorn.

" When alone, Safie resolved in her own mind the plan of conduct that it would become her to pursue in this emergency. A residence in Turkey was abhorrent to her; her religion and feelings were alike adverse to it. By some papers of her father's, which fell into her hands, she heard of the exile of her lover, and learnt the name of the spot where he then resided. She hesitated some time, but at length she formed her determination. Taking **11** with her some jewels that belonged to her, and a small sum of money, she quitted Italy, with an attendant, a native of Leghorn, but who understood the common language of Turkey, and departed for Germany.

" She arrived in safety at a town about twenty leagues from the cottage of De Lacey, when her attendant fell dangerously ill. Safie nursed her with the most devoted affection; but the poor girl died, and the Arabian was left alone, unacquainted with the language of the country, and utterly ignorant of the customs of the world. She fell, however, into good hands. The Italian had mentioned the name of the spot for which they were bound; and, after her death, the woman of the house in which they had lived took care that Safie should arrive in safety at the cot- **12** tage of her lover.

1 *a leathern portmanteau.* Coincidence, ever on the side of our author, comes to her aid once more. The found books are easy enough to accept but, as with the cloak found earlier, it is hard to believe that the clothes in the portmanteau will fit our creature.

2 *Paradise Lost.* The creature, whose native language is French, gets his education from translations. There were many French editions of each of these works. The ones available to the De Laceys in the late eighteenth century were: *Les Vies de Hommes Illustrés de Plutarque*, translated by Jacques Amyot, Paris, 1783–1787; *Les Passions du Jeune Werther*, translated by C. Aubrey (pseud.), Paris, 1797; *Le Paradis Perdu de Milton*, prose translation by N. F. Dupré de Saint-Maur, Paris, 1788.

The book list is both impressive and important, though one needs to note, as James Rieger does in his edition of *Frankenstein*, that La Fontaine's *Fables* is not mentioned, though we know that they are part of the creature's education (see p. 165, note 8).

The book list is a careful one. Each volume is intended to nurture a particular aspect of the creature's character: Goethe's *The Sorrows of Young Werther* (1774) teaches him about love; Plutarch's *Lives* instructs him in civic responsibilities, and *Paradise Lost* offers him a justification of God's ways to men.

3 *Plutarch's Lives. Plutarch's Lives*, also known as *Plutarch's Parallel Lives*. Plutarch's (A.D.45–125) biographical technique was to present the life first of a great Greek, then of an eminent Roman. The two biographies were then followed by an essay in which the lives were compared and contrasted. This technique should be of interest to readers of *Frankenstein* because Mary Shelley too presents the lives of her protagonists in parallel sets: Robert Walton and Victor Frankenstein; Victor Frankenstein and Henry Clerval; Victor Frankenstein and his creature; Justine and Elizabeth.

Percy Shelley was reading *Plutarch's Parallel Lives* on August 18–20 and again on November 17–19 and 25–27 of 1816 when Mary Shelley was well launched into writing *Frankenstein*.

4 *Sorrows of Werter.* It was a matter of some poignant interest to Mary Shelley that *The Sorrows of Young Werther* (1774) was the book that her parents, William Godwin and Mary Wollstonecraft, read together on the morning before she, Mary Shelley, was born.

CHAPTER VII.

" Such was the history of my beloved cottagers. It impressed me deeply. I learned, from the views of social life which it developed, to admire their virtues, and to deprecate the vices of mankind.

As yet I looked upon crime as a distant evil; benevolence and generosity were ever present before me, inciting within me a desire to become an actor in the busy scene where so many admirable qualities were called forth and displayed. But, in giving an account of the progress of my intellect, I must not omit a circumstance which occurred in the beginning of the month of August of the same year.

" One night, during my accustomed visit to the neighbouring wood, where I collected my own food, and brought home firing for my protectors, I found [1] on the ground a leathern portmanteau, containing several articles of dress and some books. I eagerly seized the prize, and returned with it to my hovel. Fortunately the books were written in the language the elements of which I had acquired at the cottage; they consisted of *Paradise Lost*, a volume of [2] *Plutarch's Lives*, and the *Sorrows of Werter*. The possession of these treasures gave me extreme delight; I now continually studied and exercised my mind upon these histories, whilst my [3,4]

"THE SORROWS OF WERTER."

5 *understanding it.* It will be remembered that *The Sorrows of Young Werther* recounts the increasing isolation from his fellow man experienced by the young Werther because of his hopeless love for Lotte, which leads him finally to suicide. The *Sorrows* had a tremendous impact on Europe at the time it appeared and young Werther's anguish and sometimes his end became models for the Romantic image of how young love should be endured—that is to say, with deep, deep feeling and extreme gestures.

The letters Mary Wollstonecraft wrote to William Godwin (see Introduction to this edition) were compared by him to those letters Goethe imagined for Werther. Godwin considered the Wollstonecraft letters superior to Goethe's because they savored of the reality out of which they were written, while Goethe's were works of fiction.

Godwin also considered Mary Wollstonecraft's youthful and passionate attachment to her friend Frances Blood as comparable to Werther's tragic infatuation with Lotte. Mary Shelley may have been more interested in the fact that Frances Blood, stricken by a childbed illness, died, in the fall of 1875, in Lisbon, in Mary Wollstonecraft's arms.

friends were employed in their ordinary occupations.

" I can hardly describe to you the effect of these books. They produced in me an infinity of new images and feelings, that sometimes raised me to ecstacy, but more frequently sunk me into the lowest dejection. In the *Sorrows of Werter*, besides the interest of its simple and affecting story, so many opinions are canvassed, and so many lights thrown upon what had hitherto been to me obscure subjects, that I found in it a never-ending source of speculation and astonishment. The gentle and domestic manners it described, combined with lofty sentiments and feelings, which had for their object something out of self, accorded well with my experience among my protectors, and with the wants which were for ever alive in my own bosom. But I thought Werter himself a more divine being than I had ever beheld or imagined; his character contained no pretension, but it sunk deep. The disquisitions upon death and suicide were calculated to fill me with wonder. I did not pretend to enter into the merits of the case, yet I inclined towards the opinions of the hero, whose extinction I wept, without precisely understanding it.

" As I read, however, I applied much personally to my own feelings and condition. I found myself similar, yet at the same time strangely unlike the beings concerning whom I read, and to whose conversation I was a listener. I sympathized with, and partly understood them, but I was

6 *was free*. The creature, like Victor, seems to have read Shelley's poem "Mutability," a line of which this is a paraphrase. (See p. 137, note 5.)

7 *the ancient republics*. Of Greece and Rome.

unformed in mind; I was dependent on none, and related to none. ' The path of my departure was free;' and there was none to lament my annihilation. My person was hideous, and my stature gigantic: what did this mean? Who was I? What was I? Whence did I come? What was my destination? These questions continually recurred, but I was unable to solve them.

" The volume of *Plutarch's Lives* which I possessed, contained the histories of the first founders of the ancient republics. This book had a far different effect upon me from the *Sorrows of Werter*. I learned from Werter's imaginations despondency and gloom: but Plutarch taught me high thoughts; he elevated me above the wretched sphere of my own reflections, to admire and love the heroes of past ages. Many things I read surpassed my understanding and experience. I had a very confused knowledge of kingdoms, wide extents of country, mighty rivers, and boundless seas. But I was perfectly unacquainted with towns, and large assemblages of men. The cottage of my protectors had been the only school in which I had studied human nature; but this book developed new and mightier scenes of action. I read of men concerned in public affairs governing or massacring their species. I felt the greatest ardour for virtue rise within me, and abhorrence for vice, as far as I understood the signification of those terms, relative as they were, as I applied them, to pleasure and pain alone. Induced by these feelings, I was of course

8 *Numa, Solon, and Lycurgus . . . Romulus and Theseus.* All five are subjects of biographies in *Plutarch's Lives*, a book that Mary Shelley read in 1815, and which Percy Shelley read at intervals (August 18–20, November 17–19, and November 25–27).

Numa was Numa Pompilius, the second legendary king of Rome who ruled it in the years 714–671 B.C. Solon, one of the Seven Sages of Greece, is famous for easing the tax burden of the Athenian poor, and for giving Athens a liberal constitution. Lycurgus was a Spartan lawgiver of the ninth century B.C. who, after travelling widely, returned to Sparta where he instituted reforms in Spartan law.

The creature has learned from Plutarch to admire the lawgivers in preference to Romulus and Theseus, and the reason is plain: Romulus, in addition to his fame as the first legendary founder of Rome, is notorious in classical history for having instigated the Rape of the Sabine Women. As for Theseus, the daring warrior who, among other feats, slew the Minotaur—his fame too would be tainted because, as Mary Shelley read in her Plutarch, Theseus was a practiced philanderer who not only abandoned the devoted Ariadne after she showed him how to escape from the perils of the labyrinth, but went on to make an unenviable record as a frequent rapist.

What may have been of special interest to Mary Shelley is that when the Athenians, long after Theseus's death, dug up his grave on the island of Scyros what they found were his remains in the "coffin of a man of extraordinary size" (*Plutarch's Lives*, p. 12).

9 *superior nature.* The creature is referring to Milton's *Paradise Lost*, where Adam is instructed on various occasions by the angels Raphael and Michael, as well as by God Himself. The creature might have remarked, however, that even with such superior instruction, things did not work out too well for Adam in paradise.

10 *Satan.* It is most often the creature who styles himself as Satan, as when he says, "I, like the arch fiend, bore a hell within me" (p. 196); or when he quotes from Milton's Satan "Evil thenceforth became my good" (Vol. III, p. 329). But Victor too says that "I bore a hell within me" (Vol. I, p. 120), and that "like the archangel who aspired to omnipotence, I am chained in an eternal hell" (Vol. III, p. 316).

8 led to admire peaceable law-givers, Numa, Solon, and Lycurgus, in preference to Romulus and Theseus. The patriarchal lives of my protectors caused these impressions to take a firm hold on my mind; perhaps, if my first introduction to humanity had been made by a young soldier, burning for glory and slaughter, I should have been imbued with different sensations.

" But *Paradise Lost* excited different and far deeper emotions. I read it, as I had read the other volumes which had fallen into my hands, as a true history. It moved every feeling of wonder and awe, that the picture of an omnipotent God warring with his creatures was capable of exciting. I often referred the several situations, as their similarity struck me, to my own. Like Adam, I was created apparently united by no link to any other being in existence; but his state was far different from mine in every other respect. He had come forth from the hands of God a perfect creature, happy and prosperous, guarded by the especial care of his Creator; he was allowed to converse with, and acquire knowledge from beings of a **9** superior nature : but I was wretched, helpless, and alone. Many times I **10** considered Satan as the fitter emblem of my condition; for often, like him, when I viewed the bliss of my protectors, the bitter gall of envy rose within me.

" Another circumstance strengthened and confirmed these feelings. Soon after my arrival in the hovel, I discovered some papers in the pocket of the dress which I had taken from your laboratory. At first I had neglected

11 *It was your journal.* Once again, the god of coincidence does Mary Shelley's bidding.

12 *Here they are.* One would like to have seen them. This offhand mention of documentary proof is very teasing. Both Victor and Walton will mention other important documents the reader never gets to see.

13 *disgusting circumstances.* The revulsion against what is necessary between men and women in the making of babies lurks beneath the surface of this prose. One needs to add that these emotions are intensified by the line, 'Hateful day when I received life!' since as we know in Mary Shelley's case, it meant her mother's eventual death.

14 *Satan had his companions.* Now the creature sees even Satan as more befriended than himself. Earlier (p. 186) he compared himself with a similarly befriended Adam.

FUSELI'S HEAD OF SATAN.

them; but now that I was able to decypher the characters in which they were written, I began to study them **11** with diligence. It was your journal of the four months that preceded my creation. You minutely described in these papers every step you took in the progress of your work; this history was mingled with accounts of domestic occurrences. You, doubtless, recollect **12** these papers. Here they are. Every thing is related in them which bears reference to my accursed origin; the **13** whole detail of that series of disgusting circumstances which produced it is set in view; the minutest description of my odious and loathsome person is given, in language which painted your own horrors, and rendered mine ineffaceable. I sickened as I read. 'Hateful day when I received life!' I exclaimed in agony. 'Cursed creator! Why did you form a monster so hideous that even you turned from me in disgust? God in pity made man beautiful and alluring, after his own image; but my form is a filthy type of your's, more horrid from its very resemblance. **14** Satan had his companions, fellow-devils, to admire and encourage him; but I am solitary and detested.'

" These were the reflections of my hours of despondency and solitude; but when I contemplated the virtues of the cottagers, their amiable and benevolent dispositions, I persuaded myself that when they should become acquainted with my admiration of their virtues, they would compassionate me, and overlook my personal deformity. Could they turn from their door one, however

15 *plenty reigned there.* Presumably, because of the sale of Safie's jewels, though where they could have been sold in that isolated place we are left to imagine.

16 *shade.* Rescued from its convolutions, the preceding sentence tells us that hope vanished just as the reflected image and the moonlight shadow vanished.

monstrous, who solicited their compassion and friendship? I resolved, at least, not to despair, but in every way to fit myself for an interview with them which would decide my fate. I postponed this attempt for some months longer; for the importance attached to its success inspired me with a dread lest I should fail. Besides, I found that my understanding improved so much with every day's experience, that I was unwilling to commence this undertaking until a few more months should have added to my wisdom.

" Several changes, in the mean time, took place in the cottage. The presence of Safie diffused happiness among its inhabitants; and I also found that a

15 greater degree of plenty reigned there. Felix and Agatha spent more time in amusement and conversation, and were assisted in their labours by servants. They did not appear rich, but they were contented and happy; their feelings were serene and peaceful, while mine became every day more tumultuous. Increase of knowledge only discovered to me more clearly what a wretched outcast I was. I cherished hope, it is true; but it vanished, when I beheld my person reflected in water, or my shadow in the moon-shine, even as that frail image and that inconstant

16 shade.

" I endeavoured to crush these fears, and to fortify myself for the trial which in a few months I resolved to undergo; and sometimes I allowed my thoughts, unchecked by reason, to ramble in the fields of Paradise, and dared to fancy amiable and lovely creatures sympa-

17   *Adam's supplication.* Among others, the one from *Paradise Lost* used as an epigraph to each of the three volumes of *Frankenstein:*

> Did I request thee, Maker, from my clay
> To mould me man? Did I solicit thee
> From darkness to promote me?—

thizing with my feelings and cheering my gloom; their angelic countenances breathed smiles of consolation. But it was all a dream: no Eve soothed my sorrows, or shared my thoughts; I was alone. I remembered Adam's supplication to his Creator; but where was mine? he had abandoned me, and, in the bitterness of my heart, I cursed him.

17

" Autumn passed thus. I saw, with surprise and grief, the leaves decay and fall, and nature again assume the barren and bleak appearance it had worn when I first beheld the woods and the lovely moon. Yet I did not heed the bleakness of the weather; I was better fitted by my conformation for the endurance of cold than heat. But my chief delights were the sight of the flowers, the birds, and all the gay apparel of summer; when those deserted me, I turned with more attention towards the cottagers. Their happiness was not decreased by the absence of summer. They loved, and sympathized with one another; and their joys, depending on each other, were not interrupted by the casualties that took place around them. The more I saw of them, the greater became my desire to claim their protection and kindness; my heart yearned to be known and loved by these amiable creatures: to see their sweet looks turned towards me with affection, was the utmost limit of my ambition. I dared not think that they would turn them from me with disdain and horror. The poor that stopped at their door were never driven away. I asked, it is true, for greater treasures than a little food or rest; I required

18 *into life*. The creature was "born" on November of the previous year.

19 *thoughtfulness and sadness*. Now that Safie has made Felix and presumably Agatha happy, one wonders what is the other hidden sorrow over which the old man is brooding.

kindness and sympathy; but I did not believe myself utterly unworthy of it.

" The winter advanced, and an entire revolution of the seasons had taken **18** place since I awoke into life. My attention, at this time, was solely directed towards my plan of introducing myself into the cottage of my protectors. I revolved many projects; but that on which I finally fixed was, to enter the dwelling when the blind old man should be alone. I had sagacity enough to discover, that the unnatural hideousness of my person was the chief object of horror with those who had formerly beheld me. My voice, although harsh, had nothing terrible in it; I thought, therefore, that if, in the absence of his children, I could gain the good-will and mediation of the old De Lacy, I might, by his means, be tolerated by my younger protectors.

" One day, when the sun shone on the red leaves that strewed the ground, and diffused cheerfulness, although it denied warmth, Safie, Agatha, and Felix, departed on a long country walk, and the old man, at his own desire, was left alone in the cottage. When his children had departed, he took up his guitar, and played several mournful, but sweet airs, more sweet and mournful than I had ever heard him play before. At first his countenance was illuminated with pleasure, but, as he **19** continued, thoughtfulness and sadness succeeded; at length, laying aside the instrument, he sat absorbed in reflection.

" My heart beat quick; this was the hour and moment of trial, which would

20 *'Pardon this intrusion.'* This sentence, in which we get to hear what were the creature's first spoken words, is the most superbly realized literary achievement in the whole of *Frankenstein*. To savor the tact that informs Mary Shelley's choice of phrasing here one must pause for a moment to remember what an elaborate structure of pain and self-loathing the creature's autobiography has by now become. This meeting of the visibly appalling with the blind is stunningly imagined and made graceful by the language of diffidence and courtesy in which it is couched. As an epigraph (or an epitaph) for humanity, " 'Pardon this intrusion' " is unsurpassed.

21 *De Lacy*. Mary Shelley, or her printers, as will be seen, varied the spelling of this name.

decide my hopes, or realize my fears. The servants were gone to a neighbouring fair.   All was silent in and around the cottage: it was an excellent opportunity; yet, when I proceeded to execute my plan, my limbs failed me, and I sunk to the ground.   Again I rose; and, exerting all the firmness of which I was master, removed the planks which I had placed before my hovel to conceal my retreat.   The fresh air revived me, and, with renewed determination, I approached the door of their cottage.

" I knocked. ' Who is there?' said the old man—' Come in.'

20   " I entered; ' Pardon this intrusion,' said I, ' I am a traveller in want of a little rest; you would greatly oblige me, if you would allow me to remain a few minutes before the fire.'

21   " ' Enter,' said De Lacy; ' and I will try in what manner I can relieve your wants; but, unfortunately, my children are from home, and, as I am blind, I am afraid I shall find it difficult to procure food for you.'

" ' Do not trouble yourself, my kind host, I have food; it is warmth and rest only that I need.'

" I sat down, and a silence ensued. I knew that every minute was precious to me, yet I remained irresolute in what manner to commence the interview; when the old man addressed me—

" ' By your language, stranger, I suppose you are my countryman;—are you French?'

" ' No; but I was educated by a French family, and understand that language only.   I am now going to

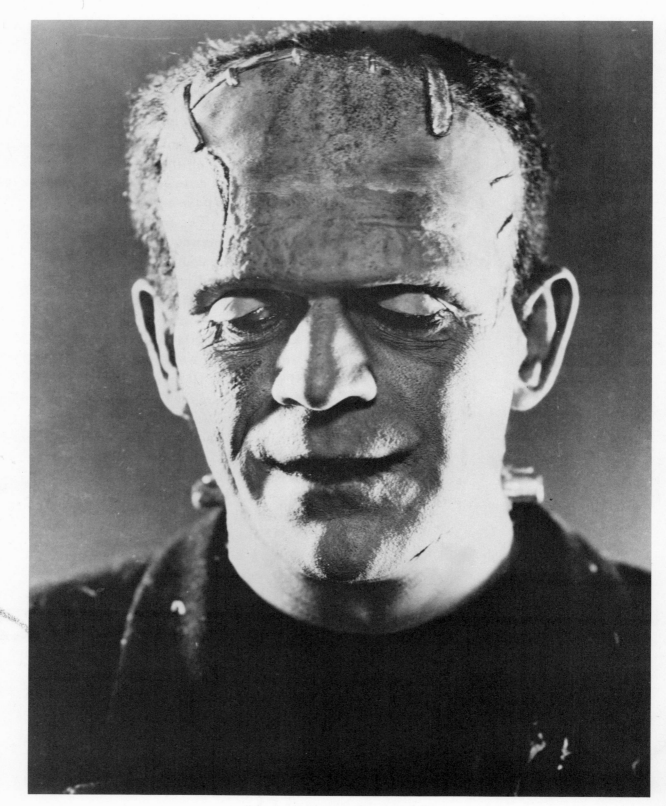

" 'PARDON THIS INTRUSION.' "

22 *monster*. The creature makes a fatal mistake. Speaking the literal truth, he forgets that his "blind" auditor will hear the word *monster* as a metaphor. The result is, as we soon see, that the creature gets advice instead of understanding.

claim the protection of some friends, whom I sincerely love, and of whose favour I have some hopes.'

" ' Are these Germans ?'

" ' No, they are French. But let us change the subject. I am an unfortunate and deserted creature ; I look around, and I have no relation or friend upon earth. These amiable people to whom I go have never seen me, and know little of me. I am full of fears ; for if I fail there, I am an outcast in the world for ever.'

" ' Do not despair. To be friendless is indeed to be unfortunate ; but the hearts of men, when unprejudiced by any obvious self-interest, are full of brotherly love and charity. Rely, therefore, on your hopes ; and if these friends are good and amiable, do not despair.'

" ' They are kind—they are the most excellent creatures in the world ; but, unfortunately, they are prejudiced against me. I have good dispositions ; my life has been hitherto harmless, and, in some degree, beneficial ; but a fatal prejudice clouds their eyes, and where they ought to see a feeling and kind friend, they behold only a detestable

22 monster.'

" ' That is indeed unfortunate ; but if you are really blameless, cannot you undeceive them ?'

" ' I am about to undertake that task ; and it is on that account that I feel so many overwhelming terrors. I tenderly love these friends ; I have, unknown to them, been for many months in the habits of daily kindness towards them ; but they believe that I wish to

23 *human creature*. Our author seems to be letting De Lacey hedge his bet. He is willing to be serviceable to a *human* creature; the creature may not fit the bill.

24 *although innocent*. Not so. De Lacey and Agatha were willing accomplices in an illegal jailbreak.

injure them, and it is that prejudice which I wish to overcome.'

" ' Where do these friends reside ?'

" ' Near this spot.'

" The old man paused, and then continued, ' If you will unreservedly confide to me the particulars of your tale, I perhaps may be of use in undeceiving them. I am blind, and cannot judge of your countenance, but there is something in your words which persuades me that you are sincere. I am poor, and an exile; but it will afford me true pleasure to be in any way ser- **23** viceable to a human creature.'

" ' Excellent man ! I thank you, and accept your generous offer. You raise me from the dust by this kindness; and I trust that, by your aid, I shall not be driven from the society and sympathy of your fellow-creatures.'

" ' Heaven forbid ! even if you were really criminal; for that can only drive you to desperation, and not instigate you to virtue. I also am unfortunate; I and my family have been condemned, **24** although innocent : judge, therefore, if I do not feel for your misfortunes.'

" ' How can I thank you, my best and only benefactor ? from your lips first have I heard the voice of kindness directed towards me ; I shall be for ever grateful ; and your present humanity assures me of success with those friends whom I am on the point of meeting.'

" ' May I know the names and residence of those friends ?'

" I paused. This, I thought, was the moment of decision, which was to rob me of, or bestow happiness on me for ever. I struggled vainly for firmness sufficient to answer him, but the effort destroyed all my remaining strength; I sank on the chair, and sobbed aloud. At that moment I heard the steps of my younger protectors. I had not a moment to lose; but, seizing the hand of the old man, I cried, ' Now is the time!—save and protect me! You and your family are the friends whom I seek. Do not you desert me in the hour of trial!'

" ' Great God!' exclaimed the old man, ' who are you?'

" At that instant the cottage door was opened, and Felix, Safie, and Agatha entered. Who can describe their horror and consternation on beholding me? Agatha fainted; and Safie, unable to attend to her friend, rushed out of the cottage. Felix darted forward, and with supernatural force tore me from his father, to whose knees I clung: in a transport of fury, he dashed me to the ground, and struck me violently with a stick. I could have torn him limb from limb, as the lion rends the antelope. But my heart sunk within me as with bitter sickness, and I refrained. I saw him on the point of repeating his blow, when, overcome by pain and anguish, I quitted the cottage, and in the general tumult escaped unperceived to my hovel.

CHAPTER VIII.

" CURSED, cursed creator! Why did I live? Why, in that instant, did I **1** not extinguish the spark of existence which you had so wantonly bestowed? I know not; despair had not yet taken possession of me; my feelings were those of rage and revenge. I could with pleasure have destroyed the cottage and its inhabitants, and have glutted myself with their shrieks and misery.

" When night came, I quitted my retreat, and wandered in the wood; and now, no longer restrained by the fear of discovery, I gave vent to my anguish in fearful howlings. I was like **2** a wild beast that had broken the toils; destroying the objects that obstructed me, and ranging through the wood with a stag-like swiftness. Oh! what a miserable night I passed! the cold stars shone in mockery, and the bare trees waved their branches above me: now and then the sweet voice of a bird burst forth amidst the universal stillness. All, save I, were at rest or in enjoyment: **3** I, like the arch fiend, bore a hell within me; and, finding myself unsympathized with, wished to tear up the trees, spread havoc and destruction around me, and then to have sat down and enjoyed the ruin.

" But this was a luxury of sensation

1 *extinguish the spark*. Both the creature and his creator have frequent thoughts of suicide. See the introduction for an account of the suicides that touched Mary Shelley's life, as well as page 21, note 7.

The phrase "extinguish the spark of existence," coupled with "which you [or I] . . . so wantonly bestowed," has now been uttered for the third time. It appears also on page 128, where Victor uses it; then again on page 140, where Victor repeats it, as he threatens his creature.

The reiteration of the idea serves to reinforce the notion, steadily growing in the course of *Frankenstein*, that the creature and his creator are aspects of each other. It does something else as well. It gives us, with some subtlety, a woman's sense of what child-begetting represents to a man—a careless and wanton gesture. That the reiterated phrases reveal Mary Shelley through her creatures is all the more likely if we remember that, according to her fiction, there was nothing either careless or wanton about Victor's long toil toward his achievement.

2 *toils*. Nets or snares.

3 *like the arch fiend.* The reference, again, is to Milton's Satan. Victor too has compared himself to that fallen archangel. (See Vol. I, p. 120.)

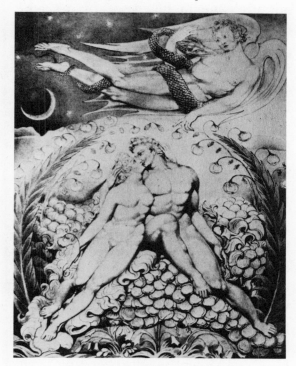

SATAN WITH ADAM AND EVE
BY WILLIAM BLAKE.

4 *everlasting war.* In Milton's *Paradise Lost*, Satan makes such a declaration after exhorting his legions in Chaos. In Book II (ll. 649–53), the fallen angel says: "Peace is despaired;/For who can think submission? War, then, War/Open or understood, must be resolved."

that could not endure; I became fatigued with excess of bodily exertion, and sank on the damp grass in the sick impotence of despair. There was none among the myriads of men that existed who would pity or assist me; and should I feel kindness towards my enemies? No: from that moment I **4** declared everlasting war against the species, and, more than all, against him who had formed me, and sent me forth to this insupportable misery.

" The sun rose; I heard the voices of men, and knew that it was impossible to return to my retreat during that day. Accordingly I hid myself in some thick underwood, determining to devote the ensuing hours to reflection on my situation.

" The pleasant sunshine, and the pure air of day, restored me to some degree of tranquillity; and when I considered what had passed at the cottage, I could not help believing that I had been too hasty in my conclusions. I had certainly acted imprudently. It was apparent that my conversation had interested the father in my behalf, and I was a fool in having exposed my person to the horror of his children. I ought to have familiarized the old De Lacy to me, and by degrees have discovered myself to the rest of his family, when they should have been prepared for my approach. But I did not believe my errors to be irretrievable; and, after much consideration, I resolved to return to the cottage, seek the old man, and by my representations win him to my party.

" These thoughts calmed me, and in

5 *females were flying.* Actually, only one was in flight. Agatha, as we have seen, collapsed on the spot.

6 *language of the country.* Presumably, their language is German.

Why these peasants, or farm laborers, are using violent gesticulations is not clear. Perhaps they are discussing the De Laceys' recent wild adventure with the creature. In any case, the countrymen disappear from the scene, and the book, forever.

the afternoon I sank into a profound sleep; but the fever of my blood did not allow me to be visited by peaceful dreams. The horrible scene of the preceding day was for ever acting be- 5 fore my eyes; the females were flying, and the enraged Felix tearing me from his father's feet. I awoke exhausted; and, finding that it was already night, I crept forth from my hiding-place, and went in search of food.

" When my hunger was appeased, I directed my steps towards the well-known path that conducted to the cottage. All there was at peace. I crept into my hovel, and remained in silent expectation of the accustomed hour when the family arose. That hour past, the sun mounted high in the heavens, but the cottagers did not appear. I trembled violently, apprehending some dreadful misfortune. The inside of the cottage was dark, and I heard no motion; I cannot describe the agony of this suspence.

" Presently two countrymen passed by; but, pausing near the cottage, they entered into conversation, using violent gesticulations; but I did not under-stand what they said, as they spoke the 6 language of the country, which differed from that of my protectors. Soon after, however, Felix approached with ano-ther man: I was surprised, as I knew that he had not quitted the cottage that morning, and waited anxiously to discover, from his discourse, the mean-ing of these unusual appearances.

" ' Do you consider,' said his com-panion to him, ' that you will be obliged to pay three months' rent, and

7 *My wife.* This is the first news we have that Felix and Safie are married—if they are. For Mary Shelley, who at the time she was writing *Frankenstein* was still Mary Godwin living in sin with Shelley, it must have been a frequent experience to be taken for or presented as Shelley's wife.

to lose the produce of your garden? I do not wish to take any unfair advantage, and I beg therefore that you will take some days to consider of your determination.'

" ' It is utterly useless,' replied Felix, ' we can never again inhabit your cottage. The life of my father is in the greatest danger, owing to the dreadful circumstance that I have related. My wife and my sister will never recover their horror. I entreat you not to reason with me any more. Take possession of your tenement, and let me fly from this place.'

" Felix trembled violently as he said this. He and his companion entered the cottage, in which they remained for a few minutes, and then departed. I never saw any of the family of De Lacy more.

" I continued for the remainder of the day in my hovel in a state of utter and stupid despair. My protectors had departed, and had broken the only link that held me to the world. For the first time the feelings of revenge and hatred filled my bosom, and I did not strive to controul them; but, allowing myself to be borne away by the stream, I bent my mind towards injury and death. When I thought of my friends, of the mild voice of De Lacy, the gentle eyes of Agatha, and the exquisite beauty of the Arabian, these thoughts vanished, and a gush of tears somewhat soothed me. But again, when I reflected that they had spurned and deserted me, anger returned, a rage of anger; and, unable to injure any thing human, I turned my fury towards

8 *at length hid.* In some sense, the creature has either entered or been driven into his own. This weird dance by moonlight with a blazing torch has all the flickering formality of a dimly understood initiation rite into an as yet undiscovered religion. The creature carefully paces his rage, delaying the fire until the moment when the watchful moon has set. With the sacrifice of the cottage, the creature gives up the possibility of devotion to the De Laceys' God and accepts himself as a creature of nature—primordial, atavistic, cruel.

inanimate objects.   As night advanced, I placed a variety of combustibles around the cottage; and, after having destroyed every vestige of cultivation in the garden, I waited with forced impatience until the moon had sunk to commence my operations.

" As the night advanced, a fierce wind arose from the woods, and quickly dispersed the clouds that had loitered in the heavens : the blast tore along like a mighty avalanche, and produced a kind of insanity in my spirits, **that burst all bounds of reason and reflection.** I lighted the dry branch of **a** tree, and danced with fury around the devoted cottage, my eyes still fixed on the western horizon, the edge of which the moon nearly touched.   A part of

8 its orb was at length hid, and I waved my brand; it sunk, and, with a loud scream, I fired the straw, and heath, and bushes, which I had collected. The wind fanned the fire, and the cottage was quickly enveloped by the flames, which clung to it, and licked it with their forked and destroying tongues.

" As soon as I was convinced **that** no assistance could save any part of the habitation, I quitted the scene, and sought for refuge in the woods.

" And now, with the world before me, whither should I bend my steps ? I resolved to fly far from the scene of my misfortunes; but to me, hated and despised, every country must be equally horrible.   At length the thought of you crossed my mind.   I learned from your papers that you were my father, **my** creator; and to whom could I apply with more fitness than to him who had given

"WITH FURY AROUND THE DEVOTED COTTAGE."

"AN OBJECT FOR THE SCORN AND
HORROR OF MANKIND."

me life? Among the lessons that Felix
had bestowed upon Safie geography
had not been omitted: I had learned
from these the relative situations of the
different countries of the earth. You
had mentioned Geneva as the name of
your native town; and towards this
place I resolved to proceed.

"But how was I to direct myself?
I knew that I must travel in a south-
westerly direction to reach my destination; but the sun was my only guide.
I did not know the names of the towns
that I was to pass through, nor could
I ask information from a single human
being; but I did not despair. From
you only could I hope for succour, although towards you I felt no sentiment
but that of hatred. Unfeeling, heartless creator! you had endowed me
with perceptions and passions, and then
cast me abroad an object for the scorn
and horror of mankind. But on you
only had I any claim for pity and re-
dress, and from you I determined to
seek that justice which I vainly attempted to gain from any other being
that wore the human form.

"My travels were long, and the sufferings I endured intense. It was late
in autumn when I quitted the district
where I had so long resided. I travelled only at night, fearful of encountering the visage of a human being.
Nature decayed around me, and the
sun became heatless; rain and snow
poured around me; mighty rivers were
frozen; the surface of the earth was
hard, and chill, and bare, and I found no
shelter. Oh, earth! how often did I im-
precate curses on the cause of my being!
The mildness of my nature had fled,

9 *were hardened*. The creature is entering his second year.

10 *possessed a map*. We learn on page 202 that the "sun was my only guide" and that he did not know the names of the towns through which he passed. His map, then, has been acquired in the interval and our author has forgotten to tell us.

11 *green*. Spring, again, of the creature's second year. It has taken him about five months to reach Switzerland from the vicinity of Ingolstadt.

and all within me was turned to gall and bitterness. The nearer I approached to your habitation, the more deeply did I feel the spirit of revenge enkindled in my heart. Snow fell, and the waters **9** were hardened, but I rested not. A few incidents now and then directed **10** me, and I possessed a map of the country; but I often wandered wide from my path. The agony of my feelings allowed me no respite: no incident occurred from which my rage and misery could not extract its food; but a circumstance that happened when I arrived on the confines of Switzerland, when the sun had recovered its warmth, and the earth again began to look **11** green, confirmed in an especial manner the bitterness and horror of my feelings.

" I generally rested during the day, and travelled only when I was secured by night from the view of man. One morning, however, finding that my path lay through a deep wood, I ventured to continue my journey after the sun had risen; the day, which was one of the first of spring, cheered even me by the loveliness of its sunshine and the balminess of the air. I felt emotions of gentleness and pleasure, that had long appeared dead, revive within me. Half surprised by the novelty of these sensations, I allowed myself to be borne away by them; and, forgetting my solitude and deformity, dared to be happy. Soft tears again bedewed my cheeks, and I even raised my humid eyes with thankfulness towards the blessed sun which bestowed such joy upon me.

" I continued to wind among the

"A YOUNG GIRL."

12 *into the wood.* This episode occurs variously in James Whales's 1931 film *Frankenstein;* in his 1935 *Bride of Frankenstein;* and in Mel Brooks's 1974 *Young Frankenstein.*

In *Frankenstein* (1931), it is transmuted into one of film's great moments. James Whale has devised a scene in which the creature comes upon a girl beside a lake who is playing with daisies. The child is too young or too innocent to be frightened by him, and invites him to play with her. One by one she throws daisies into the water and laughs delightedly as they float away. The creature too throws daisies to provoke her pleasurable laughter. When there are no more daisies, the creature, who does not understand the real world at all, throws the child into the water thinking to please her. The child drowns and the creature's doom is sealed. The climax of this scene has been cut from most copies of the film.

paths of the wood, until I came to its boundary, which was skirted by a deep and rapid river, into which many of the trees bent their branches, now budding with the fresh spring. Here I paused, not exactly knowing what path to pursue, when I heard the sound of voices, that induced me to conceal myself under the shade of a cypress. I was scarcely hid, when a young girl came running towards the spot where I was concealed, laughing as if she ran from some one in sport. She continued her course along the precipitous sides of the river, when suddenly her foot slipt, and she fell into the rapid stream. I rushed from my hiding place, and, with extreme labour from the force of the current, saved her, and dragged her to shore. She was senseless; and I endeavoured, by every means in my power, to restore animation, when I was suddenly interrupted by the approach of a rustic, who was probably the person from whom she had playfully fled. On seeing me, he darted towards me, and, tearing the girl from my arms, hastened towards the deeper parts of the wood. I followed speedily, I hardly knew why; but when the man saw me draw near, he aimed a gun, which he carried, at my body, and fired. I sunk to the ground, and my injurer, with increased swiftness, **12** escaped into the wood.

" This was then the reward of my benevolence! I had saved a human being from destruction, and, as a recompence, I now writhed under the miserable pain of a wound, which shattered the flesh and bone. The

13 *two months from this time*. The summer of the creature's second year is approaching.

feelings of kindness and gentleness, which I had entertained but a few moments before, gave place to hellish rage and gnashing of teeth. Inflamed by pain, I vowed eternal hatred and vengeance to all mankind. But the agony of my wound overcame me; my pulses paused, and I fainted.

" For some weeks I led a miserable life in the woods, endeavouring to cure the wound which I had received. The ball had entered my shoulder, and I knew not whether it had remained there or passed through; at any rate I had no means of extracting it. My sufferings were augmented also by the oppressive sense of the injustice and ingratitude of their infliction. My daily vows rose for revenge—a deep and deadly revenge, such as would alone compensate for the outrages and anguish I had endured.

" After some weeks my wound healed, and I continued my journey. The labours I endured were no longer to be alleviated by the bright sun or gentle breezes of spring; all joy was but a mockery, which insulted my desolate state, and made me feel more painfully that I was not made for the enjoyment of pleasure.

13 " But my toils now drew near a close ; and, two months from this time, I reached the environs of Geneva.

" It was evening when I arrived, and I retired to a hiding-place among the fields that surround it, to meditate in what manner I should apply to you. I was oppressed by fatigue and hunger, and far too unhappy to enjoy the gentle breezes of evening, or the prospect of

14 *companion and friend.* This may seem a strange notion, but certainly no stranger than the following: One of Helen Shelley's memories of her brother (as reported in T. J. Hogg's *Life of Shelley*, p. 27) was that "he had a wish to educate some child, and often talked seriously of purchasing a little girl for that purpose: a tumbler, who came to the back door to display her wonderful feats, attracted him, and he thought she would be a good subject for the purpose." There is also the reminiscence of Joseph Merle (which appears in Holmes, *The Pursuit*, p. 69). According to Merle, Shelley wrote him in 1811: "I wish to find two young persons of not more than four or five years of age; and should prefer females, as they are usually more precocious than males . . . I will withdraw from the world with my charge, and in some sequestered spot direct their education."

And Mary Shelley notes that in the course of her elopement journey in 1814, they had an "adventure with Marguerite Pascal—whom we would have taken with us if her father would have allowed us" (*Journal*, p. 9). Finally we note that William Godwin, while still a bachelor, did, in fact, undertake to raise a twelve-year-old second cousin named Thomas Cooper. According to Mary Shelley, the experiment was a failure.

15 *Syndic.* As noted earlier, a municipal magistrate.

the sun setting behind the stupendous mountains of Jura.

"At this time a slight sleep relieved me from the pain of reflection, which was disturbed by the approach of a beautiful child, who came running into the recess I had chosen with all the sportiveness of infancy. Suddenly, as I gazed on him, an idea seized me, that this little creature was unprejudiced, and had lived too short a time to have imbibed a horror of deformity. If, therefore, I could seize him, and edu- **14** cate him as my companion and friend, I should not be so desolate in this peo- pled earth.

"Urged by this impulse, I seized on the boy as he passed, and drew him to- wards me. As soon as he beheld my form, he placed his hands before his eyes, and uttered a shrill scream: I drew his hand forcibly from his face, and said, 'Child, what is the meaning of this? I do not intend to hurt you; listen to me.'

"He struggled violently; 'Let me go,' he cried; 'monster! ugly wretch! you wish to eat me, and tear me to pieces—You are an ogre—Let me go, or I will tell my papa.'

"'Boy, you will never see your father again; you must come with me.'

"'Hideous monster! let me go; **15** My papa is a Syndic—he is M. Fran- kenstein—he would punish you. You dare not keep me.'

"'Frankenstein! you belong then to my enemy—to him towards whom I have sworn eternal revenge; you shall be my first victim.'

"The child still struggled, and

16 *lovely lips.* The creature's view of Victor's mother has none of the brutal ambivalence that characterizes Victor's dream of her (Vol. I, p. 75). And yet his feelings for the lovely woman begin with sensual appreciation and end with the rage of sexual frustration.

loaded me with epithets which carried despair to my heart: I grasped his throat to silence him, and in a moment he lay dead at my feet.

" I gazed on my victim, and my heart swelled with exultation and hellish triumph: clapping my hands, I exclaimed, ' I, too, can create desolation; my enemy is not impregnable; this death will carry despair to him, and a thousand other miseries shall torment and destroy him.'

16 " As I fixed my eyes on the child, I saw something glittering on his breast. I took it; it was a portrait of a most lovely woman. In spite of my malignity, it softened and attracted me. For a few moments I gazed with delight on her dark eyes, fringed by deep lashes, and her lovely lips; but presently my rage returned: I remembered that I was for ever deprived of the delights that such beautiful creatures could bestow; and that she whose resemblance I contemplated would, in regarding me, have changed that air of divine benignity to one expressive of disgust and affright.

" Can you wonder that such thoughts transported me with rage? I only wonder that at that moment, instead of venting my sensations in exclamations and agony, I did not rush among mankind, and perish in the attempt to destroy them.

" While I was overcome by these feelings, I left the spot where I had committed the murder, and was seeking a more secluded hiding-place, when I perceived a woman passing near me. She was young, not indeed so beautiful

17   *youth and health*. There is an amazing erotic bent to the creature's feelings just after the murder of the child. We will see shortly to what conclusion the drift of his thoughts takes him.

18   *her dress*. If, as we were told in Volume I, page 113, Justine was "unable to rest or sleep," it seems impossible that the creature could have put the portrait in a fold of her dress without being observed. In the 1831 edition of *Frankenstein*, Mary Shelley took care of the problem by having Justine say that she managed to drop off to sleep for a second.

as her whose portrait I held, but of an agreeable aspect, and blooming in the **17** loveliness of youth and health. Here, I thought, is one of those whose smiles are bestowed on all but me; she shall not escape: thanks to the lessons of Felix, and the sanguinary laws of man, I have learned how to work mischief. I approached her unperceived, and placed the portrait securely in one of the folds **18** of her dress.

" For some days I haunted the spot where these scenes had taken place; sometimes wishing to see you, sometimes resolved to quit the world and its miseries for ever. At length I wandered towards these mountains, and have ranged through their immense recesses, consumed by a burning passion which you alone can gratify. We may not part until you have promised to comply with my requisition. I am alone, and miserable; man will not associate with me; but one as deformed and horrible as myself would not deny herself to me. My companion must be of the same species, and have the same defects. This being you must create."

CHAPTER IX.

THE being finished speaking, and fixed his looks upon me in expectation of a reply. But I was bewildered, perplexed, and unable to arrange my ideas sufficiently to understand the full extent of his proposition. He continued—

" You must create a female for me, with whom I can live in the interchange of those sympathies necessary for my being. This you alone can do; and I demand it of you as a right which you must not refuse."

The latter part of his tale had kindled anew in me the anger that had died away while he narrated his peaceful life among the cottagers, and, as he said this, I could no longer suppress the rage that burned within me.

" I do refuse it," I replied; " and no torture shall ever extort a consent from me. You may render me the most miserable of men, but you shall never make me base in my own eyes. Shall I create another like yourself, whose joint wickedness might desolate the world. Begone! I have answered you; you may torture me, but I will never consent."

" You are in the wrong,' replied the fiend; " and, instead of threatening, I am content to reason with you. I am malicious because I am miserable; am

1 *to pieces*. There has been no suggestion of such a threat but the phrase is a dramatically ironic hint of what is to come in Volume III.

2 *one creature's sake*. There is an echo here of Abraham's intercession with the Lord on the occasion of his intended destruction of Sodom and Gomorrah (See Genesis XVIII: 23–33). The exchange, it will be remembered, involves considerable bargaining between Abraham and God over how many righteous men there must be in the Cities of the Plain before the Lord will spare them. God, in a compassionate mood, is willing to forego destruction if as few as ten righteous men can be discerned in the cities but even that small number cannot be found and the fire and brimstone follow.

I not shunned and hated by all mankind? You, my creator, would tear me to pieces, and triumph; remember that, and tell me why I should pity man more than he pities me? You would not call it murder, if you could precipitate me into one of those ice-rifts, and destroy my frame, the work of your own hands. Shall I respect man, when he contemns me? Let him live with me in the interchange of kindness, and, instead of injury, I would bestow every benefit upon him with tears of gratitude at his acceptance. But that cannot be; the human senses are insurmountable barriers to our union. Yet mine shall not be the submission of abject slavery. I will revenge my injuries: if I cannot inspire love, I will cause fear; and chiefly towards you my arch-enemy, because my creator, do I swear inextinguishable hatred. Have a care: I will work at your destruction, nor finish until I desolate your heart, so that you curse the hour of your birth."

A fiendish rage animated him as he said this; his face was wrinkled into contortions too horrible for human eyes to behold; but presently he calmed himself, and proceeded—

"I intended to reason. This passion is detrimental to me; for you do not reflect that you are the cause of its excess. If any being felt emotions of benevolence towards me, I should return them an hundred and an hundred fold; for that one creature's sake, I would make peace with the whole kind! But I now indulge in dreams of bliss that cannot be realized. What I ask

"I DEMAND A CREATURE
OF ANOTHER SEX."

3 *hideous as myself.* By now, the reader has a right to wonder why, if Victor is the brilliant and skilled scientist Mary Shelley wants us to believe he is, Victor does not simply apply his various skills to remaking the creature's repulsive face, and then turn his attention to the creation of a lovely female.

The point, of course, is that the creature's ugliness is the psychological base on which *Frankenstein* rests. Its ugliness is first the metaphor for the creature's isolation, and then a clue to the source of its pain: It comes out of the "workshop of filthy creation."

of you is reasonable and moderate; I demand a creature of another sex, but **3** as hideous as myself: the gratification is small, but it is all that I can receive, and it shall content me. It is true, we shall be monsters, cut off from all the world; but on that account we shall be more attached to one another. Our lives will not be happy, but they will be harmless, and free from the misery I now feel. Oh! my creator, make me happy; let me feel gratitude towards you for one benefit! Let me see that I excite the sympathy of some existing thing; do not deny me my request!"

I was moved. I shuddered when I thought of the possible consequences of my consent; but I felt that there was some justice in his argument. His tale, and the feelings he now expressed, proved him to be a creature of fine sensations; and did I not, as his maker, owe him all the portion of happiness that it was in my power to bestow? He

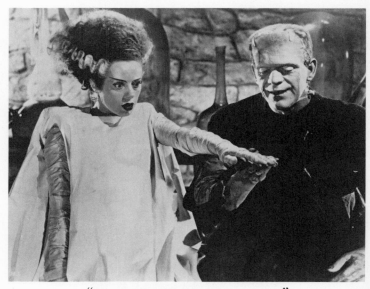

"DO NOT DENY ME MY REQUEST."

4 *nourishment.* Our being is a vegetarian, as was Percy Shelley through most of his life.

There is a story told of Peacock's concern for Shelley who, on the occasion of a boating expedition in 1815, seemed to be especially weak. Peacock, thinking Shelley's languor was the result of his vegetarian diet, prescribed a dish of mutton chops, "well-peppered." The prescription seemed to work for a time. Peacock writes: "His vegetable diet entered for something into his restlessness. When he was fixed in a place he adhered to this diet consistently and conscientiously, but it certainly did not agree with him; it made him weak and nervous, and exaggerated the sensitiveness of his imagination. Then arose those thick-coming fancies which almost invariably preceded his change of place. While he was living from inn to inn he was obliged to live, as he said, 'on what he could get'; that is to say, like other people. When he got well under this process he gave all the credit to locomotion, and held himself to have thus benefited, not in consequence of his change of regimen, but in spite of it. Once, when I was living in the country, I received a note from him wishing me to call on him in London. I did so, and found him ill in bed. He said, 'You are looking well. I suppose you go in your old way, living on animal food and fermented liquor?' I answered in the affirmative. 'And here,' he said, 'you see a vegetable feeder overcome by disease.' I said, 'Perhaps the diet is the cause.' This he would by no means allow; but it was not long before he was again posting through some yet unvisited wild, and recovering his health as usual, by living 'on what he could get' " (*Peacock's Memoirs of Shelley,* pp. 38–39).

Shelley defended a vegetable diet in his notes to "Queen Mab": "There is no disease, bodily or mental, which adoption of vegetable diet and pure water has not infallibly mitigated, wherever the experiment has been fairly tried. Debility is gradually converted into strength; disease into healthfulness; madness, in all its hideous variety, from the ravings of the fettered maniac to the unaccountable irrationalities of ill-temper, that make a hell of domestic life, into a calm and considerate evenness of temper, that alone might offer a certain pledge of the future moral reformation of society. . . . On the average, out of sixty persons four die in three years. Hopes are entertained that, in April, 1814, a statement will be given that sixty persons, all having lived more than three years on vegetables and pure water, are then in perfect health. More than two years have now elapsed; not one of them has died; no such example will be found in any sixty persons taken at random. . . . Every man forms, as it were, his god from his own character; to the divinity of one of simple habits no offering would be more acceptable than the happiness of his creatures. He would be incapable of hating or persecuting others for the love of God. He will find moreover, a system of simple diet to be a system of perfect epicurism. He will no longer be incessantly occupied in blunting and destroying those organs from which he expects his gratification. The pleasure of taste to be derived from a dinner of potatoes, beans, peas, turnips, lettuces,

saw my change of feeling, and continued—

" If you consent, neither you nor any other human being shall ever see us again: I will go to the vast wilds of South America. My food is not that of man; I do not destroy the lamb and the kid, to glut my appetite; acorns

4 and berries afford me sufficient nourishment. My companion will be of the same nature as myself, and will be content with the same fare. We shall make our bed of dried leaves; the sun will shine on us as on man, and will ripen our food. The picture I present to you is peaceful and human, and you must feel that you could deny it only in the wantonness of power and cruelty. Pitiless as you have been towards me. I now see compassion in your eyes: let me seize the favourable moment, and persuade you to promise what I so ardently desire."

" You propose," replied I, " to fly from the habitations of man, to dwell in those wilds where the beasts of the field will be your only companions. How can you, who long for the love and sympathy of man, persevere in this exile? You will return, and again seek their kindness, and you will meet with their detestation; your evil passions will be renewed, and you will then have a companion to aid you in the task of destruction. This may not be; cease to argue the point, for I cannot consent."

" How inconstant are your feelings! but a moment ago you were moved by my representations, and why do you again harden yourself to my com-

with a dessert of apples, gooseberries, strawberries, currants, raspberries, and in winter, oranges, apples and pears, is far greater than is supposed" (*The Complete Poetical Works of Percy Bysshe Shelley*, pp. 332–36.)

Mary Shelley, on the other hand, was a meat eater.

5 *by the earth.* Again we note that except for occasional interjections of the common sort in which the name of God is mentioned, serious oaths in this book are sworn in the name of aspects of the natural world as if Mary Shelley intended to keep her characters within the bonds of a loose pantheism.

6 *my dying moments.* His maker, on the other hand, will not show so much generosity in *his* dying moments. See Volume III, p. 325.

5 plaints? I swear to you, by the earth which I inhabit, and by you that made me, that, with the companion you bestow, I will quit the neighbourhood of man, and dwell, as it may chance, in the most savage of places. My evil passions will have fled, for I shall meet with sympathy; my life will flow quietly away, and, in my **6** dying moments, I shall not curse my maker."

His words had a strange effect upon me. I compassionated him, and sometimes felt a wish to console him; but when I looked upon him, when I saw the filthy mass that moved and talked, my heart sickened, and my feelings were altered to those of horror and hatred. I tried to stifle these sensations; I thought, that as I could not sympathize with him, I had no right to withhold from him the small portion of happiness which was yet in my power to bestow.

" You swear," I said, " to be harmless; but have you not already shewn a degree of malice that should reasonably make me distrust you? May not even this be a feint that will increase your triumph by affording a wider scope for your revenge?"

" How is this? I thought I had moved your compassion, and yet you still refuse to bestow on me the only benefit that can soften my heart, and render me harmless. If I have no ties and no affections, hatred and vice must be my portion; the love of another will destroy the cause of my crimes, and I shall become a thing, of whose existence every one will be ignorant.

7 *the chain of existence.* The creature is alluding to the metaphor of "The Great Chain of Being," which has its origins in Plato and Aristotle and which was singularly attractive to the eighteenth century because of the way in which it visualized creation as a hierarchically ordered, infinite series of links in a chain. In Alexander Pope's *Essay on Man* (ll. 233–41) we are told to:

> See, through this air, this ocean, and this earth,
> All matter quick, and bursting into birth.
> Above, how high progressive life may go!
> Around, how wide! how deep extend below!
> Vast Chain of Being! which from God began,
> Natures ethereal, human, angel, man,
> Beast, bird, fish, insect, what no eye can see,
> No glass can reach! from Infinite to thee,
> From thee to nothing.

My vices are the children of a forced solitude that I abhor; and my virtues will necessarily arise when I live in communion with an equal. I shall feel the affections of a sensitive being, and become linked to the chain of ex- **7** istence and events, from which I am now excluded."

I paused some time to reflect on all he had related, and the various argu- ments which he had employed. I thought of the promise of virtues which he had displayed on the opening of his existence, and the subsequent blight of all kindly feeling by the loathing and scorn which his protectors had mani- fested towards him. His power and threats were not omitted in my calcu- lations: a creature who could exist in the ice caves of the glaciers, and hide himself from pursuit among the ridges of inaccessible precipices, was a being possessing faculties it would be vain to cope with. After a long pause of re- flection, I concluded, that the justice due both to him and my fellow-crea- tures demanded of me that I should comply with his request. Turning to him, therefore, I said—

" I consent to your demand, on your solemn oath to quit Europe for ever, and every other place in the neighbour- hood of man, as soon as I shall deliver into your hands a female who will ac- company you in your exile."

" I swear," he cried, " by the sun, and by the blue sky of heaven, that if you grant my prayer, while they exist you shall never behold me again. De- part to your home, and commence your labours: I shall watch their pro- gress with unutterable anxiety; and fear not but that when you are ready I shall appear."

Saying this, he suddenly quitted me, fearful, perhaps, of any change in my sentiments. I saw him descend the mountain with greater speed than the flight of an eagle, and quickly lost him among the undulations of the sea of ice.

His tale had occupied the whole day; and the sun was upon the verge of the horizon when he departed. I knew that I ought to hasten my descent towards the valley, as I should soon be encompassed in darkness; but my heart was heavy, and my steps slow. The labour of winding among the little paths of the mountains, and fixing my feet firmly as I advanced, perplexed me, occupied as I was by the emotions 'which the occurrences of the day had produced. Night was far advanced, when I came to the half-way resting-place, and seated myself beside the fountain. The stars shone at intervals, as the clouds passed from over them; the dark pines rose before me, and every here and there a broken tree lay on the ground: it was a scene of wonderful solemnity, and stirred strange thoughts within me. I wept bitterly; and, clasping my hands in agony, I exclaimed, " Oh! stars, and clouds, and winds, ye are all about to mock me: if ye really pity me, crush sensation and memory; let me become as nought; but if not, depart, depart and leave me in darkness."

These were wild and miserable thoughts; but I cannot describe to you how the eternal twinkling of the stars weighed upon me, and how I listened

8 *siroc.* A sirocco: a hot dry wind, that travels from Africa to Italy, Spain, France.

9 *iron cowl.* The reference is to Dante's *Divine Comedy*. In Dorothy Sayers's translation ("Hell," canto XXIII, ll. 59–65), we find Dante describing a group of figures:

> Who trod their circling way with tear and groan
> And slow, slow steps, seeming subdued and faint.

They all wore cloaks, with deep hoods thrown forward

> Over their eyes, and shaped in fashion quite
> Like the great cowls the monks wear at Cologne;

Outwardly they were gilded dazzling-bright,

> But all within was lead.

8 to every blast of wind, as if it were a dull ugly siroc on its way to consume me.

Morning dawned before I arrived at the village of Chamounix; but my presence, so haggard and strange, hardly calmed the fears of my family, who had waited the whole night in anxious expectation of my return.

The following day we returned to Geneva. The intention of my father in coming had been to divert my mind, and to restore me to my lost tranquillity; but the medicine had been fatal. And, unable to account for the excess of misery I appeared to suffer, he hastened to return home, hoping the quiet and monotony of a domestic life would by degrees alleviate my sufferings from whatsoever cause they might spring.

For myself, I was passive in all their arrangements; and the gentle affection of my beloved Elizabeth was inadequate to draw me from the depth of my despair. The promise I had made to the dæmon weighed upon my mind, **9** like Dante's iron cowl on the heads of the hellish hypocrites. All pleasures of earth and sky passed before me like a dream, and that thought only had to me the reality of life. Can you wonder, that sometimes a kind of insanity possessed me, or that I saw continually about me a multitude of filthy animals inflicting on me incessant torture, that often extorted screams and bitter groans?

By degrees, however, these feelings became calmed. I entered again into the every-day scene of life, if not with interest, at least with some degree of tranquillity.

FRANKENSTEIN;

OR,

THE MODERN PROMETHEUS.

IN THREE VOLUMES.

Did I request thee, Maker, from my clay
To mould me man? Did I solicit thee
From darkness to promote me?——
PARADISE LOST.

VOL. III.

London:
PRINTED FOR
LACKINGTON, HUGHES, HARDING, MAVOR, & JONES,
FINSBURY SQUARE.

1818.

PROMETHEUS BEING STAKED TO THE CAUCASUS (HENRY FUSELI)

FRANKENSTEIN;

OR, THE

MODERN PROMETHEUS.

———

CHAPTER I.

D<small>AY</small> after day, week after week, passed away on my return to Geneva; and I could not collect the courage to recommence my work. I feared the vengeance of the disappointed fiend, yet I was unable to overcome my repugnance to the task which was enjoined me. I found that I could not compose a female without again devoting several months to profound study and laborious disquisition. I had heard of some discoveries having been made by an English philosopher, the knowledge of which was material to my success, and I sometimes thought of obtaining my father's consent to visit England for this purpose; but I clung to every pretence of delay, and could not resolve to interrupt my returning tranquillity. My health, which had hitherto declined, was now much restored; and my spirits, when unchecked by the memory of my unhappy promise, rose proportionably. My father saw this change with pleasure, and he turned his thoughts towards the best method of eradicating

1

1 *philosopher.* Scientist.

the remains of my melancholy, which every now and then would return by fits, and with a devouring blackness overcast the approaching sunshine. At these moments I took refuge in the most perfect solitude. I passed whole days on the lake alone in a little boat, watching the clouds, and listening to the rippling of the waves, silent and listless. But the fresh air and bright sun seldom failed to restore me to some degree of composure; and, on my return, I met the salutations of my friends with a readier smile and a more cheerful heart.

It was after my return from one of these rambles that my father, calling me aside, thus addressed me :—

" I am happy to remark, my dear son, that you have resumed your former pleasures, and seem to be returning to yourself. And yet you are still unhappy, and still avoid our society. For some time I was lost in conjecture as to the cause of this; but yesterday an idea struck me, and if it is well founded, I conjure you to avow it. Reserve on such a point would be not only useless, but draw down treble misery on us all."

I trembled violently at this exordium, and my father continued—

" I confess, my son, that I have always looked forward to your marriage with your cousin as the tie of our domestic comfort, and the stay of my declining years. You were attached to each other from your earliest infancy; you studied together, and appeared, in dispositions and tastes, entirely suited to one another. But so blind is the

2 *as your sister.* It has already been noted that Mary Shelley, precisely to avoid the suggestion of an incestuously close relationship between the cousins in her fiction, turned Elizabeth into a foundling in the 1831 edition of *Frankenstein*.

3 *competent fortune.* We have not been told how this came about, though it may be that Victor inherited the money from his mother or had been provided with an annuity by his father.

In 1816 the poet Shelley was in the process of realizing funds that came to him as a consequence of a complex agreement relating to his inheritance from his grandfather, Sir Bysshe Shelley, who had died the previous year. The financial settlement, which relieved Shelley's immediate economic problems, had intricate psychological implications, since it came about after a protracted and intense quarrel over the uses of the estate with Sir Timothy Shelley, the poet's father.

The immediate point is that this settlement, after 1815, helped make life easier for the Shelley household so that, by the time *Frankenstein* came to be written, the Shelleys were no longer as hard pressed financially as they had been.

experience of man, that what I conceived to be the best assistants to my plan may have entirely destroyed it. **2** You, perhaps, regard her as your sister, without any wish that she might become your wife. Nay, you may have met with another whom you may love; and, considering yourself as bound in honour to' your cousin, this struggle may occasion the poignant misery which you appear to feel."

" My dear father, re-assure yourself. I love my cousin tenderly and sincerely. I never saw any woman who excited, as Elizabeth does, my warmest admiration and affection. My future hopes and prospects are entirely bound up in the expectation of our union."

" The expression of your sentiments on this subject, my dear Victor, gives me more pleasure than I have for some time experienced. If you feel thus, we shall assuredly be happy, however present events may cast a gloom over us. But it is this gloom, which appears to have taken so strong a hold of your mind, that I wish to dissipate. Tell me, therefore, whether you object to an immediate solemnization of the marriage. We have been unfortunate, and recent events have drawn us from that every-day tranquillity befitting my years and infirmities. You are younger; yet I do not suppose, possessed as you **3** are of a competent fortune, that an early marriage would at all interfere with any future plans of honour and utility that you may have formed. Do not suppose, however, that I wish to dictate happiness to you, or that a delay on your part would cause me any se-

4 *deadly weight.* Victor is thinking of his own wedding as this fleeting allusion to *The Rime of the Ancient Mariner* crosses his mind. This is not surprising. Coleridge's *Ancient Mariner* tells his story to a wedding guest who learns from it the higher dimensions of love.

rious uneasiness. Interpret my words with candour, and answer me, I conjure you, with confidence and sincerity."

I listened to my father in silence, and remained for some time incapable of offering any reply. I revolved rapidly in my mind a multitude of thoughts, and endeavoured to arrive at some conclusion. Alas! to me the idea of an immediate union with my cousin was one of horror and dismay. I was bound by a solemn promise, which I had not yet fulfilled, and dared not break; or, if I did, what manifold miseries might not impend over me and my devoted family! Could I enter into a festival **4** with this deadly weight yet hanging round my neck, and bowing me to the ground. I must perform my engagement, and let the monster depart with his mate, before I allowed myself to enjoy the delight of an union from which I expected peace.

I remembered also the necessity imposed upon me of either journeying to England, or entering into a long correspondence with those philosophers of that country, whose knowledge and discoveries were of indispensable use to me in my present undertaking. The latter method of obtaining the desired intelligence was dilatory and unsatisfactory: besides, any variation was agreeable to me, and I was delighted with the idea of spending a year or two in change of scene and variety of occupation, in absence from my family; during which period some event might happen which would restore me to them in peace and happiness: my promise

5 *for ever.* Victor, as he has done before, is willing to soothe himself by a flight of fantasy. In Volume I, page 74, he simply ran away and left his mess behind, hoping it too might simply disappear.

6 *Strasburgh.* Strasburgh (now usually spelled Strasbourg) was French at the time the Shelley party visited it. A Roman city in the fifth century, it was destroyed by the Huns in A.D. 455. After it was rebuilt, it was a German city until it became a French possession as a result of the Treaty of Ryswick (1697). In 1871, it became German once more after the Treaty of Frankfurt (1871). In 1919, the Allied victory turned it French again until 1940 when advancing German armies turned it German. In 1944, it was French once more after the Allies freed the city.

For Mary Shelley, the daughter of politically radical and aggressively literate parents, it might have been pleasant to know (as perhaps she did) that Gutenberg is credited with having invented the printing press in Strasbourg and that Claude Rouget de Lisle, in 1792, composed "La Marseillaise" in Strasbourg.

Victor and Clerval's entire Rhine journey is a reflection of the return leg of the Shelley's 1814 elopement trip. The notes to come will have as their source both Mary Shelley's *Journal* and her *History of a Six Weeks' Tour.* In *History of a Six Weeks' Tour,* p. 64, Mary Shelley describes three of their traveling companions as students of the university at Strasbourg: "Schwitz, a rather handsome, good tempered young man; Hoff, a kind of shapeless animal, with a heavy, ugly German face; and Schneider, who was nearly an ideot [sic]."

7 *both.* That is, Victor and Elizabeth will have become wiser.

5 might be fulfilled, and the monster have departed; or some accident might occur to destroy him, and put an end to my slavery for ever.

These feelings dictated my answer to my father. I expressed a wish to visit England; but, concealing the true reasons of this request, I clothed my desires under the guise of wishing to travel and see the world before I sat down for life within the walls of my native town.

I urged my entreaty with earnestness, and my father was easily induced to comply; for a more indulgent and less dictatorial parent did not exist upon earth. Our plan was soon ar-**6**ranged. I should travel to Strasburgh, where Clerval would join me. Some short time would be spent in the towns of Holland, and our principal stay would be in England. We should return by France; and it was agreed that the tour should occupy the space of two years.

My father pleased himself with the reflection, that my union with Elizabeth should take place immediately on my return to Geneva. " These two years," said he, " will pass swiftly, and it will be the last delay that will oppose itself to your happiness. And, indeed, I earnestly desire that period to arrive, when we shall all be united, and neither hopes or fears arise to disturb our domestic calm."

" I am content," I replied, " with your arrangement. By that time we **7** shall both have become wiser, and I hope happier, than we at present are." I sighed; but my father kindly forbore

8 *the slave of my creature*. We have here the most extreme statement of the relationship of the creator to his creature. There are a series of other exchanges (Vol. II, p. 140; Vol. II, p. 210; Vol. III, pp. 250, 329) in which the roles of slave and master are traded between Victor and the creature.

9 *her understanding*. Elizabeth's diffident regret that she cannot travel is the nearest we come in *Frankenstein* to a statement of protest about the disabilities of women. Mary Shelley's mother, on the other hand, was an indefatigable traveler who, moreover, traveled not only without the protection of a man, but courageously took her infant daughter, Fanny, with her on strenuous trips through the Scandinavian countries.

to question me further concerning the cause of my dejection. He hoped that new scenes, and the amusement of travelling, would restore my tranquillity.

I now made arrangements for my journey; but one feeling haunted me, which filled me with fear and agitation. During my absence I should leave my friends unconscious of the existence of their enemy, and unprotected from his attacks, exasperated as he might be by my departure. But he had promised to follow me wherever I might go; and would he not accompany me to England? This imagination was dreadful in itself, but soothing, inasmuch as it supposed the safety of my friends. I was agonized with the idea of the possibility that the reverse of this might happen. But through the whole period

8 during which I was the slave of my creature, I allowed myself to be governed by the impulses of the moment; and my present sensations strongly intimated that the fiend would follow me, and exempt my family from the danger of his machinations.

It was in the latter end of August that I departed, to pass two years of exile. Elizabeth approved of the reasons of my departure, and only regretted that she had not the same opportunities of enlarging her experience,

9 and cultivating her understanding. She wept, however, as she bade me farewell, and entreated me to return happy and tranquil. " We all," said she, " depend upon you; and if you are miserable, what must be our feelings?"

"THE CARRIAGE THAT WAS TO
CONVEY ME AWAY."

10 *you, my friend.* The remark is addressed to Walton who, it will be remembered, is listening to Victor's recitation.

 Clerval's journal, though it is mentioned here, never plays a role in *Frankenstein*. In Mary Shelley's actual journey down the Rhine, both of her traveling companions—Percy Shelley and Claire Clairmont—did, in fact, keep journals.

I threw myself into the carriage that was to convey me away, hardly knowing whither I was going, and careless of what was passing around. I remembered only, and it was with a bitter anguish that I reflected on it, to order that my chemical instruments should be packed to go with me: for I resolved to fulfil my promise while abroad, and return, if possible, a free man. Filled with dreary imaginations, I passed through many beautiful and majestic scenes; but my eyes were fixed and unobserving. I could only think of the bourne of my travels, and the work which was to occupy me whilst they endured.

After some days spent in listless indolence, during which I traversed many leagues, I arrived at Strasburgh, where I waited two days for Clerval. He came. Alas, how great was the contrast between us! He was alive to every new scene; joyful when he saw the beauties of the setting sun, and more happy when he beheld it rise, and recommence a new day. He pointed out to me the shifting colours of the landscape, and the appearances of the sky. " This is what it is to live;" he cried, " now I enjoy existence! But you, my dear Frankenstein, wherefore are you desponding and sorrowful?" In truth, I was occupied by gloomy thoughts, and neither saw the descent of the evening star, nor the golden sun-rise reflected in the Rhine.— **10** And you, my friend, would be far more amused with the journal of Clerval, who observed the scenery with an eye of feeling and delight, than to listen to

11 *Manheim.* In 1814, Mary and Percy Shelley and Claire Clairmont stopped for a time in Mannheim, a city which is situated on the confluence of the rivers Neckar and Rhine.

In *History of a Six Weeks' Tour*, p. 66, Mary Shelley writes: "We saw on the shores few objects that called forth our attention, if I except the town of Manheim, which was strikingly neat and clean. It was situated at about a mile from the river, and the road to it was planted on each side with beautiful acacias."

12 *Mayence.* Modern Mainz.

The eloping travelers of 1814 reached Mainz on September 3 at noon. The *History of a Six Weeks' Tour* records: "The town itself is old, the streets narrow, and the houses high: the cathedral and towers of the town still bear marks of the bombardment which took place in the revolutionary war" (p. 67).

In Mary Shelley's *Journal* (p. 13), there is a happy note that she and Percy Shelley were for a time alone—without Claire.

13 *ruined castles.* In the *Journal* (p. 13) we read that "a ruined tower, with its desolated windows, stood on the summit of another hill that jutted into the river." In *History of a Six Weeks' Tour* we are told (pp. 68–69): "We were carried down by a dangerously rapid current, and saw on either side of us hills covered with vines and trees, craggy cliffs crowned by desolate towers and wooded islands, where picturesque ruins peeped from behind the foliage, and cast the shadows of their forms on the troubled waters, which distorted without deforming them."

14 *the time of the vintage.* That is, late August, early September. The Shelley party, as they made their Rhine trip in 1814, also heard the "songs of the vintagers" (*History of a Six Weeks' Tour*, p. 69).

my reflections. I, a miserable wretch, haunted by a curse that shut up every avenue to enjoyment.

We had agreed to descend the Rhine in a boat from Strasburgh to Rotterdam, whence we might take shipping for London. During this voyage, we passed by many willowy islands, and saw several beautiful towns. We staid **11** a day at Manheim, and, on the fifth from our departure from Strasburgh, **12** arrived at Mayence. The course of the Rhine below Mayence becomes much more picturesque. The river descends rapidly, and winds between hills, not high, but steep, and of beautiful forms. **13** We saw many ruined castles standing on the edges of precipices, surrounded by black woods, high and inaccessible. This part of the Rhine, indeed, presents a singularly variegated landscape. In one spot you view rugged hills, ruined castles overlooking tremendous precipices, with the dark Rhine rushing beneath; and, on the sudden turn of a promontory, flourishing vineyards, with green sloping banks, and a meandering river, and populous towns, occupy the scene.

14 We travelled at the time of the vintage, and heard the song of the labourers, as we glided down the stream. Even I, depressed in mind, and my spirits continually agitated by gloomy feelings, even I was pleased. I lay at the bottom of the boat, and, as I gazed on the cloudless blue sky, I seemed to drink in a tranquillity to which I had long been a stranger. And if these were my sensations, who can describe those of Henry? He felt as if he had

15 *priest and his mistress.* Three years after her 1814 Rhine journey, Mary Shelley in her *History of a Six Weeks' Tour* (pp. 48–49), wrote that "opposite Brunen, they tell the story of a priest and his mistress, who, flying from persecution, inhabited a cottage at the foot of the snows. One winter night an avalanche overwhelmed them, but their plaintive voices are still heard in stormy nights, calling for succour from the peasants."

16 *La Valais.* A valley extending from the source of the Rhone to Lake Geneva. In 1814 Mary Shelley was ill, passing through Valais, and, as she noted in her *Journal* (p. 11), she and her fellow travelers were heartily "tired of wheeled machines."

17 *Pays de Vaud.* In the *Letters of Percy Bysshe Shelley* (p. 353), we read that "the coasts of the Pays de Vaud, though full of villages and vineyards, present an aspect of tranquillity and peculiar beauty which well compensates for the solitude which I am accustomed to admire. The hills are very high and rocky, crowned and interspersed with woods. Waterfalls echo from the cliffs, and shine afar."

been transported to Fairy-land, and enjoyed a happiness seldom tasted by man. " I have seen," he said, " the most beautiful scenes of my own country; I have visited the lakes of Lucerne and Uri, where the snowy mountains descend almost perpendicularly to the water, casting black and impenetrable shades, which would cause a gloomy and mournful appearance, were it not for the most verdant islands that relieve the eye by their gay appearance; I have seen this lake agitated by a tempest, when the wind tore up whirlwinds of water, and gave you an idea of what the water-spout must be on the great ocean, and the waves dash with fury the base of the mountain, **15** where the priest and his mistress were overwhelmed by an avalanche, and where their dying voices are still said to be heard amid the pauses of the nightly wind; I have seen the moun- **16, 17** tains of La Valais, and the Pays de Vaud: but this country, Victor, pleases me more than all those wonders. The mountains of Switzerland are more majestic and strange; but there is a charm in the banks of this divine river, that I never before saw equalled. Look at that castle which overhangs yon precipice; and that also on the island, almost concealed amongst the foliage of those lovely trees; and now that group of labourers coming from among their vines; and that village half-hid in the recess of the mountain. Oh, surely, the spirit that inhabits and guards this place has a soul more in harmony with man, than those who pile the glacier, or retire to the inaccessible

LEIGH HUNT BY H. MEYER.

18   *poetry of nature*. The phrase is from Leigh Hunt's narrative poem *The Story of Rimini*, published in 1816. This reference to Hunt's poem is one more detail that makes it impossible for us to accept an eighteenth-century date for the action of *Frankenstein*.

Hunt played a crucial role in Percy Shelley's life. It was he who, as editor of *The Examiner*, favorably reviewed Shelley's poem *Alastor*. The review served to establish Shelley as a rising poet. Hunt was always a faithful friend to Shelley and to Mary Shelley as well, though his relationship with the poet is colored by his applications for financial help, which Shelley, for the most part, was glad to give him.

Though Mary believed that Hunt did not like her, she was, after Shelley's death, concerned enough for Hunt's welfare to intercede with Lord Byron on Hunt's behalf when Byron, disappointed by the reception of a new magazine, *The Liberal*, edited by Hunt, decided to withdraw his support from it. Mary Shelley wrote, "Consider that, however Moore may laugh at Rimini-Pimini that Hunt is a very good man—Shelley was greatly attached to him on account of his integrity."

19   *from the eye*. William Wordsworth's (1770–1850) "Lines Composed a Few Miles Above Tintern Abbey" was written on July 13, 1798. The ruins of the abbey overlook the river Wye in Monmouthshire. The poem is frequently cited by critics as the quintessential expression of the early Romantic movement in literature.

20   *perished?* Victor is getting well ahead of his story, as we will see.

peaks of the mountains of our own country."

Clerval! beloved friend! even now it delights me to record your words, and to dwell on the praise of which you are so eminently deserving.   He was a **18** being formed in the " very poetry of nature." His wild and enthusiastic imagination was chastened by the sensibility of his heart. His soul overflowed with ardent affections, and his friendship was of that devoted and wondrous nature that the worldly-minded teach us to look for only in the imagination. But even human sympathies were not sufficient to satisfy his eager mind. The scenery of external nature, which others regard only with admiration, he loved with ardour :

——————" The sounding cataract
Haunted *him* like a passion : the tall rock,
The mountain, and the deep and gloomy wood,
Their colours and their forms, were then to him
An appetite ; a feeling, and a love,
That had no need of a remoter charm,
By thought supplied, or any interest
19 Unborrowed from the eye ."

And where does he now exist ? Is this gentle and lovely being lost for ever ? Has this mind so replete with ideas, imaginations fanciful and magnificent, which formed a world, whose existence depended on the life of its **20** creator ; has this mind perished ? Does it now only exist in my memory ? No, it is not thus ; your form so divinely wrought, and beaming with beauty, has decayed, but your spirit still visits and consoles your unhappy friend

Pardon this gush of sorrow ; these ineffectual words are but a slight tri-

21 *Cologne.* The 1798 edition of the *Encyclopaedia Britannica* describes Cologne as a melancholy city with little to see but priests, friars, and students, and little to be heard but the ringing of bells.

When the Shelley *ménage* reached Cologne in 1814, Mary Shelley had nothing to say in her *Journal* about the town except that she and her companions reserved seats in the diligence [public carriage] and retired to rest (p. 14).

22 *post.* To go by public land conveyance.

EN ROUTE TO ROTTERDAM.

23 *Rotterdam.* Rotterdam, which is today the largest port in the Netherlands, did not become a great port city until the nineteenth century, after the construction of the New Waterway (1866–1872). For American readers of *Frankenstein*, the city has special significance. It was from Rotterdam that the Pilgrim Fathers set sail to try their fortunes in the New World.

Mary Shelley tells us, in her *History of a Six Weeks' Tour* (pp. 75–76), that Dutch roads "were excellent, but the Dutch have contrived as many inconveniences as possible. In our journey of the day before, we had passed by a windmill, which was so situated with regard to the road, that it was only by keeping close to the opposite side, and passing quickly, that we could avoid the sweep of its sails."

The Shelleys, in the course of their 1814 elopement journey, paid thirty English pounds as the entire cost of their travel from Switzerland down the Rhine.

24 *December.* The creature then is two years old.

This month is in conflict with what we are told on page 233.

"HOLLAND."

bute to the unexampled worth of Henry, but they soothe my heart, overflowing with the anguish which his remembrance creates. I will proceed with my tale.

21 Beyond Cologne we descended to the plains of Holland; and we resolved to

22 post the remainder of our way; for the wind was contrary, and the stream of the river was too gentle to aid us.

Our journey here lost the interest arising from beautiful scenery; but we

23 arrived in a few days at Rotterdam, whence we proceeded by sea to England. It was on a clear morning,

24 in the latter days of December, that I first saw the white cliffs of Britain. The banks of the Thames presented a new scene; they were flat, but fertile, and almost every town was marked by

25 *Tilbury Fort.* Tilbury Fort was a strategic point in the struggle between the English and the Spanish Armada in 1588. Elizabeth's commander-in-chief, the earl of Leicester, kept his main camp at Tilbury and saw to it that a boom was constructed and positioned across the Thames at that spot to thwart the Spanish army, camped across the Channel at Nieuport and Dunkirk, in their attempt to invade England and make their way up the Thames to London. On August 7, the Queen sailed down the Thames from Greenwich to Tilbury. She spent the next day reviewing the English army there, promising to join with them in defeating the Spanish invaders, not realizing that the Armada had fled and that the Spanish army across the Channel was no longer a threat.

26 *Gravesend, Woolwich, and Greenwich.* All three of these cities are situated on the south bank of the Thames. Gravesend is located at the estuary of the Thames, while the other two cities are nine miles and four and one-half miles from London respectively. They would thus be passed by any traveler who wished to reach London by boat.

GRAVESEND: A disembarkation point for travelers arriving from the Continent who intend to proceed to London. The Shelley party arrived at Gravesend at the end of the 1814 elopement trip. Mary records in her *Journal*, page 15: "We arrive at Gravesend, and with great difficulty prevail on the Captain to trust us. We go by boat to London." The difficulty was that they had arrived in England without money. The rest of their first day home was spent trying to raise enough to pay off the Channel fare.

WOOLWICH: A city known for its shipyards and docks, its magazines of war equipment (as the home of the Royal Arsenal, established 1716), and its military academy.

GREENWICH: The famous Greenwich Observatory is located here, erected by Charles II and furnished with mathematical instruments for astronomical uses. Kings Henry VII and Henry VIII had royal palaces at Greenwich and both Queen Mary and Queen Elizabeth were born here.

27 *St. Paul's.* Sir Christopher Wren rejected the idea that there was once a temple of Diana on the spot where the church designed by him was begun in 1675. The building was finally completed in 1710. To this day it is regarded as an architectural wonder.

Once there were coffeehouses in the churchyard, which were visited by notable clergy and literary figures.

28 *the Tower.* Once the chief fortress of the city of London, the Tower is best known as a place of imprisonment. Notable persons held in the Tower include Sir Walter Raleigh and Mary Queen of Scots. There was a time when the lions of the royal menagerie were kept in the Tower.

the remembrance of some story. We **25** saw Tilbury Fort, and remembered the **26** Spanish armada; Gravesend, Woolwich, and Greenwich, places which I had heard of even in my country.

At length we saw the numerous **27** steeples of London, St. Paul's towering **28** above all, and the Tower famed in English history.

CHAPTER II.

1 LONDON was our present point of rest; we determined to remain several months in this wonderful and celebrated city. Clerval desired the intercourse of the men of genius and talent who flourished at this time; but this was with me a secondary object; I was principally occupied with the means of obtaining the information necessary for the completion of my promise, and quickly availed myself of the letters of introduction that I had brought with me, addressed to the most distinguished natural philosophers.

If this journey had taken place during my days of study and happiness, it would have afforded me inexpressible pleasure. But a blight had come over my existence, and I only visited these people for the sake of the information they might give me on the subject in which my interest was so terribly profound. Company was irksome to me; when alone, I could fill my mind with the sights of heaven and earth; the voice of Henry soothed me, and I could thus cheat myself into a transitory peace. But busy uninteresting joyous faces brought back despair to my heart. I saw an insurmountable barrier placed between me and my fellow-men; this barrier was sealed with the blood of William and Justine; and to reflect on the events

1 *London*. Percy Shelley courted Mary Godwin in London, and it was to London that Mary and Percy Shelley returned with Claire after their elopement journey, only to spend the next few months pursuing or avoiding moneylenders. Even when the Shelleys no longer lived in London, Percy Shelley frequently traveled there to look after financial and publishing matters.

2 *my former self.* We have seen how the creature and Victor are aspects of each other. Now Mary Shelley offers us Clerval as part of the psychological equation.

In any event, it must be clear by now that for Mary Shelley, Clerval represents the gentler, non-demonic Victor, though it can be argued that Clerval is a kind of male Elizabeth—an idealized, and blander version of Mary Shelley herself.

3 *to collect.* Where in London he would find the materials for his "workshop of filthy creation" we are left to imagine.

4 *Scotland.* Victor's Scottish journey, described in the pages to come, undoubtedly has its origins in a childhood experience of Mary Shelley's. Because of a constitutional weakness, the fifteen-year-old Mary was sent to stay at the home of a Scottish friend named Baxter in Dundee. Life in the Baxter household, more than her own experience with Mrs. Clairmont and Godwin in London, gave Mary the sense of what a contented genial family life might be like. At Dundee, writes R. Glynn Grylls, "Mary learned to love not only the woods and mountains where she might wander at will, alone with a book or in company with Isabel and Christy, but also the atmosphere of a quiet and contented home-circle such as she had not known before" (*Mary Shelley*, p. 19).

In the Introduction to the 1831 edition of *Frankenstein*, Mary Shelley describes her Scottish experience as follows (see Appendix for complete text of this Introduction): "My habitual residence was on the blank and dreary northern shores of the Tay, near Dundee. Blank and dreary on retrospection I call them; they were not so to me then. They were the eyry of freedom, and the pleasant region where unheeded I could commune with the creatures of my fancy. . . . It was beneath the trees of the grounds belonging to our house, or on the bleak sides of the woodless mountains near, that my true composition, the airy flights of my imagination, were born and fostered."

5 *Perth.* The name of a county and its capital, situated on the eastern coast of Scotland. The county exhibits characteristics of both highlands and lowlands. Certain areas are very rich farmlands while the more mountainous areas serve as pastureland for various kinds of livestock.

The city of Perth is situated on the banks of the Tay. It was the residence of the kings of Scotland until the time of James II, who moved the court and parliament to Edinburgh.

connected with those names filled my soul with anguish.

But in Clerval I saw the image of my **2** former self; he was inquisitive, and anxious to gain experience and instruction. The difference of manners which he observed was to him an inexhaustible source of instruction and amusement. He was for ever busy; and the only check to his enjoyments was my sorrowful and dejected mien. I tried to conceal this as much as possible, that I might not debar him from the pleasures natural to one who was entering on a new scene of life, undisturbed by any care or bitter recollection. I often refused to accompany him, alleging another engagement, that I might remain alone. I now also be- **3** gan to collect the materials necessary for my new creation, and this was to me like the torture of single drops of water continually falling on the head. Every thought that was devoted to it was an extreme anguish, and every word that I spoke in allusion to it caused my lips to quiver, and my heart to palpitate.

After passing some months in London, we received a letter from a person **4** in Scotland, who had formerly been our visitor at Geneva. He mentioned the beauties of his native country, and asked us if those were not sufficient allurements to induce us to prolong our journey as far north as Perth, where **5** he resided. Clerval eagerly desired to accept this invitation; and I, although I abhorred society, wished to view again mountains and streams, and all the wondrous works with which Nature adorns her chosen dwelling-places.

"THE BEAUTIES OF HIS NATIVE COUNTRY."

6 *October.* Not if we are to believe what our author has told us on page 229, where she writes, "It was on a clear morning, in the latter days of December, that I first saw the white cliffs of Britain." Readers attempting to keep track of Victor's calendar must decide here which date to accept. For the sake of symmetry, this editor will continue to work with the October date. The choice of October seems reasonable too because it fits the assertion that Victor and Clerval spent some or several months in London.

"AS FAR NORTH AS PERTH."

6 We had arrived in England at the beginning of October, and it was now February. We accordingly determined to commence our journey towards the north at the expiration of another month. In this expedition we did not

"WE ACCORDINGLY DETERMINED
TO COMMENCE OUR JOURNEY."

7 *Edinburgh.* This picturesque city, the capital of Scotland, was described in the late eighteenth-century *Encyclopaedia Britannica* as being built on a "steep hill which rises from east to west terminating in a high and inaccessible rock. . . . Edinburgh, as not being properly a sea-port town has never been remarkable for trade. The chief advantages it enjoys arise from the supreme courts of justice which are there held; and from its college, which has become famous over Europe, particularly for physics."

Edinburgh played an important part in Percy Shelley's life. In 1810 he sent his poem "The Wandering Jew" to a publisher named Ballentine in Edinburgh, and on August 28, 1811 he was married there to Harriet Westbrook by the Reverend Joseph Robertson, a clergyman who was willing to marry young people without their parents' consent. T. J. Hogg, in his *Life of Shelley* (p. 93), describes the couple eating honeycombs shortly after their marriage. Hogg stayed with the Shelleys that week. Richard Holmes, in his *Shelley: The Pursuit* (p. 79), says that "altogether it is unlikely that Shelley was alone with Harriet for much more than seven days, three of which were spent in nonstop coach travel. It was a strange honeymoon à trois and showed from the outset Shelley's disinclination to live entirely in the company of one woman for more than a few hours at a time."

Edinburgh, in 1814, was the home of Mary Shelley's foster brother, Charles Clairmont, who worked for Constable's, a publishing house there.

8 *Windsor.* A town to the west of London in Berkshire. In the spring of 1815, shortly after the death of their baby, Percy Shelley took Mary for a brief visit to the Berkshire area, where they stayed at an inn near Windsor. Windsor was familiar country to Percy Shelley, who had lived in the region with his first wife, Harriet, and their children.

9 *Oxford.* The famous university city to the west of London on the banks of the Thames. The events referred to in this paragraph are those that took place during the British Rebellion and Civil Wars (1642–1666). Charles I surrendered to the Scots in May 1646. Edward Hyde, earl of Clarendon, was a royalist participant in the Civil War who later wrote two accounts of the period: *The History of the Rebellion and Civil Wars* and *The Life of Edward Hyde, Earl of Clarendon, by Himself.* Mary Shelley's *Journal* (pp. 65, 74) shows her reading Clarendon's *History* on September 29, 1816, and again on October 5. She was reading the *Life* on January 7, 1817. Her characterizations of Falkland, Goring, Charles I, and Henrietta Maria, his queen, are strongly influenced by Clarendon.

Oxford played an important part in the Civil Wars as a city loyal to King Charles. After the hostilities began, the royal court was moved to Oxford. Oxford, of course, played a significant role in Percy Shelley's life. He was expelled from Oxford in 1810 after sending copies of his pamphlet *The Necessity of Atheism* to officials and faculty of the university.

7
8,9 intend to follow the great road to Edinburgh, but to visit Windsor, Oxford, Matlock, and the Cumberland lakes, resolving to arrive at the completion of this tour about the end of July. I packed my chemical instruments, and the materials I had collected, resolving to finish my labours in some obscure nook in the northern highlands of Scotland.

We quitted London on the 27th of March, and remained a few days at Windsor, rambling in its beautiful forest. This was a new scene to us mountaineers; the majestic oaks, the quantity of game, and the herds of stately deer, were all novelties to us.

From thence we proceeded to Oxford. As we entered this city, our minds were filled with the remembrance of the events that had been transacted there more than a century and a half

10 before. It was here that Charles I. had collected his forces. This city had remained faithful to him, after the whole nation had forsaken his cause to join the standard of parliament and liberty. The memory of that unfortunate king,

OXFORD UNIVERSITY.

10 *Charles I.* Charles I ascended the English throne in 1625; he was executed in 1649. Clarendon admired the king and wrote glowingly of the year 1639 that Charles, "of all the princes of Europe . . . alone seemed to be seated on the pleasant promontory, that might safely view the tragic sufferings of all his neighbors about him. . . . His three kingdoms flourishing in entire peace and universal plenty, in danger of nothing but their own surfeits . . . and all these blessings under a prince of the greatest clemency and justice, and of the greatest piety and devotion, and the most indulgent to his subjects, and most solicitous for their happiness and prosperity" (Clarendon, *Selections from the History of the Rebellion and Civil Wars*, pp. 82–83).

11 *Falkland.* Lucius Cary, Viscount Falkland, was born in 1610, and died in battle in 1643. He served as secretary of state to Charles I from 1641 until his death. Clarendon writes of him: "But all his parts, abilities, and faculties, by art and industry, were not to be valued, or mentioned in comparison of his most accomplished mind and manners: his gentleness and affability was so transcendent and obliging, that it drew reverence, and some kind of compliance, from the roughest, and most unpolished, and stubborn constitutions" (Clarendon, *Selections from the History of the Rebellion and Civil Wars*, p. 67).

12 *Gower.* A misprint here for "Goring." Lord George Goring was born in 1583(?) and died in 1663. Mary Shelley, it seems clear, was impressed with Clarendon's admiring condemnation of Goring. Clarendon writes: "Goring could . . . and would, without hesitation, have broken any trust, or done any act of treachery, to have satisfied an ordinary passion or appetite; and, in truth, wanted nothing but industry (for he had wit, and courage, and understanding and ambition, uncontrolled by any fear of God or man) to have been as eminent and successful in the highest attempt in wickedness of any man in the age he lived in, or before. Of all his qualifications, dissimulation was his masterpiece; in which he so much excelled, that men were not ordinarily ashamed, or out of countenance, with being deceived but twice by him" (Clarendon, *Selections from the History of the Rebellion and Civil Wars*, p. 277).

13 *Isis.* The river Thames, north of the Oxford River.

COATS OF ARMS, VARIOUS COLLEGES, OXFORD UNIVERSITY.

11
12 and his companions, the amiable Falkland, the insolent Gower, his queen, and son, gave a peculiar interest to every part of the city, which they might be supposed to have inhabited. The spirit of elder days found a dwelling here, and we delighted to trace its footsteps. If these feelings had not found an imaginary gratification, the appearance of the city had yet in itself sufficient beauty to obtain our admiration. The colleges are ancient and picturesque; the streets are almost magnificent; and **13** the lovely Isis, which flows beside it through meadows of exquisite verdure, is spread forth into a placid expanse of waters, which reflects its majestic assemblage of towers, and spires, and domes, embosomed among aged trees.

I enjoyed this scene; and yet my en-

14 *peaceful happiness.* The creature too says that he was "benevolent and good." (See Vol. II, p. 142.)

15 *blasted tree.* We were prepared for this blasted tree as early as Volume I, page 43, where Victor sees lightning shred a beautiful oak to "thin ribbands." We were told then that it was an event that led directly to his later interest in science.

16 *the field.* Chalgrove Field.
Our author seems warmhearted enough to admire both Charles I and his adversary, but so was Clarendon, whose work affects these pages. Clarendon writes: "[Hampden] was very temperate in diet, and a supreme governor over all his passions and affections, and had thereby a great power over other men's. He was of an industry and vigilance not to be tired out, or wearied by the most laborious; and of parts not to be imposed upon by the most subtle or sharp; and of a personal courage equal to his best parts; so that he was an enemy not to be wished wherever he might have been made a friend" (Clarendon, *Selections from the History of the Rebellion and Civil Wars,* p. 84).

17 *into my flesh.* This image may well have been suggested to Mary Shelley by a visit that Byron and Percy Shelley paid to the torture chamber and dungeons at Chillon in the course of their sailing tour of Lake Geneva. There was a moment during that trip when Shelley, who could not swim, came perilously close to drowning. At Chillon the poets heard the tale of François de Bonnivard, a sixteenth-century enemy of Charles the III of Savoy, whose long imprisonment in the castle served Byron later as the impetus for his poem "The Prisoner of Chillon."

18 *Matlock.* A town in Derby. Mary Shelley's remark about the neighborhood of Matlock resembling the scenery of Switzerland is simply an inversion of what she wrote in her *Journal* (p. 51) for July 21, 1816, where she says: "The scene, at the distance of half a mile from Clusis, differs from that of Matlock in little else than the immensity of its proportions, and in its untameable, inaccessible solitude."
Percy Shelley too, in his *Letters* (p. 358), connected Matlock with Chamounix: "There is a *Cabinet d'Histoire Naturelle* at Chamouni, just as at Matlock & Keswick & Clifton."

joyment was embittered both by the memory of the past, and the anticipation of the future. I was formed for

14 peaceful happiness. During my youthful days discontent never visited my mind; and if I was ever overcome by *ennui*, the sight of what is beautiful in nature, or the study of what is excellent and sublime in the productions of man, could always interest my heart, and communicate elasticity to my spirits.

15 But I am a blasted tree; the bolt has entered my soul; and I felt then that I should survive to exhibit, what I shall soon cease to be—a miserable spectacle of wrecked humanity, pitiable to others, and abhorrent to myself.

We passed a considerable period at Oxford, rambling among its environs, and endeavouring to identify every spot which might relate to the most animating epoch of English history. Our little voyages of discovery were often prolonged by the successive objects that presented themselves. We visited the tomb of the illustrious Hampden, and

16 the field on which that patriot fell. For a moment my soul was elevated from its debasing and miserable fears to contemplate the divine ideas of liberty and self-sacrifice, of which these sights were the monuments and the remembrancers. For an instant I dared to shake off my chains, and look around me with a free and lofty spirit; but the iron had eaten

17 into my flesh, and I sank again, trembling and hopeless, into my miserable self.

We left Oxford with regret, and pro-

18 ceeded to Matlock, which was our next place of rest. The country in the

19 *Derby*. A county in the center of England. The *Encyclopaedia Britannica* for 1797 describes it as having a pleasant climate and a soil very useful for agricultural purposes, particularly the growing of grain; the western portion of the county is described as being bleaker, more susceptible to inclement winds and rain.

20 *Cumberland and Westmoreland*. These two counties in the north of England, near the Scottish border, are commonly known as the Lake District. Victor Frankenstein is not the only one to compare the Lake District to Switzerland. William Wordsworth, in his 1810 *Guide to the Lakes* (p. 106) wrote: "I am not afraid of asserting that in many points of view our LAKES, also, are much more interesting than those of the Alps; . . . from being more happily proportioned to the other features of the landscape; and next, both as being infinitely more pellucid, and less subject to agitation from the winds."

Mary Shelley would have known that the poet Shelley had spent some time in Cumberland with his first wife, Harriet, in 1811. In his *Letters* (pp. 142, 148) we read: "I have taken a long *solitary* ramble today. These gigantic mountains piled on each other, these waterfalls, these million shaped clouds tinted by the varying colors of innumerable rainbows hanging between yourself and a lake as smooth and dark as a plain of polished jet . . . Nature here sports in the awful waywardness of her solitude." And again: "These mountains are now capped with snow. The lake as I see it hence is glassy & calm. Snow vapours tinted by the loveliest colors of refraction pass far below the summits of these giant rocks. The scene even in a winter sunset is inexpressibly lovely."

21 *men of talent*. Such as the so-called Lake poets, Wordsworth, Coleridge, Southey, and De Quincey. Each of them at some time was known to, or friendly with, William Godwin and Mary Wollstonecraft.

neighbourhood of this village resembled, to a greater degree, the scenery of Switzerland; but every thing is on a lower scale, and the green hills want the crown of distant white Alps, which always attend on the piny mountains of my native country. We visited the wondrous cave, and the little cabinets of natural history, where the curiosities are disposed in the same manner as in the collections at Servox and Chamounix. The latter name made me tremble, when pronounced by Henry; and I hastened to quit Matlock, with which that terrible scene was thus associated.

19
20 From Derby still journeying northward, we passed two months in Cumberland and Westmoreland. I could now almost fancy myself among the Swiss mountains. The little patches of snow which yet lingered on the northern sides of the mountains, the lakes, and the dashing of the rocky streams, were all familiar and dear sights to me. Here also we made some acquaintances, who almost contrived to cheat me into happiness. The delight of Clerval was proportionably greater than mine; his mind expanded in the **21** company of men of talent, and he found in his own nature greater capacities and resources than he could have imagined himself to have possessed while he associated with his inferiors. " I could pass my life here," said he to me; "and among these mountains I should scarcely regret Switzerland and the Rhine."

But he found that a traveller's life is one that includes much pain amidst its enjoyments. His feelings are for

22 *I was guiltless.* The question of Victor's guilt is at least debatable. What is interesting here is the phrase itself. The poet Shelley was a great self-exculpator and fondly believed that in his dealings with mankind he was perpetually without guilt (see p. 325, note 30 for a melodramatic example). Mary Shelley once said of her husband that "it will be sufficient to say that, in all he did, at the time of doing it, he believed himself justified to his own conscience."

"I VISITED EDINBURGH."

ever on the stretch; and when he begins to sink into repose, he finds himself obliged to quit that on which he rests in pleasure for something new, which again engages his attention, and which also he forsakes for other novelties.

We had scarcely visited the various lakes of Cumberland and Westmoreland, and conceived an affection for some of the inhabitants, when the period of our appointment with our Scotch friend approached, and we left them to travel on.   For my own part I was not sorry.   I had now neglected my promise for some time, and I feared the effects of the dæmon's disappointment.   He might remain in Switzerland, and wreak his vengeance on my relatives.   This idea pursued me, and tormented me at every moment from which I might otherwise have snatched repose and peace.   I waited for my letters with feverish impatience: if they were delayed, I was miserable, and overcome by a thousand fears; and when they arrived, and I saw the superscription of Elizabeth or my father, I hardly dared to read and ascertain my fate.   Sometimes I thought that the fiend followed me, and might expedite my remissness by murdering my companion.   When these thoughts possessed me, I would not quit Henry for a moment, but followed him as his shadow, to protect him from the fancied rage of his destroyer.   I felt as if I had committed some great crime, the **22** consciousness of which haunted me.   I was guiltless, but I had indeed drawn down a horrible curse upon my head, as mortal as that of crime.

I visited Edinburgh with languid

"EDINBURGH, ITS ROMANTIC CASTLE."

23 *Arthur's Seat, St. Bernard's Well, and the Pentland Hills.*
Arthur's Seat: A hill in Edinburgh approximately eight hundred feet high. King Arthur was said to have fought a battle near here in the fifth century.

Saint Bernard's Well: This circular, templelike monument was commissioned by Lord Gardenstone in 1790 in gratitude for the benefits he received from drinking the well's mineral spring waters.

Pentland Hills: These mountains south of Edinburgh extend for some ten miles south, separating the city from the countryside beyond.

24 *Coupar.* In Mary Shelley's time, Coupar, in the northwestern division of Fifeshire, on the southern shore of the Tay, had a population of two thousand. Coupar was a regularly constituted Scottish "burch" well before the end of the fourteenth century. The tale is that Macduff's wife and children (Shakespeare's *Macbeth*, Act IV, Scene 2, ll. 74–89) were murdered in Coupar Castle.

25 *St. Andrews.* Saint Andrews is a seaboard parish in the county of Fife looking out on Saint Andrews Bay. The town is famous for its university, its cathedral, and its castle. In the light of the grisly tale Mary Shelley has written, it may be worth repeating here a local legend of Saint Andrews, which she may have known:

A certain Greek monk named Regulus was instructed three times to visit the shrine of Saint Andrews and to take certain relics of that saint to the edge of the world. Regulus, with the help of his friends, made the long journey from Greece and stole an arm bone and three fingers of the right hand of the crucified saint. Then he set sail for the world's edge, but misfortune dogged him. Two years later, he would have sailed over the edge of the world into ultima Thule but was saved by being wrecked on the coast of Fife. There, with the help of Ungus, son of Urguist, king of the Picts, he built the chapel and tower of Saint Regulus.

eyes and mind; and yet that city might have interested the most unfortunate being. Clerval did not like it so well as Oxford; for the antiquity of the latter city was more pleasing to him. But the beauty and regularity of the new town of Edinburgh, its romantic castle, and its environs, the most delightful in the world, Arthur's Seat, St. Bernard's Well, and the Pentland Hills, compensated him for the change, and filled him with cheerfulness and admiration. But I was impatient to arrive at the termination of my journey.

We left Edinburgh in a week, passing through Coupar, St. Andrews, and

23

24,25

"ST. BERNARD'S WELL."

"THE PENTLAND HILLS."

COUPAR, ON THE EDEN RIVER.

A CONTEMPORARY VIEW
OF COUPAR AND THE EDEN RIVER.

FAIR AT ST. ANDREW'S.

ST. ANDREW'S UNIVERSITY.

RUINS AT ST. ANDREW'S.

A VIEW OF PERTH.

26 *Tay.* This river, the largest in Scotland, flows through Perthshire and Dundee. We have already remarked on Mary Shelley's memories of this area and the river Tay (see p. 232, note 4).

26 along the banks of the Tay, to Perth, where our friend expected us.   But I was in no mood to laugh and talk with strangers, or enter into their feelings or plans with the good humour expected from a guest; and accordingly I told Clerval that I wished to make the tour of Scotland alone. "Do you," said I, "enjoy yourself, and let this be our rendezvous.   I may be absent a month or two; but do not interfere with my motions, I entreat you: leave me to peace and solitude for a short time; and when I return, I hope it will be with a lighter heart, more congenial to your own temper."

Henry wished to dissuade me; but, seeing me bent on this plan, ceased to remonstrate.   He entreated me to write often.   " I had rather be with you," he said, " in your solitary rambles, than with these Scotch people, whom I do not know: hasten then, my dear friend, to return, that I may again feel myself somewhat at home, which I cannot do in your absence."

Having parted from my friend, I determined to visit some remote spot of Scotland, and finish my work in solitude.   I did not doubt but that the

"THE REMOTEST OF THE ORKNEYS."

27 *remotest of the Orkneys.* Which of the Orkneys fits this description it is difficult to say. In the twentieth century, the islands are neither as desolate nor as poverty stricken as our author describes them, and are, in fact, most famous for having been the scene of the scuttling of the German fleet at Scapa Flow in 1917.

The 1797 edition of the *Encyclopaedia Britannica* says of the poorer inhabitants of the Orkneys that they wore pieces of sealskin for shoes, lived primarily on salt fish, and were very superstitious.

It is too bad for Victor that he was unaware of the curiosities to be found on some of the Orkney Islands: on the isle of Sanda and in Westray human bones have been found far exceeding normal human size. Mary Shelley too may have heard that the Orkneys were remarkable for producing men of gigantic stature.

"HARDLY MORE THAN A ROCK."

28 *gaunt and scraggy limbs.* Hardly a description of the contemporary Orcadian who, except in the winter, is given to a hearty cheerfulness characterized by the sprightly greeting in the streets, "Aye, aye," spoken quickly and with a perceptible lilt.

monster followed me, and would discover himself to me when I should have finished, that he might receive his companion.

With this resolution I traversed the **27** northern highlands, and fixed on one of the remotest of the Orkneys as the scene labours. It was a place fitted for such a work, being hardly more than a rock, whose high sides were continually beaten upon by the waves. The soil was barren, scarcely affording pasture for a few miserable cows, and oatmeal for its inhabitants, which consisted of **28** five persons, whose gaunt and scraggy limbs gave tokens of their miserable fare. Vegetables and bread, when they indulged in such luxuries, and even fresh water, was to be procured from

AN ORKANDER AT WORK.

29 *the main land.* If Mary Shelley meant that this remote island was five miles from the mainland of Scotland, then it is impossible to identify it precisely. However, if she knew that the large middle island in the Orkney group was called The Mainland, then we can say with some certainty that Victor took up his abode on the Brough of Bifa.

30 *ungazed at and unmolested.* Unmolested, perhaps. Ungazed at is most unlikely. If the Orkney island is as desolate as Mary Shelley describes it, and if its inhabitants are as squalidly poor, they must surely have gazed in wonder at this foreign-speaking rich man who brought furniture and chemical apparatus to their dreary world, not to mention whatever God-forsaken materials would be necessary to furnish his "workshop of filthy creation."

ANOTHER NINETEENTH-CENTURY
VIEW OF THE ORKNEYS.

29 the main land, which was about five miles distant.

On the whole island there were but three miserable huts, and one of these was vacant when I arrived. This I hired. It contained but two rooms, and these exhibited all the squalidness of the most miserable penury. The thatch had fallen in, the walls were unplastered, and the door was off its hinges. I ordered it to be repaired, bought some furniture, and took possession; an incident which would, doubtless, have occasioned some surprise, had not all the senses of the cottagers been benumbed by want and squalid poverty.

30 As it was, I lived ungazed at and unmolested, hardly thanked for the pittance of food and clothes which I gave; so much does suffering blunt even the coarsest sensations of men.

In this retreat I devoted the morning to labour; but in the evening, when the weather permitted, I walked on the stony beach of the sea, to listen to the waves as they roared, and dashed at my feet. It was a monotonous, yet ever-changing scene. I thought of Switzerland; it was far different from this desolate and appalling landscape. Its hills are covered with vines, and its cottages are scattered thickly in the plains. Its fair lakes reflect a blue and gentle sky; and, when troubled by the winds, their tumult is but as the play of a lively infant, when compared to the roarings of the giant ocean.

In this manner I distributed my occupations when I first arrived; but, as I proceeded in my labour, it became

31 *filthy process.* Once more, the work of creation is described as filthy. How Victor acquired and transported with him the materials he needed for his work is left unspecified.

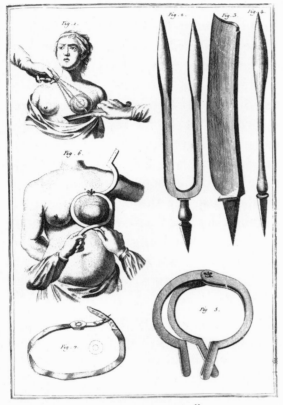

"A FILTHY PROCESS."

every day more horrible and irksome to me. Sometimes I could not prevail on myself to enter my laboratory for several days; and at other times I toiled day and night in order to complete my work. It was indeed a filthy process in which I was engaged. During my first experiment, a kind of enthusiastic frenzy had blinded me to the horror of my employment; my mind was intently fixed on the sequel of my labour, and my eyes were shut to the horror of my proceedings. But now I went to it in cold blood, and my heart often sickened at the work of my hands.

31

Thus situated, employed in the most detestable occupation, immersed in a solitude where nothing could for an instant call my attention from the actual scene in which I was engaged, my spirits became unequal; I grew restless and nervous. Every moment I feared to meet my persecutor. Sometimes I sat with my eyes fixed on the ground, fearing to raise them lest they should encounter the object which I so much dreaded to behold. I feared to wander from the sight of my fellow-creatures, lest when alone he should come to claim his companion.

In the mean time I worked on, and my labour was already considerably advanced. I looked towards its completion with a tremulous and eager hope, which I dared not trust myself to question, but which was intermixed with obscure forebodings of evil, that made my heart sicken in my bosom.

CHAPTER III.

I SAT one evening in my laboratory; the sun had set, and the moon was just rising from the sea; I had not sufficient light for my employment, and I remained idle, in a pause of consideration of whether I should leave my labour for the night, or hasten its conclusion by an unremitting attention to it. As I sat, a train of reflection occurred to me, which led me to consider the effects of what I was now doing. Three years before I was engaged in the same manner, and had created a fiend whose unparalleled barbarity had desolated my heart, and filled it for ever with the bitterest remorse. I was now about to form another being, of whose dispositions I was alike ignorant; she might become ten thousand times more malignant than her mate, and delight, for its own sake, in murder and wretchedness. He had sworn to quit the neighbourhood of man, and hide himself in deserts; but she had not; and she, who in all probability was to become a thinking and reasoning animal, might refuse to comply with a compact made before her creation. They might even hate each other; the creature who already lived loathed his own deformity, and might he not conceive a greater abhorence for it when it came before his eyes in the

1 *hate each other.* This possibility is developed in the films *The Bride of Frankenstein* as well as in the television film *Frankenstein: The True Story.*

2 *superior beauty of man.* As she does in *The Bride of Frankenstein* (1935) and again in the television film *Frankenstein: The True Story*, though it might be argued that Elsa Lanchester facing Boris Karloff in the former had more to fear than Jane Seymour confronting Michael Sarrazin in the latter.

"A RACE OF DEVILS WOULD BE PROPAGATED."

3 *as their pest.* The word *pest* means plague. We will recall that long ago (Vol. I, p. 67) Victor dreamed of being blessed by future generations.

female form? She also might turn with **2** disgust from him to the superior beauty of man; she might quit him, and he be again alone, exasperated by the fresh provocation of being deserted by one of his own species.

Even if they were to leave Europe, and inhabit the deserts of the new world, yet one of the first results of those sympathies for which the dæmon thirsted would be children, and a race of devils would be propagated upon the earth, who might make the very existence of the species of man a condition precarious and full of terror. Had I a right, for my own benefit, to inflict this curse upon everlasting generations? I had before been moved by the sophisms of the being I had created; I had been struck senseless by his fiendish threats: but now, for the first time, the wickedness of my promise burst upon me; I shuddered to think that future ages might curse **3** me as their pest, whose selfishness had not hesitated to buy its own peace at the price perhaps of the existence of the whole human race.

I trembled, and my heart failed within me; when, on looking up, I saw, by the light of the moon, the dæmon at the casement. A ghastly grin wrinkled his lips as he gazed on me, where I sat fulfilling the task which he had allotted to me. Yes, he had followed me in my travels; he had loitered in forests, hid himself in caves, or taken refuge in wide and desert heaths; and he now came to mark my progress, and claim the fulfilment of my promise.

As I looked on him, his countenance

4 *tore to pieces.* There is an uncanny echo in this scene of the story told about the great rabbi Solomon ibn Gabirol (A.D. 1021–1058) who, being charged with sorcery for having created a female golem, saved himself from the death penalty by dismantling his creature before his judges. Whether Mary Shelley knew this tale is not certain.

expressed the utmost extent of malice and treachery. I thought with a sensation of madness on my promise of creating another like to him, and, trembling with passion, tore to pieces the thing on which I was engaged. The wretch saw me destroy the creature on whose future existence he depended for happiness, and, with a howl of devilish despair and revenge, withdrew.

I left the room, and, locking the door, made a solemn vow in my own heart never to resume my labours; and then, with trembling steps, I sought my own apartment. I was alone; none were near me to dissipate the gloom, and relieve me from the sickening oppresion of the most terrible reveries.

Several hours past, and I remained near my window gazing on the sea; it was almost motionless, for the winds were hushed, and all nature reposed under the eye of the quiet moon. A few fishing vessels alone specked the water, and now and then the gentle breeze wafted the sound of voices, as the fishermen called to one another. I felt the silence, although I was hardly conscious of its extreme profundity until my ear was suddenly arrested by the paddling of oars near the shore, and a person landed close to my house.

In a few minutes after, I heard the creaking of my door, as if some one endeavoured to open it softly. I trembled from head to foot; I felt a presentiment of who it was, and wished to rouse one of the peasants who dwelt in a cottage not far from mine; but I was overcome by the sensation of helplessness, so often felt in frightful dreams,

(OVERLEAF) "TREMBLING WITH PASSION, [I] TORE TO PIECES THE THING ON WHICH I WAS ENGAGED."

5 *of the Rhine*. We have seen how Victor and Clerval's journey down the Rhine parallels Mary and Percy Shelley's elopement journey. It is time now to suggest that just as in real life there were three persons making the Rhine journey—Mary, Percy Shelley, and Claire Clairmont—so in the fictional voyage there are three travelers, Henry, Victor, and the unseen creature.

The fascinating question, of course, is which of the real people are represented by which fictional ones? Particularly, one would like to guess who among the real people represents the creature? Claire?

In a May 1836 letter to Edward Trelawny, Mary Shelley described her relationship with Claire as follows: "We were never friends—Now I would not go to Paradise, with her for a companion—she poisoned my life when young . . . she has still the faculty of making me more uncomfortable than any human being" (*Shelley and His Circle*, III, pp. 400–401).

6 *period of your power is arrived*. Victor is speaking. To the modern ear this sentence sounds like a contradiction, but to a nineteenth-century listener it meant "your power is now ended."

when you in vain endeavour to fly from an impending danger, and was rooted to the spot.

Presently I heard the sound of footsteps along the passage; the door opened, and the wretch whom I dreaded appeared. Shutting the door, he approached me, and said, in a smothered voice—

" You have destroyed the work which you began; what is it that you intend? Do you dare to break your promise? I have endured toil and misery: I left Switzerland with you; I crept **5** along the shores of the Rhine, among its willow islands, and over the summits of its hills. I have dwelt many months in the heaths of England, and among the deserts of Scotland. I have endured incalculable fatigue, and cold, and hunger; do you dare destroy my hopes?"

" Begone! I do break my promise; never will I create another like yourself, equal in deformity and wickedness."

" Slave, I before reasoned with you, but you have proved yourself unworthy of my condescension. Remember that I have power; you believe yourself miserable, but I can make you so wretched that the light of day will be hateful to you. You are my creator, but I am your master;—obey!"

" The hour of my weakness is past, **6** and the period of your power is arrived. Your threats cannot move me to do an act of wickedness; but they confirm me in a resolution of not creating you a companion in vice. Shall I, in cool blood, set loose upon

7 *on your wedding-night*. Lest the lofty language of the previous paragraph has obscured what the issue is between the creature and his creator, this clean threat illuminates it in a lightning flash. The issue is sex. Victor has doomed the creature to a life of sexual frustration, and the creature promises to repay in kind.

the earth a dæmon, whose delight is in death and wretchedness. Begone! I am firm, and your words will only exasperate my rage."

The monster saw my determination in my face, and gnashed his teeth in the impotence of anger. "Shall each man," cried he, "find a wife for his bosom, and each beast have his mate, and I be alone? I had feelings of affection, and they were requited by detestation and scorn. Man, you may hate; but beware! Your hours will pass in dread and misery, and soon the bolt will fall which must ravish from you your happiness for ever. Are you to be happy, while I grovel in the intensity of my wretchedness? You can blast my other passions; but revenge remains— revenge, henceforth dearer than light or food! I may die; but first you, my tyrant and tormentor, shall curse the sun that gazes on your misery. Beware; for I am fearless, and therefore powerful. I will watch with the wiliness of a snake, that I may sting with its venom. Man, you shall repent of the injuries you inflict."

" Devil, cease; and do not poison the air with these sounds of malice. I have declared my resolution to you, and I am no coward to bend beneath words. Leave me; I am inexorable."

"It is well. I go; but remember, I shall be with you on your wedding-night."

I started forward, and exclaimed, " Villain! before you sign my death-warrant, be sure that you are yourself safe."

I would have seized him; but he eluded me, and quitted the house with precipitation : in a few moments I saw him in his boat, which shot across the waters with an arrowy swiftness, and was soon lost amidst the waves.

All was again silent; but his words rung in my ears. I burned with rage to pursue the murderer of my peace, and precipitate him into the ocean. I walked up and down my room hastily and perturbed, while my imagination conjured up a thousand images to torment and sting me. Why had I not followed him, and closed with him in mortal strife ? But I had suffered him to depart, and he had directed his course towards the main land. I shuddered to think who might be the next victim sacrificed to his insatiate revenge. And then I thought again of his words—" *I will be with you on your wedding-night.*" That then was the period fixed for the fulfilment of my destiny. In that hour I should die, and at once satisfy and extinguish his malice. The prospect did not move me to fear ; yet when I thought of my beloved Elizabeth,—of her tears and endless sorrow, when she should find her lover so barbarously snatched from her,—tears, the first I had shed for many months, streamed from my eyes, and I resolved not to fall before my enemy without a bitter struggle.

The night passed away, and the sun rose from the ocean ; my feelings became calmer, if it may be called calmness, when the violence of rage sinks into the depths of despair. I left the house, the horrid scene of the last night's contention, and walked on the beach of the sea, which I almost re-

8 *deep sleep*. Shortly after bringing his creature to life, Victor abandoned it and went off to his bedroom, where he took refuge in sleep. Now, having made and destroyed the female creature, he has recourse to sleep once more. The first sleep, following creation, was fitful and was climaxed by a nightmare. This sleep, following destruction, is described as refreshing.

9 *oaten cake*. A staple of Scottish life. I am indebted to Meg Louttit of Stromness, the Orkneys, for her recipe. She says: "You take four cupfuls of oatmeal, less than half a cup of flour, a teaspoonful of baking soda, rather less than one-half teaspoon of salt. Add one half tablespoon of cooking oil and enough chilled water to make a mixture that can be handled. For people who like their oat cakes brown, a wee jam spoonful of sugar can be added.

"Roll the mixture into a ball, then roll it out on a floured board (I used to have a roller, but the drawer wouldn't take it, so I use a milk bottle), roll it out as thick or as thin as you like. Put it in the oven and don't let it go brown or it will turn bitter. A hottish oven (400 degrees). Touch your cakes from time to time to see if they are drying nicely." The oatcakes are good hot or cold though hot, and spread with jam, is best.

garded as an insuperable barrier between me and my fellow-creatures; nay, a wish that such should prove the fact stole across me. I desired that I might pass my life on that barren rock, wearily it is true, but uninterrupted by any sudden shock of misery. If I returned, it was to be sacrificed, or to see those whom I most loved die under the grasp of a dæmon whom I had myself created.

I walked about the isle like a restless spectre, separated from all it loved, and miserable in the separation. When it became noon, and the sun rose higher, I lay down on the grass, and **8** was overpowered by a deep sleep. I had been awake the whole of the preceding night, my nerves were agitated, and my eyes inflamed by watching and misery. The sleep into which I now sunk refreshed me; and when I awoke, I again felt as if I belonged to a race of human beings like myself, and I began to reflect upon what had passed with greater composure; yet still the words of the fiend rung in my ears like a death-knell, they appeared like a dream, yet distinct and oppressive as a reality.

The sun had far descended, and I still sat on the shore, satisfying my appetite, which had become ravenous, **9** with an oaten cake, when I saw a fishing-boat land close to me, and one of the men brought me a packet; it contained letters from Geneva, and one from Clerval, entreating me to join him. He said that nearly a year had elapsed since we had quitted Switzerland, and France was yet unvisited. He en-

10 *in a week.* It is clear that the journey from the Orkneys to Perth, or vice versa, takes a week. This will prove important to us later.

treated me, therefore, to leave my **10** solitary isle, and meet him at Perth, in a week from that time, when we might arrange the plan of our future proceedings. This letter in a degree recalled me to life, and I determined to quit my island at the expiration of two days.

Yet, before I departed, there was a task to perform, on which I shuddered to reflect: I must pack my chemical instruments; and for that purpose I must enter the room which had been the scene of my odious work, and I must handle those utensils, the sight of which was sickening to me. The next morning, at day-break, I summoned sufficient courage, and unlocked the door of my laboratory. The remains of the half-finished creature, whom I had destroyed, lay scattered on the floor, and I almost felt as if I had mangled the living flesh of a human being. I paused to collect myself, and then entered the chamber. With trembling hand I conveyed the instruments out of the room; but I reflected that I ought not to leave the relics of my work to excite the horror and suspicion of the peasants, and I accordingly put them into a basket, with a great quantity of stones, and laying them up, determined to throw them into the sea that very night; and in the mean time I sat upon the beach, employed in cleaning and arranging my chemical apparatus.

Nothing could be more complete than the alteration that had taken place in my feelings since the night of the appearance of the dæmon. I had before regarded my promise with a

11 *two and three in the morning.* A little less than twenty-four hours after he had gathered together the parts for the female.

12 *the moment of darkness.* Victor, like the creature, cannot bear to do his wickedness by moonlight (see Vol. II, p. 200).

gloomy despair, as a thing that, with whatever consequences, must be fulfilled; but I now felt as if a film had been taken from before my eyes, and that I, for the first time, saw clearly. The idea of renewing my labours did not for one instant occur to me; the threat I had heard weighed on my thoughts, but I did not reflect that a voluntary act of mine could avert it. I had resolved in my own mind, that to create another like the fiend I had first made would be an act of the basest and most atrocious selfishness; and I banished from my mind every thought that could lead to a different conclusion.

11 Between two and three in the morning the moon rose; and I then, putting my basket aboard a little skiff, sailed out about four miles from the shore. The scene was perfectly solitary: a few boats were returning towards land, but I sailed away from them. I felt as if I was about the commission of a dreadful crime, and avoided with shuddering anxiety any encounter with my fellow-creatures. At one time the moon, which had before been clear, was suddenly overspread by a thick cloud, and **12** I took advantage of the moment of darkness, and cast my basket into the sea; I listened to the gurgling sound as it sunk, and then sailed away from the spot. The sky became clouded; but the air was pure, although chilled by the north-east breeze that was then rising. But it refreshed me, and filled me with such agreeable sensations, that I resolved to prolong my stay on the water, and fixing the rudder in a direct position, stretched myself at the bottom

13 *mounted considerably.* This is now the third day since the female creature was destroyed.

of the boat. Clouds hid the moon, every thing was obscure, and I heard only the sound of the boat, as its keel cut through the waves; the murmur lulled me, and in a short time I slept soundly.

13 I do not know how long I remained in this situation, but when I awoke I found that the sun had already mounted considerably. The wind was high, and the waves continually threatened the safety of my little skiff. I found that the wind was north-east, and must have driven me far from the coast from which I had embarked. I endeavoured to change my course, but quickly found that if I again made the attempt the boat would be instantly filled with water. Thus situated, my only resource was to drive before the wind. I confess that I felt a few sensations of terror. I had no compass with me, and was so little acquainted with the geography of this part of the world that the sun was of little benefit to me. I might be driven into the wide Atlantic, and feel all the tortures of starvation, or be swallowed up in the immeasurable waters that roared and buffeted around me. I had already been out many hours, and felt the torment of a burning thirst, a prelude to my other sufferings. I looked on the heavens, which were covered by clouds that flew before the wind only to be replaced by others: I looked upon the sea, it was to be my grave. " Fiend," I exclaimed, " your task is already fulfilled!" I thought of Elizabeth, of my father, and of Clerval; and sunk into a reverie, so despairing and frightful, that even now, when the

14 *I entered.* Victor, having drifted twelve to fourteen hours, arrives on the evening of the fourth day since he destroyed the female creature.

scene is on the point of closing before me for ever, I shudder to reflect on it.

Some hours passed thus; but by degrees, as the sun declined towards the horizon, the wind died away into a gentle breeze, and the sea became free from breakers. But these gave place to a heavy swell; I felt sick, and hardly able to hold the rudder, when suddenly I saw a line of high land towards the south.

Almost spent, as I was, by fatigue, and the dreadful suspense I endured for several hours, this sudden certainty of life rushed like a flood of warm joy to my heart, and tears gushed from my eyes.

How mutable are our feelings, and how strange is that clinging love we have of life even in the excess of misery! I constructed another sail with a part of my dress, and eagerly steered my course towards the land. It had a wild and rocky appearance; but as I approached nearer, I easily perceived the traces of cultivation. I saw vessels near the shore, and found myself suddenly transported back to the neighbourhood of civilized man. I eagerly traced the windings of the land, and hailed a steeple which I at length saw issuing from behind a small promontory. As I was in a state of extreme debility, I resolved to sail directly towards the town as a place where I could most easily procure nourishment. Fortunately I had money with me. As I turned the promontory, I perceived a small neat town and a good harbour, **14** which I entered, my heart bounding with joy at my unexpected escape.

15 *the Irish.* Mary Shelley herself never visited Ireland, though she had an aunt who lived there. Mary Wollstonecraft's mother was Irish, and Mary Wollstonecraft was employed as a governess in Ireland for several months.

On the other hand, Percy Shelley visited Ireland with his first wife, Harriet, and her sister Elizabeth in 1812. His intention, as he expressed it in a letter to William Godwin (*Letters*, p. 231), was "principally to forward as much as we can the Catholic Emancipation." It was a wild-eyed and abortive journey.

As I was occupied in fixing the boat and arranging the sails, several people crowded towards the spot. They seemed very much surprised at my appearance; but, instead of offering me any assistance, whispered together with gestures that at any other time might have produced in me a slight sensation of alarm. As it was, I merely remarked that they spoke English; and I therefore addressed them in that language: " My good friends," said I, " will you be so kind as to tell me the name of this town, and inform me where I am ?"

" You will know that soon enough," replied a man with a gruff voice. " May be you are come to a place that will not prove much to your taste; but you will not be consulted as to your quarters, I promise you."

I was exceedingly surprised on receiving so rude an answer from a stranger; and I was also disconcerted on perceiving the frowning and angry countenances of his companions. " Why do you answer me so roughly ?" I replied: " surely it is not the custom of Englishmen to receive strangers so inhospitably."

" I do not know," said the man, " what the custom of the English may be; but it is the custom of the Irish to hate villains."

While this strange dialogue continued, I perceived the crowd rapidly increase. Their faces expressed a mixture of curiosity and anger, which annoyed, and in some degree alarmed me. I inquired the way to the inn; but no one replied. I then moved forward, and a murmuring sound arose

15

16 *last night*. The gentleman, then, was found murdered on the third evening after the dismemberment of the female.

from the crowd as they followed and surrounded me; when an ill-looking man approaching, tapped me on the shoulder, and said, " Come, Sir, you must follow me to Mr. Kirwin's, to give an account of yourself."

" Who is Mr. Kirwin? Why am I to give an account of myself? Is not this a free country?"

" Aye, Sir, free enough for honest folks. Mr. Kirwin is a magistrate; and you are to give an account of the death of a gentleman who was found **16** murdered here last night."

This answer startled me; but I presently recovered myself. I was innocent; that could easily be proved: accordingly I followed my conductor in silence, and was led to one of the best houses in the town. I was ready to sink from fatigue and hunger; but, being surrounded by a crowd, I thought it politic to rouse all my strength, that no physical debility might be construed into apprehension or conscious guilt. Little did I then expect the calamity that was in a few moments to overwhelm me, and extinguish in horror and despair all fear of ignominy or death.

I must pause here; for it requires all my fortitude to recall the memory of the frightful events which I am about to relate, in proper detail, to my recollection.

CHAPTER IV.

1 *ten o'clock.* To put in perspective our sense of time elapsed since the dismemberment of the female creature, the following summary table may be useful:

	Event	Time
Day I	Day of dismemberment.	Late evening—moonlight.
	Confrontation with creature.	Hours later—same night.
	Creature leaves by sea.	Later—same night.
Day II	Victor sleeps on beach.	Midday.
	Victor eats oatcake.	Evening.
	Victor receives packet.	Evening.
Day III	Victor packs, gathers remnants of female creature.	Morning.
Day IV	Victor takes skiff and female remains.	2 or 3 A.M.
	Drops remains into water,	4 A.M.?
	Victor wakes, scudding toward southwest.	Late morning.
	Arrives Ireland.	Evening.

Given this calendar, Daniel Nugent's story must be set on the night of day three, while Victor was still on shore in the Orkneys.

The name Nugent may have reached Mary Shelley via Percy Shelley who, with his first wife, Harriet, maintained a friendship with Catherine Nugent of Dublin.

I was soon introduced into the presence of the magistrate, an old benevolent man, with calm and mild manners. He looked upon me, however, with some degree of severity; and then, turning towards my conductors, he asked who appeared as witnesses on this occasion.

About half a dozen men came forward; and one being selected by the magistrate, he deposed, that he had been out fishing the night before with his son and brother-in-law, Daniel Nugent, when, about ten o'clock, they observed a strong northerly blast rising, and they accordingly put in for port. It was a very dark night, as the moon had not yet risen; they did not land at the harbour, but, as they had been accustomed, at a creek about two miles below. He walked on first, carrying a part of the fishing tackle, and his companions followed him at some distance. As he was proceeding along the sands, he struck his foot against something, and fell all his length on the ground. His companions came up to assist him; and, by the light of their lantern, they found that he had fallen on the body of a man, who was to all appearance dead. Their first supposition was, that it was the corpse of some person who had been drowned, and was thrown on shore by the waves;

2 *not then cold*. If this detail is to be believed, our creature must be the world's speediest murderer. Having threatened Victor on the evening of Day I (see calendar in note 1), he has managed to zoom off to Perth, a distance of better than 150 miles, and, not counting the sea crossing from the Orkneys, catch up with his victim and bring him alive to this unknown port in northern Ireland, all within the space of two days.

3 *from my manner*. Throughout this book we have seen how facial expressions carry significance to the people who view them. Justine's manner in the course of her trial was deemed significant, and Victor, as he was being led to Mr. Kirwin, "thought it politic to rouse all my strength, that no physical debility might be construed into apprehension or conscious guilt" (p. 259).

Mary Shelley was aware of the highly popular *Principles of Physiognomy* (1775–1778; Eng: 1789–1798) by Johann Kaspar Lavater (1741–1801), a work that had interested Godwin; and her mother, Mary Wollstonecraft, had reviewed one of Lavater's books.

R. Glynn Grylls in her *Mary Shelley* (p. 10–11) cites a Lavaterian analysis of the infant Mary Godwin's face, which gives us some sense of how much credence Lavaterian enthusiasts placed in his system. Mr. Nicholson, a friend of the Godwins, examined the three-week-old Mary and analyzed her features as follows:

1. The outline of the head viewed from above, its profile, the outline of the forehead, seen from behind and in its horizontal positions, are such as I have invariably and exclusively seen in subjects who possessed considerable memory and intelligence.

2. The base of the forehead, the eyes and eyebrows, are familiar to me in subjects of quick sensibility, irritable, scarcely irascible, and surely not given to rage. That part of the outline of the forehead, which is very distinct in patient investigators, is less so in her. I think her powers of themselves, would lead to speedy combination, rather than continued research.

3. The lines between the eyes have much expression, but I had not time to develop them. They simply confirmed to me the inductions in the late paragraph.

4. The form of the nose, the nostrils, its insertion between the eyes, and its changes by muscular action, together with the side of the face in which the characteristic marks of affection are most prominent, were scarcely examined. Here also is much room for meditation and remark.

6. The mouth was too much employed to be well observed. It has the outlines of intelligence. She was displeased, and it denoted much more of resigned vexation than either scorn or rage.

On this imperfect sight it would be silly to risk a character; for which reason I will only add that I conjecture that her manner may be petulant in resistance, but cannot be sullen.

2 but, upon examination, they found that the clothes were not wet, and even that the body was not then cold. They instantly carried it to the cottage of an old woman near the spot, and endeavoured, but in vain, to restore it to life. He appeared to be a handsome young man, about five and twenty years of age. He had apparently been strangled; for there was no sign of any violence, except the black mark of fingers on his neck.

The first part of this deposition did not in the least interest me; but when the mark of the fingers was mentioned, I remembered the murder of my brother, and felt myself extremely agitated; my limbs trembled, and a mist came over my eyes, which obliged me to lean on a chair for support. The magistrate observed me with a keen eye, and of course drew an unfavourable **3** augury from my manner.

The son confirmed his father's account: but when Daniel Nugent was called, he swore positively that, just before the fall of his companion, he saw a boat, with a single man in it, at a short distance from the shore; and, as far as he could judge by the light of a few stars, it was the same boat in which I had just landed.

A woman deposed, that she lived near the beach, and was standing at the door of her cottage, waiting for the return of the fishermen, about an hour before she heard of the discovery of the body, when she saw a boat, with only only one man in it, push off from that part of the shore where the corpse was afterwards found.

Another woman confirmed the ac-

count of the fishermen having brought
the body into her house; it was not
cold. They put it into a bed, and
rubbed it; and Daniel went to the
town for an apothecary, but life was
quite gone.

Several other men were examined
concerning my landing; and they
agreed, that, with the strong north
wind that had arisen during the night,
it was very probable that I had beaten
about for many hours, and had been
obliged to return nearly to the same
spot from which I had departed. Besides, they observed that it appeared
that I had brought the body from another place, and it was likely, that as
I did not appear to know the shore, I
might have put into the harbour ignorant of the distance of the town of
———— from the place where I had de-
posited the corpse.

Mr. Kirwin, on hearing this evidence, desired that I should be taken
into the room where the body lay for
interment that it might be observed
what effect the sight of it would produce upon me. This idea was probably suggested by the extreme agitation
I had exhibited when the mode of the
murder had been described. I was accordingly conducted, by the magistrate
and several other persons, to the inn.
I could not help being struck by the
strange coincidences that had taken
place during this eventful night; but,
knowing that I had been conversing
with several persons in the island I
had inhabited about the time that the
body had been found, I was perfectly
tranquil as to the consequences of the
affair.

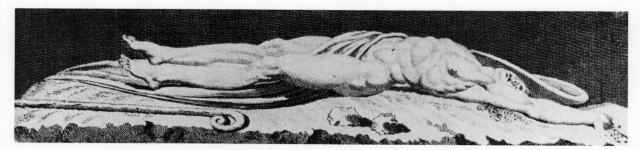

THE DEATH OF HENRY CLERVAL (FUSELI'S THE DEATH OF ABEL).

4 *Two.* William and Justine. Victor does not include the female creature in the list of those he has destroyed.

I entered the room where the corpse lay, and was led up to the coffin. How can I describe my sensations on beholding it? I feel yet parched with horror, nor can I reflect on that terrible moment without shuddering and agony, that faintly reminds me of the anguish of the recognition. The trial, the presence of the magistrate and witnesses, passed like a dream from my memory, when I saw the lifeless form of Henry Clerval stretched before me. I gasped for breath; and, throwing myself on the body, I exclaimed, " Have my murderous machinations deprived you also, my dearest Henry,

4 of life? Two I have already destroyed; other victims await their destiny: but you, Clerval, my friend, my benefactor"——

The human frame could no longer support the agonizing suffering that I endured, and I was carried out of the room in strong convulsions.

A fever succeeded to this. I lay for two months on the point of death: my ravings, as I afterwards heard, were frightful; I called myself the murderer of William, of Justine, and of Clerval. Sometimes I entreated my attendants to assist me in the destruction of the fiend by whom I was tormented; and,

5 *native language*. French.

6 *was I made*. Victor here talks like the creature with whom, it should by now be clear, he frequently identifies.

7 *turnkeys*. Prison guards.

at others, I felt the fingers of the monster already grasping my neck, and screamed aloud with agony and terror. **5** Fortunately, as I spoke my native language, Mr. Kirwin alone understood me; but my gestures and bitter cries were sufficient to affright the other witnesses.

Why did I not die? More miserable than man ever was before, why did I not sink into forgetfulness and rest? Death snatches away many blooming children, the only hopes of their doating parents: how many brides and youthful lovers have been one day in the bloom of health and hope, and the next a prey for worms and the decay **6** of the tomb! Of what materials was I made, that I could thus resist so many shocks, which, like the turning of the wheel, continually renewed the torture.

But I was doomed to live; and, in two months, found myself as awaking from a dream, in a prison, stretched on a wretched bed, surrounded by gaolers, **7** turnkeys, bolts, and all the miserable apparatus of a dungeon. It was morning, I remember, when I thus awoke to understanding: I had forgotten the particulars of what had happened, and only felt as if some great misfortune had suddenly overwhelmed me; but when I looked around, and saw the barred windows, and the squalidness of the room in which I was, all flashed across my memory, and I groaned bitterly.

This sound disturbed an old woman who was sleeping in a chair beside me. She was a hired nurse, the wife of one

8 *whole series.* Sequence.

of the turnkeys, and her countenance expressed all those bad qualities which often characterize that class. The lines of her face were hard and rude, like that of persons accustomed to see without sympathizing in sights of misery. Her tone expressed her entire indifference; she addressed me in English, and the voice struck me as one that I had heard during my sufferings:

"Are you better now, Sir?" said she.

I replied in the same language, with a feeble voice, "I believe I am; but if it be all true, if indeed I did not dream, I am sorry that I am still alive to feel this misery and horror."

"For that matter," replied the old woman, "if you mean about the gentleman you murdered, I believe that it were better for you if you were dead, for I fancy it will go hard with you; but you will be hung when the next sessions come on. However, that's none of my business, I am sent to nurse you, and get you well; I do my duty with a safe conscience, it were well if every body did the same."

I turned with loathing from the woman who could utter so unfeeling a speech to a person just saved, on the very edge of death; but I felt languid, and unable to reflect on all that had 8 passed. The whole series of my life appeared to me as a dream; I sometimes doubted if indeed it were all true, for it never presented itself to my mind with the force of reality.

As the images that floated before me became more distinct, I grew feverish; a darkness pressed around me; no one was near me who soothed me with the gentle voice of love; no dear hand supported me. The physician came and prescribed medicines, and the old woman prepared them for me; but utter carelessness was visible in the first, and the expression of brutality was strongly marked in the visage of the second. Who could be interested in the fate of a murderer, but the hangman who would gain his fee?

These were my first reflections; but I soon learned that Mr. Kirwin had shewn me extreme kindness. He had caused the best room in the prison to be prepared for me (wretched indeed was the best); and it was he who had provided a physician and a nurse. It is true, he seldom came to see me; for, although he ardently desired to relieve the sufferings of every human creature, he did not wish to be present at the agonies and miserable ravings of a murderer. He came, therefore, sometimes to see that I was not neglected; but his visits were short, and at long intervals.

One day, when I was gradually recovering, I was seated in a chair, my eyes half open, and my cheeks livid like those in death, I was overcome by gloom and misery, and often reflected I had better seek death than remain miserably pent up only to be let loose in a world replete with wretchedness. At one time I considered whether I should not declare myself guilty, and suffer the penalty of the law, less innocent than poor Justine had been. Such were my thoughts, when the door of my apartment was opened, and Mr.

9 *criminal charge*. There is a contradiction here. Mr. Kirwin is now willing to believe that evidence exists that will free Victor from a criminal charge, and yet earlier we were told that Mr. Kirwin came rarely to visit the delirious Victor because "he did not wish to be present at the agonies and miserable ravings of a murderer" (p. 266).

Kirwin entered. His countenance expressed sympathy and compassion; he drew a chair close to mine, and addressed me in French—

"I fear that this place is very shocking to you; can I do any thing to make you more comfortable?"

"I thank you; but all that you mention is nothing to me: on the whole earth there is no comfort which I am capable of receiving."

"I know that the sympathy of a stranger can be but of little relief to one borne down as you are by so strange a misfortune. But you will, I hope, soon quit this melancholy abode; **9** for, doubtless, evidence can easily be brought to free you from the criminal charge."

"That is my least concern: I am, by a course of strange events, become the most miserable of mortals. Persecuted and tortured as I am and have been, can death be any evil to me?"

"Nothing indeed could be more unfortunate and agonizing than the strange chances that have lately occurred. You were thrown, by some surprising accident, on this shore, renowned for its hospitality: seized immediately, and charged with murder. The first sight that was presented to your eyes was the body of your friend, murdered in so unaccountable a manner, and placed, as it were, by some fiend across your path."

As Mr. Kirwin said this, notwithstanding the agitation I endured on this retrospect of my sufferings, I also felt considerable surprise at the knowledge he seemed to possess concerning me. I suppose some astonishment was exhibited in my countenance; for Mr. Kirwin hastened to say—

" It was not until a day or two after your illness that I thought of examining your dress, that I might discover some trace by which I could send to your relations an account of your misfortune and illness. I found several letters, and, among others, one which I discovered from its commencement to be from your father. I instantly wrote to Geneva: nearly two months have elapsed since the departure of my letter.—But you are ill; even now you tremble: you are unfit for agitation of any kind."

" This suspense is a thousand times worse than the most horrible event: tell me what new scene of death has been acted, and whose murder I am now to lament."

" Your family is perfectly well," said Mr. Kirwin, with gentleness; " and some one, a friend, is come to visit you."

I know not by what chain of thought the idea presented itself, but it instantly darted into my mind that the murderer had come to mock at my misery, and taunt me with the death of Clerval, as a new incitement for me to comply with his hellish desires. I put my hand before my eyes, and cried out in agony—

" Oh! take him away! I cannot see him; for God's sake, do not let him enter!"

Mr. Kirwin regarded me with a troubled countenance. He could not help regarding my exclamation as a presumption of my guilt, and said, in rather a severe tone—

" I should have thought, young man, that the presence of your father would have been welcome, instead of inspiring such violent repugnance."

" My father!" cried I, while every feature and every muscle was relaxed from anguish to pleasure. " Is my father, indeed, come? How kind, how very kind. But where is he, why does he not hasten to me?"

My change of manner surprised and pleased the magistrate; perhaps he thought that my former exclamation was a momentary return of delirium, and now he instantly resumed his former benevolence. He rose, and quitted the room with my nurse, and in a moment my father entered it.

Nothing, at this moment, could have given me greater pleasure than the arrival of my father. I stretched out my hand to him, and cried—

" Are you then safe—and Elizabeth—and Ernest?"

My father calmed me with assurances of their welfare, and endeavoured, by dwelling on these subjects so interesting to my heart, to raise my desponding spirits; but he soon felt that a prison cannot be the abode of cheerfulness. " What a place is this that you inhabit, my son!" said he, looking mournfully at the barred windows, and wretched appearance of the room. " You travelled to seek happiness, but a fatality seems to pursue you. And poor Clerval—"

The name of my unfortunate and murdered friend was an agitation too great to be endured in my weak state; I shed tears.

10 *my friends*. Mr. Kirwin and Victor's father.

11 *assizes*. Court sessions held in British counties for the jury trial of both criminal and civil cases.

" Alas! yes, my father," replied I; " some destiny of the most horrible kind hangs over me, and I must live to fulfil it, or surely I should have died on the coffin of Henry."

We were not allowed to converse for any length of time, for the precarious state of my health rendered every precaution necessary that could insure tranquillity. Mr. Kirwin came in, and insisted that my strength should not be exhausted by too much exertion. But the appearance of my father was to me like that of my good angel, and I gradually recovered my health.

As my sickness quitted me, I was absorbed by a gloomy and black melancholy, that nothing could dissipate. The image of Clerval was for ever before me, ghastly and murdered. More than once the agitation into which these reflections threw me made **10** my friends dread a dangerous relapse. Alas! why did they preserve so miserable and detested a life? It was surely that I might fulfil my destiny, which is now drawing to a close. Soon, oh, very soon, will death extinguish these throbbings, and relieve me from the mighty weight of anguish that bears me to the dust; and, in executing the award of justice, I shall also sink to rest. Then the appearance of death was distant, although the wish was ever present to my thoughts; and I often sat for hours motionless and speechless, wishing for some mighty revolution that might bury me and my destroyer in its ruins.

11 The season of the assizes approached. I had already been three months in

prison; and although I was still weak,
and in continual danger of a relapse, I
was obliged to travel nearly a hundred
miles to the county-town, where the
court was held. Mr. Kirwin charged
himself with every care of collecting
witnesses, and arranging my defence.
I was spared the disgrace of appearing
publicly as a criminal, as the case was
not brought before the court that de-
cides on life and death. The grand
jury rejected the bill, on its being
proved that I was on the Orkney Islands
at the hour the body of my friend was
found, and a fortnight after my re-
moval I was liberated from prison.

My father was enraptured on finding
me freed from the vexations of a criminal charge, that I was again allowed
to breathe the fresh atmosphere, and
allowed to return to my native country.
I did not participate in these feelings;
for to me the walls of a dungeon or a
palace were alike hateful. The cup of
life was poisoned for ever; and although the sun shone upon me, as upon
the happy and gay of heart, I saw
around me nothing but a dense and
frightful darkness, penetrated by no
light but the glimmer of two eyes that
glared upon me. Sometimes they were
the expressive eyes of Henry, languish-
ing in death, the dark orbs nearly
covered by the lids, and the long black
lashes that fringed them; sometimes it
was the watery clouded eyes of the monster, as I first saw them in my chamber
at Ingolstadt.

My father tried to awaken in me the
feelings of affection. He talked of
Geneva, which I should soon visit—of

THE RHONE ENTERING LAKE GENEVA.

12 *put an end to.* These suicide attempts must then have been restrained by Victor's father, since he was no longer in prison.

13 *Dublin.* The 1771 *Encyclopaedia Britannica* describes eighteenth-century Dublin as a "large and beautiful city, pleasantly situated; having a view of the sea on one side, and of a fine country on the other."

Percy Shelley, in his radical activist youth, went to Dublin (in 1812) to work for Catholic Emancipation and against the Irish Union with Great Britain. Shelley spent some two months in Ireland working for his causes. Jean Overton Fuller, one of Shelley's biographers, suggests that it was "Godwin [who] called him off, telling him his action was misconceived" (*Shelley: A Biography*, p. 117).

While Mary Shelley certainly knew that Jonathan Swift, the great satirist, was born in Dublin, she would never know that her great colleague in terror literature, Bram Stoker, the author of *Dracula*, would be born in Dublin in 1847, four years before her own death.

Elizabeth, and Ernest; but these words only drew deep groans from me. Sometimes, indeed, I felt a wish for happiness; and thought, with melancholy delight, of my beloved cousin; or longed, with a devouring *maladie du pays*, to see once more the blue lake and rapid Rhone, that had been so dear to me in early childhood: but my general state of feeling was a torpor, in which a prison was as welcome a residence as the divinest scene in nature; and these fits were seldom interrupted, but by paroxysms of anguish and despair. At these moments I often endeavoured to

12 put an end to the existence I loathed; and it required unceasing attendance and vigilance to restrain me from committing some dreadful act of violence.

I remember, as I quitted the prison, I heard one of the men say, " He may be innocent of the murder, but he has certainly a bad conscience." These words struck me. A bad conscience! yes, surely I had one. William, Justine, and Clerval, had died through my infernal machinations; " And whose death," cried I, " is to finish the tragedy? Ah! my father, do not remain in this wretched country; take me where I may forget myself, my existence, and all the world."

My father easily acceded to my desire; and, after having taken leave of

13 Mr. Kirwin, we hastened to Dublin. I felt as if I was relieved from a heavy weight, when the packet sailed with a fair wind from Ireland, and I had quitted for ever the country which had been to me the scene of so much misery.

14 *laudanum.* A sedative hydroalcoholic solution containing either 1 percent morphine or 10 percent opium. Laudanum, in the nineteenth century, was easily available and widely used to calm the nerves. A carafe of laudanum at one's bedside was not unusual.

We have already noted that Percy Shelley was a frequent laudanum user. Fanny Godwin, Mary Shelley's half-sister, it will be remembered, committed suicide by taking an overdose of laudanum.

Victor's frequent seizures of despair have much in common with the typical withdrawal symptoms of an opium addict.

It was midnight. My father slept in the cabin; and I lay on the deck, looking at the stars, and listening to the dashing of the waves. I hailed the darkness that shut Ireland from my sight, and my pulse beat with a feverish joy, when I reflected that I should soon see Geneva. The past appeared to me in the light of a frightful dream; yet the vessel in which I was, the wind that blew me from the detested shore of Ireland, and the sea which surrounded me, told me too forcibly that I was deceived by no vision, and that Clerval, my friend and dearest companion, had fallen a victim to me and the monster of my creation. I repassed, in my memory, my whole life; my quiet happiness while residing with my family in Geneva, the death of my mother, and my departure for Ingolstadt. I remembered shuddering at the mad enthusiasm that hurried me on to the creation of my hideous enemy, and I called to mind the night during which he first lived. I was unable to pursue the train of thought; a thousand feelings pressed upon me, and I wept bitterly.

Ever since my recovery from the fever I had been in the custom of taking every **14** night a small quantity of laudanum; for it was by means of this drug only that I was enabled to gain the rest necessary for the preservation of life. Oppressed by the recollection of my various misfortunes, I now took a double dose, and soon slept profoundly. But sleep did not afford me respite from thought and misery; my dreams presented a thousand objects that scared me. Towards morning I was possessed by a kind of night-mare; I felt the

15 *Holyhead.* The customary point of departure or arrival between England and Dublin. Mary Wollstonecraft sailed from Holyhead on the way to her position as a governess in Ireland; Percy Shelley returned from his stay in Ireland by way of Holyhead. The usual time for the passage from England to Ireland was twelve hours.

fiend's grasp in my neck, and could not free myself from it; groans and cries rung in my ears. My father, who was watching over me, perceiving my restlessness, awoke me, and pointed to the 15 port of Holyhead, which we were now entering.

CHAPTER V.

WE had resolved not to go to London,
but to cross the country to Portsmouth,
and thence to embark for Havre. I
preferred this plan principally because
I dreaded to see again those places in
which I had enjoyed a few moments of
tranquillity with my beloved Clerval.
I thought with horror of seeing again
those persons whom we had been accustomed to visit together, and who
might make inquiries concerning an
event, the very remembrance of which
made me again feel the pang I endured
when I gazed on his lifeless form in
the inn at ————.

As for my father, his desires and exertions were bounded to the again seeing me restored to health and peace of
mind. His tenderness and attentions
were unremitting; my grief and gloom
was obstinate, but he would not despair.
Sometimes he thought that I felt deeply
the degradation of being obliged to
answer a charge of murder, and he endeavoured to prove to me the futility of
pride.

" Alas! my father," said I, " how
little do you know me. Human beings,
their feelings and passions, would indeed be degraded, if such a wretch as
I felt pride. Justine, poor unhappy
Justine, was as innocent as I, and she
suffered the same charge; she died

1 *Portsmouth.* A port city on the southeast coast of England.

On their return from the continent in 1816, the Shelley party chose to land in Portsmouth, thinking it would be less awkward than arriving in London with a pregnant Claire Clairmont.

2 *Havre.* A seaport town in Normandy, on the English Channel.

Le Havre was the port from which the Shelleys and Claire Clairmont departed Europe for Portsmouth in England in early September of 1816, after their summer in Switzerland. Shelley carried the manuscript of Byron's *Childe Harold*, intending to deliver it to Byron's publishers. Claire, of course, was already pregnant with Byron's child.

Le Havre also had other associations for Mary Shelley. Her mother, Mary Wollstonecraft, gave birth to Fanny Imlay at Le Havre while Charles Imlay, Fanny's father, was in London doing what he could to avoid renewing his relationship with the child's mother.

for it; and I am the cause of this—I murdered her.   William, Justine, and Henry—they all died by my hands."

My father had often, during my imprisonment, heard me make the same assertion; when I thus accused myself, he sometimes seemed to desire an explanation, and at others he appeared to consider it as caused by delirium, and that, during my illness, some idea of this kind had presented itself to my imagination, the remembrance of which I preserved in my convalescence.   I avoided explanation, and maintained a continual silence concerning the wretch I had created.   I had a feeling that I should be supposed mad, and this for ever chained my tongue, when I would have given the whole world to have confided the fatal secret.

Upon this occasion my father said, with an expression of unbounded wonder, "What do you mean, Victor? are you mad?   My dear son, I entreat you never to make such an assertion again."

"I am not mad," I cried energetically; "the sun and the heavens, who have viewed my operations, can bear witness of my truth.   I am the assassin of those most innocent victims; they died by my machinations.   A thousand times would I have shed my own blood, drop by drop, to have saved their lives; but I could not, my father, indeed I could not sacrifice the whole human race."

The conclusion of this speech convinced my father that my ideas were deranged, and he instantly changed the

"PROCEEDED TO PARIS."

3 *Paris.* The Shelleys too stopped in Paris on their way to Switzerland: once in 1814 and again in 1816. They spent their first visit seeing the usual places of interest (the Tuileries, the Louvre, and Notre Dame) and, with the help of various acquaintances, trying to find the money necessary for their further travels. In 1816 their financial situation was much improved, and it was for the purpose of obtaining the proper official signatures for their passports that they were delayed two days in Paris.

A PARIS STREET SCENE.

subject of our conversation, and endeavoured to alter the course of my thoughts. He wished as much as possible to obliterate the memory of the scenes that had taken place in Ireland, and never alluded to them, or suffered me to speak of my misfortunes.

As time passed away I became more calm: misery had her dwelling in my heart, but I no longer talked in the same incoherent manner of my own crimes; sufficient for me was the consciousness of them. By the utmost self-violence, I curbed the imperious voice of wretchedness, which sometimes desired to declare itself to the whole world; and my manners were calmer and more composed than they had ever been since my journey to the sea of ice.

3 We arrived at Havre on the 8th of May, and instantly proceeded to Paris, where my father had some business which detained us a few weeks. In this city, I received the following letter from Elizabeth:—

" *To* VICTOR FRANKENSTEIN.

" MY DEAREST FRIEND,

" It gave me the greatest pleasure to receive a letter from my uncle dated at Paris; you are no longer at a formidable distance, and I may hope to see you in less than a fortnight. My poor cousin, how much you must have suffered! I expect to see you looking even more ill than when you quitted Geneva. This winter has been passed most miserably, tortured as I have been by anxious suspense; yet I hope to see peace in your countenance, and to find that your heart is not totally devoid of comfort and tranquillity.

" Yet I fear that the same feelings now exist that made you so miserable a year ago, even perhaps augmented by time. I would not disturb you at this period, when so many misfortunes weigh upon you; but a conversation that I had with my uncle previous to his departure renders some explanation necessary before we meet.

" Explanation! you may possibly say; what can Elizabeth have to explain? If you really say this, my questions are answered, and I have no more to do than to sign myself your affectionate cousin. But you are distant from me, and it is possible that you may dread, and yet be pleased with this explanation; and, in a probability of this being the case, I dare not any longer postpone writing what, during your absence, I have often wished to express to you, but have never had the courage to begin.

" You well know, Victor, that our union had been the favourite plan of your parents ever since our infancy. We were told this when young, and taught to look forward to it as an event that would certainly take place. We were affectionate playfellows during childhood, and, I believe, dear and valued friends to one another as we grew older. But as brother and sister often entertain a lively affection towards each other, without desiring a more intimate union, may not such also be our case? Tell me, dearest Victor. Answer me, I conjure you, by our mu-

4 *interested*. That is, an affection marked by self-interest.

tual happiness, with simple truth — Do you not love another?

" You have travelled; you have spent several years of your life at Ingolstadt; and I confess to you, my friend, that when I saw you last autumn so unhappy, flying to solitude, from the society of every creature, I could not help supposing that you might regret our connexion, and believe yourself bound in honour to fulfil the wishes of your parents, although they opposed themselves to your inclinations. But this is false reasoning. I confess to you, my cousin, that I love you, and that in my airy dreams of futurity you have been my constant friend and companion. But it is your happiness I desire as well as my own, when I declare to you, that our marriage would render me eternally miserable, unless it were the dictate of your own free choice. Even now I weep to think, that, borne down as you are by the cruelest misfortunes, you may stifle, by the word *honour*, all hope of that love and happiness which would alone restore you to yourself. I, who have so

4 interested an affection for you, may increase your miseries ten-fold, by being an obstacle to your wishes. Ah, Victor, be assured that your cousin and playmate has too sincere a love for you not to be made miserable by this supposition. Be happy, my friend; and if you obey me in this one request, remain satisfied that nothing on earth will have the power to interrupt my tranquillity.

" Do not let this letter disturb you; do not answer it to-morrow, or the

5   *but free*. The scene described is not a speculative metaphor. Mary and Percy Shelley, on their 1814 elopement journey through France, passed through villages that had been destroyed in the Napoleonic wars. On August 11, Mary wrote in her *Journal* (pp. 7, 8): "From Provins we came to Nogent. The town was entirely desolated by the Cossacks; the houses were reduced to heaps of white ruins, and the bridge was destroyed. Proceeding on our way we left the great road and arrived at S. Aubin, a beautiful little village situated among trees. This village was also completely destroyed. The inhabitants told us the Cossacks had not left one cow in the village." The next day, she wrote: "At Echemine we rested. This village is entirely ruined by the Cossacks; . . . went on to Pavillon, a beautiful place, but also desolated by the Cossacks; and, in fact, we did not see a cottage on the road but had been burnt. The account they gave at Pavillon was that they took the cows, sheep, and poultry, and tore down the houses for wood for fires . . . we met on the road a man whose children had been murdered by the Cossacks."

next day, or even until you come, if it will give you pain. My uncle will send me news of your health; and if I see but one smile on your lips when we meet, occasioned by this or any other exertion of mine, I shall need no other happiness.

"   ELIZABETH LAVENZA.

"Geneva, May 18th, 17—."

This letter revived in my memory what I had before forgotten, the threat of the fiend—"*I will be with you on your wedding-night!*" Such was my sentence, and on that night would the dæmon employ every art to destroy me, and tear me from the glimpse of happiness which promised partly to console my sufferings. On that night he had determined to consummate his crimes by my death. Well, be it so; a deadly struggle would then assuredly take place, in which if he was victorious, I should be at peace, and his power over me be at an end. If he were vanquished, I should be a free man. Alas! what freedom? such as the peasant enjoys when his family have been massacred before his eyes, his cottage burnt, his lands laid waste, and he is turned adrift, homeless, pennyless, and alone, but free. Such would be my liberty, except that in my Elizabeth I possessed a treasure; alas! balanced by those horrors of remorse and guilt, which would pursue me until death.

Sweet and beloved Elizabeth! I read and re-read her letter, and some softened feelings stole into my heart, and dared to whisper paradisaical dreams of love and joy; but the apple

THE EXPULSION FROM EDEN
BY WILLIAM BLAKE.

6 *from all hope.* The reference is both biblical and Miltonic. In the Bible version of the story, God himself drives out Adam, after which he places cherubim at the eastern gate of Eden, armed with a flaming sword to bar the path to the Tree of Life. In Book XII of Milton's *Paradise Lost*, it is the archangel Michael who takes the erring parents to the eastern slope of Eden from which

They, hand in hand, with wandering steps and slow,
Through Eden took their solitary way. (ll. 891–901)

Neither Genesis nor Milton speaks of an apple.

6 was already eaten, and the angel's arm bared to drive me from all hope. Yet I would die to make her happy. If the monster executed his threat, death was inevitable; yet, again, I considered whether my marriage would hasten my fate. My destruction might indeed arrive a few months sooner; but if my torturer should suspect that I postponed it, influenced by his menaces, he would surely find other, and perhaps more dreadful means of revenge. He had vowed *to be with me on my wedding-night*, yet he did not consider that threat as binding him to peace in the mean time; for, as if to shew me that he was not yet satiated with blood, he had murdered Clerval immediately after the enunciation of his threats. I resolved, therefore, that if my immediate union with my cousin would conduce either to her's or my father's happiness, my adversary's designs against my life should not retard it a single hour.

In this state of mind I wrote to Elizabeth. My letter was calm and affectionate. " I fear, my beloved girl," I said, " little happiness remains for us on earth; yet all that I may one day enjoy is concentered in you. Chase away your idle fears; to you alone do I consecrate my life, and my endeavours for contentment. I have one secret, Elizabeth, a dreadful one; when revealed to you, it will chill your frame with horror, and then, far from being surprised at my misery, you will only wonder that I survive what I have endured. I will confide this tale of misery and terror to you the day after

7 *to it*. Victor must rank as one of literature's most irresponsible human beings. He has abandoned the creature of his own hands at the moment of its birth; he has destroyed before the creature's very eyes its one hope of happiness; now in response to a letter as filled with love as it is with nobility, he confides an inchoate secret into Elizabeth's ear that can do nothing but terrify her.

our marriage shall take place; for, my sweet cousin, there must be perfect confidence between us.   But until then, I conjure you, do not mention or allude **7   to** it.   This I most earnestly entreat, and I know you will comply."

In about a week after the arrival of Elizabeth's letter, we returned to Geneva.   My cousin welcomed me with warm affection; yet tears were in her eyes, as she beheld my emaciated frame and feverish cheeks.   I saw a change in her also.   She was thinner, and had lost much of that heavenly vivacity that had before charmed me; but her gentleness, and soft looks of compassion, made her a more fit companion for one blasted and miserable as I was.

The tranquillity which I now enjoyed did not endure.   Memory brought madness with it; and when I thought on what had passed, a real insanity possessed me; sometimes I was furious, and burnt with rage, sometimes low and despondent.   I neither spoke or looked, but sat motionless, bewildered by the multitude of miseries that overcame me.

Elizabeth alone had the power to draw me from these fits; her gentle voice would soothe me when transported by passion, and inspire me with human feelings when sunk in torpor. She wept with me, and for me.   When reason returned, she would remonstrate, and endeavour to inspire me with resignation.   Ah! it is well for the unfortunate to be resigned, but for the guilty there is no peace.   The agonies of remorse poison the luxury there is otherwise sometimes found in indulging the excess of grief.

Soon after my arrival my father spoke of my immediate marriage with my cousin. I remained silent.

"Have you, then, some other attachment?"

"None on earth. I love Elizabeth, and look forward to our union with delight. Let the day therefore be fixed; and on it I will consecrate myself, in life or death, to the happiness of my cousin."

"My dear Victor, do not speak thus. Heavy misfortunes have befallen us; but let us only cling closer to what remains, and transfer our love for those whom we have lost to those who yet live. Our circle will be small, but bound close by the ties of affection and mutual misfortune. And when time shall have softened your despair, new and dear objects of care will be born to replace those of whom we have been so cruelly deprived."

Such were the lessons of my father. But to me the remembrance of the threat returned: nor can you wonder, that, omnipotent as the fiend had yet been in his deeds of blood, I should almost regard him as invincible; and that when he had pronounced the words, "*I shall be with you on your wedding-night,*" I should regard the threatened fate as unavoidable. But death was no evil to me, if the loss of Elizabeth were balanced with it; and I therefore, with a contented and even cheerful countenance, agreed with my father, that if my cousin would consent, the ceremony should take place in ten days, and thus put, as I imagined, the seal to my fate.

Great God! if for one instant I

8 *a friendless outcast*. This is, of course, the same as the creature's condition.

9 *nicer*. More precise.

10 *Cologny*. Cologny is a village on the southern shore of Lake Geneva. Maison Chapuis, the house in which the Shelleys lived while in Switzerland in 1816, was very near the village of Cologny.

"CONGRATULATORY VISITS WERE RECEIVED."

had thought what might be the hellish intention of my fiendish adversary, I would rather have banished myself for ever from my native country, and wan-**8** dered a friendless outcast over the earth, than have consented to this miserable marriage.   But, as if possessed of magic powers, the monster had blinded me to his real intentions; and when I thought that I prepared only my own death, I hastened that of a far dearer victim.

As the period fixed for our marriage drew nearer, whether from cowardice or a prophetic feeling, I felt my heart sink within me.   But I concealed my feelings by an appearance of hilarity, that brought smiles and joy to the coun- tenance of my father, but hardly de- **9** ceived the ever-watchful and nicer eye of Elizabeth.   She looked forward to our union with placid contentment, not unmingled with a little fear, which past misfortunes had impressed, that what now appeared certain and tangible happiness, might soon dissipate into an airy dream, and leave no trace but deep and everlasting regret.

Preparations were made for the event; congratulatory visits were received; and all wore a smiling appearance.   I shut up, as well as I could, in my own heart the anxiety that preyed there, and entered with seeming earnestness into the plans of my father, although they might only serve as the decorations of my tragedy.   A house was purchased **10** for us near Cologny, by which we should enjoy the pleasures of the country, and yet be so near Geneva as to see my father every day; who would

11 *Evian.* Also called Évian-les-Bains, a suburb of Thonon, on the shore of Lake Geneva. In late June 1816, Shelley and Byron set out in their boat to sail around Lake Geneva. In a letter to his friend Peacock (*Letters of Percy Bysshe Shelley,* p. 482), Shelley describes Évian as follows: "The appearance of the inhabitants of Évian is more wretched, diseased and poor, than I ever recollect to have seen. . . . They have mineral waters here, *eaux savonneuses,* they call them. In the evening we had some difficulty about our passports, but so soon as the syndic heard my companion's rank and name, he apologized for the circumstance. The inn was good. During our voyage, on the distant height of a hill, covered with pine-forests, we saw a ruined castle, which reminded me of those on the Rhine."

EVIAN.

still reside within the walls, for the benefit of Ernest, that he might follow his studies at the schools.

In the mean time I took every precaution to defend my person, in case the fiend should openly attack me. I carried pistols and a dagger constantly about me, and was ever on the watch to prevent artifice; and by these means gained a greater degree of tranquillity. Indeed, as the period approached, the threat appeared more as a delusion, not to be regarded as worthy to disturb my peace, while the happiness I hoped for in my marriage wore a greater appearance of certainty, as the day fixed for its solemnization drew nearer, and I heard it continually spoken of as an occurrence which no accident could possibly prevent.

Elizabeth seemed happy; my tranquil demeanour contributed greatly to calm her mind. But on the day that was to fulfil my wishes and my destiny, she was melancholy, and a presentiment of evil pervaded her; and perhaps also she thought of the dreadful secret, which I had promised to reveal to her the following day. My father was in the mean time overjoyed, and, in the bustle of preparation, only observed in the melancholy of his niece the diffidence of a bride.

After the ceremony was performed, a large party assembled at my father's; but it was agreed that Elizabeth and I should pass the afternoon and night at **11** Evian, and return to Cologny the next morning. As the day was fair, and the wind favourable, we resolved to go by water.

12 *Montalêgre.* Near the village of Cologny where the Shelleys rented their residence in the summer of 1816.

13 *yet endure.* There is an echo here of Coleridge's *Ancient Mariner:*

The man hath penance done,
And penance more will do. (Part V, ll. 408–9)

Those were the last moments of my life during which I enjoyed the feeling of happiness. We passed rapidly along: the sun was hot, but we were sheltered from its rays by a kind of canopy, while we enjoyed the beauty of the scene, sometimes on one side of the lake, where we saw Mont Salêve, the plea- **12** sant banks of Montalêgre, and at a dis- tance, surmounting all, the beautiful Mont Blânc, and the assemblage of snowy mountains that in vain endea- vour to emulate her ; sometimes coast- ing the opposite banks, we saw the mighty Jura opposing its dark side to the ambition that would quit its native country, and an almost insurmountable barrier to the invader who should wish to enslave it.

I took the hand of Elizabeth : " You are sorrowful, my love. Ah ! if you knew what I have suffered, and what I may **13** yet endure, you would endeavour to let me taste the quiet, and freedom from despair, that this one day at least per- mits me to enjoy."

" Be happy, my dear Victor," re- plied Elizabeth ; " there is, I hope, nothing to distress you ; and be assured that if a lively joy is not painted in my face, my heart is contented. Something whispers to me not to depend too much on the prospect that is opened before us ; but I will not listen to such a si- nister voice. Observe how fast we move along, and how the clouds which sometimes obscure, and sometimes rise above the dome of Mont Blânc, render this scene of beauty still more interest- ing. Look also at the innumerable fish that are swimming in the clear

14 *The river Drance.* The river Drance was another of the points of interest mentioned by Shelley in his 1816 description to Peacock (*Letters of Percy Bysshe Shelley*, p. 354): "We saw the River Drance, which descends from between a chasm in the mountains, and makes a plain near the lake, intersected by its divided streams. Thousands of besolets, beautiful water-birds, like sea-gulls, but smaller, with purple on their backs, take their station on the shallows where its waters mingle with the lake."

waters, where we can distinguish every pebble that lies at the bottom. What a divine day! how happy and serene all nature appears!"

Thus Elizabeth endeavoured to divert her thoughts and mine from all reflection upon melancholy subjects. But her temper was fluctuating; joy for a few instants shone in her eyes, but it continually gave place to distraction and reverie.

The sun sunk lower in the heavens; 14 we passed the river Drance, and observed its path through the chasms of the higher, and the glens of the lower hills. The Alps here come closer to the lake, and we approached the amphitheatre of mountains which forms its eastern boundary. The spire of Evian shone under the woods that surrounded it, and the range of mountain above mountain by which it was overhung.

The wind, which had hitherto carried us along with amazing rapidity, sunk at sunset to a light breeze; the soft air just ruffled the water, and caused a pleasant motion among the trees as we approached the shore, from which it wafted the most delightful scent of flowers and hay. The sun sunk beneath the horizon as we landed; and as I touched the shore, I felt those cares and fears revive, which soon were to clasp me, and cling to me for ever.

CHAPTER VI.

1 *The moon.* As our book rushes to its climax, Mary Shelley, following the lead of the great terror writers who preceded her, makes the natural world an accompanist to her catastrophe.

2 *pistol.* One wonders how Elizabeth explained to herself the presence of this bulky implement in her husband's bosom.

Peacock, in his *Memoirs* (p. 25), relates a curious incident having to do with pistols and a wedding night. Percy Shelley and Harriet, his first wife, had arrived in Edinburgh to be married, but without money. They found lodgings, and Shelley confided that they were penniless to the landlord, who agreed to lend them the money to be married and to hold his own bill on condition that Shelley celebrate the occasion by treating the landlord and his friends to supper. Peacock writes: "It was arranged accordingly; but the man was more obtrusive and officious than Shelley was disposed to tolerate. The marriage was concluded, and in the evening Shelley and his bride were alone together, when the man tapped at their door. Shelley opened it, and the landlord said to him—'It is customary here at weddings for the guests to come in, in the middle of the night, and wash the bride with whisky.' 'I immediately,' said Shelley, 'caught up my brace of pistols, and pointing them both at him said to him,—I have had enough of your impertinence; if you give me any more of it I will blow your brains out.' " These dueling pistols were Percy Shelley's dear possessions. In T. J. Hogg's *Life of Percy Bysshe Shelley*, we learn that Shelley got them while at Oxford and that he frequently carried them with him along with a "good store of powder and ball." Hogg says (pp. 60–61) that "the duelling pistols were a most discordant interruption of the repose of a quiet country walk; besides, he handled them with such inconceivable carelessness, that I had perpetually reason to apprehend that . . . he would shoot himself, or me, or both of us. How often have I lamented that Nature, which so rarely bestows upon the world a creature endowed with such marvellous talents, ungraciously rendered the gift less precious by implanting a fatal taste for perilous recreations." Holmes, in his biography of Shelley, tells us that these same pistols were packed, along with laudanum, the manuscript of a pamphlet, a collection of poems, and other belongings, to be taken with Percy and Harriet Shelley on their trip to Ireland.

IT was eight o'clock when we landed; we walked for a short time on the shore, enjoying the transitory light, and then retired to the inn, and contemplated the lovely scene of waters, woods, and mountains, obscured in darkness, yet still displaying their black outlines.

The wind, which had fallen in the south, now rose with great violence in the west. The moon had reached her summit in the heavens, and was beginning to descend; the clouds swept across it swifter than the flight of the vulture, and dimmed her rays, while the lake reflected the scene of the busy heavens, rendered still busier by the restless waves that were beginning to rise. Suddenly a heavy storm of rain descended.

I had been calm during the day; but so soon as night obscured the shapes of objects, a thousand fears arose in my mind. I was anxious and watchful, while my right hand grasped a pistol which was hidden in my bosom; every sound terrified me; but I resolved that I would sell my life dearly, and not relax the impending conflict until my own life, or that of my adversary, were extinguished.

Elizabeth observed my agitation for some time in timid and fearful silence; at length she said, " What is it that

3 *very dreadful.* Elizabeth is being asked to bear a very heavy burden. This is hard language for a bride to hear who is approaching her marriage bed.

It should be said, however, that wedding night terror was common to the Romantic imagination. Brides died or were carried off by specter bridegrooms with great frequency. A formidable example is Bürger's *Lenore,* which Percy Shelley had seen illustrated by Lady Diana Beauclerk. Medwin, in his *Life of Percy Bysshe Shelley* (p. 45), writes that the poem "produced on Shelley a powerful effect; and I have in my possession a copy of the whole poem, which he made with his own hand."

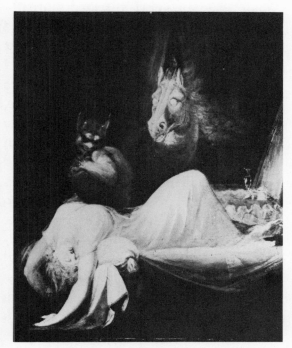

THE NIGHTMARE BY HENRY FUSELI.

agitates you, my dear Victor? What is it you fear?"

"Oh! peace, peace, my love," replied I, **3** "this night, and all will be safe: but this night is dreadful, very dreadful."

I passed an hour in this state of mind, when suddenly I reflected how dreadful the combat which I momentarily expected would be to my wife, and I earnestly entreated her to retire, resolving not to join her until I had obtained some knowledge as to the situation of my enemy.

She left me, and I continued some time walking up and down the passages of the house, and inspecting every corner that might afford a retreat to my adversary. But I discovered no trace of him, and was beginning to conjecture that some fortunate chance had intervened to prevent the execution of his menaces; when suddenly I heard a shrill and dreadful scream. It came from the room into which Elizabeth had retired. As I heard it, the whole truth rushed into my mind, my arms dropped, the motion of every muscle and fibre was suspended; I could feel the blood trickling in my veins, and tingling in the extremities of my limbs. This state lasted but for an instant; the scream was repeated, and I rushed into the room.

Great God! why did I not then expire! Why am I here to relate the destruction of the best hope, and the purest creature of earth. She was there, lifeless and inanimate, thrown across the bed, her head hanging down, and her pale and distorted features half

4 *I fainted.* This entire scene vibrates with erotic overtones. It is Elizabeth's wedding night, and she is the object of contention between two lovers. One of them, her husband, is weak, pale, frail, frightened. The other, the creature, is tall, vigorous, and vital. In such a situation, the only solution for a woman of honor and sensibility is death. And so we see her, lying in an attitude that strangely resembles that of an exhausted voluptuary, having escaped both dishonor and experience.

Mary Shelley's description of Elizabeth's death bears comparison with Henry Fuseli's treatment of the sleeping woman in his painting *The Nightmare*.

Structurally, this scene may have served Bram Stoker as a model for an important moment in his novel *Dracula* (1897). It is the scene in which Dr. Van Helsing and his cohorts break into the Harker bedroom and find Jonathan Harker supine and unconscious beside his wife while Dracula, the glutted vampire, stands triumphantly over a just-ravished Mina Harker (pp. 249–50). There is the same inertness of a husband, the same nearly lascivious sprawl of the woman, and, of course, the same presence (or near presence) of the unacknowledged third member of the *ménage à trois*, the vampire/monster.

THE DEATH OF ELIZABETH
(FUSELI'S THE EZZELINO BRACCIA -
FERRON AND THE DEAD MEDUNA).

covered by her hair. Every where I turn I see the same figure—her bloodless arms and relaxed form flung by the murderer on its bridal bier. Could I behold this, and live? Alas! life is obstinate, and clings closest where it is most hated. For a moment only did **4** I lose recollection; I fainted.

When I recovered, I found myself surrounded by the people of the inn; their countenances expressed a breathless terror: but the horror of others appeared only as a mockery, a shadow of the feelings that oppressed me. I escaped from them to the room where lay the body of Elizabeth, my love, my wife, so lately living, so dear, so worthy. She had been moved from the posture in which I had first beheld her; and now, as she lay, her head upon her arm, and a handkerchief thrown across her face and neck, I might have supposed her asleep. I rushed towards her, and embraced her with ardour; but the deathly languor and coldness of the limbs told me, that what I now held in my arms had ceased to be the Elizabeth whom I had loved and cherished. The murderous mark of the fiend's grasp was on her neck, and the breath had ceased to issue from her lips.

While I still hung over her in the agony of despair, I happened to look up. The windows of the room had before been darkened; and I felt a kind of panic on seeing the pale yellow light of the moon illuminate the chamber. The shutters had been thrown back; and, with a sensation of horror not to be described, I saw at the open window a figure the most hideous and

5 *to jeer*. The creature gloats here at this staging of a scene which, in its own way, parallels the one in which Victor destroyed the creature's intended bride.

Richard Holmes, Percy Shelley's biographer, thinks that the presence of the jeering creature reflects an incident in the poet's life when, on February 26, 1813, an intruder into the Shelley household fired his pistol at Shelley. The event is described by Harriet Shelley in *The Letters of Percy Bysshe Shelley* (pp. 355–56): "Bysshe then fired, but it flashed in the pan. The man then knocked Bysshe down, and they struggled on the ground. Bysshe then fired his second pistol, which he thought wounded him in the shoulder, as he uttered a shriek, and got up, when he said these words: By God I will be revenged; I will murder your wife. I will ravish your sister. By God. I will be revenged. He then fled—as we hoped for the night."

"DRAWING A PISTOL FROM MY BOSOM, SHOT."

abhorred. A grin was on the face of the **5** monster; he seemed to jeer, as with his fiendish finger he pointed towards the corpse of my wife. I rushed towards the window, and drawing a pistol from my bosom, shot; but he eluded me, leaped from his station, and, running with the swiftness of lightning, plunged into the lake.

The report of the pistol brought a crowd into the room. I pointed to the spot where he had disappeared, and we followed the track with boats; nets were cast, but in vain. After passing several hours, we returned hopeless, most of my companions believing it to have been a form conjured by my fancy. After having landed, they proceeded to search the country, parties going in different directions among the woods and vines.

I did not accompany them; I was exhausted: a film covered my eyes, and my skin was parched with the heat of fever. In this state I lay on a bed, hardly conscious of what had happened; my eyes wandered round the room, as if to seek something that I had lost.

At length I remembered that my father would anxiously expect the return of Elizabeth and myself, and that I must return alone. This reflection brought tears into my eyes, and I wept for a long time; but my thoughts rambled to various subjects, reflecting on my misfortunes, and their cause. I was bewildered in a cloud of wonder and horror. The death of William, the execution of Justine, the murder of Clerval, and lastly of my wife; even

(OVERLEAF) "A GRIN WAS ON THE FACE OF THE MONSTER; HE SEEMED TO JEER, AS WITH HIS FIENDISH FINGER HE POINTED TOWARDS THE CORPSE OF MY WIFE."

at that moment I knew not that my only remaining friends were safe from the malignity of the fiend; my father even now might be writhing under his grasp, and Ernest might be dead at his feet. This idea made me shudder, and recalled me to action. I started up, and resolved to return to Geneva with all possible speed.

There were no horses to be procured, and I must return by the lake; but the wind was unfavourable, and the rain fell in torrents. However, it was hardly morning, and I might reasonably hope to arrive by night. I hired men to row, and took an oar myself, for I had always experienced relief from mental torment in bodily exercise. But the overflowing misery I now felt, and the excess of agitation that I endured, rendered me incapable of any exertion. I threw down the oar; and, leaning my head upon my hands, gave way to every gloomy idea that arose. If I looked up, I saw the scenes which were familiar to me in my happier time, and which I had contemplated but the day before in the company of her who was now but a shadow and a recollection. Tears streamed from my eyes. The rain had ceased for a moment, and I saw the fish play in the waters as they had done a few hours before; they had then been observed by Elizabeth. Nothing is so painful to the human mind as a great and sudden change. The sun might shine, or the clouds might lour; but nothing could appear to me as it had done the day before. A fiend had snatched from me every hope of future happiness: no

6 *apoplectic fit.* "Apopletic fit" is the colloquial term for the effects of cerebral hemorrhage, thrombosis, embolism, or vasospasm. It is what people mean when they speak of a "stroke."

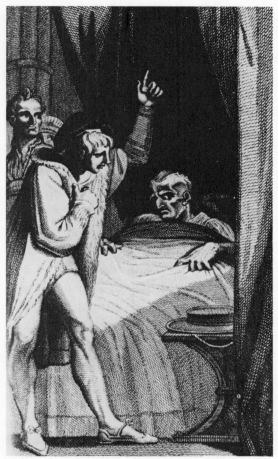

"AN APOPLECTIC FIT WAS BROUGHT ON"
(FUSELI'S DEATH OF CARDINAL
BEAUFORT).

creature had ever been so miserable as I was; so frightful an event is single in the history of man.

But why should I dwell upon the incidents that followed this last overwhelming event. Mine has been a tale of horrors; I have reached their *acme*, and what I must now relate can but be tedious to you. Know that, one by one, my friends were snatched away; I was left desolate. My own strength is exhausted; and I must tell, in a few words, what remains of my hideous narration.

I arrived at Geneva. My father and Ernest yet lived; but the former sunk under the tidings that I bore. I see him now, excellent and venerable old man! his eyes wandered in vacancy, for they had lost their charm and their delight—his niece, his more than daughter, whom he doated on with all that affection which a man feels, who, in the decline of life, having few affections, clings more earnestly to those that remain. Cursed, cursed be the fiend that brought misery on his grey hairs, and doomed him to waste in wretchedness! He could not live under the horrors that were accumulated around him; an apoplectic fit was brought on, and in a few days he died in my arms.

What then became of me? I know not; I lost sensation, and chains and darkness were the only objects that pressed upon me. Sometimes, indeed, I dreamt that I wandered in flowery meadows and pleasant vales with the friends of my youth; but awoke, and found myself in a dungeon. Melancholy followed, but by degrees I gained

A MADHOUSE.

"THE MAGISTRATE LISTENED TO ME."

a clear conception of my miseries and situation, and was then released from my prison. For they had called me mad; and during many months, as I understood, a solitary cell had been my habitation.

But liberty had been a useless gift to me had I not, as I awakened to reason, at the same time awakened to revenge. As the memory of past misfortunes pressed upon me, I began to reflect on their cause—the monster whom I had created, the miserable dæmon whom I had sent abroad into the world for my destruction. I was possessed by a maddening rage when I thought of him, and desired and ardently prayed that I might have him within my grasp to wreak a great and signal revenge on his cursed head.

Nor did my hate long confine itself to useless wishes; I began to reflect on the best means of securing him; and for this purpose, about a month after my release, I repaired to a criminal judge in the town, and told him that I had an accusation to make; that I knew the destroyer of my family; and that I required him to exert his whole authority for the apprehension of the murderer.

The magistrate listened to me with attention and kindness: " Be assured, sir," said he, " no pains or exertions on my part shall be spared to discover the villain."

" I thank you," replied I; " listen, therefore, to the deposition that I have to make. It is indeed a tale so strange, that I should fear you would not credit it, were there not something in truth

7 *on his countenance.* One is puzzled to know why Victor favored this magistrate with his story. Until now he has refrained from confiding in anyone because he believed that his tale was so bizarre that he would be considered mad for telling it. It may be that having finally achieved madness in the course of his illness, Victor has lost his fear of the word.

which, however wonderful, forces conviction. The story is too connected to be mistaken for a dream, and I have no motive for falsehood." My manner, as I thus addressed him, was impressive, but calm; I had formed in my own heart a resolution to pursue my destroyer to death; and this purpose quieted my agony, and provisionally reconciled me to life. I now related my history briefly, but with firmness and precision, marking the dates with accuracy, and never deviating into invective or exclamation.

The magistrate appeared at first perfectly incredulous, but as I continued he became more attentive and interested; I saw him sometimes shudder with horror, at others a lively surprise, unmingled with disbelief, was painted

7 on his countenance.

When I had concluded my narration, I said. " This is the being whom I accuse, and for whose detection and punishment I call upon you to exert your whole power. It is your duty as a magistrate, and I believe and hope that your feelings as a man will not revolt from the execution of those functions on this occasion."

This address caused a considerable change in the physiognomy of my auditor. He had heard my story with that half kind of belief that is given to a tale of spirits and supernatural events; but when he was called upon to act officially in consequence, the whole tide of his incredulity returned. He, however, answered mildly, " I would willingly afford you every aid in your pursuit; but the creature of whom you

8 *chamois*. The chamois (*Rupicapra rupicapra*) is a goatlike creature found only in the mountains of Europe. Both sexes are horned. The chamois stands about thirty inches high and can weigh between fifty-five and one hundred and ten pounds. In Mary Shelley's *Journal* entry for July 26 (p. 54), she writes that the men of the Chamounix region "hunt the chamois, an occupation they delight in. They think themselves lucky if they kill three in the season, which they are glad to sell for 24 or 25 francs, and if they cannot, they eat it themselves in the winter."

speak appears to have powers which would put all my exertions to defiance. Who can follow an animal which can traverse the sea of ice, and inhabit caves and dens, where no man would venture to intrude? Besides, some months have elapsed since the commission of his crimes, and no one can conjecture to what place he has wandered, or what region he may now inhabit."

"I do not doubt that he hovers near the spot which I inhabit; and if he has indeed taken refuge in the Alps, he may be hunted like the chamois, and destroyed as a beast of prey. But I perceive your thoughts: you do not credit my narrative, and do not intend to pursue my enemy with the punishment which is his desert."

As I spoke, rage sparkled in my eyes; the magistrate was intimidated; "You are mistaken," said he, "I will exert myself; and if it is in my power to seize the monster, be assured that he shall suffer punishment proportionate to his crimes. But I fear, from what you have yourself described to be his properties, that this will prove impracticable, and that, while every proper measure is pursued, you should endeavour to make up your mind to disappointment."

"That cannot be; but all that I can say will be of little avail. My revenge is of no moment to you; yet, while I allow it to be a vice, I confess that it is the devouring and only passion of my soul. My rage is unspeakable, when I reflect that the murderer,

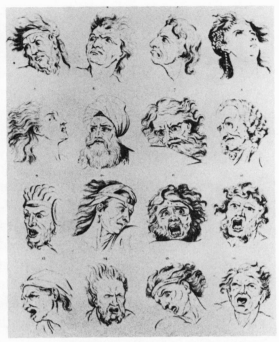

THE PASSIONS BY FUSELI, AFTER LAVATER.

whom I have turned loose upon society, still exists.   You refuse my just
demand: I have but one resource; and
I devote myself, either in my life or
death, to his destruction."

I trembled with excess of agitation
as I said this; there was a phrenzy in
my manner, and something, I doubt
not, of that haughty fierceness, which
the martyrs of old are said to have possessed.   But to a Genevan magistrate,
whose mind was occupied by far other
ideas than those of devotion and
heroism, this elevation of mind had
much the appearance of madness.   He
endeavoured to soothe me as a nurse
does a child, and reverted to my tale
as the effects of delirium.

"Man," I cried, "how ignorant
art thou in thy pride of wisdom!
Cease; you know not what it is you
say."

I broke from the house angry and
disturbed, and retired to meditate on
some other mode of action.

CHAPTER VII.

My present situation was one in which all voluntary thought was swallowed up and lost. I was hurried away by fury; revenge alone endowed me with strength and composure; it modelled my feelings, and allowed me to be calculating and calm, at periods when otherwise delirium or death would have been my portion.

My first resolution was to quit Geneva for ever; my country, which, when I was happy and beloved, was dear to me, now, in my adversity, became hateful. I provided myself with a sum of money, together with a few 1 jewels which had belonged to my mother, and departed.

And now my wanderings began, which are to cease but with life. I have traversed a vast portion of the earth, and have endured all the hardships which travellers, in deserts and barbarous countries, are wont to meet. How I have lived I hardly know; many times have I stretched my failing limbs upon the sandy plain, and prayed for death. But revenge kept me alive; I dared not die, and leave my adversary in being.

When I quitted Geneva, my first labour was to gain some clue by which I might trace the steps of my fiendish

1 *jewels.* We have been told (p. 221) that Victor is a man of independent means. Presumably, then, these jewels are taken for their sentimental value, and not to provide funds for the journey.

2 *mourner.* Graveyards had a special meaning for our author. When, as a child, she returned to her father's house from Scotland, one of her frequent pastimes was to visit Saint Pancras Churchyard, where her mother, Mary Wollstonecraft, was buried. Percy and Mary Shelley carried on their illicit courtship in the graveyard, where they sat on her mother's gravestone for hours on end.

enemy. But my plan was unsettled; and I wandered many hours around the confines of the town, uncertain what path I should pursue. As night approached, I found myself at the entrance of the cemetery where William, Elizabeth, and my father, reposed. I entered it, and approached the tomb which marked their graves. Every thing was silent, except the leaves of the trees, which were gently agitated by the wind; the night was nearly dark; and the scene would have been solemn and affecting even to an uninterested observer. The spirits of the departed seemed to flit around, and to cast a shadow, which was felt but seen not, around the head of the

2 mourner.

The deep grief which this scene had at first excited quickly gave way to rage and despair. They were dead, and I lived; their murderer also lived, and to destroy him I must drag out my weary existence. I knelt on the grass, and kissed the earth, and with quivering lips exclaimed, " By the sacred earth on which I kneel, by the shades that wander near me, by the deep and eternal grief that I feel, I swear; and by thee, O Night, and by the spirits that preside over thee, I swear to pursue the dæmon, who caused this misery, until he or I shall perish in mortal conflict. For this purpose I will preserve my life: to execute this dear revenge, will I again behold the sun, and tread the green herbage of earth, which otherwise should vanish from my eyes for ever. And I call on you, spirits of the dead; and on you, wandering ministers of vengeance, to aid and con-

3 *torments me.* Here, as in the oath the creature swears (Vol. II, p. 214), the name of God is resolutely avoided. The powers invoked are those of the natural world and the ghosts of the departed dead.

4 *the furies.* The word is being used here as a specific reference to the Eumenides, who in classical mythology were given the task of avenging unpunished crimes. The three goddesses are named Megaera, Tisiphone, and Alecto.

5 *miserable existence.* The significance of this moment in our fiction must not be overlooked. The creature laughs, thereby acknowledging that he has heard Victor's vengeful oath, and the laughter saves Victor's life as it lets him know that his bitter challenge has been accepted. From here on, creator and creature perform the movements of a dance of unification in which each one is essential to the symmetry of the dance as they merge toward fusion with each other.

Mary Shelley may have had the concluding lines of her husband's 1815 poem "Oh! there are spirits of the air" in mind as she was writing this scene. Percy Shelley writes:

Thine own soul still is true to thee,
But changed to a foul fiend through misery.

This fiend, whose ghastly presence ever
  Beside thee like a shadow hangs,
Dream not to chase;—the mad endeavour
  Would scourge thee to severer pangs.
(ll. 29–34)

In what is to come, Victor ignores that good advice.

6 *pursued him.* The metaphor of pursuit occurs frequently in Percy Shelley's poetry. It is the central element in his poem *Alastor or the Spirit of Solitude.* The following pages of *Frankenstein* are closely linked to that poem with the difference that in *Alastor* the poet pursues a dream vision of his *idealized* woman rather than a monster man. The intensity of the pursuit is the same in both cases. Shelley writes:

. . . At night the passion came,
Like the fierce fiend of a distempered dream,
And shook him from his rest, and led him forth
Into the darkness. . . .   (ll. 224–27)
. . . wildly he wandered on,
Day after day a weary waste of hours,
Bearing within his life the brooding care
That ever fed on its decaying flame.
And now his limbs were lean; his scattered hair
Sered by the autumn of strange suffering
Sung dirges in the wind; his listless hand
Hung like dead bone within its withered skin;
Life, and the lustre that consumed it, shone
As in a furnace burning secretly
From his dark eyes alone.   (ll. 244–54)

In *Alastor*, the poet hero dies, having wasted his vitality in a vain pursuit of the ideal.

duct me in my work. Let the cursed and hellish monster drink deep of agony; let him feel the despair that **3** now torments me."

I had begun my adjuration with solemnity, and an awe which almost assured me that the shades of my murdered friends heard and approved **4** my devotion; but the furies possessed me as I concluded, and rage choaked my utterance.

I was answered through the stillness of night by a loud and fiendish laugh. It rung on my ears long and heavily; the mountains re-echoed it, and I felt as if all hell surrounded me with mockery and laughter. Surely in that moment I should have been possessed by phrenzy, and have destroyed my **5** miserable existence, but that my vow was heard, and that I was reserved for vengeance. The laughter died away: when a well-known and abhorred voice, apparently close to my ear, addressed me in an audible whisper—" I am satisfied: miserable wretch! you have determined to live, and I am satisfied."

I darted towards the spot from which the sound proceeded; but the devil eluded my grasp. Suddenly the broad disk of the moon arose, and shone full upon his ghastly and distorted shape, as he fled with more than mortal speed.

6,7 I pursued him; and for many months this has been my task. Guided by a slight clue, I followed the windings of **8** the Rhone, but vainly. The blue Mediterranean appeared; and, by a strange chance, I saw the fiend enter

William Godwin's *Caleb Williams* too is organized around the image of a pursuit.

7 *many months.* "Many months" is an insufficient clue for how long Victor and the creature moved together in their trajectory toward a climax, but given the vast expanses of space traversed, combined with what we know of the pace of travel in Victor's day, we are entitled to suppose that eighteen months is the very lowest estimate of the time needed for the epic journeys described below.

8 *the Rhone.* The river Rhone flows through Geneva into Lake Geneva.

9 *inspirited me.* Is Victor remembering the fifth verse of the Twenty-third Psalm in which David says to God that "thou preparest a table before me in the presence of mine enemies"?

The feeding of Victor and the way in which the creature later tends to him has certain analogies to what happens to the prophet Elijah in the first book of Kings. Victor is looked after by good spirits. the prophet Elijah, it will be recalled, fleeing the wrath of Ahab, took refuge by the brook Cherith where, according to the Lord's promise, he was fed when he was hungry by three ravens (I Kings xvii: 6). Later (I Kings xvii: 10–15), a widow cooked for him; and later still, in another desert near Beersheba, Elijah was fed by an angel under a juniper tree (I Kings xix: 4–6). The angel that looked after Elijah, like the spirit of good now nourishing Victor, fed a despairing and suicidal man.

by night, and hide himself in a vessel bound for the Black Sea. I took my passage in the same ship; but he escaped, I know not how.

Amidst the wilds of Tartary and Russia, although he still evaded me, I have ever followed in his track. Sometimes the peasants, scared by this horrid apparition, informed me of his path; sometimes he himself, who feared that if I lost all trace I should despair and die, often left some mark to guide me. The snows descended on my head, and I saw the print of his huge step on the white plain. To you first entering on life, to whom care is new, and agony unknown, how can you understand what I have felt, and still feel? Cold, want, and fatigue, were the least pains which I was destined to endure; I was cursed by some devil, and carried about with me my eternal hell; yet still a spirit of good followed and directed my steps, and, when I most murmured, would suddenly extricate me from seemingly insurmountable difficulties. Sometimes, when nature, overcome by hunger, sunk under the exhaustion, a repast was prepared for me in the desert, that restored and

9 inspirited me. The fare was indeed coarse, such as the peasants of the country ate; but I may not doubt that it was set there by the spirits that I had invoked to aid me. Often, when all was dry, the heavens cloudless, and I was parched by thirst, a slight cloud would bedim the sky, shed the few drops that revived me, and vanish.

I followed, when I could, the courses of the rivers; but the dæmon generally

10 *sleep.* The line echoes Coleridge's *The Rime of the Ancient Mariner*, where we read:

> Oh sleep! it is a gentle thing,
> Beloved from pole to pole!
> To Mary Queen the praise be given!
> She sent the gentle sleep from Heaven,
> That slid into my Soul.   (part V, ll. 291–96)

avoided these, as it was here that the population of the country chiefly collected. In other places human beings were seldom seen; and I generally subsisted on the wild animals that crossed my path. I had money with me, and gained the friendship of the villagers by distributing it, or bringing with me some food that I had killed, which, after taking a small part, I always presented to those who had provided me with fire and utensils for cooking.

My life, as it passed thus, was indeed **10** hateful to me, and it was during sleep alone that I could taste joy. O blessed sleep! often, when most miserable, I sank to repose, and my dreams lulled me even to rapture. The spirits that guarded me had provided these moments, or rather hours, of happiness, that I might retain strength to fulfil my pilgrimage. Deprived of this respite, I should have sunk under my hardships. During the day I was sustained and inspirited by the hope of night: for in sleep I saw my friends, my wife, and my beloved country; again I saw the benevolent countenance of my father, heard the silver tones of my Elizabeth's voice, and beheld Clerval enjoying health and youth. Often, when wearied by a toilsome march, I persuaded myself that I was dreaming until night should come, and that I should then enjoy reality in the arms of my dearest friends. What agonizing fondness did I feel for them! how did I cling to their dear forms, as sometimes they haunted even my waking hours, and persuade myself that they still lived! At such moments vengeance, that burned within me, died in my heart, and I pursued my path towards the destruction of the dæmon, more as a task enjoined by heaven, as the mechanical impulse of some power of which I was unconscious, than as the ardent desire of my soul.

What his feelings were whom I pursued, I cannot know. Sometimes, indeed, he left marks in writing on the barks of the trees, or cut in stone, that guided me, and instigated my fury. " My reign is not yet over," (these words were legible in one of these inscriptions) ; " you live, and my power is complete. Follow me ; I seek the everlasting ices of the north, where you will feel the misery of cold and frost, to which I am impassive. You will find near this place, if you follow not too tardily, a dead hare ; eat, and be refreshed. Come on, my enemy ; we have yet to wrestle for our lives ; but many hard and miserable hours must you endure, until that period shall arrive."

Scoffing devil! Again do I vow vengeance ; again do I devote thee, miserable fiend, to torture and death. Never will I omit my search, until he or I perish ; and then with what ecstacy shall I join my Elizabeth, and those who even now prepare for me the reward of my tedious toil and horrible pilgrimage.

As I still pursued my journey to the northward, the snows thickened, and the cold increased in a degree almost too severe to support. The peasants were shut up in their hovels, and only a few of the most hardy ventured forth to seize the animals whom starvation had forced from their hiding-places to

11   *the Greeks wept.* The reference is to the culminating moment in the course of the famous March of the Ten Thousand into Persia and back to Greece at the end of the fifth century B.C. Xenophon describes the scene to which Mary Shelley refers. In his *The Persian Expedition* (pp. 164–65), he writes that the Greeks "came to the mountain on the fifth day, the name of the mountain being Thekes. When the men in front reached the summit and caught sight of the sea there was great shouting. Xenophon and the rearguard heard it and thought that there were some more enemies attacking in the front, since there were natives of the country they had ravaged following them up behind, and the rearguard had killed some of them and made prisoners of others in an ambush, and captured about twenty raw ox-hide shields, with the hair on. However, when the shouting got louder and drew nearer, and those who were constantly going forward started running toward the men in front who kept on shouting, and the more there were of them the more shouting there was, it looked then as though this was something of considerable importance. So Xenophon mounted his horse and, taking Lycus and the cavalry with him, rode forward to give support, and, quite soon, they heard the soldiers shouting out 'The sea! The sea!!' and passing the word down the column. Then certainly they all began to run, the rearguard and all, and drove on the baggage animals and the horses at full speed; and when they had all got to the top, the soldiers, with tears in their eyes, embraced each other and their generals and captains."

"A SLEDGE AND DOGS."

seek for prey. The rivers were covered with ice, and no fish could be procured; and thus I was cut off from my chief article of maintenance.

The triumph of my enemy increased with the difficulty of my labours. One inscription that he left was in these words: " Prepare! your toils only begin: wrap yourself in furs, and provide food, for we shall soon enter upon a journey where your sufferings will satisfy my everlasting hatred."

My courage and perseverance were invigorated by these scoffing words; I resolved not to fail in my purpose; and, calling on heaven to support me, I continued with unabated fervour to traverse immense deserts, until the ocean appeared at a distance, and formed the utmost boundary of the horizon. Oh! how unlike it was to the blue seas of the south! Covered with ice, it was only to be distinguished from land by its superior wildness and ruggedness. **11** The Greeks wept for joy when they beheld the Mediterranean from the hills of Asia, and hailed with rapture the boundary of their toils. I did not weep; but I knelt down, and, with a full heart, thanked my guiding spirit for conducting me in safety to the place where I hoped, notwithstanding my adversary's gibe, to meet and grapple with him.

Some weeks before this period I had procured a sledge and dogs, and thus traversed the snows with inconceivable speed. I know not whether the fiend possessed the same advantages; but I found that, as before I had daily lost ground in the pursuit, I now

12 *inquired.* One would give much to know in what language, since by now both the creature and Victor are in Russia.

"INHABITANTS."

gained on him; so much so, that when I first saw the ocean, he was but one day's journey in advance, and I hoped to intercept him before he should reach the beach. With new courage, therefore, I pressed on, and in two days arrived at a wretched hamlet on the sea-**12** shore. I inquired of the inhabitants concerning the fiend, and gained accurate information. A gigantic monster, they said, had arrived the night before, armed with a gun and many pistols; putting to flight the inhabitants of a solitary cottage, through fear of his terrific appearance. He had carried off their store of winter food, and, placing it in a sledge, to draw which he had seized on a numerous drove of trained dogs, he had harnessed them, and the same night, to the joy of the horror-struck villagers, had pursued his journey across the sea in a direction that led to no land; and they conjectured that he must speedily be destroyed by the breaking of the ice, or frozen by the eternal frosts.

On hearing this information, I suffered a temporary access of despair. He had escaped me; and I must commence a destructive and almost endless journey across the mountainous ices of the ocean,—amidst cold that few of the inhabitants could long endure, and which I, the native of a genial and sunny climate, could not hope to survive. Yet at the idea that the fiend should live and be triumphant, my rage and vengeance returned, and, like a mighty tide, overwhelmed every other feeling. After a slight repose, during which the spirits of the dead hovered round, and

"IMMENSE AND RUGGED MOUNTAINS OF ICE."

instigated me to toil and revenge, I prepared for my journey.

I exchanged my land sledge for one fashioned for the inequalities of the frozen ocean; and, purchasing a plentiful stock of provisions, I departed from land.

I cannot guess how many days have passed since then; but I have endured misery, which nothing but the eternal sentiment of a just retribution burning within my heart could have enabled me to support. Immense and rugged mountains of ice often barred up my passage, and I often heard the thunder of the ground sea, which threatened my destruction. But again the frost came, and made the paths of the sea secure.

By the quantity of provision which I had consumed I should guess that I had passed three weeks in this journey; and the continual protraction of hope, returning back upon the heart, often wrung bitter drops of despondency and grief from my eyes. Despair had indeed almost secured her prey, and I should soon have sunk beneath this misery; when once, after the poor animals that carried me had with incredible toil gained the summit of a sloping ice mountain, and one sinking under his fatigue died, I viewed the expanse before me with anguish, when suddenly my eye caught a dark speck upon the dusky plain. I strained my sight to discover what it could be, and uttered a wild cry of ecstacy when I distinguished a sledge, and the distorted proportions of a well-known form within. Oh! with what a burning

"A SCATTERED PIECE OF ICE."

gush did hope revisit my heart! warm tears filled my eyes, which I hastily wiped away, that they might not intercept the view I had of the dæmon; but still my sight was dimmed by the burning drops, until, giving way to the emotions that oppressed me, I wept aloud.

But this was not the time for delay; I disencumbered the dogs of their dead companion, gave them a plentiful portion of food; and, after an hour's rest, which was absolutely necessary, and yet which was bitterly irksome to me, I continued my route. The sledge was still visible; nor did I again lose sight of it, except at the moments when for a short time some ice rock concealed it with its intervening crags. I indeed perceptibly gained on it; and when, after nearly two days' journey, I beheld my enemy at no more than a mile distant, my heart bounded within me.

But now, when I appeared almost within grasp of my enemy, my hopes were suddenly extinguished, and I lost all trace of him more utterly than I had ever done before. A ground sea was heard; the thunder of its progress, as the waters rolled and swelled beneath me, became every moment more ominous and terrific. I pressed on, but in vain. The wind arose; the sea roared; and, as with the mighty shock of an earthquake, it split, and cracked with a tremendous and overwhelming sound. The work was soon finished: in a few minutes a tumultuous sea rolled between me and my enemy, and I was left drifting on a scattered piece of ice, that was continually lessening, and thus preparing for me a hideous death.

13 *swear to me, Walton.* This is a request that surely strains a friendship of such short duration. Victor wants nothing less from Walton than a vow to commit murder.

14 *wretch as I am.* Though Victor is speaking metaphorically, it is fascinating to see how Mary Shelley endows him with the recognition that the creature is now, as Victor has been, able to make "another such a wretch." The symbolic fusion of Victor and the creature is all but complete.

In this manner many appalling hours passed; several of my dogs died; and I myself was about to sink under the accumulation of distress, when I saw your vessel riding at anchor, and holding forth to me hopes of succour and life. I had no conception that vessels ever came so far north, and was astounded at the sight. I quickly destroyed part of my sledge to construct oars; and by these means was enabled, with infinite fatigue, to move my ice-raft in the direction of your ship. I had determined, if you were going southward, still to trust myself to the mercy of the seas, rather than abandon my purpose. I hoped to induce you to grant me a boat with which I could still pursue my enemy. But your direction was northward. You took me on board when my vigour was exhausted, and I should soon have sunk under my multiplied hardships into a death, which I still dread,—for my task is unfulfilled.

Oh! when will my guiding spirit, in conducting me to the dæmon, allow me the rest I so much desire; or must

13 I die, and he yet live? If I do, swear to me, Walton, that he shall not escape; that you will seek him, and satisfy my vengeance in his death. Yet, do I dare ask you to undertake my pilgrimage, to endure the hardships that I have undergone? No; I am not so selfish. Yet, when I am dead, if he should appear; if the ministers of vengeance should conduct him to you, swear that he shall not live—swear that he shall not triumph over my accumulated woes, and live to make

14 another such a wretch as I am. He is

15 *manes*. The spirits of the dead.

16 *steel aright*. Victor's narrative ends here. From this point on Mary Shelley abandons chapter headings and falls back on the earlier pretense that we are reading Walton's letters to his sister.

17 *The letters of Felix*. These letters were indeed promised to Victor by the creature early in the course of their conversation in the hut on the Mer de Glace. Here is the evidence that they were delivered, though in what manner remains obscure. Equally obscure is how letters said to be copies (see Vol. II, p. 177) can in any way validate either the creature's or Victor's stories.

Dr. Marc A. Rubenstein, a Freudian psychiatrist, in a closely reasoned article in *Studies in Romanticism*, XV, no. 2, argues that these fictional letters represented for Mary Shelley some intimate love letters exchanged between her father and mother, which she took with her at the time she eloped with Percy Shelley in 1814.

eloquent and persuasive; and once his words had even power over my heart: but trust him not. His soul is as hellish as his form, full of treachery and fiend-like malice. Hear him not;

15 call on the manes of William, Justine, Clerval, Elizabeth, my father, and of the wretched Victor, and thrust your sword into his heart. I will hover near,

16 and direct the steel aright.

WALTON, *in continuation.*

August 26th, 17—.

You have read this strange and terrific story, Margaret; and do you not feel your blood congealed with horror, like that which even now curdles mine? Sometimes, seized with sudden agony, he could not continue his tale; at others, his voice broken, yet piercing, uttered with difficulty the words so replete with agony. His fine and lovely eyes were now lighted up with indignation, now subdued to downcast sorrow, and quenched in infinite wretchedness. Sometimes he commanded his countenance and tones, and related the most horrible incidents with a tranquil voice, suppressing every mark of agitation; then, like a volcano bursting forth, his face would suddenly change to an expression of the wildest rage, as he shrieked out imprecations on his persecutor.

His tale is connected, and told with an appearance of the simplest truth;

17 yet I own to you that the letters of Felix and Safie, which he shewed me, and the apparition of the monster,

18 *Are you mad.* He would need to be to suppose that by merely asking, he could get the formula for the creation of a human being. Leaving to one side the psychological density shown by Walton, who has heard this long tale of misery without drawing the proper moral from it, Walton seems to suppose that being a failed poet and a hapless explorer are sufficient training to prepare him for feats of biochemical skill beyond the reach of all but one tragic mortal.

19 *corrected and augmented.* If one is looking for points of similarity between Victor and Percy Bysshe Shelley, here is a further one. Percy Shelley was so deeply concerned to make *Frankenstein* a success that he wrote the Preface with which the book begins. He served too as an assiduous copy editor of the manuscripts. Mary Shelley first mentions Shelley's work on the manuscript in her journal entry for May 14, 1817: "Shelley . . . corrects Frankenstein. Write Preface. Finis."

In one of his earliest letters to Lackington & Hughes, the publishers of *Frankenstein*, Shelley wrote: "I ought to have mentioned that the novel which I sent you is not my own production, but that of a friend who not being present in England cannot make the correction you suggest. As to any mere inaccuracies of language I should feel myself authorized to amend them when revising proofs" (*The Letters of Percy Bysshe Shelley*, p. 553).

In September 1817, Mary Shelley wrote to the poet: "I send you my dearest another proof [*Frankenstein*]—which arrived tonight. In looking it over there appeared to me some abruptness which I have endeavoured to supply—but I am tired and not very clear headed so I give you carte blanche to make what alterations you please" (*Letters of Mary Shelley*, p. 31).

In October 1817, Shelley wrote to Lackington & Hughes twice:

On October 23 he wrote: "You are of course aware how much depends upon extensive & judicious advertising: a part of the question which you are the most competent to understand. I have paid considerable attention to the correction of such few instances of baldness of style as necessarily occur in the production of a young writer" (*Letters of Percy Bysshe Shelley*, p. 565).

On October 28, he wrote: "I thought it necessary just to say that I shall not find it necessary in future to trouble the printer with any considerable alterations such as he will find in the present sheet & that which immediately preceded it. But the alterations will be found of the last importance to the interest of the tale" (*Letters of Percy Bysshe Shelley*, p. 565).

seen from our ship, brought to me a greater conviction of the truth of his narrative than his asseverations, however earnest and connected. Such a monster has then really existence; I cannot doubt it; yet I am lost in surprise and admiration. Sometimes I endeavoured to gain from Frankenstein the particulars of his creature's formation; but on this point he was impenetrable.

18 "Are you mad, my friend?" said he, "or whither does your senseless curiosity lead you? Would you also create for yourself and the world a demoniacal enemy? Or to what do your questions tend? Peace, peace! learn my miseries, and do not seek to increase your own."

Frankenstein discovered that I made notes concerning his history: he asked **19** to see them, and then himself corrected and augmented them in many places; but principally in giving the life and spirit to the conversations he held with his enemy. "Since you have preserved my narration," said he, "I would not that a mutilated one should go down to posterity."

Thus has a week passed away, while I have listened to the strangest tale that ever imagination formed. My thoughts, and every feeling of my soul, have been drunk up by the interest for my guest, which this tale, and his own elevated and gentle manners have created. I wish to soothe him; yet can I counsel one so infinitely miserable, so destitute of every hope of consolation, to live? Oh, no! the only joy that he can now know will be when he composes his shattered feelings to peace and death.   Yet he enjoys one comfort, the offspring of solitude and delirium: he believes, that, when in dreams he holds converse with his friends, and derives from that communion consolation for his miseries, or excitements to his vengeance, that they are not the creations of his fancy, but the real beings who visit him from the regions of a remote world.   This faith gives a solemnity to his reveries that render them to me almost as imposing and interesting as truth.

Our conversations are not always confined to his own history and misfortunes.   On every point of general literature he displays unbounded knowledge, and a quick and piercing apprehension.   His eloquence is forcible and touching; nor can I hear him, when he relates a pathetic incident, or endeavours to move the passions of pity or love, without tears.   What a glorious creature must he have been in the days of his prosperity, when he is thus noble and godlike in ruin.   He seems to feel his own worth, and the greatness of his fall.

" When younger," said he, " I felt as if I were destined for some great enterprise.   My feelings are profound; but I possessed a coolness of judgment that fitted me for illustrious achievements.   This sentiment of the worth of my nature supported me, when others would have been oppressed; for I deemed it criminal to throw away in useless grief those talents that might be useful to my fellow-creatures.   When I reflected on the work I had completed,

20 *projectors*. Scientists.

21 *I fell*. Our author is insisting rather mechanically on Victor's fall to prepare us to see him as an Aristotelian tragic figure. Aristotle's famous description of dramatic tragedy, it will be remembered, requires that it be a story of a great, good man who falls from a high place because of a fatal flaw, and whose destiny raises in us, and then purges, the emotions of pity and terror.

22 *such a one*. Walton is presumptuous. We have no evidence that Victor loves Walton.

no less a one than the creation of a sensitive and rational animal, I could not rank myself with the herd of common **20** projectors. But this feeling, which supported me in the commencement of my career, now serves only to plunge me lower in the dust. All my speculations and hopes are as nothing; and, like the archangel who aspired to omnipotence, I am chained in an eternal hell. My imagination was vivid, yet my powers of analysis and application were intense; by the union of these qualities I conceived the idea, and executed the creation of a man. Even now I cannot recollect, without passion, my reveries while the work was incomplete. I trod heaven in my thoughts, now exulting in my powers, now burning with the idea of their effects. From my infancy I was imbued with high hopes and a lofty ambition; but how am I sunk! Oh! my friend, if you had known me as I once was, you would not recognize me in this state of degradation. Despondency rarely visited my heart; a high **21** destiny seemed to bear me on, until I fell, never, never again to rise."

Must I then lose this admirable being? I have longed for a friend; I have sought one who would sympathize with and love me. Behold, on these **22** desert seas I have found such a one; but, I fear, I have gained him only to know his value, and lose him. I would reconcile him to life, but he repulses the idea.

"I thank you, Walton," he said, "for your kind intentions towards so miserable a wretch; but when you speak of new ties, and fresh affections,

think you that any can replace those who are gone? Can any man be to me as Clerval was; or any woman another Elizabeth? Even where the affections are not strongly moved by any superior excellence, the companions of our childhood always possess a certain power over our minds, which hardly any later friend can obtain. They know our infantine dispositions, which, however they may be afterwards modified, are never eradicated; and they can judge of our actions with more certain conclusions as to the integrity of our motives. A sister or a brother can never, unless indeed such symptoms have been shewn early, suspect the other of fraud or false dealing, when another friend, however strongly he may be attached, may, in spite of himself, be invaded with suspicion. But I enjoyed friends, dear not only through habit and association, but from their own merits; and, wherever I am, the soothing voice of my Elizabeth, and the conversation of Clerval, will be ever whispered in my ear. They are dead; and but one feeling in such a solitude can persuade me to preserve my life. If I were engaged in any high undertaking or design, fraught with extensive utility to my fellow-creatures, then could I live to fulfil it. But such is not my destiny; I must pursue and destroy the being to whom I gave existence; then my lot on earth will be fulfilled, and I may die."

September 2d.

MY BELOVED SISTER,

I write to you, encompassed by peril, and ignorant whether I am ever

23 *doomed.* Fated.

"I AM SURROUNDED BY MOUNTAINS OF ICE."

24 *Seneca.* The Roman philosopher (A.D.2–65), teacher and adviser to the Emperor Nero. After the conspiracy of Piso (A.D.65), Nero ordered the philosopher to kill himself. Sir William Smith, in his *Smaller Classical Dictionary* (p. 264), writes that Seneca took the order "without alarm . . . Seneca cheered his friends reminding them of the lessons of philosophy" and opened his veins calmly, as if death by suicide was a perfectly reasonable matter. Seneca's stoicism in the event is frequently praised. Perhaps Mary Shelley took note of the fact that Seneca's wife, Pompeia Paulina, who was not quite so calm on the occasion, chose to die by the same stroke of the knife that killed her husband.

23 doomed to see again dear England, and the dearer friends that inhabit it. I am surrounded by mountains of ice, which admit of no escape, and threaten every moment to crush my vessel. The brave fellows, whom I have persuaded to be my companions, look towards me for aid; but I have none to bestow. There is something terribly appalling in our situation, yet my courage and hopes do not desert me. We may survive; and if we do not, I will repeat **24** the lessons of my Seneca, and die with a good heart.

Yet what, Margaret, will be the state of your mind? You will not hear of my destruction, and you will anxiously await my return. Years will pass, and you will have visitings of despair, and yet be tortured by hope. Oh! my beloved sister, the sickening failings of your heart-felt expectations are, in prospect, more terrible to me than my own death. But you have a husband, and lovely children; you may be happy: heaven bless you, and make you so!

My unfortunate guest regards me with the tenderest compassion. He endeavours to fill me with hope; and talks as if life were a possession which he valued. He reminds me how often the same accidents have happened to other navigators, who have attempted this sea, and, in spite of myself, he fills me with cheerful auguries. Even the sailors feel the power of his eloquence: when he speaks, they no longer despair; he rouses their energies, and, while they hear his voice, they believe these vast mountains of ice are mole-hills, which will vanish before the resolutions of man. These feelings are transitory; each day's expectation delayed fills them with fear, and I almost dread a mutiny caused by this despair.

September 5th.

A scene has just passed of such uncommon interest, that although it is highly probable that these papers may never reach you, yet I cannot forbear recording it.

We are still surrounded by mountains of ice, still in imminent danger of being crushed in their conflict. The cold is excessive, and many of my unfortunate comrades have already found a grave amidst this scene of desolation. Frankenstein has daily declined in health: a feverish fire still glimmers in his eyes; but he is exhausted, and, when suddenly roused to any exertion, he speedily sinks again into apparent lifelessness.

I mentioned in my last letter the fears I entertained of a mutiny. This morning, as I sat watching the wan countenance of my friend—his eyes half closed, and his limbs hanging listlessly,—I was roused by half a dozen of the sailors, who desired admission into the cabin. They entered; and their leader addressed me. He told me that he and his companions had been chosen by the other sailors to come in deputation to me, to make me a demand, which, in justice, I could not refuse. We were immured in ice, and should probably never escape; but they feared that if, as was possible, the ice should dissipate, and a free passage be opened, I should be rash enough to continue

25 *this demand?* Though it has been clear almost from the beginning of this fiction that our author has meant to link Walton and Victor thematically, only at this moment can it be said that their lives are actually alike. Walton, we see, is as responsible for the fate of the men he commands as Victor has been for the destiny of his creature.

26 *of your species.* This is the language Victor used when he described his ambitions as a creator of human life. (See Vol. I, p. 67.)

my voyage, and lead them into fresh dangers, after they might happily have surmounted this. They desired, therefore, that I should engage with a solemn promise, that if the vessel should be freed, I would instantly direct my course southward.

This speech troubled me. I had not despaired; nor had I yet conceived the idea of returning, if set free. Yet could I, in justice, or even in possibility, refuse this demand? I hesitated before I answered; when Frankenstein, who had at first been silent, and, indeed, appeared hardly to have force enough to attend, now roused himself; his eyes sparkled, and his cheeks flushed with momentary vigour. Turning towards the men, he said—

" What do you mean? What do you demand of your captain? Are you then so easily turned from your design? Did you not call this a glorious expedition? and wherefore was it glorious? Not because the way was smooth and placid as a southern sea, but because it was full of dangers and terror; because, at every new incident, your fortitude was to be called forth, and your courage exhibited; because danger and death surrounded, and these dangers you were to brave and overcome. For this was it a glorious, for this was it an honourable undertaking. You were hereafter to be hailed as the benefactors of your species; your name adored, as belonging to brave men who encountered death for honour and the benefit of mankind. And now, behold, with the first imagination of danger, or, if you will, the first

27 *the foe.* James Rieger, in his edition of *Frankenstein* (p. 263), notes that "this speech echoes that in which Dante's Ulysses persuades his sailors to join him in a fatal, westward voyage of discovery." The passage in Dante's Inferno reads:

"Brothers," said I, "that have come valiantly
    Through hundred thousand jeopardies undergone
    To reach the West, you will not now deny

To this last little vigil left to run
    Of feeling life, the new experience
    Of the uninhabited world behind the sun.

Think of your breed; for brutish ignorance
    Your mettle was not made; you were made men
    To follow after knowledge and excellence."
                        (Canto XXVI, ll. 112–20)

mighty and terrific trial of your courage, you shrink away, and are content to be handed down as men who had not strength enough to endure cold and peril; and so, poor souls, they were chilly, and returned to their warm fire-sides. Why, that requires not this preparation; ye need not have come thus far, and dragged your captain to the shame of a defeat, merely to prove yourselves cowards. Oh! be men, or be more than men. Be steady to your purposes, and firm as a rock. This ice is not made of such stuff as your hearts might be; it is mutable, cannot withstand you, if you say that it shall not. Do not return to your families with the stigma of disgrace marked on your brows. Return as heroes who have fought and conquered, and who know not what it is to turn their backs on **27** the foe."

He spoke this with a voice so modulated to the different feelings expressed in his speech, with an eye so full of lofty design and heroism, that can you wonder that these men were moved. They looked at one another, and were unable to reply. I spoke; I told them to retire, and consider of what had been said: that I would not lead them further north, if they strenuously desired the contrary; but that I hoped that, with reflection, their courage would return.

They retired, and I turned towards my friend; but he was sunk in languor, and almost deprived of life.

How all this will terminate, I know not; but I had rather die, than return shamefully,—my purpose unfulfilled.

28 *The die is cast.* This is, of course, Julius Caesar's famous remark as he led his army across the Rubicon. The utterance is recorded by Suetonius in his *Life of Caesar* (I, 32). Mary Shelley was reading Suetonius in May 1817. Percy Shelley read him in December 1814.

As we see, Walton's earlier heroic rhetoric did not sustain him long. It is only two days since he proclaimed that he would rather die than return home shamefully.

29 *September 19th.* A misprint for September 9.

Yet I fear such will be my fate; the men, unsupported by ideas of glory and honour, can never willingly continue to endure their present hardships.

September 7th.

28 The die is cast; I have consented to return, if we are not destroyed. Thus are my hopes blasted by cowardice and indecision; I come back ignorant and disappointed. It requires more philosophy than I possess, to bear this injustice with patience.

September 12th.

It is past; I am returning to England. I have lost my hopes of utility and glory;—I have lost my friend. But I will endeavour to detail these bitter circumstances to you, my dear sister; and, while I am wafted towards England, and towards you, I will not despond.

29 September 19th, the ice began to move, and roarings like thunder were heard at a distance, as the islands split and cracked in every direction. We were in the most imminent peril; but, as we could only remain passive, my chief attention was occupied by my unfortunate guest, whose illness increased in such a degree, that he was entirely confined to his bed. The ice cracked behind us, and was driven with force towards the north; a breeze sprung from the west, and on the 11th the passage towards the south became perfectly free. When the sailors saw this, and that their return to their native country was apparently assured, a shout of tumultuous joy broke from them, loud and long-continued. Frankenstein, who was dozing, awoke, and asked the cause of the tumult. "They shout," I said, "because they will soon return to England."

"Do you then really return?"

"Alas! yes; I cannot withstand their demands. I cannot lead them unwillingly to danger, and I must return."

"Do so, if you will; but I will not. You may give up your purpose; but mine is assigned to me by heaven, and I dare not. I am weak; but surely the spirits who assist my vengeance will endow me with sufficient strength." Saying this, he endeavoured to spring from the bed, but the exertion was too great for him; he fell back, and fainted.

It was long before he was restored; and I often thought that life was entirely extinct. At length he opened his eyes, but he breathed with difficulty, and was unable to speak. The surgeon gave him a composing draught, and ordered us to leave him undisturbed. In the mean time he told me, that my friend had certainly not many hours to live.

His sentence was pronounced; and I could only grieve, and be patient. I sat by his bed watching him; his eyes were closed, and I thought he slept; but presently he called to me in a feeble voice, and, bidding me come near, said—"Alas! the strength I relied on is gone; I feel that I shall soon die, and he, my enemy and persecutor, may still be in being. Think not, Walton, that in the last moments

30 *it blameable*. This final fit of self-exculpation sounds very like the poet Shelley, who confidently believed for most of his life that he was always in the right, or at the very least, that there were always others who behaved worse than he did. There is an appalling letter of Shelley's on the occasion of his wife Harriet's suicide in which he writes: "It seems that this poor woman [Harriet]—the most innocent of her abhorred & unnatural family—was driven from her father's house, & descended the steps of prostitution until she lived with a groom of the name of Smith, who deserting her, she killed herself—There can be no question that the beastly viper her sister, unable to gain profit from her connection with me—has secured to herself the fortune of the old man [Harriet's father]—who is now dying—by the murder of this poor creature. Everything tends to prove, however, that beyond the mere shock of so hideous a catastrophe having fallen on a human being once so nearly connected with me, there would, in any case have been little to regret. Hookham, Longdill—every one does *me* full justice;—bears testimony to the uprightness & liberality of my conduct to her" (*The Letters of Percy Bysshe Shelley*, p. 521).

The wild charges against Harriet intended in this letter have not been substantiated.

30 of my existence I feel that burning hatred, and ardent desire of revenge, I once expressed, but I feel myself justified in desiring the death of my adversary. During these last days I have been occupied in examining my past conduct; nor do I find it blameable. In a fit of enthusiastic madness I created a rational creature, and was bound towards him, to assure, as far as was in my power, his happiness and wellbeing. This was my duty; but there was another still paramount to that. My duties towards my fellow-creatures had greater claims to my attention, because they included a greater proportion of happiness or misery. Urged by this view, I refused, and I did right in refusing, to create a companion for the first creature. He shewed unparalleled malignity and selfishness, in evil: he destroyed my friends; he devoted to destruction beings who possessed exquisite sensations, happiness, and wisdom; nor do I know where this thirst for vengeance may end. Miserable himself, that he may render no other wretched, he ought to die. The task of his destruction was mine, but I have failed. When actuated by selfish and vicious motives, I asked you to undertake my unfinished work; and I renew this request now, when I am only induced by reason and virtue.

" Yet I cannot ask you to renounce your country and friends, to fulfil this task; and now, that you are returning to England, you will have little chance of meeting with him. But the consideration of these points, and the well-

31 *succeed.* These are Victor's last words and they are at least ambiguous.

balancing of what you may esteem your duties, I leave to you; my judgment and ideas are already disturbed by the near approach of death. I dare not ask you to do what I think right, for I may still be misled by passion.

"That he should live to be an instrument of mischief disturbs me; in other respects this hour, when I momentarily expect my release, is the only happy one which I have enjoyed for several years. The forms of the beloved dead flit before me, and I hasten to their arms. Farewell, Walton! Seek happiness in tranquillity, and avoid ambition, even if it be only the apparently innocent one of distinguishing yourself in science and discoveries. Yet why do I say this? I have myself been blasted in these hopes, yet another may **31** succeed."

His voice became fainter as he spoke; and at length, exhausted by his effort, he sunk into silence. About half an hour afterwards he attempted again to speak, but was unable; he pressed my hand feebly, and his eyes closed for ever, while the irradiation of a gentle smile passed away from his lips.

Margaret, what comment can I make on the untimely extinction of this glorious spirit? What can I say, that will enable you to understand the depth of my sorrow? All that I should express would be inadequate and feeble. My tears flow; my mind is overshadowed by a cloud of disappointment. But I journey towards England, and I may there find consolation.

I am interrupted. What do these sounds portend? It is midnight; the breeze blows fairly, and the watch on deck scarcely stir. Again; there is a sound as of a human voice, but hoarser; it comes from the cabin where the remains of Frankenstein still lie. I must arise, and examine. Good night, my sister.

Great God! what a scene has just taken place! I am yet dizzy with the remembrance of it. I hardly know whether I shall have the power to detail it; yet the tale which I have recorded would be incomplete without this final and wonderful catastrophe.

I entered the cabin, where lay the remains of my ill-fated and admirable friend. Over him hung a form which I cannot find words to describe; gigantic in stature, yet uncouth and distorted in its proportions. As he hung over the coffin, his face was concealed by long locks of ragged hair; but one vast hand was extended, in colour and apparent texture like that of a mummy. When he heard the sound of my approach, he ceased to utter exclamations of grief and horror, and sprung towards the window. Never did I behold a vision so horrible as his face, of such loathsome, yet appalling hideousness. I shut my eyes involuntarily, and endeavoured to recollect what were my duties with regard to this destroyer. I called on him to stay.

He paused, looking on me with wonder; and, again turning towards the lifeless form of his creator, he seemed to forget my presence, and every feature and gesture seemed instigated by

32 *in his murder.* The creature, like Victor, is eagerly willing to be guilty. Victor was not murdered. He died of natural causes brought on by his own decision to pursue vengeance.

33 *have lived.* Walton's taunt is as superfluous as it is cruel.

34 *the deed.* Which deed? The creation of the creature? Victor's death?

the wildest rage of some uncontrollable passion.

32 " That is also my victim !" he exclaimed ; in his murder my crimes are consummated ; the miserable series of my being is wound to its close ! Oh, Frankenstein ! generous and self-devoted being ! what does it avail that I now ask thee to pardon me ? I, who irretrievably destroyed thee by destroying all thou lovedst. Alas ! he is cold ; he may not answer me."

His voice seemed suffocated ; and my first impulses, which had suggested to me the duty of obeying the dying request of my friend, in destroying his enemy, were now suspended by a mixture of curiosity and compassion. I approached this tremendous being ; I dared not again raise my looks upon his face, there was something so scaring and unearthly in his ugliness. I attempted to speak, but the words died away on my lips. The monster continued to utter wild and incoherent self-reproaches. At length I gathered resolution to address him, in a pause of the tempest of his passion : " Your repentance," I said, " is now superfluous If you had listened to the voice of conscience, and heeded the stings of remorse, before you had urged your diabolical vengeance to this extremity,

33 Frankenstein would yet have lived."

" And do you dream ?" said the dæmon ; " do you think that I was then dead to agony and remorse ?—He," he continued, pointing to the corpse, " he suffered not more in the consummation

34 of the deed ;—oh ! not the ten-thousandth portion of the anguish that was mine during the lingering detail of its

35 *love and sympathy*. Both Victor and the creature have frequently sounded this refrain.

36 *After the murder*. This entire paragraph deserves careful reading. It is charged and surcharged with the language of sexual ambiguity: "unspeakable torments," "impotent envy," "insatiable thirst."

execution. A frightful selfishness hurried me on, while my heart was poisoned with remorse. Think ye that the groans of Clerval were music to my ears? My heart was fashioned to
35 be susceptible of love and sympathy; and, when wrenched by misery to vice and hatred, it did not endure the violence of the change without torture, such as you cannot even imagine.

36   " After the murder of Clerval, I returned to Switzerland, heart-broken and overcome. I pitied Frankenstein; my pity amounted to horror: I abhorred myself. But when I discovered that he, the author at once of my existence and of its unspeakable torments, dared to hope for happiness; that while he accumulated wretchedness and despair upon me, he sought his own enjoyment in feelings and passions from the indulgence of which I was for ever barred, then impotent envy and bitter indignation filled me with an insatiable thirst for vengeance. I recollected my threat, and resolved that it should be accomplished. I knew that I was preparing for myself a deadly torture; but I was the slave, not the master of an impulse, which I detested, yet could not disobey. Yet when she died!—nay, then I was not miserable. I had cast off all feeling, subdued all anguish to riot in the excess of my despair. Evil thenceforth became my good. Urged thus far, I had no choice but to adapt my nature to an element which I had willingly chosen. The completion of my demoniacal design became an insatiable passion. And now it is ended; there is my last victim!"

    I was at first touched by the expres-

37 *powers of eloquence.* A characteristic frequently attributed to Frankenstein himself. (See Vol. I, p. 27; Vol. III, p. 315; Vol. III, p. 319).

38 *lament the fall.* This is not a mere metaphor since Walton, having heard Victor's tale, knows that the creature did, in fact, burn the De Laceys' cottage.

sions of his misery; yet when I called to mind what Frankenstein had said of **37** his powers of eloquence and persuasion, and when I again cast my eyes on the lifeless form of my friend, indignation was re-kindled within me. " Wretch !" I said, " it is well that you come here to whine over the desolation that you have made. You throw a torch into a pile of buildings, and when they are consumed you sit among **38** the ruins, and lament the fall. Hypocritical fiend ! if he whom you mourn still lived, still would he be the object, again would he become the prey of your accursed vengeance. It is not pity that you feel ; you lament only because the victim of your malignity is withdrawn from your power."

" Oh, it is not thus—not thus," interrupted the being; " yet such must be the impression conveyed to you by what appears to be the purport of my actions. Yet I seek not a fellow-feeling in my misery. No sympathy may I ever find. When I first sought it, it was the love of virtue, the feelings of happiness and affection with which my whole being overflowed, that I wished to be participated. But now, that virtue has become to me a shadow, and that happiness and affection are turned into bitter and loathing despair, in what should I seek for sympathy ? I am content to suffer alone, while my sufferings shall endure : when I die, I am well satisfied that abhorrence and opprobrium should load my memory. Once my fancy was soothed with dreams of virtue, of fame, and of enjoyment. Once I falsely hoped to meet with beings, who, pardoning my outward form, would love me for the excellent qualities which I was capable of bringing forth. I was nourished with high thoughts of honour and devotion. But now vice has degraded me beneath the meanest animal. No crime, no mischief, no malignity, no misery, can be found comparable to mine. When I call over the frightful catalogue of my deeds, I cannot believe that I am he whose thoughts were once filled with sublime and transcendant visions of the beauty and the majesty of goodness. But it is even so; the fallen angel becomes a malignant devil. Yet even that enemy of God and man had friends and associates in his desolation; I am quite alone.

" You, who call Frankenstein your friend, seem to have a knowledge of my crimes and his misfortunes. But, in the detail which he gave you of them, he could not sum up the hours and months of misery which I endured, wasting in impotent passions. For whilst I destroyed his hopes, I did not satisfy my own desires. They were for ever ardent and craving; still I desired love and fellowship, and I was still spurned. Was there no injustice in this? Am I to be thought the only criminal, when all human kind sinned against me? Why do you not hate Felix, who drove his friend from his door with contumely? Why do you not execrate the rustic who sought to destroy the saviour of his child? Nay, these are virtuous and immaculate beings! I, the miserable and the abandoned, am an abortion, to be spurned

39 *no more.* To paraphrase this obtuse sentence: The creature longs for the time (presumably after death) when he can look at his own hands without being guiltily reminded of his evil deeds.

40 *of the globe.* The creature, who once promised to travel south for his union with a female like himself, now promises to move north, where he will consummate a transcendant union with Victor.

Where, in the vicinity of the North Pole, he expects to find wood enough to make a funeral pyre is a detail that did not trouble Mary Shelley. Perhaps it should not trouble us.

at, and kicked, and trampled on. Even now my blood boils at the recollection of this injustice.

" But it is true that I am a wretch. I have murdered the lovely and the helpless; I have strangled the innocent as they slept, and grasped to death his throat who never injured me or any other living thing. I have devoted my creator, the select specimen of all that is worthy of love and admiration among men, to misery; I have pursued him even to that irremediable ruin. There he lies, white and cold in death. You hate me; but your abhorrence cannot equal that with which I regard myself. I look on the hands which executed the deed; I think on the heart in which the imagination of it was conceived, and long for the moment when they will meet my eyes, when it will haunt my thoughts, no **39** more.

" Fear not that I shall be the instrument of future mischief. My work is nearly complete. Neither your's nor any man's death is needed to consummate the series of my being, and accomplish that which must be done; but it requires my own. Do not think that I shall be slow to perform this sacrifice. I shall quit your vessel on the ice-raft which brought me hither, and shall seek the most northern extremity **40** of the globe; I shall collect my funeral pile, and consume to ashes this miserable frame, that its remains may afford no light to any curious and unhallowed wretch, who would create such another as I have been. I shall die. I shall no longer feel the agonies

41 *death?* The second half of this paragraph is a fine recapitulation of the details we were long ago given of the creature's first coming to consciousness.

which now consume me, or be the prey of feelings unsatisfied, yet unquenched. He is dead who called me into being; and when I shall be no more, the very remembrance of us both will speedily vanish. I shall no longer see the sun or stars, or feel the winds play on my cheeks. Light, feeling, and sense, will pass away; and in this condition must I find my happiness. Some years ago, when the images which this world affords first opened upon me, when I felt the cheering warmth of summer, and heard the rustling of the leaves and the chirping of the birds, and these were all to me, I should have wept to die; now it is my only consolation. Polluted by crimes, and torn by the bitterest remorse, where can I find rest but in **41** death?

" Farewell! I leave you, and in you the last of human kind whom these eyes will ever behold. Farewell, Frankenstein! If thou wert yet alive, and yet cherished a desire of revenge against me, it would be better satiated in my life than in my destruction. But it was not so; thou didst seek my extinction, that I might not cause greater wretchedness; and if yet, in some mode unknown to me, thou hast not yet ceased to think and feel, thou desirest not my life for my own misery. Blasted as thou wert, my agony was still superior to thine; for the bitter sting of remorse may not cease to rankle in my wounds until death shall close them for ever.

" But soon," he cried, with sad and solemn enthusiasm, " I shall die, and what I now feel be no longer felt.

42 *the end.* Critics generally have taken the creature's word for the deed and have assumed that he has indeed gone off to die. But there is a hovering uncertainty about the matter, a poignant puzzle made particularly baffling because all the other deaths in this book have been so direct and unambiguous. Then why, since the author of a book has merely to write a fictive death to accomplish it, has the creature been left in the limbo of his own promise to die? It would have taken but a couple of strokes of the pen to have Walton shoot the creature, thereby carrying out Victor's dearest wish (see p. 310). Yet, Mary Shelley is reticent, as if she could not bring herself to murder this most unfortunate creature of her brain.

ARCTIC FOX.

Soon these burning miseries will be extinct.   I shall ascend my funeral pile triumphantly, and exult in the agony of the torturing flames.   The light of that conflagration will fade away; my ashes will be swept into the sea by the winds.   My spirit will sleep in peace; or if it thinks, it will not surely think thus.   Farewell."

He sprung from the cabin-window, as he said this, upon the ice-raft which lay close to the vessel. He was soon borne away by the waves, and lost in darkness and distance.

42   THE END.

APPENDIXES

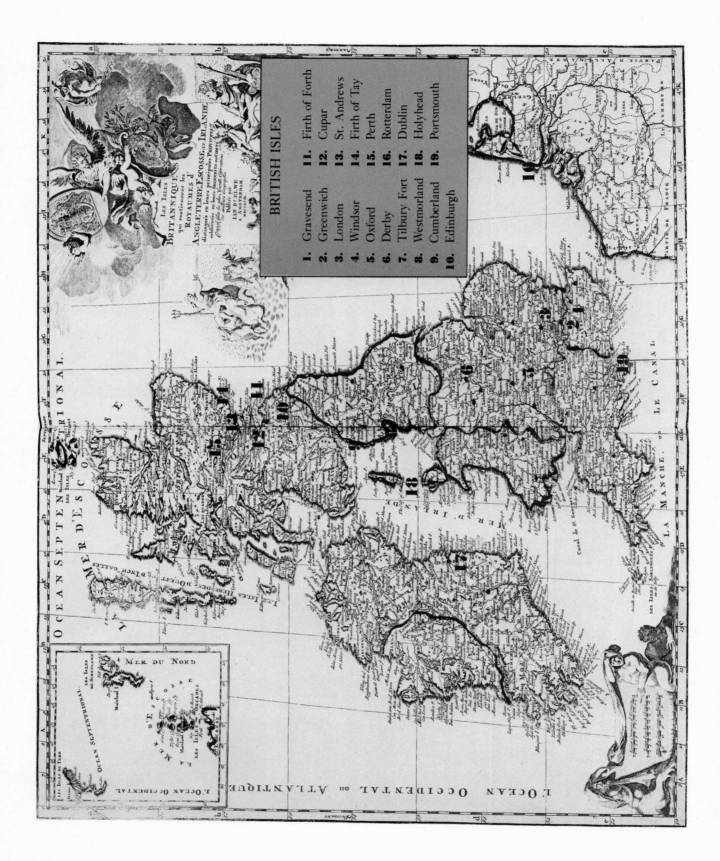

BRITISH ISLES

1. Gravesend	**11.** Firth of Forth
2. Greenwich	**12.** Cupar
3. London	**13.** St. Andrews
4. Windsor	**14.** Firth of Tay
5. Oxford	**15.** Perth
6. Derby	**16.** Rotterdam
7. Tilbury Fort	**17.** Dublin
8. Westmorland	**18.** Holyhead
9. Cumberland	**19.** Portsmouth
10. Edinburgh	

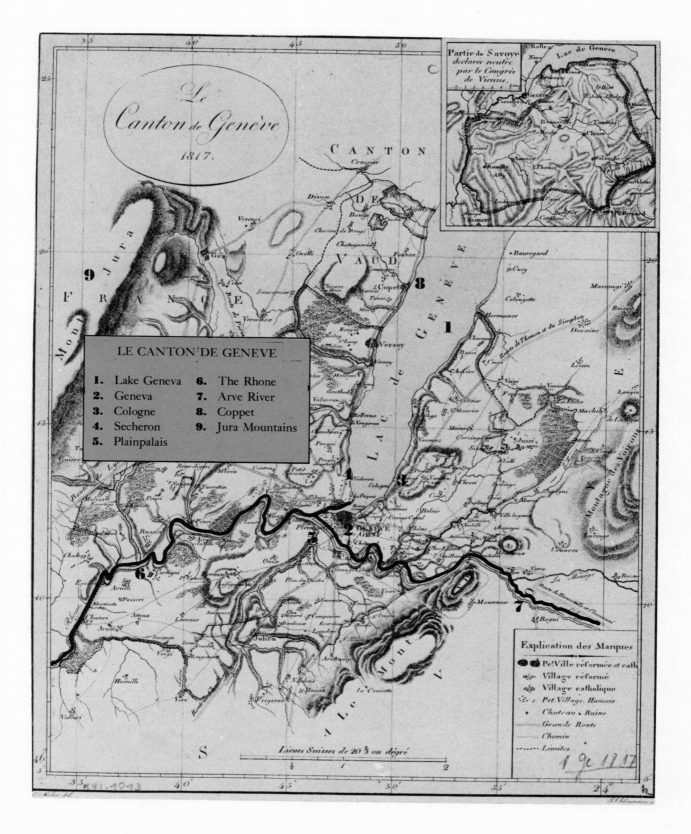

LE CANTON DE GENEVE

1. Lake Geneva   6. The Rhone
2. Geneva   7. Arve River
3. Cologne   8. Coppet
4. Secheron   9. Jura Mountains
5. Plainpalais

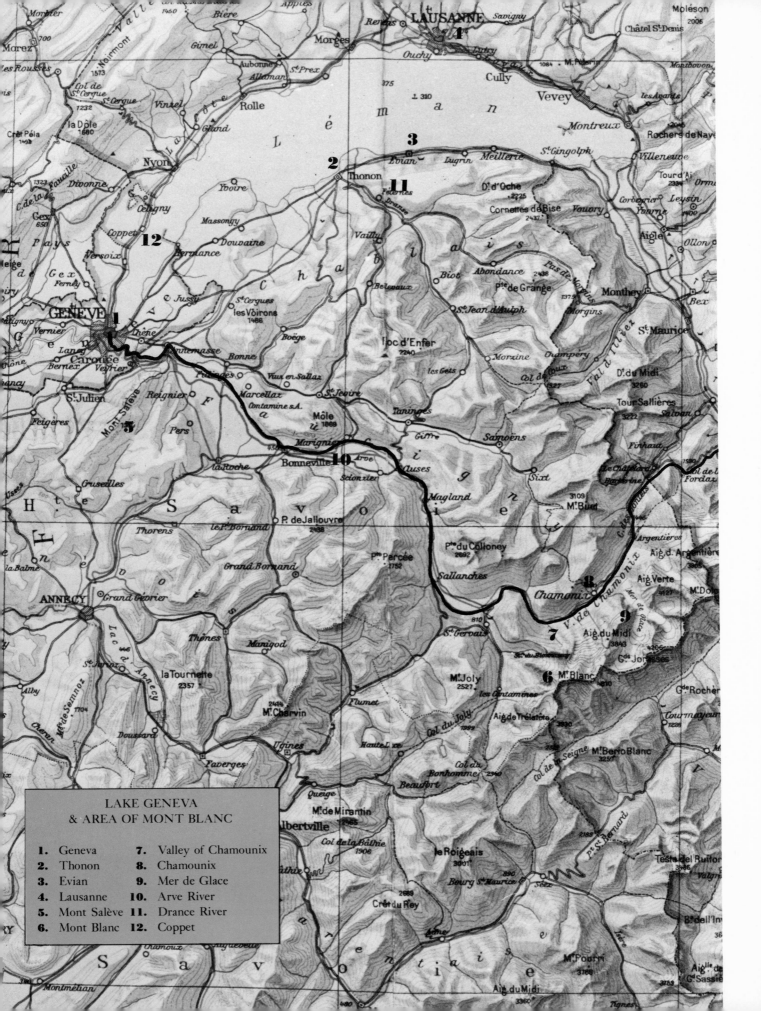

LAKE GENEVA
& AREA OF MONT BLANC

1. Geneva   7. Valley of Chamounix
2. Thonon   8. Chamounix
3. Evian   9. Mer de Glace
4. Lausanne   10. Arve River
5. Mont Salève   11. Drance River
6. Mont Blanc   12. Coppet

SWITZERLAND

1. Geneva
2. Lake Geneva
3. Lake Como

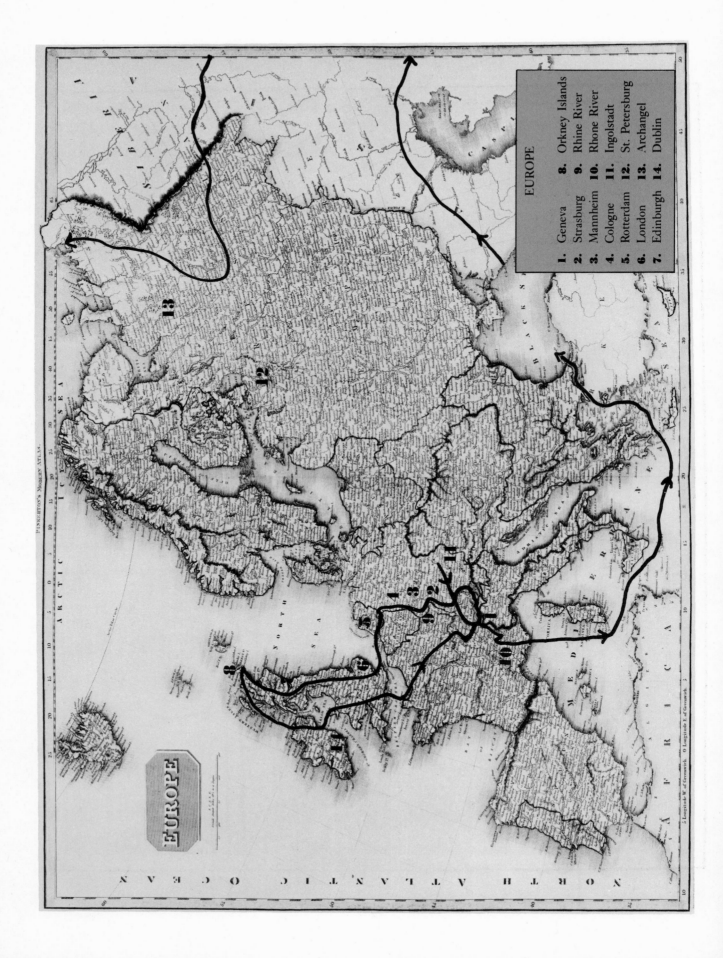

EUROPE

1. Geneva	**8.**	Orkney Islands
2. Strasburg	**9.**	Rhine River
3. Mannheim	**10.**	Rhone River
4. Cologne	**11.**	Ingolstadt
5. Rotterdam	**12.**	St. Petersburg
6. London	**13.**	Archangel
7. Edinburgh	**14.**	Dublin

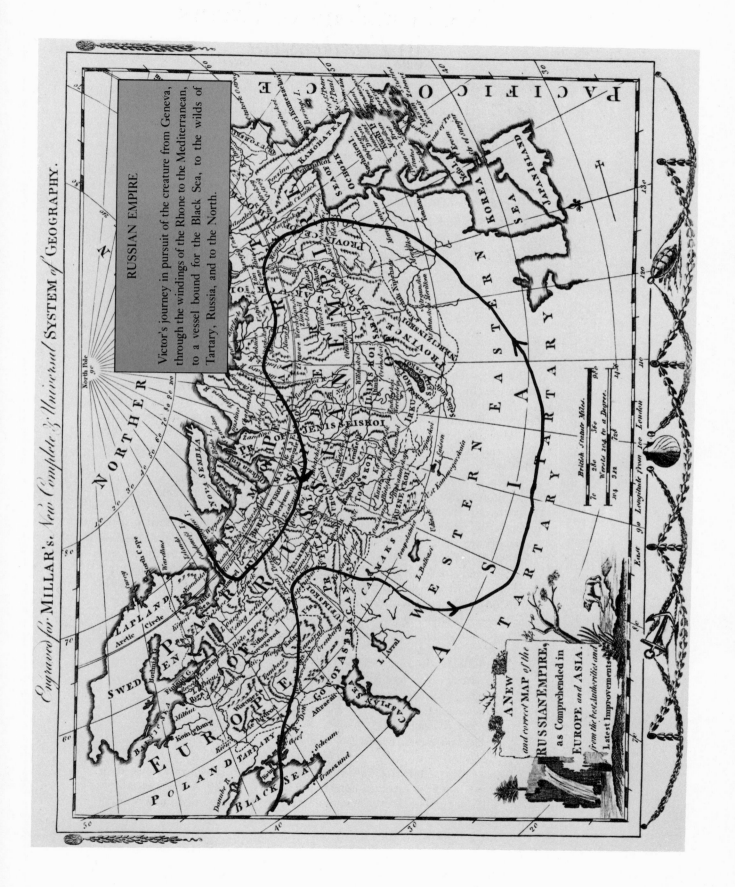

Engraved for MILLAR's New Complete & Universal SYSTEM of GEOGRAPHY.

RUSSIAN EMPIRE

Victor's journey in pursuit of the creature from Geneva, through the windings of the Rhone to the Mediterranean, to a vessel bound for the Black Sea, to the wilds of Tartary, Russia, and to the North.

A NEW
and correct MAP of the
RUSSIAN EMPIRE,
as Comprehended in
EUROPE and ASIA.
from the best Authorities and
Latest Improvements.

A Chronology of Events
in *Frankenstein*

An effort has been made to discover a rational calendar for the action of *Frankenstein* that would permit one to say accurately that any given date was a particular day of the week, either in a possible late eighteenth-century year or in an imaginary but orderly lunar year. There are two clues to work with. In Robert Walton's fourth letter, dated August 5, we are told that the preceding Monday was July 31; and in Alphonse Frankenstein's letter to Victor giving him the news of William's death, we are told that William died on Thursday, May 7.

If we consult a perpetual calendar, we learn that in the late eighteenth century

May 7 fell on a Thursday in:	*July 31 fell on a Monday in:*
1761	1758
1767	1769
1772	1775
1778	1780
1789	1786
1795	1797

The question then is whether a single calendar can be created to accommodate the certain dates with which we started. Since we know that four years have elapsed between the murder of William and the time when Walton sees the creature on the Arctic ice, we should expect our extrapolation to carry us neatly from Thursday, May 7, 17——, to Monday, July 31, 17—— + 4. Sadly enough, that does not happen. There is no way to bring our two dates into a single calendar.

Given the impasse, it has been thought better simply to provide readers with a chronological sequence of events based on such clues as the text gives us. We know, for example, that Victor was four years old when the "infant" Elizabeth was brought into his family (Vol. I, p. 35, this edition); that Justine came to live with the Frankensteins when she was twelve years old and that she served the family for five years before returning home "a few months after your [Victor's] departure for Ingolstadt" when they were both seventeen (Vol. I, p. 87). The chronology that follows, then, is simple enough. It begins with Victor's birth and ends with his death.

Readers who like to know how old some of the characters are at any point in the book may want to remember that Victor is:

twenty-one years older than	the creature
sixteen years older than	William
three years older than	Elizabeth
the same age as	Justine
a year younger than	Walton
thirty-one years younger (approximately)	than Waldman

Madness, illness and death are identified in the chronology because their frequency is a matter of critical interest, and because, in the view of this editor, they reflect Mary Shelley's experiences in the years that preceded the writing of *Frankenstein*.

Victor's Age	Time or Season	Event	Volume/page number (this edition)
		Victor's birth	I/32
4		Elizabeth is brought to live with the Frankensteins	I/35
12		Victor's mother brings Justine to household as servant	I/86
13		Victor begins to study work of "exploded" scientists	I/39
		Walton decides to become a poet	I/16
14		Walton inherits his cousin's fortune	I/12
15		Victor sees oak tree destroyed by lightning	I/43
17		■ Elizabeth contracts scarlet fever	I/47
		■ ■ Victor's mother contracts scarlet fever and dies	I/47–48
		■ Justine contracts scarlet fever	I/87
		Victor leaves for Ingolstadt	I/51
		Justine goes to live with her mother	I/87
19		Victor attains fame at the university	I/61
21		Walton decides to go to sea	I/12
		■ Victor sick with nervous exhaustion	I/71
	November	Victor finishes the creature	I/72
	next day	Henry arrives in Ingolstadt	I/78
		■ Victor becomes sick with nervous fever	I/81
	early winter	■ ■ Justine's mother, in nervous fit, dies	I/88
	2 weeks later	creature in forest, learns use of senses	II/145–146
	2 weeks later	creature in forest, discovers fire	II/149
	3 days later	■ creature wounded by villagers' stones	II/152
	same day	creature arrives at cottage	II/152
	winter	creature learns a few words and cottagers' names	II/58–59
22	May	Victor regains his senses	I/82
	May 18	Elizabeth's letter to Victor	I/84
	2 weeks later	Victor introduces Henry to professors	I/90
	late spring	Safie arrives at cottage	II/167
	2 months later	creature has learned French	II/170
	August	creature finds three books	II/183
	fall	Victor and Henry study Oriental languages	I/91
	late fall	creature reveals himself to De Lacey and flees	II/191–195
		■ creature sick with nervous exhaustion and despair	II/196
		■ De Lacey in shock, health ruined	II/198–199
		■ creature, frustrated, destroys cottage	II/199–200
	winter	creature wanders in general direction of Geneva	II/202
23	early spring	■ creature shot after saving girl from drowning	II/134
	May	Victor and Henry tour Ingolstadt	I/92–93
	May 7	creature arrives in Geneva	II/205
	May 7	■ William murdered by creature	II/207
		■ Justine sick with grief over murder	I/111
	May 12	Alphonse's letter to Victor	I/95–97
	May/June	Victor returns to Geneva	I/99
	June	Justine convicted of William's death	I/116
	mid-August	Frankensteins take 6-day vacation in Chamounix	II/131
		Victor and creature meet on glacier	II/139
	end of August	Victor leaves Geneva	III/224
		Victor and Henry meet in Strasburgh	III/225

■ indicates illness   ■ indicates madness   ■ indicates death

Victor's Age	Time or Season	Event	Volume/page number (this edition)
	end of December	Victor and Henry arrive in England	III/229
24	March 27	Victor and Henry leave London	III/234
	2 months	Victor and Henry stay at Oxford	III/236
	2 months	Victor and Henry stay in Cumberland and Westmoreland	III/237
	beg. August	Victor goes to Orkneys; Henry stays in Perth	III/239–243
	August	Victor creates, then destroys, female creature	III/245–247
	end of August	Henry's letter to Victor, wanting to resume tour	III/253–254
		■ Henry murdered by creature	III/260–261
	next day	Victor leaves Orkney Islands	III/255
		▪ Victor is seasick	III/257
	that night	Victor arrested for Henry's murder	III/259
	2 months later	▪ Victor, sick with convulsions and fever, is in prison	III/263–264
	late October	Victor's father arrives at prison	III/268
	late November	Victor's trial; Victor acquitted	III/270–271
	December	Victor released from prison	III/271
		Victor and his father travel across England	III/272–274
	May 8	Victor and his father arrive in Le Havre	III/277
	May 18	Elizabeth's letter to Victor in Paris	III/277–280
	June	Victor and his father arrive in Geneva	III/282
	June	Victor and Elizabeth are married	III/285
	that night	■ Elizabeth is murdered by the creature	III/288–290
		▪ Victor is grief-stricken	III/290
		Victor returns to Geneva	III/294–295
	few days later	■ ▪ Alphonse, Victor's father, dies in apoplectic fit	III/295
	many months later	▪ ■ Victor mad with grief and shock; released from prison	III/295–296
	1 month later	Victor tells magistrate about the creature	III/296–297
26	January	Victor begins pursuit of creature	III/300
	December 10	Walton arrives in Saint Petersburg	I/7
	December 11	Walton's first letter to Mrs. Saville	I/7–14
27	March 28	Walton's second letter to Mrs. Saville (Archangel)	I/15–19
	June	Victor and creature use sleds to travel	III/306
	July 7	Walton's third letter to Mrs. Saville (at sea)	I/20–21
	Monday, July 31	ship surrounded by ice; crew sights creature	I/22–23
	August 1	Victor rescued by Walton's ship	I/23–24
		▪ Victor sick from exposure	I/24–25
	August 5	Walton's fourth letter to Mrs. Saville	I/22–31
	August 20	Victor begins his story	I/32
	August 26	continuation of letter; Victor's story ends	III/311
	September 2	ship is surrounded by ice	III/309–310
	September 5	crew insists ship be sailed south if passage opened	III/319
	September 7	Walton agrees to return to England, if possible	III/321
	September 9	ice begins to shift	III/321
	September 11	passage to south is free	III/321
	September 11	■ Victor dies	III/324
	September 12	continuation of Walton's letter	III/321
	September 12	creature boards Walton's ship, sees Victor's body, speaks a eulogy, is "borne away by the waves, and lost in darkness and distance."	III/325–332

Selected Filmography

Mary Shelley's creature, and his creator, have moved across the movie screens of the world since 1910. For decades, the creature has been destroyed and ingeniously resurrected in scores of films. There is every reason to think that he and his creator will go on leading their shadowy movie lives for generations to come.

The list of films that follows is not a record of excellence, though there are great films on it. Instead, it is a collection of those titles that have helped to define or to enlarge the by-now substantial film lore of *Frankenstein*. This should help to explain how it is that fine productions like James Whale's *Frankenstein*, Jack Smight's *Frankenstein: The True Story*, Andy Warhol's (Paul Morrissey's) *Frankenstein*, and Mel Brooks's *Young Frankenstein* appear on the same page with such dreary films as Charles T. Barton's *Abbot & Costello Meet Frankenstein* and William Beaudine's *Jesse James Meets Frankenstein's Daughter*.

Date	Title	Director	Studio	Creature Played By
1910	*Frankenstein*	J. Searle Dowley	Edison (U.S.)	Charles Ogle
1915	*Life without Soul*	Joseph W. Smiley	Ocean (U.S.)	Percy Darrell Standing
1920	*Mostro di Frankenstein, Il*	Eugenio Testa	Albertini (Italy)	Umberto Guarracino
1931	*Frankenstein*	James Whale	Universal (U.S.)	Boris Karloff
1935	*Bride of Frankenstein*	James Whale	Universal (U.S.)	Boris Karloff
1939	*Son of Frankenstein*	Rowland Lee	Universal (U.S.)	Boris Karloff
1942	*Ghost of Frankenstein*	Erle C. Kenton	Universal (U.S.)	Lon Chaney, Jr.
1943	*Frankenstein Meets The Wolfman*	Roy William Neill	Universal (U.S.)	Bela Lugosi
1944	*House of Frankenstein*	Erle C. Kenton	Universal (U.S.)	Glenn Strange
1945	*House of Dracula*	Erle C. Kenton	Universal (U.S.)	Glenn Strange

Date	Title	Director	Studio	Creature Played By
1948	Abbot & Costello Meet Frankenstein	Charles T. Barton	Universal (U.S.)	Glenn Strange
1957	Curse of Frankenstein	Terence Fisher	Hammer (G.B.)	Christopher Lee
1957	Horrors of Frankenstein	Tony Brezinski	Adventure (U.S.)	Ken Carroll
1957	I Was a Teenage Frankenstein	Herbert L. Strock	Santa Rosa (U.S.)	Gary Conway
1958	Frankenstein 1970	Howard W. Koch	Allied Artists (U.S.)	Mike Lane
1958	Frankenstein's Daughter	Dick Curha	Layton (U.S.)	Sally Todd
1958	The Revenge of Frankenstein	Terence Fisher	Hammer (G.B.)	Michael Gwynn
1963	Kiss Me Quick	Russ Meyer	Fantasy (U.S.)	Fred Coe
1964	The Evil of Frankenstein	Freddie Francis	Hammer (G.B.)	Kiwi Kingston
1965	Frankenstein Conquers the World	Inoshiro Honda	Toho (Japan)	Tadao Takashina
1965	Jesse James Meets Frankenstein's Daughter	William Beaudine	Embassy (U.S.)	Cal Bolder
1966	Frankenstein Created Woman	Terence Fisher	Hammer (G.B.)	Susan Denberg & Robert Morris
1966	Munster Go Home!	Earl Bellamy	Universal (U.S.)	Fred Gwynne
1970	The Horror of Frankenstein	Jimmy Sangster	Hammer (G.B.)	David Prowse
1971	Dracula Contra El Dr. Frankenstein	Jesus Franco	Fenix (Spain)	Fernando Bilbao
1971	Dracula vs. Frankenstein	Al Adamson	Independent Int. (U.S.)	John Bloom
T.V.–1973	Frankenstein	Glenn Jordan	Dan Curtis Prod. (U.S.)	Bo Svenson
T.V.–1973	Frankenstein: The True Story	Jack Smight	Universal (U.S.)	Michael Sarrazin
1974	Flesh for Frankenstein (Andy Warhol's Frankenstein)	Paul Morrissey	Bryanston	Srdjan Zelenovic
1974	Frankenstein and the Monster from Hell	Terence Fisher	Hammer (G.B.)	David Prowse
1974	Young Frankenstein	Mel Brooks	Twentieth Century-Fox (U.S.)	Peter Boyle

A Survey of British, American, and Foreign-language Editions of *Frankenstein*

BRITISH EDITIONS

Date	Publisher	Place of Publication	Date	Publisher	Place of Publication
1818	Lackington, Hughes, Harding, Mayor & Jones	London	1932	Readers' Library	London
1823	G. & W. B. Whitaker	London	1933	J. M. Dent (Everyman Edition)	London
*1831	H. Colburn & R. Bentley	London	1960	J. M. Dent (Everyman Edition)	London
*1849	R. Bentley	London	1963	J. M. Dent (Everyman Edition)	London
1856	The Parlour Library	London	1968	J. M. Dent (Everyman Edition)	London
1882	G. Routledge & Sons	London	1968	Penguin Edition	London
1886	G. Routledge & Sons (Introduction by H. R. Haweis)	London	*1969	Oxford University (Introduction by N. K. Joseph)	London
1888	G. Routledge & Sons, Pocket Editions	London	1973	Arrow Books	London
1891	G. Routledge & Sons	London	1974	Pan Books (Edited by Richard J. Anobile)	London
1906	J. M. Dent (First Everyman Edition)	London			
1912	J. M. Dent (Everyman Edition)	London			
1921	J. M. Dent (Everyman Edition)	London			

AMERICAN EDITIONS

Date	Publisher	Place of Publication	Date	Publisher	Place of Publication
1833	Carey, Lea & Blanchard	Philadelphia	*193?	Grosset & Dunlap (Illustrations from the Universal *Frankenstein* film)	New York
1845	H. G. Daggers	New York			
1882	J. W. Lovell Company	New York	†1933	E. P. Dutton	New York
†1891	E. P. Dutton	New York	*1934	The Limited Editions Club (Illustrations by Everett Henry)	New York
1910	J. Pott & Company	New York			
†1912	E. P. Dutton (Introduction by R. E. Dowse & D. J. Palmer)	New York	*1934	Harrison Smith & Robert Haas (Illustrations by Lynd Ward)	New York
19??	Caxton House, Popular Classics of the World	New York			
*1932	Illustrated Editions (Illustrations by Nino Carbe)	Garden City			

*Illustrated edition.

†The E. P. Dutton editions are the American versions of the British J. M. Dent texts.

Date	Publisher	Place of Publication	Date	Publisher	Place of Publication
1942	U.S. Armed Forces in Germany (Issued by the Council of Books in Wartime)	New York	1973	Doubleday (*Dracula* included)	Garden City
1949	Halcyon House	Garden City	1974	Bobbs-Merrill (The 1818 text edited with an Introduction by James Rieger)	Indianapolis
1957	Pyramid Books	New York	1974	Universe Books (Edited by Richard J. Anobile)	New York
1960	Doubleday	Garden City	1974	Clarkson N. Potter, Inc. (Illustrated by Robert Andrew Parker)	New York
†1960	E. P. Dutton	New York			
1969	Oxford University (Introduction by M. K. Joseph)	New York			

FOREIGN-LANGUAGE EDITIONS

Date	Publisher	Place of Publication	Date	Publisher	Place of Publication
French			*Greek*		
1821	Coréard (Translation by Jules Saladin)	Paris	1971	Ekodseis Galia (Translation by Rozitas Sàkou)	Athens
1932	Édition Cosmopolite (Universal Film Scenerio et Adaptation)		*Hindi-Urdu*		
1922	La Renaissance du Livre (Introduction, D. d'Hangest)	Paris	1959	Nasim Book Department (Translation by Mazhar-ul-Haw 'Alvi)	Lucknow
1946	Le Scribe (Adaptation de Henry Langon)	Brussels	*Italian*		
196?	Verviers, Gerard (Translation by Joe Cevruorst)	Paris	1944	D. de Luigi (Translation by Ranieri Cochetti)	Rome
1964	Union Générale d'Éditions	Paris	1953	Rizzoli (Translation by Bruno Tasso)	Milan
*1968	Cercle du Bibliophile (Illustrated by Christian Broutin. Translation by Hannah Bejeman. Introduction and Filmography by Michel Boujet)	Paris	*Sanskrit*		
			1959	Kozhikode Bros. (Translation by M. R. Narayana Pilla)	?
*1969	Éditions d'Érable (Illustrated by Claude Selva. Translation by Raymonde de Gans)	Geneva	*Spanish*		
			1947	Lautaro (Translation by Laura Marazal)	Madrid
			1947	————	Buenos Aires
German			1953	Janes	Madrid
1910	H. Schroth (Translation by Karl Henkelman)	Darmstadt	1959	Aguilar (Translation by Antonio Gobernada)	Madrid
1912	Ahmann (Translation by Heinz Widtmann)	Leipzig	1969	Brujula (Translation by Hermengildo Sabat)	Buenos Aires
1970	S. Hauser (Translation by F. Polakovics)	?	*Swedish*		
1975	Wagenbach	Berlin	1959	Christofer's (Translation by Monica Stolpe)	Stockholm

A Note on the Illustrated Editions of *Frankenstein*

Curiously enough, for a book that has been as frequently reprinted and is as visually powerful as *Frankenstein*, there are relatively few editions of it that have been illustrated. In 1818, when the book was first published, there were no pictures at all. In the revised edition of 1831, there were two mildly gloomy drawings by Chevalier which served as the frontispiece and title page decoration (see p. 74 and p. 50, respectively, of this edition). The frontispiece shows a not at all loathsome creature coming to life in the presence of a book, a skull, and a piece of laboratory equipment. The title page decoration shows a dark-clad Victor taking leave of a doleful Elizabeth. These illustrations were occasionally included in later printings of the 1831 text, but it was not until the twentieth century that *Frankenstein* attracted illustrators of stature.

The heavy period of *Frankenstein* illustration comes in the 1930s, no doubt as a consequence of the popularity of the 1931 Universal Pictures film.[1] Nino Carbe's stark woodcuts, made for the 1932 Illustrated Editions printing of the book, remain as strong, as poignant, and as tactful as ever. Carbe captured both the sense of muscle distortion and psychological rigidity that are such integral elements in Mary Shelley's masterpiece. In 1934 there were two other illustrated editions. Lynd Ward's woodcuts for the Harrison Smith-Robert Haas edition add a megalithic quality to the story, as if immovable ancient evil meant to lurch through the tale; while Everett Henry's pastels, made for the Limited Editions Club printing of the book, are considerably at war with the simplicities of light and dark contending with each other on the pages he is illustrating. Curiously enough, the creature does not fully appear in Henry's drawings. Instead, his presence is hinted at either with a looming shadow, or in a glimpse of him behind a powerfully outstretched arm.

More than thirty years were to pass before *Frankenstein* appeared again with pictures. In 1968 Christian Broutin made a number of sleek, but intense pen and ink drawings for the French Cercle du Bibliophile edition; and in 1969 Claude Selva's darkly intimate drawings accompanied the Swiss Éditions d'Érable text of *Frankenstein*. In 1976 the distinguished Robert Andrew Parker made a number of watercolor illustrations that brooded handsomely through the pages of the *Illustrated Frankenstein*, issued by Clarkson N. Potter, Inc.

---

[1] In an unspecified year in the thirties, Grosset & Dunlap published an edition of *Frankenstein* that was illustrated with stills taken from the Universal Pictures photoplay.

NINO CARBE.

Illustrators Of
Mary Shelley's Frankenstein

CHRISTIAN BROUTIN.

EVERETT HENRY.

LYND WARD.

ROBERT ANDREW PARKER.

BIBLIOGRAPHY

The list of books that follows is in no sense either a Mary Shelley bibliography or a bibliography of the Frankenstein myth. Instead, it is a record of books consulted by an editor doing what he can to answer a host of sometimes unrelated questions posed by Mary Shelley's masterpiece.

Aeschylus. *Plays*. Translated by G. M. Cookson. New York: E. P. Dutton, 1967.

————. *The Tragedies of Aeschylus*. Translated by R. Potter. London: T. & J. Allman, 1819.

Agrippa von Nettesheim, Heinrich Cornelius. *Three Books of Occult Philosophy or Magic*. New York: Samuel Welzer, Inc., 1897, 1971.

Aldiss, Brian. *Billion Year Spree: The True History of Science Fiction*. New York: Doubleday, 1973.

————. *Frankenstein Unbound*. New York: Fawcett-Crest, 1975.

Anobile, Richard J., ed. *Frankenstein*. New York: Avon, 1974.

Babinski, Hubert F. *The Mazeppa Legend in European Romanticism*. New York and London: Columbia University Press, 1974.

Baker, Carlos. *Shelley's Major Poetry: The Fabric of a Vision*. Princeton, New Jersey: Princeton University Press, 1948.

Ballard, Joseph. *England in 1815*. Boston and New York: Houghton Mifflin Co., 1913.

Barry, George Rev. D.D. *History of the Orkney Islands*. London: Longman, Hurst, Rees and Orme, 1808.

Beck, Calvin. *Heroes of the Horrors*. New York: Collier Books, 1972.

Biermann, Berthold, ed. *Goethe's World as Seen in Letters and Memoirs*. New York: New Directions, 1949.

Blake, E. Vale, ed. *Arctic Experiences*. New York: Harper, 1874.

Britton, John, and Shepherd, Thomas H. *Modern Athens: Or Edinburgh in the Nineteenth Century*. New York and London: Benjamin Blom, Inc., 1831, 1969.

Brown, Ford K. *The Life of William Godwin*. London: J. M. Dent & Sons, Ltd., 1926.

Burgess, Anthony. *Coaching Days of England*. London: Paul Elek, 1966.

Burroughs, Edgar Rice. *Tarzan of the Apes*. New York: Ballantine Books, 1972.

Buxton, John. *Byron and Shelley: The History of a Friendship*. Melbourne, Toronto and London: Macmillan & Co., 1968.

Byron, Lord George Gordon. *Childe Harold's Pilgrimage and Other Romantic Poems*. New York: The Odyssey Press, 1936.

————. *Poetical Works of George Lord Byron*. With original life and notes by A. C. Cunningham, Esq. New York and Auburn: Miller, Orton & Mulligan, 1856.

Cameron, Kenneth Neill, ed. *Shelley and His Circle*. Vols. 1–4. Cambridge, Massachusetts: Harvard University Press, 1961, 1970.

————. *Shelley: The Golden Years*. Cambridge, Massachusetts: Harvard University Press, 1974.

Carpenter, Ed, and Barnfield, George. *Psychology of the Poet Shelley*. London: Allen & Unwin Ltd., 1925. New York: E. P. Dutton, 1925.

Chancellor, E. Beresford. *Life in Regency and Early Victorian Times*. London: B. T. Batsford, Ltd., n.d.

Christy, Miller. *The Voyages of Captain Luke Fox of Hull and Captain Thomas James of Bristol.* 2 vols. London: Hakluyt Society, 1633. New York: Burt Franklin, n.d.

Church, Richard. *Mary Shelley.* Folcroft, Pennsylvania: The Folcroft Press, Inc., 1928, 1969.

Clairmont, Claire. *The Journals of Claire Clairmont.* Edited by Marion Kingston Stocking. Cambridge, Massachusetts: Harvard University Press, 1968.

Clarendon, Earl of (Edward Hyde). *The History of the Great Rebellion.* Edited by Roger Lockyer. London: Oxford University Press, 1967.

————. *Selections from the History of the Rebellion and Civil Wars and the Life By Himself.* Edited by G. Huehus. London: Oxford University Press, 1966.

Clarke, Isabel C. *Shelley and Byron: A Tragic Friendship.* London: Hutchinson and Co., 1934.

Cohen, John. *Human Robots in Myth and Science.* London: George Allen & Unwin, Ltd., 1966.

Coleridge, Samuel Taylor. *The Complete Poetical Works of Samuel Taylor Coleridge.* Edited by James Dykes Campbell. London: Macmillan and Co., Ltd., 1899.

Cook, Dr. Frederick A. *My Attainment of the Pole.* New York and London: Mitchell Kinnerley, 1912.

Dante Alighieri. *The Comedy of Dante Alighieri.* Translated by Dorothy Sayers. Harmondsworth, Middlesex: Penguin Books, 1950.

Darnton, Robert. *Mesmerism and the end of the Enlightenment in France.* Cambridge, Massachusetts: Harvard University Press, 1968.

Darwin, Erasmus, M.D. *The Botanic Garden.* London: Jones & Co., 1825.

————. *The Essential Writings of Erasmus Darwin.* Edited by Desmond King-Hele. London: Macgibbon & Kee, Ltd., 1968.

de Volney, Constantin François Chasseboeuf. *Oeuvres Completes.* Paris: Firmin Didot Frères, Fils, 1868.

Douglas, Drake. *Horror!* New York: Macmillan & Co., 1966.

Dowden, Edward. *Percy Bysshe Shelley.* London: Kegan Paul, Trench, Trubner & Co., Ltd., n.d.

Egede, Hans. *A Description of Greenland.* 2nd. ed. Millwood, New York: Kraus Reprint Co., 1818, 1973.

Eisner, Lotte H. *The Haunted Screen.* Translated by Roger Greaves. Berkeley and Los Angeles: University of California Press, 1969.

Enscoe, Gerald. *Eros and the Romantics.* Mouton: The Hague, Paris, 1967.

Fantasmagoriana: ou Reçueil Histoires d'Apparitions. Traduit de l'allemand, par un Amateur (J. B. B. Eyries). Paris: F. Schoell, 1812.

Farber, Edward. *The Evolution of Chemistry.* New York: Ronald Press Co., 1969.

Flexner, Eleanor. *Mary Wollstonecraft: A Biography.* New York: Coward, McCann & Geoghegan, 1972.

Florescu, Radu. *In Search of Frankenstein.* New York: Warner Edition, 1976.

de la Fontaine, Jean. *Oeuvres Choisies.* Introduction, etc., par G. Le Bidois. Paris: Librairie A. Hatier, 1947.

Forman, H. Buxton. *Note Books of Percy Bysshe Shelley.* Boston: The Bibliophile Society, 1911.

Franklin, Captain John. *Narrative of a Second Expedition.* New York: Greenwood Press, Publishers, 1969.

Fuller, Jean Overton. *Shelley: A Biography.* London: Jonathan Cape, 1968.

Füssli, Johann Heinrich. *Gemalde und Zeichnungen.* Int. R. Wheli. Zurich: Kunsthaus Zürich and Schweizerisches Institut für Kunstwissenschaft, 1969.

Gerson, Noel B. *Daughter of Earth and Water: A Biography of Mary Wollstonecraft Shelley.* New York: William Morrow and Co., 1972.

Godwin, Mary Wollstoncraft. *Posthumous Works.* Clifton: Augustus M. Kelley, Publisher, 1972.

Godwin, William. *The Adventures of Caleb Williams.* Edited by Herbert Van Thal. Int. Walter Allen. London: Cassell, 1794, 1966.

Goethe, Wolfgang Amadeus. *Faust, A Tragedy.* Translated by Bayard Taylor. Boston: Houghton Mifflin, 1912.

————. *The Sorrow of Young Werther.* Text translated by Elizabeth Mayer and Louise Bogan. Poems translated by W. H. Auden. Foreword by W. H. Auden. New York: Vintage Books, 1973.

Goldsmith, Oliver. *The Vicar of Wakefield.* Int. Frederick W. Hilles. New York: E. P. Dutton & Co., Inc., 1951.

Grabo, Carl. *The Magic Plant.* Chapel Hill: The University of North Carolina Press, 1936.

————. *A Newton Among Poets.* New York: Gordian Press, Inc., 1968.

————. *Prometheus Unbound: An Interpretation.* New York: Gordian Press, Inc., 1968.

————. *Shelley's Eccentricities.* University of New Mexico Publications in Language and Literature No. 5. Albuquerque: The University of New Mexico Press, 1950.

Grylls, R. Glynn. *Mary Shelley, A Biography.* London, New York, and Toronto: Oxford University Press, 1938.

————. *Trelawny.* London: Constable, 1950.

————. *William Godwin & His World.* Longacre, London: Odhams Press, Ltd., 1953.

Hadfield, Alice Mary. *Time to Finish the Game.* London: Phoenix House, 1964.

Hakluyt, Richard. *The Principal Navigations, Voyages, Traffics & Discoveries of the English Nations.* 12 vols. Reprint: New York: AMS Press, 1965.

Hall, Captain Charles Francis. *Life with the Esquimaux.* Rutland, Vermont and Tokyo, Japan: Charles E. Tuttle Co., 1970.

Harper, Henry H., ed. *Letters of Mary W. Shelly.* Folcroft, Pennsylvania: Folcroft Library Editions, 1918, 1972.

————. *The Romance of Mary W. Shelley, John Howard Payne and Washington Irving*. Folcroft, Pennsylvania: Folcroft Library Editions, 1908, 1972.

Herodotus. *The Histories*. Translated by Aubrey de Selincourt. Baltimore, Maryland: Penguin Books, 1968.

Hill, Douglas. *A Hundred Years of Georgian London*. London: Macdonald & Co., Ltd., 1920.

Hogg, Thomas Jefferson. *The Life of Percy Bysshe Shelley*. Introduction by Humbert Wolfe. London: J. M. Dent & Son, Ltd., 1933.

Holmes, Richard. *Shelley: The Pursuit*. London: Weidenfeld and Nicholson, 1974.

Hudson, Gladys W. *Paradise Lost: A Concordance*. Detroit: Gale Research Co., 1970.

Hunt, Leigh, *Lord Byron and Some of His Contemporaries*. New York: AMS Press, Inc., 1828, 1966.

Ingpen, Roger. *Shelley in England*. Boston and New York: Houghton Mifflin, 1917.

Irving, Washington. *Tour in Scotland 1817 and Other Manuscript Notes*. Edited by Stanley T. Williams. New Haven: Yale University Press, 1927.

Isherwood, Christopher, and Bachardy, Don. *Frankenstein: The True Story*. New York: Avon Co., 1973.

James, D. G., M. A. *Byron and Shelley*. Folcroft, Pennsylvania: Folcroft Library Editions, 1951, 1971.

James, Ivor. *The Source of the Ancient Mariner*. Cardiff, England: Daniel Owen and Co., Ltd., 1890.

Jones, Frederick L., ed. *The Letters of Mary W. Shelley*. Norman, Oklahoma: University of Oklahoma Press, 1944.

————. *The Letters of P. B. Shelley*. Oxford: Oxford University Press, 1964.

————. *Mary Shelley's Journal*. Norman, Oklahoma: University of Oklahoma Press, 1947.

Jones, Lawrence F., and Lonn, George. *Pathfinders of the North*. Toronto: Pitt Publishing Co., Ltd., 1970.

Kant, Elisha Kent. *The U.S. Grinnell Expedition in Search of Sir John Franklin*. New York: Harper & Bros., Publisher, 1854.

Keats, John. *The Poetical Works of John Keats*. Edited by William T. Arnold. London: Macmillan and Co., 1925.

Keay, Carolyn. *Henry Fuseli*. London: Academy Editions, 1974.

Kiely, Robert. *The Romantic Novel in England*. Cambridge, Massachusetts: Harvard University Press, 1972.

La Croix, Paul. *Science and Literature in the Middle Ages and at the Period of the Renaissance*. London: Bickers and Son, 1878.

Laing, Lloyd. *Orkney and Shetland: An Archeological Guide*. London: David and Charles, Newton Abbot, 1974.

Landes, David Saul. *The Unbound Prometheus*. Cambridge: Cambridge University Press, 1969.

Langhorne, John and William. *Plutarch's Lives*. London: George Routledge and Sons, Ltd., 1890.

Lavater, J. C. *Physiognomy*. London: William Tegg, 1867.

Lee, Walt. *Reference Guide to Fantastic Films*. Los Angeles: Chelsea-Lee Books, 1972.

Lem, Stanislaw. *The Cyberiad*. New York: Seabury Press, 1974.

Lewis, Bernard. *Istanbul and the Civilization of the Ottoman Empire*. Norman: University of Oklahoma Press, 1963.

Lovejoy, Arthur O. *The Great Chain of Being*. Cambridge, Massachusetts: Harvard University Press, 1970.

Lowes, John Livingston. *The Road to Xanadu, A Study in the Ways of the Imagination*. Boston and New York: Houghton Mifflin Co., 1927.

Marchand, Leslie A. *Byron, A Biography*. 3 vols. New York: Alfred A. Knopf, 1957.

Margetson, Stella. *Journey by Stages*. London: Cassell & Co., 1967.

Marlowe, Derek. *A Single Summer with Lord Byron*. New York: The Viking Press, 1969.

Marshall, Mrs. Julian. *The Life and Letters of Mary Wollstonecraft Shelley*. 2 vols. New York: Haskell House Publishers, Ltd., 1970.

Martineau, Harriet. *Harriet Martineau's Autobiography with Memorials by Maria Weston Chapman*. 3rd ed. London: Smith, Elder & Co., 1877.

Mason, Eudo C., ed. *The Mind of Henry Fuseli*. London: Routledge & Kegan Paul, 1951.

Medwin, Thomas. *The Life of Percy Bysshe Shelley*. Introduction by J. Buxton Forman. London: Oxford University Press, Humphrey Milford, 1913.

Millar, A. H. F. S. A. Scot. *Fife: Pictorial and Historical*. Edinburgh: A. Westwood and Son, 1895.

Mirsky, Jeannette. *To the Arctic!* Introduction by Vilhjalmur Stefanson. New York: Alfred A. Knopf, 1948.

Moers, Ellen. *Literary Women*. Garden City, New York: Doubleday & Co., Inc., 1976.

Monro, D. H. *Godwin's Moral Philosophy*. London: Oxford University Press, 1953.

Moritz, Karl Philipp. *Travels of Karl Philipp Moritz*. Introduction by P. E. Matheson. London: Oxford University Press, 1795, 1924.

Mowatt, Farley. *Ordeal by Ice*. Toronto: McClelland & Stewart, Ltd., 1973.

————. *The Polar Passion: The Quest for the North Pole*. Boston and Toronto: Atlantic Monthly Press Book: Little, Brown & Co., 1967.

Newman, Irving White. *Shelley*. 2 vols. New York: Alfred A. Knopf, 1940.

New Shelley Letters. Edited by W. S. Scott. New Haven: Yale University Press, 1949.

Nitchie, Elizabeth. *Mary Shelley Author of Frankenstein*. Westport, Connecticut: Greenwood Press, 1953.

Orr, Sutherland, Mrs. *A Handbook to the Works of Robert*

Browning. 3rd ed. revised. London: George Bell & Sons, 1887.

Paracelsus, pseudonym. Theophrastus Bombastus. *Selected Writings.* Translated by Norbert Guterman. Bollingen Series XXVIII. New York: Pantheon Books, 1951.

Paul, Kegan. *William Godwin: His Friends and Contemporaries.* 2 vols. Boston: Roberts Brothers, 1876.

Peacock, Thomas Love. *Peacock's Memoirs of Shelley with Shelley's Letters to Peacock.* Edited by H. F. B. Borett-Smith. London: Henry Frowde, 1909.

Penzer, N. M. *The Harem.* Philadelphia: J. B. Lippincott Co., 1937.

Perkins, David, ed. *English Romantic Writers.* New York: Harcourt, Brace & World, 1967.

Powell, Nicholas. *The Drawings of Henry Fuseli.* London: Faber & Faber, 1951.

Praz, Mario. *The Romantic Agony.* Cleveland & New York: World Publishing Co., 1965.

Rawcliffe, D. A. *Illusions and Delusions of the Supernatural and the Occult.* New York: Dover, 1959.

Rieger, James. *The Mutiny Within.* New York: George Braziller, 1967.

de la Rochefoucauld, François. *A Frenchman in England.* Translated by S. C. Roberts. Cambridge: Cambridge University Press, 1933.

Rodway, A. E., ed. *Godwin and the Age of Transition.* London: George S. Harrap & Co., Ltd., 1952.

Ross, Sir John. *Appendix to the Narrative of a Second Voyage.* Vols. I and II. New York: Greenwood Press, Publishers, 1969.

Rossetti, Lucy Madox. *Mrs. Shelley.* Folcroft, Pennsylvania: The Folcroft Press, Inc., 1969.

Rousseau, Jean-Jacques. *La Nouvelle Héloïse.* Translated and abridged by Judith H. McDowell. University Park: Pennsylvania State University, 1968.

Sachs, Hans. *Creative Unconscious.* Cambridge, Mass.: Science-Art Publishers, 1951.

Sayers, Dorothy. *The Comedy of Dante Alighieri.* Harmondsworth, England: Penguin, 1949.

Schiff, Gert. *Henry Fuseli–1741–1825.* Translated by Sarah Twohig. London: Tate Gallery, 1975.

———. *Johan Heinrich Füssli's Milton Galerie.* Zurich/Stuttgart: Fritz & Wasmuth Verlag, 1963.

———, and Hoffman, Werner. *Johann Heinrich Füssli.* München: Prestel, 1974.

Scott, Sidney Walter. *Percy Bysshe Shelley, Harriet and Mary.* Folcroft, Pennsylvania: Folcroft Library, 1974.

Shelley, Lady Jane (Gibson), ed. *Shelley Memorials: From Authentic Sources.* Boston: Ticknor and Fields, 1859.

Shelley, Mary. *Falkner A Novel by the Author of 'Frankenstein.'* London: Saunders and Otley, 1837.

———. *The Fortunes of Perkin Warbeck, A Romance.* London: Henry Colburn and Richard Bentley, 1830.

———. *Frankenstein.* London: H. Dolburn & R. Bentley, 1831.

———. *Frankenstein.* Edited by James Rieger. Indianapolis: Bobbs Merrill, 1974.

———. *Frankenstein; or, the Modern Prometheus.* Illustrated by Nino Carbe. New York: Illustrated Editions, 1932.

———. *Frankenstein; or, the Modern Prometheus.* With engravings by Lynd Ward. New York: Harrison Smith & Robert Haas, 1934.

———. *Frankenstein; or, the Modern Prometheus.* Introduction by Edmund Lester Pearson. Illustrated by Everett Henry. New York: Heritage Press, 1934.

———. *Frankenstein; or, the Modern Prometheus.* London: Lackington, Hughes, Harding, Mayor, & Jones, 1818.

———. *Frankenstein; or, the Modern Prometheus.* Edited by M. K. Joseph. London: Oxford University Press, 1969.

———. *History of a Six Weeks' Tour.* London: T. Hookham Jun, 1817.

———. *The Last Man.* Edited by Hugh J. Luke, Jr. Lincoln: University of Nebraska Press, 1965.

———. *The Last Man by the Author of Frankenstein.* London: Henry Colburn, 1826.

———. *The Letters of Mary W. Shelley.* Edited by Frederick L. Jones. 2 vols. Norman: University of Oklahoma Press, 1946.

———. *Letters of Mary W. Shelley, Mostly Unpublished.* Introduction and notes by Henry H. Harper. Folcraft, Pennsylvania: Folcroft Library Editions, 1972.

———. *Lives of Eminent Literary and Scientific Men of Italy, Spain and Portugal.* London: Lardner, 1835–37.

———. *Lodore, by the Author of 'Frankenstein.'* London: Richard Bentley, 1835.

———. *Mary Shelley's Journal.* Edited by Frederick L. Jones. Norman: University of Oklahoma Press, 1947.

———. *Mathilda.* Edited by Elizabeth Nitchie. Chapel Hill: University of North Carolina Press, 1959.

———. *My Best Mary: The Selected Letters of Mary Wollstonecraft Shelley.* Edited by Muriel Spark and Derek Stanford. London: Folcroft Library Editions: Allan Wingate, 1972.

———. *Perkin Warbeck.* London: Colburn and Bentley, 1830.

———. *Rambles in Germany and Italy in 1840, 1842, and 1843.* London: Edward Moxon, 1844.

———. *The Romance of Mary W. Shelley, John Howard Payne and Washington Irving.* Edited by H.H.H. Boston: Folcroft Library Editions, Bibliophile Society, 1907.

———. *Tales and Stories.* Edited by Richard Garnett. Philadelphia: William Patterson and Co., 1891.

———. *Valperga: Or the Life and Adventures of Castruccio.* London: G. and W. B. Whittaker, 1823.

Shelley, Percy Bysshe. *The Complete Poetical Works of Percy Bysshe Shelley.* Edited by Thomas Hutchinson. London, New York, Toronto: Oxford University Press, 1952.

————. *The Complete Poetical Works of Percy Bysshe Shelley.* Edited by Neville Rogers. Oxford: Clarendon Press, 1975.

————. *The Complete Works of Percy Bysshe Shelley.* 10 vols. Edited by Roger Ingpen and W. E. Peck. London: Julian Edition, 1926–1930.

————. *Essays and Letters by Percy Bysshe Shelley.* Ernest Rhys, ed. Freeport, New York: Books for Libraries Press, 1971.

————. *The Letters of Percy Bysshe Shelley.* Vols. I and II. Edited by Roger Ingpen. London: G. Bell and Sons, Ltd. 1914.

————. *The Letters   Percy Bysshe Shelley.* 2 vols. Frederick L. Jones, ed. Oxford: Clarendon Press, 1964.

————. *Shelley at Oxford.* Walter Sidney Scott, ed. London: The Golden Cockerel Press, 1944.

————. *Shelley's Critical Prose.* B. R. McElderry, ed. Lincoln: University of Nebraska Press, 1967.

Shepherd, Thomas H., and Britton, John. *Modern Athens . . . Edinburgh in the Nineteenth Century.* New York: Benjamin Blom, Inc., 1969.

Small, Christopher. *Mary Shelley's Frankenstein: Tracing the Myth.* Pittsburgh: University of Pittsburgh Press, 1972.

Southey, Robert. *Journal of a Tour in Scotland in 1819.* Edinburgh: James Thin, 1972.

Spark, Muriel. *Child of Light.* Essex: Tower Bridge Publications, 1951.

————, and Stanford, Derek, eds. *My Best Mary.* London: Allan Wingate, 1953.

Stillman, John Maxson. *The Story of Alchemy and Early Chemistry.* New York: Dover Publications, Inc., 1960.

Stoker, Bram. *Dracula (The Annotated Dracula).* Edited by Leonard Wolf. New York: Clarkson N. Potter, Inc., 1975.

Sunstein, Emily. *A Different Face. The Life of Mary Wollstonecraft.* New York: Harper & Row, 1975.

Swift, Jonathan. *The Writings of Jonathan Swift.* Robert A. Greenberg and William B. Piper, eds. New York: W. W. Norton & Co., Inc., 1973.

Thousand and One Nights, The. 3 vols. Translated by Edward W. Lane. Illustrated by William Harry. London: Chatto and Windus, 1889.

Tomalin, Claire. *The Life and Death of Mary Wollstonecraft.* New York: Harcourt Brace Jovanovich, 1974.

Tomory, Peter. *The Life and Art of Henry Fuseli.* London: Thames and Hudson, 1972.

Trelawny, Edward John. *Trelawny's Recollections of the Last Days of Shelley and Byron.* Introduction by Edward Dowden. London: Henry Frowde, 1906.

Tristram, W. Outram. *Coaching Days and Coaching Ways.* Illustrated by Herbert Railton and Hugh Thomson. London: Macmillan and Co., 1888.

Tropp, Martin. *Mary Shelley's Monster.* Boston: Houghton Mifflin, 1976.

Turner, J. M. W., R.A. *Liber Fluviorum; or, River Scenery of France.* London: Henry G. Bohn, 1853.

Vallance, Aymer. *The Old Colleges of Oxford.* London: B. T. Batsford, n.d.

Varma, Devendra. *The Gothic Flame.* London: Arthur Barker, Ltd., 1957.

Walling, William A. *Mary Shelley.* New York: Tayne Publishers, 1972.

Wardle, Ralph M., ed. *Godwin and Mary. Letters of William Godwin and Mary Wollstonecraft.* Lawrence, Kansas: The University of Kansas Press, 1966.

Weizenbaum, Joseph. *Computer Power and Human Reason: From Judgment to Calculation.* San Francisco: W. H. Freeman & Co., 1976.

White, Newman I. *Shelley.* New York: Alfred A. Knopf, 1940.

Wingfield-Stratford, Esme. *King Charles and King Pym 1637–1643.* Westport, Connecticut: Greenwood Press Publishers, 1949, 1975.

Wollstonecraft, Mary. *Letters Written During a Short Residence in Sweden, Norway and Denmark.* Sussex: Centaur Press, Ltd., 1970.

————. *Maria: The Wrongs of Woman.* Introduction by Moira Ferguson. New York: Norton, 1798, 1975.

————. *Mary: A Fiction.* Introduction by Gina Luria. New York: Garland Publishing Inc., 1788, 1974.

Woodcock, George. *William Godwin: A Biographical Study.* London: The Porcupine Press, 1946.

Wordsworth, Dorothy. *Recollections of a Tour Made in Scotland A.D. 1803.* J. C. Shairp, L.L.D., ed. New York: AMS Press, Inc., 1874, 1973.

Xenophon. *The Persian Expedition.* Translated by Rex Warner. Baltimore: Penguin Books, 1957.

INDEX

Page numbers in italics indicate illustrations